Root Causes of Terrorism

Addressing the causes of a problem is often more effective than trying to fight its symptoms and effects. In *Root Causes of Terrorism*, a team of international experts analyses the possibilities and limitations of preventing and reducing terrorism by addressing the factors that give rise to it and sustain it. The questions raised include:

- What are the main circumstances that provide preconditions for the emergence of various types of terrorism?
- What are the typical precipitants that trigger terrorist campaigns?
- To what extent is it possible to reduce the problem of terrorism by influencing these causes and circumstances?
- Should we address those factors that sustain terrorist campaigns rather than root causes?

Tore Bjørgo is Senior Research Fellow at the Norwegian Institute of International Affairs (NUPI), and Research Director and Professor of Police Science at the Norwegian Police University College.

Root Causes of Terrorism

Myths, reality and ways forward

Edited by Tore Bjørgo

Routledge
Taylor & Francis Group

LONDON AND NEW YORK

First published 2005
by Routledge
2 Park Square, Milton Park, Abingdon, Oxon OX14 4RN

Simultaneously published in the USA and Canada
by Routledge
270 Madison Avenue, New York, NY 10016

Routledge is an imprint of the Taylor & Francis Group

© 2005 Tore Bjørgo for selection and editorial matter;
individual authors for their contributions

Typeset in Garamond
by Bookcraft Ltd, Stroud, Gloucestershire
Printed and bound in Great Britain
by MPG Books Ltd, Bodmin

British Library Cataloguing in Publication Data
A catalogue record for this book is available from the British Library

Library of Congress Cataloging in Publication Data
Root causes of terrorism: myths, reality, and ways forward / edited by Tore Bjørgo.
    p. cm.
    1. Terrorism. I. Bjørgo, Tore.
    HV6431.R66 2005
    303.6'25–dc22

                                                        2005003573

ISBN 0-415-35149-9 (hbk)
ISBN 0-415-35150-2 (pbk)

Contents

Figures

Tables

Contributors

Hisham H. Ahmed is an Associate Professor of Political Science at Birzeit University, Palestine. Born in 1963 in the Deheisheh refugee camp near Bethlehem, Dr Ahmed finished two years of university education in Palestine before he travelled to the USA where he obtained a BA degree in political science from Illinois State University in 1985. He obtained his MA and Ph.D. degrees, also in political science, at the University of California, Santa Barbara, in 1986 and 1988, respectively. Unable to immediately return to his homeland because of political turmoil during the 1987 Intifada, he taught political science at the Florida International University in Miami, Florida from 1989–91 and at the University of North Dakota from 1991–3, before returning to Palestine as a Fulbright scholar. In Palestine, Dr Ahmed has taught at several universities and colleges. In addition to his teaching career, Dr Ahmed is the author of a number of studies dealing with the Middle East, Islamic movements and American foreign policy.

Tore Bjørgo is Research Director and Professor of Police Science at the Norwegian Police University College, and Senior Research Fellow at the Norwegian Institute of International Affairs (NUPI), where he is heading a research group on terrorism and international crime. A social anthropologist by training, he received his doctoral degree from the University of Leiden, where he was a research associate. Currently, his main fields of research are political extremism and terrorism, racist and right-wing violence, delinquent youth gangs, and international crime. He has authored or edited nine books, including *Racist and Right-wing Violence in Scandinavia: Patterns, Perpetrators and Responses* (1997) and *Terror from the Extreme Right* (1995).

Dipak K. Gupta is a Professor in the Department of Political Science at San Diego State University, Co-director of the Institute for International Security and Conflict Resolution (IISCOR) and a Research Associate of the Fred J. Hansen Institute for World Peace. He is the author of five books and over 70 articles. He has been a visiting Fellow and has lectured in many universities around the world. His primary areas of research include various aspects of political violence and terrorism.

Wilhelm Heitmeyer is Professor for Socialization at the University of Bielefeld, Germany, the Director of the Institute for Interdisciplinary Research on Conflict and Violence and head of various research programmes on right-wing extremism, violence, xenophobia and ethnic-cultural conflict. He is also a member of the Council and Theory Sections of the German Sociological Association, a member of the editorial board of the series *International Studies of Childhood and Adolescence* at Verlag de Gruyter. He also edits several series including *Jugendforschung* (Youth Research) and *Konflikt und Gewaltforschung* (Research on Conflict and Violence) at Juventa Verlag and *Kultur und Konflikt* (Culture and Conflict) at Suhrkamp Verlag.

John Horgan is a forensic psychologist and lecturer at the Department of Applied Psychology, University College, Cork, Ireland. He teaches on the psychology of terrorism in universities and colleges around the world, and frequently gives lectures to law enforcement, army, intelligence and other government audiences. His work on terrorism and related forensic issues is published widely. Dr Horgan's books include *The Future of Terrorism* (with Max Taylor 1999) and *The Psychology of Terrorism* (2005).

Alison Jamieson is an independent consultant and author who has written extensively in English and Italian on issues of political violence, organized crime and drugs. Her books include two school texts on terrorism for Wayland publishers (UK 1991 and 1995), *The Heart Attacked: Terrorism and Conflict in the Italian State* (1989) and *The Anti-Mafia: Italy's Fight against Organized Crime* (2000). Between 1992 and 1997 she was a regular guest lecturer at the NATO Defence College in Rome. She has worked as a consultant to the United Nations Drug Control Programme (UNDCP), and to the International Narcotics Control Board. She was principal author of the UNDCP's *World Drug Report* (1997). She was born and educated in Scotland but has lived in Italy since 1984.

Shri D.R. Kaarthikeyan is an advisor on law, human rights and corporate affairs. Born to a farming family, he became a lawyer and later joined the elite Indian Police Service. In that capacity he held several positions including District Superintendent of Police of the largest problematic districts, Director of the Police Training Academy, Chief of Intelligence and Security, Director-General of the Central Reserve Police Force (the largest paramilitary force in India), Chief of Investigation of the former Prime Minister Rajiv Gandhi assassination case, Director of the Central Bureau of Investigation of India, Director of Trade Promotion in Australia with headquarters in Sydney, Diplomat and Head of Chancery in the Indian Embassy in Moscow (then USSR), and Director-General in the National Human Rights Commission. He is currently Professor emeritus in several prestigious universities, President of *Life Positive* magazine, Chairperson/Advisor/Member in several voluntary organizations, including the World Community Service Centre, the National Agriculturist Awareness Movement, the Indian Human Rights Organization, the National Alliance for Fundamental Right Education, the Academy for a Better World, the All-India Conference of Intellectuals, the World Congress for

Peace and Harmony, the Indian Council of Arbitration, the Association of Asian Union and the ORG Institute of Polity and Governance.

Farid el Khazen is Professor and Chair of the Department of Political Studies and Public Administration at the American University of Beirut. He is also a former editor of the academic journal *al-Abhath*. His recent publications include *The Breakdown of the State in Lebanon, 1967–76* (2000), *Parliamentary Elections in Post-war Lebanon: Democracy with No Choice* (2000, in Arabic) and *Lebanon's Political Parties and Democratic Practice* (2002, in Arabic). He has also published several other books and numerous articles on Lebanese and Middle Eastern politics.

Jitka Malečková is an Associate Professor at the Institute for Middle Eastern and African Studies at Charles University in Prague. She has written extensively on nationalism and on gender history in the Middle East and in Eastern Europe. Her recent publications include *Fertile Soil: Women Save the Nation* (2002). Together with the economist Alan Krueger from Princeton University, she has published articles on the relationship between poverty and terrorism, including 'Education, Poverty and Terrorism: Is There a Causal Connection?' in the *Journal of Economic Perspectives*.

Ariel Merari is a member of the Department of Psychology at Tel Aviv University and the Director of the Political Violence Research Unit. He received a BA degree in Psychology and Economics from the Hebrew University in Jerusalem, and a Ph.D. in Psychology from the University of California, Berkeley. He was a visiting Professor at Berkeley and Harvard, and Senior Fellow at the Kennedy School's BCSIA. He has studied political terrorism and other forms of political violence for more than 25 years and has authored, co-authored or edited several books and many articles, monographs and chapters on these subjects.

Abdullah Yousef Sahar Mohammad is a Professor of International Relations at the Political Science department of Kuwait University. He graduated from Kuwait University in 1985 with a BA in Political Science. He obtained his MA in International Affairs from Florida State University in 1988. He obtained a Ph.D. from the University of Kentucky in 1994 and has also been a visiting Professor at the London School of Economics and Political Science in 1997–8. Among his area of interests are non-governmental organizations, security studies, political economy, and studies of political Islam. His publications have dealt with matters such as the Orientalism school and the Western policy toward Muslim and Arab, the impact of globalization on the Third World, the Arab–Israeli conflict, terrorism, Iran foreign policy, and Western involvement in oil-related issues in the Gulf.

Jerrold M. Post is Professor of Psychiatry, Political Psychology and International Affairs and Director of the Political Psychology Program at The George Washington University. He has devoted his entire career to the field of political psychology. Dr Post accepted this position after a 21-year career with the Central Intelligence Agency where he was the founding director of the Center for the Analysis of Personality and Political Behavior. Dr Post has published widely on crisis decision making, leadership, and on the psychology of political violence and terrorism. His most recent book is *Leaders and their Followers in a Dangerous World: The Psychology of Political Behavior* (2004). He is a frequent commentator in the international media on terrorism and the political psychology of rogue leaders, such as Osama bin Laden, Saddam Hussein and Kim Jong-Il.

Fernando Reinares is Professor and Chair in Political Science, as well as Director of the Unit for Documentation and Analysis on Terrorism, at Universidad Rey Juan Carlos in Madrid. On May 2004 he was appointed Senior Advisor on Anti-terrorist Policy to the Minister of Interior, Government of Spain. He is a contrib-uting editor of *Studies in Conflict and Terrorism*, and a member of the International Advisory Board of Terrorism and Political Violence and also belongs to the academic committee of the Queen Sofía Center for the Study of Violence. His recent books include *Terrorismo y Antiterrorismo* (Terrorism and Anti-terrorism, 1998), *European Democracies Against Terrorism: Governmental Policies and Inter-governmental Cooperation* (2000), *Patriotas de la Muerte: Quiénes han militado en ETA y por qué* (Patriots of Death: Who Joined ETA and Why, 2001), *Terrorismo Global* (Global Terrorism, 2003), and *El Nuevo Terrorismo Islamista* (The New Islamist Terrorism, 2004).

Louise Richardson is Executive Dean of the Radcliff Institute for Advanced Study at Harvard University. From 1989 to 2001, she was Assistant and Associate Professor of Government at Harvard. A political scientist by training she has specialized in international security with an emphasis on terrorist movements. Her publications include *When Allies Differ* (1996) and a wide range of articles on international terrorism, foreign and defence policy, security institutions, and international rela-tions. Dean Richardson teaches these subjects at Harvard College, Graduate School and Law School. Richardson's current research projects involve a study of the patterns of terrorist violence and a study on the counter-terrorism lessons to be derived from earlier experiences with terrorism. She is also the co-editor of the SUNY Press series on terrorism.

Alex P. Schmid is a historian by training but has later worked in the fields of soci-ology, political science and human rights. He held the Synthesis Chair on Conflict Resolution at the Erasmus University in Rotterdam. He taught International Rela-tions at the Department of Political Sciences of Leiden University and was an Einstein Fellow at the Center for International Affairs, Harvard University. Dr Schmid was Research Coordinator of the Interdisciplinary Research Programme on the Causes of Human Rights Violations (PIOOM) at Leiden University and one of the founding members of FEWER, the London-based Forum on Early Warning and Early Response. Dr Schmid has authored and edited more than one hundred publications, including the award-winning *Political Terrorism*. From 1999 to 2003, he served as Officer-in-Charge of the United Nations Terrorism Prevention Branch in Vienna where he currently holds the position of a Senior Crime Prevention and Criminal Justice Officer at the Office on Drugs and Crime. Dr Schmid is a Corresponding Member of the Royal Academy of Sciences of the Netherlands.

Andrew Silke has a background in forensic psychology and has worked both in academia and for government. He has published widely on the subject of terrorism, with recent books including *Terrorists, Victims and Society* (2003) and *Research on Terrorism: Trends, Achievements and Failures* (2004). Dr Silke is an Honorary Senior Research Associate of the Centre for the Study of Terrorism and Political Violence at the University of St Andrews and is a Fellow of the University of Leicester. He is a member of the International Association for Counter-terrorism and Security Professionals and serves on the United Nations Roster of Terrorism Experts.

Joshua Sinai, a senior terrorism specialist at ANSER (Analytical Services) at Arlington, Virginia, and is on detail to the US Government. His work on terrorism has focused on analysing and developing conceptual frameworks and tools to model and forecast the proclivity of terrorist groups to embark on a spectrum of warfare, ranging from conventional low-impact to WMD warfare, as well as new approaches to pre-emptively resolving protracted terrorist insurgencies. He has published in the *Armed Forces Journal, Defense News, Jane's Intelligence Review*, the *Journal of Counter-terrorism & Homeland Security International*, and the *Encyclopedia of World Terrorism*. He also writes the *Terrorism Bookshelf* book review column on the Terrorism Research Center website (http://www.terrorism.com). Dr Sinai had previously worked at SAIC (1998–9) and the Federal Research Division of the Library of Congress (1986–8 and 1991–7). He obtained his MA and Ph.D. from the Political Science Department at Columbia University.

Michael Stohl is Professor of Communication at the University of California, Santa Barbara (UCSB). Prior to this appointment in January 2002, Professor Stohl was Dean of International Programs from 1992 and Professor of Political Science at Purdue University in West Lafayette, Indiana, where he had taught since 1972. Dr Stohl's research focuses on international relations and political communication with special reference to terrorism and human rights. He is the author or co-author of more than 60 articles and the author, editor or co-editor of 12 books including *The Politics of Terrorism* (1988).

Peter Waldmann is Professor Emeritus at the University of Augsburg. He studied law and social sciences at Munich and Paris, finishing his law degree before definitely opting for the career of a sociologist. He has worked extensively in Latin America (especially Argentina and Colombia) and Spain, and his main research fields are sociology of law and crime, marginal groups and ethnic minorities, and the different forms of political violence (including governmental repression). He was visiting professor at numerous universities, including Buenos Aires, Santiago, Madrid, Bern and Harvard. Most of the eight books and nearly 90 articles written by him have been translated into Spanish, but only few into English. Among his latest publications are *Terrorismus: Provokation der Macht* (Terrorism: Provocation of authority, 1998) and *Der anomische Staat: Über Recht, Unsicherheit und Alltag in Lateinamerika* (The Anomic State: Law, Insecurity and Everyday Life in Latin America, 2002).

Preface

Is it possible to identify the main root causes of the various forms of terrorism? Will terrorism decline or disappear if such root causes are removed and grievances are addressed? Is the root cause approach to reducing terrorism a fruitful and realistic way to deal with this problem?

These are questions asked by policy-makers as well academic researchers and students of terrorism. The answers given may have great bearings on how we respond to the problem of terrorism, which has become a main challenge to international security and civil society. However, a one-sided focus on military means and repressive responses may become a greater threat to civil society and the process of democratization in many countries than the threat posed by terrorist violence itself. For that reason, there is a need to search for alternative approaches. This book represents an effort by leading experts in the field to explore and analyse the factors and circumstances that give rise to terrorism, and to seek the possibilities and limitations of reducing terrorism by addressing its causes.

This book has evolved out of a meeting of some 30 international experts on terrorism, who gathered in Oslo on 9–11 June 2003. Organized by the Norwegian Institute of International Affairs (NUPI), this expert meeting on *Root Causes of Terrorism* was initiated and financed by the Norwegian Government. The purpose of the meeting was to summarize and document what leading academics within the community of terrorism research know regarding the causes of terrorism, and to pass on this information to the high-level conference *Fighting Terrorism for Humanity*, which was held in New York on 22 September 2003.

This book is based on a selection of the papers presented at the Oslo expert meeting. These contributions were thoroughly revised and edited to fit into this collection. We believe the book will fill a need not only among academic experts and policy-makers in the field, but also serve well as a textbook for undergraduate and graduate courses on terrorism.

I wish to extend my thanks to the Prime Minister of Norway, Kjell Magne Bondevik, for his initiative, and to ambassador Morten Wetland and coordinator Erik Giercksky at the Norwegian Foreign Ministry for their generous support and collaboration in making the expert meeting possible. Anja K. Bakken and Anders Romarheim at the Norwegian Institute of International Affairs provided invaluable assistance before, during and after the Oslo conference. I also want to thank Vibeke Sand, Liv Høivik, Jan Risvik, Susan Høivik, Geir Arne Fredriksen and Ole Dahl Gulliksen for their assistance at various stages in the process of realizing this book. Finally, I express my gratitude to the international experts who have contributed their knowledge and insights.

Tore Bjørgo

1   Introduction

Tore Bjørgo

In the aftermath of September 11 and the declaration of the 'War on Terrorism', some would say that it is irrelevant and apologetic to address root causes of terrorism. Terrorism, they stress, is evil, and it must be crushed and uprooted. This is not the time to show understanding of its causes.[1] Others argue that if we focus solely on the symptoms of terrorism, without addressing the conditions that produce it and provide fertile ground in which extremism and violence can grow and take root, then the war on terrorism will only produce more terrorism. Some even point to a specific root cause which they see as 'the mother of all terrorism', be it poverty, the festering Israeli–Palestinian conflict, state sponsorship of terrorism, or some other favourite reason. Only if that particular problem is solved, they argue, will terrorism come to an end.

A complex picture

Terrorism, however, is an extremely complex set of phenomena, covering a great diversity of groups with different origins and causes. Thus, it is *not* the ambition of this book to come up with any new magic bullets. The aim should rather be to provide a more nuanced discussion on the causes of terrorism and, it is hoped, indicate some possibilities for influencing factors that may actually have an impact on the level of terrorism.

Identifying these root causes is a complex task, for several reasons. The many failed attempts to find one common definition of terrorism have been frustrated by the fact that the label 'terrorism' is used to cover a wide range of rather different phenomena. Rebellious groups and powerful states may both use terrorist methods to intimidate target groups, but the nature of 'terror from above' and 'terror from below' differs in several fundamental ways. Moreover, left-wing revolutionary terrorists use terrorist means in different ways and for different strategic and tactical purposes than do religiously motivated terrorists. Obviously, we will not be able to identify one set of root causes that will cover all forms of terrorism.

The statements 'researchers have identified more than 200 definitions of terrorism but failed to agree on any one'[2] and 'one person's terrorist is another person's freedom fighter' have become clichés. However, there is actually a growing consensus among researchers as well as among governments about the *core* meaning of the concept of terrorism. Most agree that terrorism is a set of methods or strategies of combat rather than an identifiable ideology or movement, and that terrorism involves premeditated use of violence against (at least primarily) non-combatants in order to achieve a psychological effect of fear on others than the immediate targets. However, beyond this core meaning of terrorism, there is heated disagreement regarding the delimitation of the phenomenon of terrorism, and particularly when it comes down to which specific groups or violent campaigns should be included or excluded under the label 'terrorism'. Some definitions specifically exclude state actors as possible terrorists, whereas others include states. Some definitions restrict the notion of terrorism to attacks on civilians only, whereas other definitions would include military and police targets under non-war conditions. Some limit terrorism to violent acts with a political purpose, whereas others also include terrorism for criminal purposes. Most definitions (implicitly or explicitly) consider terrorism as an illegitimate method, irrespective of its political goals or purposes. However, a few (rather exceptional) definitions specifically claim that armed struggle for certain just purposes is legitimate, irrespective of means.[3] The emerging consensus, however, is that terrorism is primarily an extremism of means, not one of ends.[4]

This book will focus mainly on terrorism by non-state actors. Although state terrorism may be seen as a different phenomenon, it is nevertheless addressed in several chapters, partly because state sponsorship is frequently considered a root cause of terrorism but also because brutal state repression may be a significant trigger of oppositional terrorism.

Among researchers, there is also a growing agreement that there is not one single 'terrorism', but several different 'terrorisms'. Because there are different types of terrorism with highly disparate foundations, there are very diverse types of causes and levels of causation.[5] The notion that there is one single 'prime mover' behind terrorism is therefore not tenable. Terrorism occurs in poor countries as well as in rich ones, in authoritarian societies as well as in democracies. What seems likely is that certain forms of terrorism are outcomes of certain combinations of factors: some of which may be more fundamental than others.

One basic question we need to address is whether the concept of 'root causes of terrorism' is really useful at all. The notion of 'root causes' is taken more from the realm of political discourse than from terrorism research and social theory. The idea is that no long-term success in the 'war on terrorism' can be expected as long as the root causes remain, continuing to spawn new terrorist actors. The underlying, and some would say naive, assumption is that if we can manage to identify and remove these root causes, then terrorism will end.

One problem with this assumption is that the more deep-rooted a cause (as with 'poverty' or 'modernization'), the more general it becomes, and the less directly it is related to terrorism.[6] Such causes act to produce all kinds of social outcomes, of which terrorism is just one. Moreover, some of the 'root causes' that we can see as preconditions to international terrorism, such as modern news media and various modernization and globalization processes, have both positive and negative (side) effects; and these should not or cannot be 'removed'.

A counterpart to such deep-seated and general root causes is what is sometimes called 'trigger causes': those immediate circumstances and events that provoke people to have recourse to terrorist action. Here there is a short and direct link between cause and outcome. Examples are the police killing of a student, Benny Ohnesorg, in West Berlin in 1967, which helped to trigger the formation of the Red Army Faction; the 'Bloody Sunday' massacre by British soldiers in Belfast (1972), which unleashed a wave of IRA bombings; and Ariel Sharon's 2000 visit to the Temple Mount/al-Aqsa Mosque in Jerusalem, which set off the Second Intifada. Although such triggering events have very direct causal relations to terrorist action, they will have such effects only if other, more basic, preconditions for terrorism are also present. Terrorism tends to be the product of a long process of radicalization that prepares a group of people for such extreme action.

Another limitation of the 'root cause' approach is that it may give the impression that terrorists are merely passive objects of social, economic and psychological forces: puppets obeying what these 'causes' compel them to do. It may be more useful to see terrorists as rational and intentional actors who develop deliberate strategies in order to achieve political objectives. They make their choices between different options, on the basis of the limitations and possibilities the situation offers.[7] When applying such an actor-oriented approach we would be interested in understanding dynamic processes rather than focusing on more or less static causes.

Levels of causation

With these reservations in mind, let us look at the various levels of causes of terrorism, some of which are more remotely and some more closely and directly linked with terrorism. The simplest way to organize them is to make a distinction between preconditions of terrorism and precipitants of terrorism. Preconditions set the stage for terrorism in the long run, whereas precipitants are the specific events or phenomena that immediately precede or trigger the outbreak of terrorism.[8] This can be further differentiated, as follows:

- *Structural causes* (demographic imbalances, globalization, rapid modernization, transitional societies, increasing individualism with rootlessness and atomization, relative deprivation, class structure, etc.) are causes which affect people's lives in ways that they may or may not comprehend, at a rather abstract macro level.
- *Facilitator* (or *accelerator*) *causes* make terrorism possible or attractive, without being prime movers. Examples include the evolution of modern news media, transportation, weapons technology, weak state control of territory, etc. Proponents of the so-called 'ecology of terrorism thesis' even claim that international terrorism occurs mainly because modern circumstances have made it exceptionally easy to employ terrorist methods.[9]
- *Motivational causes* are the actual grievances that people experience at a personal level, motivating them to act. Ideologues and political leaders are sometimes able to translate causes from a structural level up to a motivational level, thereby moving

people to act. The role of ideology and rhetoric is to explain how things really are, and persuade individuals and groups to take action. Motivational causes may also be seen as concrete 'symptoms' of more fundamental structural causes.

- *Triggering causes* are the direct precipitators of terrorist acts. They may be momentous or provocative events, a political calamity, an outrageous act committed by the enemy, or some other events that call for revenge or action. Even peace talks may trigger opponents of political compromise to carry out terrorist action in order to undermine negotiations and discredit moderates.

Another way to organize the various causes of terrorism is to distinguish between explanations at the individual and group level, explanations at the societal and national level, and explanations at the systemic or international level.[10]

Some root factors may impact differently on various types of terrorist groups, and on individuals with different positions within a group. For example, it has been found (in the context of Europe) that the level of modernization makes a strong significant impact on the level of ideological terrorism in a country, whereas there is almost no systematic relationship between modernization and ethnonational terrorism.[11] It is also likely that in such organizations as al-Qaeda, relative deprivation has differing impacts on the well-educated, upper-middle-class leaders and on the less-educated, lower-class foot soldiers. It is also a well-known phenomenon in the history of terrorism that middle-class students and well-paid professionals take on roles as representatives and champions of the poor and repressed of the world. They are not deprived themselves, but they use (some would say exploit) the issue of poverty as a justification for terrorism.

In many cases, terrorist groups emerge due to one set of causes, and continue to operate over time for quite different reasons. Similarly, individuals may remain in a terrorist group for reasons other than what led them to join in the first place. Domestic terrorism and international terrorism are also likely to emerge for different reasons.

In most cases, terrorism is an extension and radicalization of various types of conflicts (between different ethnonational groups, between ethnic minorities and governments, between ideological groups and governments, between rival ideological groups, etc.).[12] Obviously, the root causes of such conflicts are also root causes of terrorism. On the other hand, most conflicts, even many armed conflicts, do not lead to terrorism, which is a set of more specific violent strategies, differing from civil war or guerrilla warfare.[13] A main task of this book should be to identify the factors, processes and circumstances that tend to produce such a radicalization into terrorism; as well as to find which factors tend to prevent such conflicts from generating terrorism.

Questions to address

This book will address a number of questions, although we will hardly be able to provide all the answers. Still, we may start to identify some of the more promising avenues, and rule out others as blind alleys. The authors were asked to address the following questions:

- Are there some root causes or fundamental processes that are common to all (or most) forms of terrorism? Or do different types of terrorism reflect only superficial similarities in their forms of violent expression, whereas their origins and basic processes are totally dissimilar?
- Why do some dissident groups or movements radicalize into using terrorist means? And why do people join such militant groups? Some of these motivations and processes may be relatively similar across different types of terrorist groups.
- Is religious fundamentalism by itself a root cause of terrorism? Or is it just a reflection of more fundamental political and social tensions? What is the role of religion in conflicts leading to terrorism? Are religious differences a fundamental cause, or merely an organizing principle of violent conflicts between social groups? Some conflicts involving terrorism are organized along religious lines, even if the fundamental causes are more social than religious. Examples here are conflicts in the former Yugoslavia and Northern Ireland. How and at what stage does religion become a factor in itself?
- Is radicalized ideology a root cause of terrorism, or is it adopted subsequently so as to justify acts of terror carried out for other reasons? What roles do ideological leaders and entrepreneurs play in channelling people's frustrations and anger into a terrorist movement?
- What role does the weakness or strength of the state play in spawning local terrorist groups? And to what extent can international terrorist groups be seen as products and instruments of states? Is state sponsorship actually causing terrorist groups to emerge, or is it just a way to reinforce (and perhaps influence) groups that are already committing terrorism for their own reasons?
- Why do some terrorist groups globalize their agendas or their operations, whereas others choose to remain local?
- We should also try to identify possible vicious circles that act to reinforce and perpetuate terrorism. What role do notions of revenge or retaliation play in such circles? And how do overreactions to terrorism by the state reinforce terrorism? Are there any possibilities for breaking the vicious circle?

All the experts invited to contribute to this book have been asked to try to identify the main causes behind the terrorism they describe in their papers. Which of these causes or processes can be influenced through various forms of policies of prevention or intervention? Which are more promising for achieving a reduction in terrorism? And what alleged 'root causes' are dead ends that will lead to nothing, either because the causal relationship to terrorism is weak, or because this cause is something that either cannot or should not be removed or dealt with?

Is the notion of 'root causes' really useful? Is it meaningful to distinguish a 'root' cause from less 'rooted' causes or factors in the complex processes of generating terrorism? Perhaps our recommendation to the politicians should be that they drop the 'root' part from their discourse, and focus instead on more specific and immediate causes of terrorism? Or could it be that the concept of 'root causes' leads us astray by inducing us to look for very general social ills that actually have little to do with causing terrorism? It is likely that the more general we make the problem, the more impossible it becomes to address and handle the more specific causes of terrorism by targeted intervention or preventive measures.

The organization of this book

The purpose of this book is to address a wide range of relevant causes of terrorism in order to assess their relative importance in producing terrorist outcomes, and to provide the basis for a comprehensive discussion on which causes are amenable for intervention. The chapters are organized in a thematic sequence, where adjacent chapters provide supplementary perspectives and examples to what comes before and after.

Following this Introduction, in Chapter 2, *Exploring roots of terrorism*, Dipak Gupta asks why are people participating in collective action in general, and in terrorist action in particular? What are the rationalities and motivations for joining terrorist organizations and being involved in violent action, frequently at great personal cost? He points to the importance of ideology and the role of political entrepreneurs in providing prospective terrorists with a coherent motivation. However, in any movement we will find that different types of participants are involved for highly different reasons. Some are 'true believers' motivated by ideology and the cause, others are 'mercenaries' who are in it for their own selfish interests, whereas a third type are the 'captive participants' who are involved for the fear of not going along with the group. Based on his discussion on motivations for joining terrorist organizations, he ends up with a list of suggestions for dealing more effectively with terrorist organizations. In particular, he advises that we must devote much greater effort to understanding the dynamics of their demise.

In Chapter 3, *Impoverished terrorists: stereotype or reality?*, Jitka Malečková addresses one of the most commonly held ideas about the root cause of terrorism, particularly popular with politicians and even some scholars: the idea that people become terrorists because of poverty and despair caused by economic deprivation. However, her critical examination of available data lends little support to this thesis. Specifically, she and her colleague Alan Krueger have investigated the determinants of participation in militant activities in the Middle East, in particular suicide terrorists. They also looked at cross-country data on the connection between economic conditions on the national level and the occurrence of terrorism by individuals from various countries, and analysed public opinion polls on the strength of support for attacks against Israeli targets in the West Bank and Gaza Strip. Their investigation suggests that any connection between poverty and terrorism is indirect and probably quite weak. In fact, most of their results point in the opposite direction: a higher living standard is positively associated with support for or participation in terrorism. The roots of terrorism, and thus also the possible ways and means to stop it, should therefore be sought elsewhere. Malečková argues that terrorists are more likely to come from countries that lack civil liberties, suggesting that freedom of expression may provide an alternative to terrorism.

The next three chapters address the root causes of terrorism from social and psychological perspectives. In Chapter 4, John Horgan discusses *The social and psychological characteristics of terrorism and terrorists*. He calls for a measure of realism in our expectations to prevent terrorism by addressing its root causes. We are usually not in a position to address terrorist grievances per se until the terrorist campaign has developed, he argues. At the social and psychological level, the question of what causes people to act as they do is very complex, depending on the stage in the process of terrorist group membership. Why and how persons become involved in a terrorist group may have little bearing on what they do in different roles as terrorists. And what keeps people involved with a terrorist organization may have surprisingly little, if any, bearing on what subsequently sees them disengaging from the organization. Thus, unless we recognize these different stages in the process of involvement in terrorism, we may force our answers to the question of 'What are the root causes of terrorism?' into misleading singular explanations. Thus, terrorism must be seen as a complex process, and our efforts to prevent it must reflect this complexity. Furthermore, Horgan dismisses the common idea that terrorists represent a special type of person, with personal traits or characteristics that make them special or very different from the rest of us: a point also made in the two following chapters.

In Chapter 5, Jerrold M. Post describes *The socio-cultural underpinnings of terrorist psychology*. He shows that different types of terrorist groups (namely the social-revolutionary terrorists, the nationalist-separatist terrorists, and the religious fundamentalist terrorists) have fundamentally different pathways into terrorism. Although attempts have been made to identify a terrorist personality, in fact terrorists are not mentally disturbed. Indeed, terrorist groups regularly exclude emotionally disturbed individuals, who represent a security risk. Rather, it is to social psychology (the psychology of groups, organizations, and indeed societies) that we must turn to understand what impels these individuals. And insofar as the process of socialization to hate the enemy and justify violence against them begins in childhood, Post argues that countering terrorism must have as a central component combating the 'war for hearts and minds', with four central elements being: inhibiting potential terrorists from joining the group in the first place; creating dissension in the group; facilitating exit from the group; and reducing support for the group and its leadership.

In Chapter 6, *Social, organizational and psychological factors in suicide terrorism*, Ariel Merari claims that attempts to explain suicide terrorist attacks have so far been speculative, and have focused on religious fanaticism, 'brainwashing', and personality factors. Empirical evidence, however, leads to different conclusions: religion is neither a prerequisite nor a major factor in the etiology of suicide terrorism. In fact, until recently, most suicide attacks have been perpetrated by secular terrorist groups. Terrorist suicides tend to be young, unmarried persons. In Islamic groups they are almost exclusively males, except for Chechen rebels, among whom females have constitued about 40 per cent. Other than that, they have no common psychological and demographic profile. Terrorist suicides do not fit the characteristics of 'ordinary' suicides. There is no evidence that the wish to take revenge for personal suffering plays a major role in an individual's readiness to carry out a suicide attack. Terrorist suicide is not associated with poverty. Merari concludes that suicide terrorism is the product of manipulative group influences, rather than the result of individual characteristics.

In Chapter 7, *Palestinian resistance and 'suicide bombing': causes and consequences*, the Palestinian political scientist Hisham H. Ahmed provides findings and perspectives that are in support of, as well as in contrast to, those of his Israeli colleague in the preceding chapter. Ahmed agrees that religious motivation is not the decisive factor in causing young Palestinians to blow themselves up in 'martyrdom operations', and that these young people are not suicidal or committing suicide in the usual sense. In Palestinian society and culture these actions have a completely different meaning: they are acts of self-sacrifice. However, in Ahmad's analysis, the main motivation for committing these extreme acts of self-sacrifice is found not so much in group processes as in the heavy repression of the Israeli occupation as experienced in Palestinian everyday life. Coupled with the failure of the political process in bringing relief and hope, the overwhelming force of the occupation regime has caused general despair and frustration among the Palestinians. Traditional forms of military resistance have been seen as futile. However, 'martyrdom operations' in the form of 'intelligent human bombs' represented a tactic of asymmetric warfare that had a prospect of equalizing Israeli hi-tech military power, shaking Israeli society and morale. Ahmed describes how such 'martyrdom operations' were seen as justified by the Palestinian public as well as by Islamic scholars. The misery and personal traumas caused by living under a brutalizing occupation and seeing children being killed and family members humiliated, created an immense anger, bitterness and hatred. Ahmad argues that suicide bombing should be seen as an act of ultimate despair, a horrific reaction to extremely inhumane conditions in a seriously damaged environment of hopelessness.

In Chapter 8, Abdullah Sahar Mohammad analyses *The roots of terrorism in the Middle East: internal pressures and international constraints*. He provides a critique of Western 'terrorology', and gives a useful survey of what Arab analysts have to say about the causes of terrorism in the Middle East. He then sets out to apply a multi-dimensional cause–effect methodology to study these causes. He investigates how the levels of four main variables – socio-economic development, literacy, democracy and extremism – relate to the level of terrorist violence in Arab countries. Regardless of highly different levels of economic well-being, all Arab societies experience a certain degree of social and economic injustice. In the vast majority of these countries, a feeling of inequality is felt among the general population. Still, those who have committed terrorist actions in countries like Kuwait, Saudi Arabia or Egypt have never based the justification for their actions upon economic factors of any kind, but rather on issues of foreign policy, such as American involvement in the region or the conflict (or peace) with Israel. Mohammad also points out that in spite of growing levels of literacy in the Middle East, terrorism has grown. One possible explanation is that education reinforces people's awareness of the surrounding political ills, such as frustrating economic and social conditions. Regarding democratization, Arab countries lag far behind, and the lack of regime legitimacy and pathways for opposition are likely to cause people to turn to violence. Still, small measures towards democratization in countries like Kuwait and Jordan have not minimized terrorist incidents. Concerning extremism, Mohammad shows how it has spread in different forms throughout the Middle East. Islamic extremism became increasingly attractive as a political alternative due to lack of regime legitimacy and effectiveness. Islamic groups provided credible alternatives for interpreting political realities as well as for action. Mohammad concludes that terrorist incidents occur in almost all the Arab states regardless of their levels of societal dissatisfaction, economic injustice, political liberalization or extremism. He then sets out to construct a multidimensional model to explain this puzzle.

The next two chapters address ethnonationalist terrorism. In Chapter 9, Fernando Reinares discusses *Nationalist separatism and terrorism in comparative perspective.* Nationalist movements often include political organizations seeking the separation of a certain territory and its population from the state or states under which they are currently governed. However, only some independentist or irredentist organizations engage in violence. Reinares states that nationalist separatism does not in itself explain nationalist separatist terrorism. Exclusionary ethnic nationalisms are more likely to justify terrorism than moderate and inclusive civic nationalisms. The radicalization of nationalist protest into terrorism is more likely under authoritarian regimes and in the context of democratic transitions. Consensual democracies seem to have been less affected by nationalist separatist terrorism than majoritarian democracies. Terrorism is typically adopted by nationalist separatist organizations expelled from relevant public decision-making processes as a result of state coercion or pluralistic competition. Unless there is some kind of external sponsorship or assistance, the persistence of any independentist or irredentist terrorist organization depends on the support or tolerance mobilized among its population of reference, particularly among people from the lower social classes. These terrorist organizations tend to follow a logic of self maintenance. This has implications for governmental initiatives aiming at peaceful regulation of nationalist conflicts. Reinares argues that democratic governments must make decisions considering the plurality of collective identities and political allegiances existing among the citizens affected. Such plurality may well limit the scope of nationalist achievements and make it impossible to satisfy the expectations of independentist and irredentist terrorist organizations.

In Chapter 10, D.R. Kaarthikeyan provides *A case study of the Tamil insurgency and the LTTE,* discussing the root causes of this bloody conflict and the possible pathways out of it. He argues that the rise and growth of the Tamil insurgency in Sri Lanka and particularly the growth of the LTTE, *Liberation Tigers of Tamil Elam* (known as the *Tamil Tigers*) was born out of systematic discrimination against the Tamil minority, bred under oppression and strengthened through orchestrated state violence. The leaders of the LTTE, on their part, ruthlessly killed off leaders of rival Tamil organizations, thereby getting rid of the more moderate voices of Tamil rights. The LTTE's campaign remains one of the longest lasting insurgencies in contemporary politics. It commenced fighting for a separate homeland and continues to do so, unlike other similar outfits that have adapted their goals to suit the evolving dynamics of state and international politics. After having identified the various causal factors that have spawned the growth of the LTTE, Kaarthikeyan discuss the two main options before the Sri Lankan government. The first one is to give up peace talks and to continue with the military option in order to suppress or subjugate the Tamil rebels. This military option has been tried for two decades, at great cost, but has not worked. The other option is to continue peace talks, accommodate the LTTE's more reasonable demands and go for a genuine democratic federal solution. Kaarthikeyan argues that addressing the root causes of the conflict in this way is the only viable option.

The next three chapters discuss the use of terrorism by right-wing, left-wing and organized crime groups, respectively. In Chapter 11, *Right-wing terrorism*, Wilhelm Heitmeyer points out that there are very different forms of right-wing violence and perpetrators. In Europe, the groups have been small and violence has been directed mostly against ethnic minorities and the democratic system in general. In South and Central America the right-wing terror in the 1970s was much more comprehensive and the central aim was to stabilize the dictatorships. Thus, different explanations are needed. In the European situation, Heitmeyer points to several constellations: a violent form of right-wing extremism is more likely to develop where there is no political representation through political parties or channelling mechanism in the form of electoral success at national level. However, right-wing extremist violence can exist or develop without electoral successes for the far Right, but can never survive without xenophobic and right-wing moods and attitudes among the population. The greater the level of violence perpetrated by right-wing extremist groups, the lower is the political weight attached to legitimate power-sharing. And finally, political marginalization of right-wing extremist parties and groups produces variable results. In some cases it leads to fragmentation of the extreme Right, while in others it may lead to radicalization into violence and even terrorism. The process of radicalization into terrorism is a function of political interaction. The role of the state is crucial in this interaction because both underreaction and overreaction may well accelerate this escalation process.

In Chapter 12, Peter Waldmann makes a comparative analysis of *Social-revolutionary terrorism in Latin America and Europe* to assess whether it is a promising path to try to discover the 'root causes' of these two varieties of terrorist movements. He argues that the structural conditions in which the European and Latin American groups emerged were vastly different in terms of economic development as well as level of democratization in their respective countries. The social-revolutionary terrorists themselves have, in the vast majority of cases, a middle-class academic background. The decision to employ terrorist violence depends less on deep-rooted 'causes' than on the social and geographic opportunity structures under which the violent groups have to operate. Waldmann claims that 'subjective' factors (rooted in frustrated career expectations, status problems, generation conflict, affinity to global ideological currents, etc.) offer a far better key for understanding the violent behaviour of these groups and their members than 'objective' factors such as social misery and injustice, corrupt governments and so on. The appearance of terrorist groups must be seen in the broader context of a general predisposition to apply political violence. Whether this predisposition takes the concrete form of a protest movement, a guerrilla campaign or terrorist attacks depends less on specific 'causes' than on strategic decisions of the leaders of these groups when coping with the structural conditions of a given situation. Without a hinterland to retire to and hide in, and a sympathetic peasant population to provide support functions, running a guerrilla campaign is not possible, thus making terrorism or protest movements more realistic alternatives to social-revolutionary rebels.

In Chapter 13, *The use of terrorism by organized crime*, Alison Jamieson argues that organized crime and terrorism should always be viewed as quite distinct phenomena in terms of motivation, operational tactics and ultimate objectives. In cases where these phenomena overlap, Jamieson distinguishes between (a) the self-financing of terrorist groups by typical 'organized crime-type' activities, (b) pragmatic collaboration between terrorist and organized crime groups for mutually beneficial ends, and (c) the use of terrorism by organized crime groups for political purposes. Essentially, the terrorist is a revolutionary seeking to overthrow the political order, whereas organized crime actors tend to be inherently conservative, tending to resist political upheaval and seeking conditions of stability that are more conducive to their ultimate goal of financial accumulation. In her discussion about the Sicilian Mafia, the *Cosa Nostra*, she argues that their recourse to a car bomb campaign on the Italian mainland in 1993 was atypical, and marked the collapse of a long-standing equilibrium between the privatized Mafia state and the public or institutional state. The aim of the campaign was to intimidate and destabilize Italy's institutions and open up space for mediation with new political interlocutors. Jamieson also makes a comparison with the left-wing *Brigate Rosse* (the Red Brigades), discussing the significance of group identity, the relationship to violence and the importance of consensus. *Cosa Nostra* has survived by adherence to core values and a capacity to adapt and modernize whereas inflexibility and alienation from their intended constituency of support led to internal dissent and the defeat of the *Brigate Rosse*.

The following three chapters discuss the role of the state in facilitating, sponsoring or perpetrating terrorism. In Chapter 14, Farid el Khazen analyses *Patterns of state failure: the case of Lebanon*. States fail for several reasons ranging from the loss of monopolistic control over the means of legitimate coercion to the failure to deliver and regulate services. There are also different degrees of state failure. First, one extreme degree of state failure is when centralized authority within internationally recognized borders of the state collapse (e.g. Somalia) or where a recognized authority exists but no borders are defined and the 'state' is ruled by another country (e.g. Palestine, and Kuwait in 1990–1). A second degree is represented by deficit in the capacity of the state to exercise power (e.g. Cambodia, Sri Lanka, Haiti, Columbia). A third degree is states kept together only by an authoritarian order (Tibet under Chinese rule, Iraq, the former Soviet Union). During the war years in Lebanon, 1975–90, a number of local militias, international foreign and guerrilla organizations and foreign armies could operate more or less at will, without a central government able to enforce a monopoly of violence. However, el Khazen argues that the state in post-war Lebanon does not present a classic case of a failed state but a state that provides an arena for armed conflict involving several regional state and non-state actors. But unlike patterns of failure forced upon the state for political and/or military reasons, (e.g. Somalia, Liberia, Afghanistan, Indonesia), state failure in post-war Lebanon is 'engineered' by the state to the benefit of another state (Syria) fighting proxy wars in Lebanon and/or pursuing political objectives ranging from relations with the USA to a multifaceted regional agenda that includes the Arab–Israeli conflict, Iran, and Arab countries. If not contained, this state-designed security vacuum provides the possibility of armed conflict and political violence: terrorism or otherwise. Only when the vacuum is filled would the state in Lebanon be held accountable for its deeds and for whatever developments occur over its territories.

In Chapter 15, *State sponsorship: a root cause of terrorism?*, Louise Richardson argues that, contrary to the prevailing view of the US administration in the 1980s (a view that has re-emerged in the present Bush administration), state sponsorship is not a root cause of terrorism. For various reasons, these administrations have preferred to consider terrorism primarily as a problem of rogue states, sponsoring and directing their terrorist clients. However, states across the political spectrum have used terrorism as an instrument of foreign policy; even impeccably liberal democracies have been known to do so. In these instances, states have capitalized on pre-existing terrorist movements rather than created them. Relationships between terrorists and their sponsors in fact can be quite nuanced, and range from alliances of convenience occasioned by sharing an enemy at one extreme, to covert actions of agents of the state masquerading as terrorists, on the other. Terrorist movements, rather than states, have often been the initiators of these relationships and have been known to play off one state against another. The popularity of the view that state sponsorship is a root cause of terrorism is largely attributable to the fact that it is easier for a state to retaliate against another state with military means than against a more inchoate enemy. That said, state sponsorship can, and on many occasions does, significantly enhance the lethality of terrorist groups by providing resources, training and safe havens.

In Chapter 16, *Expected utility and state terrorism*, Michael Stohl explores the conditions under which states have resorted to the use of violence, repression and terrorism against their own and others' populations. He also sets out to detect the conditions that resulted in these behaviours and explore different forms of state terrorist behaviour in both domestic and international affairs. The argument is that a regime is more likely to employ terrorism as a means of governance when it believes that terrorism is more effective relative to other means of governance, and when costs associated with the behaviours are relatively low. This approach locates terrorism as a strategy of action in a conflict situation. State terrorism within the domestic context presupposes a regime in conflict with at least some of its citizenry which estimates that terrorism will perform better than alternative means in eliminating or quieting some actual or perceived potential challenge or threat. Within the international realm, the same logic applies. Stohl asserts that states (and other terrorist actors) might choose terrorism paradoxically both when they perceive themselves as powerless – in the sense that other policy instruments of rule are unavailable or less useful – and when they are in a situation that may be labelled confident strength – when the costs were perceived as low and the probability of success believed high in relation to other means. Two forms of costs are identified.

Firstly, the response costs associated with the reaction of targeted groups and bystanders (domestic and international) and secondly, production costs, which are the actual material as well as psychic costs of performing acts which are generally defined as unacceptable. The approach suggests that this will generally place socially marginal or socially distant groups at the greatest risk because the response and production costs associated with these groups as a target are relatively low in comparison to their vulnerability, and the perceived chances of success for policies directed against them are considered relatively high because of their relative powerlessness and marginalization. However, Stohl's perspective also provides insight in how bystanders and audiences can increase the cost and hence the utility of terrorist behaviour.

The final four chapters seek to extract from our understandings of root causes of terrorism lessons that can be translated into policies to prevent the emergence of terrorism or to reduce actual terrorist campaigns.

In Chapter 17, Joshua Sinai sets out to provide *A conceptual framework for resolving terrorism's causes* by assessing the spectrum of response measures, whether coercive or conciliatory, that are appropriate to resolve a terrorist-type conflict's underlying root causes. A primary assumption is that when a terrorist rebellion succeeds in gaining the support of a significant segment of the population and in protracting the insurgency, and the government's coercive measures are unable either to decisively defeat the insurgents on the battlefield or to resolve the insurgency peacefully, then a new counter-terrorism strategy is required to resolve the conflict. In a situation of such a protracted 'hurting stalemate' that is damaging to both sides, long-term resolution can only come about when governments begin to address a conflict's underlying root causes; but only when the insurgents' grievances are considered to be legitimate and grounded in some aspects of international law. It is also up to the insurgents to incorporate into their demands, grievances and other objectives that are amenable to the 'give-and-take' of compromise and negotiations.

In Chapter 18, *Prevention of terrorism: towards a multi-pronged approach*, Alex P. Schmid briefly discusses trends and perceptions of terrorism and the UN draft definition of terrorism. He then introduces a 'toolbox' of eight types of counter-terrorism measures. In particular, he discusses *Political and Governance Measures*, where he pleads for anti-terrorism policies based on (a) good governance, (b) democracy, (c) rule of law, and (d) social justice. Concerning *Economic and Social Measures*, he tests statistically whether or not poverty is a causal factor by comparing UNDP poverty indicators with a self-developed terrorism index. Data show that the correlation between poverty and terrorism is much weaker than the correlation between (the lack of) rule of law and terrorism.

In Chapter 19, *Fire of Iolaus: the role of state countermeasures in causing terrorism and what needs to be done*, Andrew Silke draws an analogy between counter-terrorism measures and the myth of the Hydra. When Hercules chopped off a head of the Hydra, more simply grew in its place. On the verge of defeat in his battle with the creature, Hercules was only saved when his nephew, Iolaus, used fire to cauterize the Hydra's wounds and thus prevented more heads from growing. Silke's paper considers why some counter-terrorism and anti-terrorism policies and tactics have proven so unsuccessful and have often seemed to create more terrorism than they stopped or prevented. Examples of such counter-productive strategies include extra-legal assassinations (e.g. South Africa, Israel); military retaliations (e.g. USA against Libya 1986); and internment without trial (e.g. Northern Ireland). The paper considers the circumstances in which such policies have been adopted by various states. An argument is made that a better understanding of human psychology, particularly as it relates to the needs for retribution and punishment, provides the key for an objective understanding of the impact of high-risk counter-terrorism policies. The paper ends with a consideration of the lessons to be taken away from such experiences.

In the final chapter, the editor reviews the main findings of the book. One main set of findings concerns several widely held assumptions of what causes terrorism: the alleged causal relationship between poverty and terrorism; that state sponsorship is a root cause of terrorism; that suicide terrorism is predominantly motivated by religion; and that terrorists are insane and irrational actors. These assumptions get little or no support from the data on which the present studies were based. Although it is, as expected, not possible to identify a single root cause that explains the emergence of most terrorist campaigns, the authors identified a number of preconditions that often set the stage for the emergence of terrorism, and several more specific precipitants (types of specific events or situations that immediately precede, motivate or trigger the outbreak of terrorism). However, terrorism is often sustained for reasons other than those which gave birth to it in the first place. This chapter ends with a discussion about the possibilities and limitations of reducing terrorism by addressing its root causes.

Notes

1   Politically, this opposition to the root causes approach has been articulated by, for example, some 'neo-cons' within the present Bush administration, although these circles also frequently emphasize certain root causes (such as rogue states and lack of democracy) as essential to address in order to fight terrorism. From academic quarters, Walter Laqueur (2003a, Chapter 1) has expressed strong scepticism about the utility of preventing terrorism by addressing its root causes.

2   The figure is provided by Silke (2003: 2).

3   The Arab League Convention on the Suppression of Terrorism from 1998 states that 'All cases of struggle by whatever means, including armed struggle, against foreign occupation and aggression for liberation and self-determination, in accordance with the principles of international law, shall not be regarded as an offence' (UN Office of Legal Affairs 2001: 153–4). A more moderate version of this argument was expressed in the Convention of the Organization of the Islamic Conference on Combating International Terrorism (2000).

4   Schmid and Jongman's handbook on terrorism research (1988: 14) contains a highly influential analysis and discussion on the definitions of terrorism.

5   For a good overview and discussion, see Lia and Skjølberg (2000).

6   For example, research has not been able to establish a direct linear relationship between the level of poverty and the level of terrorism. This does not mean, however, that there are not important links, rather that these relationships are of a more complex kind. Thus, some studies have found significant relationships between the degree of unequal distribution of wealth and the level of terrorism in various European countries (see Engene 1994, 1998). Others, focusing on relative deprivation, have shown that in countries with rapid economic growth, the gap between increasing expectations and

insufficient satisfaction generates frustration, which in turn may lead to collective civil violence and terrorism (Gurr 1970; Huntington 1968).

7   For a discussion of terrorism as strategic choice and as sets of strategies, see Crenshaw (1990) and Bjørgo and Heradstveit (1993).
8   See Lia and Skjølberg (2000) and Crenshaw (1990).
9   See Kegley (1990: 105ff), Laqueur (2003b), and Lia and Skjølberg (2000: 22–4).
10 Lia and Skjølberg (2000) provide a detailed and useful discussion of different theoretical perspectives on the causes of terrorism.
11 See Engene (1994, 1998).
12 There is an extensive literature within the peace and conflict research tradition exploring the various causes of armed conflict. For an overview, see The World Bank (2003, Appendix 2: 'A selected bibliography of civil war and rebellion').
13 For a discussion of typologies of terrorism, see Schmid and Jongman (1988, Chapter 1).

Bibliography

Bjørgo, T. and Heradstveit, D. (1993) *Politisk Terrorisme*. Oslo: TANO.

Crenshaw, M. (1990) 'The Logic of Terrorism: Terrorist Behaviour as a Product of Strategic Choice', in Reich (1990): 7–24.

Crenshaw, M. (2003) 'The Causes of Terrorism', in Kegley (2003).

Engene, J.O. (1994) *Europeisk terrorisme. Vold, stat og legitimitet*. Oslo: TANO.

Engene, J.O. (1998) *Patterns of Terrorism in Western Europe 1950–95*. Bergen: Department of Comparative Politics, University of Bergen (doctoral dissertation).

Gurr, T.R. (1970) *Why Men Rebel*. Princeton, NJ: Princeton University Press.

Huntington, S.P. (1968) *Political Order in Changing Societies*. New Haven, CT: Yale University Press.

Kegley, C. Jr. (ed.) (1990) *International Terrorism: Characteristics, Causes and Controls*. New York, London: St Martin's Press.

Kegley, C. Jr. (ed.) (2003) *The New Global Terrorism: Characteristics, Causes, Controls*. Upper Saddle River, NJ: Prentice Hall.

Laqueur, W. (2003a) *No End to War: Terrorism in the Twenty-first Century*. New York: Continuum.

Laqueur, W. (2003b) 'Postmodern Terrorism', in Kegley (2003).

Lia, B. and Skjølberg, K.H.-W. (2000) *Why Terrorism Occurs: A Survey of Theories and Hypotheses on the Causes of Terrorism*. Norway: Kjeller (FFI/Rapport – 2000/02769), also available at http://www.nupi.no/IPS/filestore/02769.pdf

Reich, W. (ed.) (1990) *Origins of Terrorism: Psychologies, Ideologies, Theologies, States of Mind*. Cambridge: Cambridge University Press.

Schmid, A.P. and Jongman, A.J. (1988) *Political Terrorism: A New Guide to Actors, Authors, Concepts, Databases, Theories and Literature*. Amsterdam: SWIDOC, North Holland Publishing Company.

Silke, A. (ed.) (2003) *Terrorism Research: Trends, Achievements and Failures*. London: Frank Cass.

The World Bank (2003) *Breaking the Conflict Trap: Civil War and Development Policy*. Washington, DC: The World Bank Group (policy research report).

UN Office of Legal Affairs (2001) *International Instruments Related to the Prevention and Suppression of International Terrorism*. New York: United Nations.

2 Exploring roots of terrorism

Dipak K. Gupta

Factors of individual motivation

Terrorism has a long history, but its systematic analysis has a short past. Within this relatively brief period of time, spanning perhaps not much longer than three decades, analytical literature on the causes of terrorism has mushroomed.[1] The rate of publication of academic and journalistic books and articles is even more accelerated since the days when the USA and other Western countries started to feel terrorism's nefarious effects. If there are a few thin but resolute threads running through this rapidly burgeoning literature, despite its sheer volume and diversity, they are:

- It is nearly impossible to define 'terrorism'.
- The link between socio-political and economic structural factors, such as poverty, lack of economic opportunity, etc. and terrorism is weak.
- There is no single profile of a 'terrorist'.

All of these above conclusions define the contours of not what we know, but what we don't know about terrorism. In favour of this meagre harvest, we may do well to recall the Socratic wisdom: 'What you know may be less important than what you don't know'.

Facing such a conundrum in looking for the 'root causes' of terrorism, in this chapter, I would like to start with a different approach. Any act of 'terrorism', however defined, is a collective action, a quintessentially political act taken in the name of a group based on ethnicity, religion, nationalism or ideological orientation.[2] If it were not, it would fall under the category of common criminal behaviour, undertaken solely for the enrichment of the participants. Hence, in our quest for the 'root causes' I begin by asking the question, 'Why do people participate in collective actions?'.

A comparison between what an individual might feel in the midst of a deeply religious or ideological movement or during horrific sectarian violence, and what psychiatrists and psychologists might call 'paranoia', 'schizophrenia' or 'delusion' is inevitable. For instance, Glass (1985: 38) notes, 'It occurs to me after listening for several months to the delusional utterances that some connection may exist between internal emotional structures and construction of ethical, political systems of belief'.

He further adds that in their delusion, his patients, similar to demagogues and their followers all over the world, develop a more or less coherent belief system. This belief system is characterized by inner images of sharp dichotomies between 'good/bad, God/devil, American/communists, black/white' (ibid.: 61), and so on. A number of psychiatrists have sought causes of abnormal behaviour, which allows people to target innocent people through individual personality traits (Akhtar 1999; Haroun 1999). Investigations by other clinical psychologists have also produced a mixed bag of tangible outcomes. For instance, Sarraj (2002), a noted Palestinian psychologist argues that the primary motivations behind suicide bombing are a mix of guilt, shame, and an overwhelming desire to avenge the perceived injustice wrought to their land by the Israeli authorities.[3] Others have found evidence of repressed sexual fantasies in the young men (Konet 2001) and women (Morgan 2002) in their decision to participate in the acts of self-immolation. Yet, the problem with such analyses is that two separate individuals are not chased by the same demon; mental illness, unlike infectious disease, does not contaminate an entire population.

Among social scientists, only economists make explicit behavioural assumptions. They argue that individuals participate in an action if, in their estimation, their benefits resulting from their involvement outweighs the costs. That is:

$$\text{Benefits} - \text{Cost} > 0 \tag{1}$$

The introduction of a 'rational choice' hypothesis has expanded the domain of economics significantly. Originally developed to explain market behaviour, economic principles have been used to explain a vast array of human activities from criminal behaviour (Becker 1976) to marriage (Grossbard-Sechtman 1993), and even to the choice of religious faith (Innaccone 2002). The assumption of self-utility maximization, however, runs into two interrelated conceptual problems in explaining collective action (Olson 1965). First, the problem with explaining collective action with the assumption of self-interest is that these acts are undertaken for the welfare of the entire group. Hence, the benefits stemming from their attainment cannot be restricted to those who would be participating. Second, to the participants, the outcome is not directly linked to the effort, particularly when the group size is large. Let me explain the problems.

Suppose, there are two individuals both of whom would benefit from a political change (e.g. the removal of a tyrant from power, or even going to vote in a national election to choose a candidate). One has decided to participate in an act of political dissidence, the other has not. In our formulation this would appear as:

$$\text{Participant} = \text{Benefit} - \text{Cost} \tag{2}$$

$$\text{Non-participant} = \text{Benefit} \tag{3}$$

As we can see from these formulations, since a non-participant does not have to pay any cost (from loss of time, income to even loss of life) to get benefits from a collective good, there is no reason for any rational human being to participate in a collective action. Furthermore, as the group size increases, a single participant's contribution to the cause becomes increasingly insignificant. A single voter cannot affect the outcome of a national election. Nor can a single Islamic suicide bomber expect to establish a global Islamic state with his or her sacrifice. Therefore, nobody would have any reason to contribute to a collective cause. Thus, the conclusion of this line of argument is that having realized the insignificance of his or her own participation, for instance in bringing about a free Palestinian state, no rational Palestinian would ever join an act of rebellion against Israel. As a result, no collective action will be undertaken, no war will ever be fought, and much of what we see around us as public goods will cease to exist. In the literature, this is known as Olson's Paradox or, alternatively, Social Dilemma (Olson 1965). The reason it is important to start from this theoretical perspective is because otherwise, while looking for 'root causes' of terrorism, we would have to assume that those who take part in the acts of dissidence while sacrificing their own welfare are either irrational beings or are masking their ulterior motives of selfish goals with claims of ideology, religion, or nationalism (Tullock 1971). The most pressing problem with the traditional economic assumption of self-utility maximization is that it provides us with a truncated view of a human rationality, which ultimately can lead to faulty policy prescriptions for eliminating the threats of terrorism.

In order to overcome the Paradox, I have proposed an expanded behavioural assumption, which combines individuals' self-utility along with their desire for a greater welfare of the groups in which they choose to belong (Gupta 1990, 2001, 2002). In my expanded formulation, individuals maximize their self-utility (personal welfare) as well as what they perceive as their group-utility or the welfare of their entire group. Thus, my expanded formulation states:

$$\text{Participant} = \text{Personal benefit} + \text{Group benefit} - \text{Cost} \qquad (4)$$

Therefore, according to my assumption of human behaviour, a rational individual can join a collective action even if his or her own net personal welfare is negative, as long as the perceived benefit to the group is large enough to compensate for these losses. I argue that unless we understand the need for an individual to belong to a group and strive for its betterment, we will not understand the motivation of human beings as social animals. Furthermore, the perception of group welfare is the result of a number of external factors, such as socialization process, religious beliefs, culture and, perhaps most importantly, the influence of a leader, known in the literature as a 'political entrepreneur'. These 'political entrepreneurs', from Carlos Marighela to Osama bin Laden, mix history, religion and mythology to 'frame' an issue, thereby creating a coherent story, replete with the archetypes of 'good' and 'evil', that resonates with a large number of people.[4] Their vision defines the contours of the group identity for their followers, who respond with violent actions (Gupta 2001). These visions are spread through fiery sermons in the mosques, taught in the *madrasas* (religious schools) and through political speeches (Stern 2003; Juergensmeyer, 2000). For instance, having interviewed 35 incarcerated terrorists in the Middle East, Post, Sprinzak, and Denny (2003: 176) correctly observe that in the process of becoming a soldier for a cause a recruit submerges his/her identity to the collective: 'As an individual succumbs to the organization, there is no room for individual ideas, individual identity and individual decision-making'. Hence a proper understanding of the root causes of terrorism must include both economic as well as socio-psychological dimensions of human motivations.

This expanded behavioural precept carries two broad implications. First, it implies that political grievance is a necessary factor but not a sufficient cause for terrorism. In other words, there can be wide-ranging social, political, economic, and even religious grievances in the society, but, following the predictions of Olson's Paradox, these will not necessarily lead to violence. Political violence takes place when a leader gives voice to the frustration by formulating a well-defined social construction of collective identity and paints in vivid colour the images of 'us' and 'them'. Since factors of structural deprivation are the only necessary conditions, any attempt to correlate terrorism and other acts of political violence with poverty and lack of political or religious freedom will only produce a weak statistical correlation. By drawing the same line of reasoning we can clearly see why researchers fail to find a stable profile of a terrorist. None of the 19 perpetrators of the 9/11 attacks suffered from poverty, lack of education or lack of exposure to the privileged lifestyle of the Western world. Few of them were literal followers of the Qur'an. The reason they took part in this action is because they felt inspired by a group of Islamic preachers and revolutionaries, like Osama bin Laden.[5] Since the existence of a 'political entrepreneur' presents us with the 'sufficient' cause, and the rise of these individuals cannot be predicted, it will not be possible to develop a predictive model for the rise of terrorism based on factors of deprivation alone. However, at the same time, when a group is formed, it would follow its interests, which would include among other factors, the advancement of its ideological position, the increase of influence among its constituents, and the promotion of power, influence, and even the financial gains of the group and its leader(s).

Second, my expanded behavioural model indicates that those who would participate in acts of political dissidence would not have a single motivating factor. By examining my proposed formulation in equation (4), we can see that in any movement, there will be those who would participate because participation offers them opportunities for promoting their selfish interests, by offering them the ability to loot, rape, acquire power or, simply, the respect of their followers. I call them the 'mercenaries'. Also, in any political movement, we are likely to encounter those for whom the primary motivating force is ideology or the desire to enhance the welfare of the entire group. I call them the 'ideologues' or 'true believers'. Finally, we will find a group of participants whose presence can be accounted for by their fear (cost) of not going along with the group. I call them the 'captive participants'. It is important to point out that these three basic sources of motivation – greed (self-utility), ideology (group-utility), and fear (cost) – are often indistinguishable from each other. We can only gauge their importance by analysing the revealed preferences of the group members. For instance, one cannot say, without invoking a serious flaw of circular reasoning, that those who are taking part in suicide bombings are doing so to maximize their individual utility. Similarly, when groups engage in kidnapping and drug trafficking, many of their members become more interested in their own selfish interests. The infusion of large sums of money can truly change the character of a political movement. Reflecting the multiplicity of motivations, primarily between ideology and profit motive, we can see that terrorist groups all over the world engage in combating their adversaries based on their most favoured tactics.

The global pattern of violent protest

Although data on terrorism are difficult to obtain, recently a number of research outfits are engaged in collecting relevant information. In this chapter, I have used data provided by the Israeli-based International Policy Institute for Counter-Terrorism. The Institute's website (ICT 2005) provides the most comprehensive information on each event of terrorism that is available in public domain. Also, Pape (2003) provides us with a dataset on suicide attacks. For this study, I have combined the two sources to create a more complete dataset.

Based on the dataset compiled by the ICT I have presented activities of a number of significant terrorist organizations around the world in Table 2.1. This table presents a thumbnail portrait of these groups indicating their specialized nature. Each cell of the table indicates the percentage of each activity for a particular group. The last row presents the sum of the three most prevalent acts of violence as a percentage of each group's total activities. From this list we can easily discern the specialized nature of the various groups. For instance, the Basque Fatherland and Liberty (ETA) and the Irish Republican Army's activities are primarily concentrated on bombings, car bombings and shootings (96 per cent and 94 per cent of their total activities, respectively). The Peruvian group *Sendero Luminoso* (the Shining Path) prefers car bombing, shooting and kidnapping (90 per cent). The Islamic rebel group of the Philippines (the Abu Sayyaf group) and the Revolutionary Armed Forces of Colombia (FARC), on the other hand, specialize in kidnapping and hostage taking. These comprise 91 per cent and 82 per cent of their respective activities.

Only a handful of the world's terrorist organizations engage in suicide bombings: of the 52 major groups listed by the ICT, only 10 engage in suicide bombings. It is apparent from the table that the Hamas and the PIJ follow the path of violence by choosing to concentrate on suicide bombings, shootings and knife attacks. Thus, we can clearly see that violent opposition groups do not choose their weapons of terror in a random fashion but are guided by their internal organizational logic. It is also interesting to note that among the major groups listed in Table 2.1, only the Kurdish Workers' Party, *Patiay Karkeren Kurdestan* (PKK) seems to be less specialized in its choice of terrorist activities. Their top three activities comprise a relatively low 62.1 per cent of their total activities. Since suicide attacks are a specialized activity, I have presented their frequencies in Table 2.2.

In order to empirically establish the clustering of terrorist activities, I performed a Principal Component Factor Analysis on the data from the 17 most active groups in the world.[6] The results, shown in Table 2.3, clearly demonstrate the validity of our hypothesis. I have arranged the components according to their highest loading

Table 2.1 Comparison of profiles of 10 terrorist groups (1980–2002). (Percentage of total activities.)

Activities	Hamas	Abu Sayyaf Group	al-Qaeda	ETA	FARC	LTTE	PIJ	IRA	PKK	Sendero Luminoso
Bombing	6.1	27.3	13.3	37.3	7.9	20.7	9.3	25.0	27.6	5.0
Car bomb	4.3	—	33.3	35.3	5.3	10.3	18.5	37.5	—	45.0
Hand grenade	2.6	—	6.7	2.0	—	—	1.9	—	3.4	—
Hijacking	—	—	6.7	—	2.6	—	—	—	3.4	—
Hostage taking	—	18.2	—	—	7.9	—	—	—	—	5.0
Incendiary devices	—	9.1	—	—	—	—	—	—	10.3	—
Kidnapping	5.2	45.5	—	—	65.8	6.9	1.9	—	20.7	10.0
Knife attack	7.8	—	—	—	—	3.4	1.9	—	—	—
Letter bomb	—	—	—	2.0	—	—	1.9	—	—	—
Mortar attack	—	—	—	—	5.3	3.4	—	6.2	—	—
Rocket attack	—	—	6.7	—	2.6	3.4	—	—	—	—
Shooting	37.4	—	6.7	23.5	2.6	10.3	27.8	31.5	13.8	35.0
Suicide bombing	34.8	—	26.7	—	—	41.4	35.2	—	13.8	—
Vandalism	—	—	—	—	—	—	—	—	3.4	—
Arson	—	—	—	—	—	—	—	—	3.4	—
Chemical attack	—	—	—	—	—	—	—	—	—	—
Stoning	—	—	—	—	—	—	1.9	—	—	—
Vehicle attack	1.7	—	—	—	—	—	—	—	—	—

continued on next page

Table 2.1 Comparison of profiles of 10 terrorist groups (1980–2002). (Percentage of total activities.) (continued from previous page)

Activities	Hamas	Abu Sayyaf Group	al-Qaeda	ETA	FARC	LTTE	PIJ	IRA	PKK	Sendero Luminoso
Lynching	—	—	—	—	—	—	—	—	—	—
Approx. total	100.0	100.0	100.0	100.0	100.0	100.0	100.0	100.0	100.0	100.0
Top three activities (%)	80.0	91.0	73.3	96.1	81.6	72.4	81.5	94.0	62.1	90.0

Source: ICT 2005

within their factor in the five categories. This table further bolsters the argument that dissident groups do not choose their activities randomly, but do so with careful consideration; they pick those which are closest to their ideology, expertise, opportunity and the general modus operandi. Let us look at the logic of association of violent activities as identified by Factor Analysis. We may gain a deeper understanding of the categories by focusing on the activities that have the highest loading within each category. Thus, suicide bombings define the first category and we can call them ideological terrorist acts, since they are inspired by ideological fervour (Hamas), religious extremism (the PIJ and al-Qaeda) and the personal charisma of a leader (the LTTE). I call them 'ideological' because, apart from the technical know-how and complex logistical needs required to carry out successful suicide attacks, they need supremely dedicated cadres who would be willing to give their lives for the cause. This is so rare in the world of violent conflict that only a handful of the groups can have a ready supply of suitable candidates. If we examine the other activities within this factor, we see that shootings and grenade attacks require being physically close to the target, which indicates the assumption of considerable personal risk by the attacker.

In contrast, the second category of attacks is designed for groups with specific professional skills. They include bombings and car bombings, which involve a number of specialized skills, but usually are seldom motivated by acts of religious zealotry, although religion may be one of their principal reasons for conflict. These attacks are usually done with remote control devices, which allow the attackers time to escape. The IRA (see Coogan 2002) and the ETA (Alexander *et al.* 2002) fall in this category. I call these groups 'professional terrorists'.

The third category of activities is promoted primarily by a group's need to make financial gain. The preferences of groups such as the FARC in Colombia (Pulido and Alberto 1996) and the Abu Sayyaf in the Philippines (Roger 2004) are revealed through hostage taking and kidnapping. Their vehicle attacks are usually related to the attempts at taking hostages. Since the hostages are held for ransom, and usually for quite a large amount, we may conjecture that those taking part in these activities are motivated primarily by their personal pecuniary considerations. In other words, we may expect to find a larger proportion of what I call 'mercenaries' among these groups. We may call them 'anomic terrorists', since they attempt to operate within an environment of anomie or lawlessness and thrive in failed states or in nations with weakened central control.

We may call the fourth group 'hooligan terrorists' since their activities (arson and vandalism) do not usually require specialized skill or disciplined self-sacrifice. Although, in the Factor Analysis, they form a separate category, I can find no groups in our list that depend primarily of these activities.

The fifth group consists of two separate components, each with a single activity: lynching and stoning. We can conceptually consider them to be expressions of a single type, which I call 'vigilante terrorists'. These activities require a large number of participants indulging more in mob violence than small bands of people involved in the acts of covert planning and execution typical of other terrorist acts.

Table 2.2 Incidents of suicide attacks, 1980–2002

Groups	Number of attacks	Percentage of total
al-Aqsa Brigade	14	6.9
al-Qaeda	6	3.0
Chechen rebel groups	4	1.9
Fatah	2	1.0
Fatah-Tanzim	1	0.5
Hamas	39	18.9
Hezbollah	30	14.5
Kashmiri Separatist groups	3	1.4
Kurdistan Workers' Party	9	4.3
Palestine Islamic Jihad	19	9.2
Popular Front For The Liberation of Palestine (PFLP)	1	0.5
Tamil Tigers of Sri Lanka (LTTE)	75	36.2
Unknown	4	1.9
Total	207	100.0

Sources: Pape 2003 and ICT 2005.

Figure 2.1 summarizes my categorization of the various terrorist groups and their operations. Based on a-priori logic this diagram presents a picture that shows the typical need for organizational capability and ideological strength in carrying out various kinds of terrorist activity. We can safely conjecture that it takes the greatest amount of organizational skills along with ideological strength to turn individual followers into a living H(uman)-bomb: the smartest of weapons in the arsenal of any nation. We may also hypothesize that as we move from right to left along the *x*-axis, violent acts of political dissidence turn increasingly from a law and order problem to a political problem.

Empirical evidence suggests (Gupta *et al.* 1993) that the relationship between government coercion and political violence is essentially shaped like an inverted U; lower levels of coercion only add fuel to the fire of dissent, while dissident activities can be brought down beyond a certain point of high violence and high coercion by resorting to extreme forces of brutality.[7] This research also found that this point of draconian force is generally beyond the capabilities of democratic nations. Thus, what Stalin, Mao, Pol Pot and their likes could do to bring down political opposition cannot be done within the constitutional limits imposed by liberal democracies.[8] Therefore, in democracies, a solution to the problems of terrorism with a high ideological content must be sought within the political arena and not the battle field.

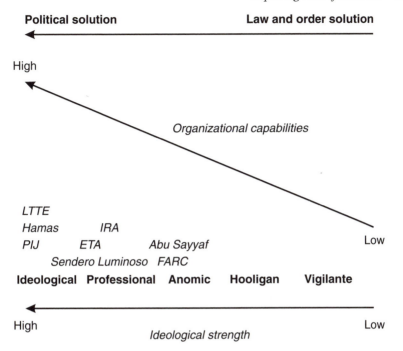

Figure 2.1 Classification of terrorist groups and their ideologies.

Evolution of choice of terrorist strategies

In our pursuit of the 'root causes' of terrorism I have presented a complex picture of multiple motivations. The world of terrorism that is currently threatening the basic fabric of the Western world cannot be understood without shedding some of the popular misperceptions that are drawn from the media, which portray them as religious fanatics or simply bloodthirsty sociopaths. Tamil Tigers are not inspired by religious fanaticism. Nor can many of the suicide bombers be comfortably classified as religious fanatics. It is religion and ethnic nationalism that are being used by the political entrepreneurs which give rise to acts of terrorism.

The most interesting question that can be raised from our taxonomy of the terrorist groups and their motivations is whether these groups evolve over time from a low level of terrorism, based on widespread feelings of frustration and anger, to the most destructive kind, inspired by deep ideological orientation, group cohesion, overreaction to their adversaries and/or attachment to a charismatic leader. For instance, available data lend limited support to the hypothesis that a number of terrorist groups start out with lesser attacks and then due to repression and other external events change to more deadly forms of attacks: the Tamil Tigers of Sri Lanka evolved from a small band of rebels to a full-blown terrorist organization with an estimated income of $100 million per year (Gunaratna 2001: 188). As the movement progressed so did their terrorism strategies (Hellmann-Rajanayagam 1994; Narayan Swamy 1994).

Table 2.3 Factor analysis of violent activities by selected terrorist groups 1980–2002

	Component factors					
Activities	Ideological terrorists	Professional terrorists	Anomic terrorists	Hooligan terrorists	Vigilante terrorists	
Shooting	**0.759**	−0.228	0.338	0.050	0.414	0.242
Knife attack	**0.698**	0.710	0.599	0.083	−0.236	−0.084
Grenade attack	**0.678**	0.377	0.302	0.391	−0.187	−0.062
Vehicle attack	**0.661**	0.284	0.650	0.156	−0.039	−0.045
Suicide bombing	**0.659**	0.128	0.502	0.052	0.179	0.021
Bombing	0.274	**0.631**	−0.444	0.307	0.313	−0.099
Car bombing	0.403	**0.621**	0.590	−0.112	0.204	−0.135
Letter bombing	0.358	**0.452**	−0.698	−0.021	0.195	0.275
Mortar attack	−0.561	**0.384**	0.308	0.438	0.191	0.066
Rocket attack	−0.459	**0.364**	0.301	−0.362	0.110	−0.230
Kidnapping	−0.519	0.257	**0.528**	−0.107	0.184	0.400
Hostage taking	−0.601	0.246	**0.308**	−0.338	−0.044	0.303
Arson	−0.331	−0.005	0.017	**0.928**	0.076	0.046
Vandalism	−0.331	−0.005	0.017	**0.928**	0.076	0.046
Incendiary devices	−0.387	−0.005	0.012	**0.887**	0.004	0.060
Lynching	0.129	−0.631	0.100	−0.112	**0.726**	0.123
Stoning	0.271	−0.062	−0.329	0.062	−0.349	**0.729**
Percentage of variance	**26.91**	**18.81**	**16.68**	**13.12**	**6.83**	**5.78**
Cumulative percentage	**26.91**	**45.72**	**62.40**	**75.52**	**82.34**	**88.12**

Note: Cumulative percentage of explained variance 89.0%.

To illustrate the point of evolving strategy, I have provided a plot of suicide bombing within Israel (Figure 2.2). This figure shows that Hamas, a product of the First Intifada movement, was involved in small scale-attack events in the late 1980s. However, the demonstrated effectiveness of Hezbollah's suicide attacks in Lebanon in driving out the Americans and then the Israelis contributed toward the choice of suicide bombings by the Hamas in the early 1990s. The successes of Hamas prompted a much smaller radical group, the Palestinian Islamic Jihad, to adopt the same tactics. Being increasingly sidelined by the Israelis and the PLO during the Oslo peace process, the Hamas and the Palestinian Islamic Jihad responded with a sustained series of suicide bombings.[9] However, when it became apparent that the peace process had come to a dead end, in desperation to maintain support among the disaffected youths in the West Bank and Gaza Strip, the PLO-affiliated groups, the Fatah, Fatah-Tanzim, the Popular Front for the Liberation of Palestine (PFLP) and the newly created al-Aqsa Brigade unleashed a relentless campaign of suicide bombings.[10]

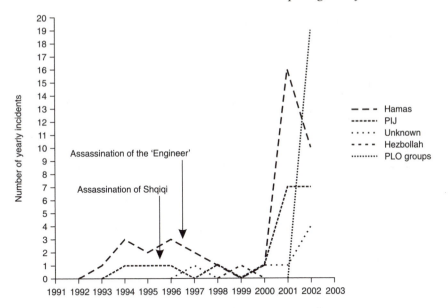

Figure 2.2 Suicide bombings by the rebel groups within Israel and the Palestine territories.

Discussion of findings

Serious study of terrorism must start with the proper understanding of human motivations for joining a terrorist organization. In this chapter, I have attempted to fuse economic reasoning with those of social psychology to formulate a more comprehensive framework within which the 'root causes' of terrorism can be understood. Based on my theoretical model, along with the findings of the existing literature on terrorism, the following conclusions may be drawn:

- *Distinguish among ideologies.* We have to learn to distinguish among ideologies that threaten and those that do not threaten the Western world and the larger global community. For instance, the transnational ideologies of Pan Islamism of today, professed by the likes of Osama bin Laden, similar to the ideology of global communism of the 1970s, pose a far greater threat to the Western world than does the nationalistic fervour of groups such as the Hamas and the LTTE of Sri Lanka. However, the dangers emanating from these latter groups with a limited global objective may menace the world in a different way through their nexus with organized crime.
- *Not all grievances are baseless.* In our zeal to fight terrorist atrocities, it is easy to disregard legitimate grievances. Although absolute poverty and other aspects of economic deprivation have a weak link to terrorism, a pervasive sense of humiliation and hopelessness does not. The global community must recognize the need to address the legitimate grievances of disaffected people in a meaningful way. Not addressing the legitimate grievances of a large segment of the populace will only add fuel to the fire of resentment and will increase threats of terrorism.

- *Recognize the power of communication.* Since it is extremely important to have the presence of a strong ideology to overcome the collective action problem, we must realize the power of political discourse that reduces another group of people as contemptible enemies. It is indeed difficult for Western democracies, established on the foundation of free speech, to recognize the danger resulting for it. However, the incendiary potential of unrestrained incitement to a small group of people cannot be minimized. Hence, we must pay a great deal of attention to hate speech coming from the leadership of various groups from all around the world. Whenever possible, the global community must find ways of discouraging the sponsorship of hate.

- *Don't play with people's extreme emotions.* If we look at the history of most of the extremist groups, particularly those that are based on religious fundamentalism, we find that they were promoted by governments as a strategic deterrent to some other force. For instance, the USA found it expedient to befriend religious zealots and to direct their fury toward the Soviet occupiers of Afghanistan. India's Prime Minister Indira Gandhi found a Sikh religious extremist group to be a good ally against a moderate political party that was about to defeat the Indian Congress Party in a state election. There is evidence to suggest that for some time the Israeli government saw the Hamas as a counterweight to Mr Arafat and the PLO. In each of these cases, it backfired; the US support for the *mujahidin* produced Osama bin Laden and the Taliban, Indira Gandhi was assassinated by the Sikh extremists, Hamas became the largest source of suicide attacks within Israel.

- *Don't overreact.* Understand the aims of the extremists. The causes of the extremist groups are best served when the society becomes polarized. For instance Hamas routinely stages suicide bombings and other acts designed to create outrage among the Israelis at critical points of peace process and national elections. In such a situation, the organized governments must resist the temptation to dig into national anger and mete out collective punishment. Instead, they may do well to draw upon the natural wellspring of human sympathy at the sight of tragedy to promote the moderate middle.

- *Reach political accommodation whenever possible.* There are limits to power when it comes to applying coercion within a constitutional democracy. Therefore, democracies cannot hope to bring order through police and military action alone. Whenever possible, it is best to come to a political compromise with the dissident groups, particularly when there is a broad-based popular support for the groups' stated goals.

- *Constrict the life-blood of the terrorist groups by restricting money.* Money is the life-blood of any organization, including the ones waging clandestine wars. These funds come from both illegitimate and legitimate sources. Studies of terrorist group funding reveal a consistent pattern of fund raising. Some of the funds come from trafficking in drugs, cigarettes, alcohol, etc. Others are raised through small contributions by the domestic constituents as well as the diaspora. Also, it is not unusual for a dissident group to acquire a few extremely wealthy financiers. Money can also be raised by laundering money and investing it into legitimate businesses. Finally, many terrorist groups are funded by state sponsorship. If we are to stop the scourge of international terrorism, the political leadership must develop a global consensus to stop the flow of money.

- *Fight terrorism on ideological grounds.* The battle against terrorism cannot be fought only on military grounds. We must recognize that the allure of such movements is also group-centric. Therefore, if there is any hope of controlling terrorism it must come also by offering ideological alternatives to the people. This may require long-term planning in the educational system, social service delivery, and the use of the media promoting ideals of tolerance.

- *Use more human intelligence rather than scientific surveillance.* Terrorists wage people-oriented wars. From the earliest writings on terrorism and guerrilla warfare, it has been recognized that the terrorists use their ability to melt into the general populace. Therefore, its suppression would require infiltration and other aspects of surveillance based on human assets.

- *No country can address the issue of multinational terrorism unilaterally.* Since terrorism is rarely confined within the political boundaries of a single nation, we need to recognize the need for a multinational approach for its suppression. Given the fact no country wants to give up its political and/or ideological position by defining terrorism (evinced by the absence of a universal definition of terrorism accepted by the United Nations), the international community should at least consider terrorism, case by case, and act multilaterally to suppress its most virulent forms, particularly those which deliberately aim at mass murder of civilians.

- *Be realistic in expectation.* We must know that while terrorism may never be totally eradicated, in time the allure of specific ideologies may wane. In the past, there were many terrorist movements, particularly the radical Marxist groups, that posed great threats to the global community, but these ultimately became spent forces. As scholars, we must devote a much greater effort to understand the dynamics of their demise. The most troubling aspect of terrorism is that, with the advent of technology in the areas of communication, transportation and the capability of the weapons, the ability of the future terrorist groups to bring widespread death and destruction is going to increase. Given this frightening scenario, the government leaders are well advised to increase their support of terrorism studies.

- *Know what we are fighting against and what we are fighting for.* If the clash is about conflicting world views, we cannot win by attempting to destroy political extremism by becoming extremists ourselves. Our fight must be waged under the universally accepted norms and standards of human rights and procedural justice. If there is a conflict between civilizations, in our fight against terrorism, we must not lose sight of what we are fighting for.

Notes

1   For some of the earlier behavioural explanations of political violence, see Feierabend, Feierabend and Nesvold (1969), Gurr (1970) and Hibbs (1973).

2   Although there is no general official definition of terrorism, there are many functional descriptions. For instance Wilkinson (2001: 206) describes it as a special form of political violence with five characteristics: 1) it is premeditated and aims to create a climate of extreme fear or terror; 2) it is directed at a

wider audience or target than the immediate victims of the violence; 3) it inherently involves attacks on random or symbolic targets, including civilians; 4) the acts of violence committed are seen by the society in which they occur as extra-normal, in the literal sense that they breach social norms, thus causing a sense of outrage; and 5) terrorism is generally used to try to influence political behaviour in some way, for example to force opponents into conceding some or all of the perpetrators' demands, to provoke an overreaction, to serve as a catalyst for more general conflict or to publicize a political or religious cause, to inspire followers to emulate violent attacks, to give vent to deep hatred and the thirst for revenge, and to help undermine governments and institutions designated as enemies by the terrorists.

3   See also Butler (2002).

4   The importance of 'framing' with the use of symbols has been extremely well researched. For a theoretical discussion see Schuessler (2000) and for empirical verifications in the area of political science see Nelson and Oxley (1999).

5   It is interesting to note that followers of al-Qaeda offer a substantially different socio-economic profile from those groups in Israel. For instance the study by Post *et al.* (2003) reveals the portrait of an individual without much hope, whilst Sageman (2004) finds quite a different profile of the al-Qaeda operatives.

6   These groups include the Abu Sayyaf Group (the Philippines), al-Aqsa Brigade, al-Qaeda, the Basque Homeland and Freedom Party (ETA in Spain), Fatah, Fatah-Tanzim, the Front for the Liberation of Palestine (PFLP), Hamas, Hezbollah, The Irish Republican Army (IRA), the Kurdish Workers' Party (PKK in Turkey), Lashkar-e-Toiba (Kashmiri separatist group), the Liberation Tigers of Tamil Eelam (LTTE in Sri Lanka), the Palestine Islamic Jihad (PIJ), the Revolutionary Armed Forces of Columbia (FARC) and *Sendero Luminoso* (Shining Path in Peru).

7   For an alternative explanation of the relationship between repression and dissent see Moore (1998).

8   It is interesting to note that while extreme coercion may work to put down active opposition in the most repressive regimes in the short run, it is questionable whether such policies would ever succeed over a longer period of time. Pol Pot was defeated, the Soviet system eventually collapsed and the future prospect of the rule of the Chinese Communist Party is difficult to predict.

9   For a rational choice explanation of strategic behaviour by the rebel groups see Kydd and Walter (2002). Also see Pape (2003).

10   For a detailed discussion see Gupta and Mundra (2003).

Bibliography

Akhtar, S. (1999) 'The psychodynamic dimensions of terrorism', *Psychiatric Annals*, **29**(6), 350–6.

Alexander, Y., Swetnam, M.S. and Levine, H.M. (2001) *ETA: Profile of a Terrorist Group*. Ardsley, NY: Transnational Press.

Becker, G. (1976) *The Economic Approach to Human Behavior*. Chicago, IL: University of Chicago Press.

Butler, L. (2002) 'Suicide bombers: dignity, despair and the need for hope. An interview with Eyad el Sarraj', *Journal of Palestinian Studies*, **31**(4), 71–6.

Chomsky, N. (2002) 'Terror and Just Response', in Rai, M. (ed.) *War Plan Iraq: Ten Reasons Against War on Iraq*. New York: Verso (originally published in 2001).

Coogan, T.P. (2002) *The IRA*. New York: St Martin's Press.

Feierabend, I., Feierabend, R. and Nesvold, B.A. (1969) 'Social Change and Political Violence: Cross-national Patterns', in Graham, H.D. and Gurr, T.R. (eds) *Violence in America: Historical and Comparative Perspectives*. New York: Signet Books.

Glass, J.M. (1985) *Delusion: Internal Dimensions of Political Life*. Chicago, IL: University of Chicago Press.

Grossbard-Sechtman, S. (1993) *On Economics of Marriage*. Boulder, CO: Westview Press.

Gunaratna, R. (2001) 'The lifeblood of terrorist organizations: evolving terrorist financing strategies', in *Countering terrorism through international cooperation*. Proceedings of the *International Conference on Countering Terrorism Through Enhanced International Cooperation*, Courmayeur Mont Blanc, Italy, pp. 180–205.

Gupta, D.K. (1990) *Economics of Political Violence*. Westport, CT: Praeger.

Gupta, D.K. (2001) *Path to Collective Madness: A Study in Social Order and Political Pathology*. Westport, CT: Praeger.

Gupta, D.K. (2002) 'Economics and Social Psychology: Explaining Collective Action', in Grossbard-Sechtman S. and Clague, C. (eds) *The Expansion of Economics: Towards a More Inclusive Social Science*. Armonk, NY: M.E. Sharpe, pp. 239–65.

Gupta, D.K. and Mundra, K. (2003) *Suicide Bombing as a Rational Strategy: An Empirical Investigation*. Department of Political Science, San Diego State University.

Gupta, D.K., Singh, H. and Sprague, T. (1993) 'Government coercion of dissidents: deterrence or provocation?', *Journal of Conflict Resolution*, **37**(2), 301–40.

Gurr, T.R. (1970) *Why Men Rebel*. New Haven, CT: Yale University Press.

Haroun, A. (1999) 'Psychiatric aspects of terrorism', *Psychiatric Annals*, **29**(6), 335–6.

Hellmann-Rajanayagam, D. (1994) *The Tamil Tigers: Armed Struggle for Identity*. Berlin: F. Steiner.

Hibbs, D.P. (1973) *Mass Political Violence: A Cross-national Causal Analysis*. New York: Wiley.

ICT (2005) http://www.ict.org.il

Innaccone, L.R. (2002) 'A Marriage Made in Heaven? Economic Theory and Religious Study', in Grossbard-Sechtman, S. and Clague, C. (eds) *The Expansion of Economics: Towards a More Inclusive Social Science*. Armonk, NY: M.E. Sharpe, pp. 203–26.

Juergensmeyer, M. (2000) *Terror in the Mind of God : The Global Rise of Religious Violence*. Berkeley: University of California Press.

Konet, R. (2001) *Sexual Fantasies of a Suicide Bomber*, http://www.israelinsider.com

Kydd, A. and Walter, B. (2002) 'Sabotaging the peace: the politics of extremist violence', *International Organization*, **56**(2), 263–96.

Moore, W. (1998) 'Repression and dissent: substitution, context and timing', *American Journal of Political Science*, **42**(3), 851–73.

Morgan, R. (2002) 'The demon lover syndrome', *MS*, **13**(3), p. 17.

Narayan Swamy, M.R. (1994) *Tigers of Lanka: From Boys to Guerrillas*. New Delhi: South Asia Publishing.

Nelson, T.E., and Oxley, Z.M. (1999) 'Issue framing effects on belief importance and opinion', *The Journal of Politics*, **61**(4), Nov. 1999, 1040–67.

Olson, M. (1965) *The Logic of Collective Action: Public Goods and the Theory of Groups*. Cambridge: MA: Harvard University Press.

Pape, R. (2003) 'The strategic logic of suicide terrorism', *American Political Science Review*, **97**(3), 343–61.

Post, J.M., Sprinzak, E. and Denny, L.M. (2003). 'The terrorists in their own words: interviews with 35 incarcerated Middle Eastern terrorists', *Terrorism and Political Violence*, **15**(1), 171–84.

Pulido, V. and Alberto, L. (1996) *The FARC Cartel*. S.l.: Ediciones el Faraón.

Rapoport, D. (2003) 'The Four Waves of Rebel Terror and September 11', in Kegley, C.W. (ed.) *The New Global Terrorism: Characteristics, Causes, Controls*. Upper Saddle River, NJ: Prentice-Hall, pp. 36–52.

Roger, S. (2004) 'Beyond the Abu Sayyaf', *Foreign Affairs*, **83**(1) Jan/Feb, 5–21.

Sageman, M. (2004) *Understanding Terror Networks*. University of Pennsylvania Press.

Sarraj, E. (2002) 'Why we blow ourselves up', *Time Magazine*, **159**(14), 8 April, 35-42

Schmid, A.P. and Graaf, J.D. (1982) *Violence As Communication: Insurgent Terrorism and the Western News Media*. Beverly Hills, CA: Sage Publications.

Schuessler, A. (2000) *A Logic of Expressive Choice*. Princeton, NJ: Princeton University Press.

Stern, J. (2003) *Terror in the Name of God: Why Religious Militants Kill*. New York: Harper Collins.

Tullock, G. (1971) 'The paradox of revolution', *Public Choice*, **11**, 89–99.

Wilkinson, P. (2001) 'Response to terrorism from the toolbox of liberal democracies: Their applicability to other types of regimes', in *Countering Terrorism Through International Cooperation*, Proceedings of the *International Conference on Countering Terrorism Through Enhanced International Cooperation*, Courmayeur Mont Blanc, Italy, pp. 206–13.

3   Impoverished terrorists

Stereotype or reality?

Jitka Malečková

The stereotype

Despite much evidence to the contrary in the scholarly literature, a common stereotype of a terrorist is nonetheless that of a poor (usually male and often Muslim) youth with low education, if not illiterate. Such stereotypes tend to perpetuate themselves, narrow our vision, and can misdirect public policy.

If there is one view concerning terrorism on which public opinion, media and politicians from opposing political camps seem to agree it is that poverty is a root cause of terrorism. This consensus is not new, but it was further strengthened after September 11. American politicians, including George W. Bush and Al Gore, and other public figures, emphasized that the fight against poverty is necessary in order to defeat terrorism. 'At the bottom of terrorism is poverty. That is the main cause', stated the South Korean Nobel Peace Prize laureate Kim Dae-Jung, and his view is shared by other Nobel Peace Prize winners. (Jai 2001)

Scholars also aligned themselves with the economic explanations of terrorism, though their appeals for a new Marshall plan to fight terrorism were more complex. In December 2001, Laura Tyson, then Dean of the Haas School of Business at the University of California at Berkeley, called for the removal of political tyranny and intolerance and the eradication of crushing poverty because in the interconnected world 'poverty and despair in a remote region can harbor a network of terrorism dedicated to our destruction' (Tyson 2001).

Richard Sokolsky and Joseph McMillan, research fellows at the National Defense University's Institute for National Strategic Studies, wrote in February 2002:

> To crush this threat, we need a program of tightly focused foreign aid to address the economic, political and social conditions that will otherwise continue breeding new terrorists ... Although there is a great deal we do not understand about the causes of terrorism, one major factor is clear: the historic failure of development in a swath of countries running from North Africa to Pakistan. Our foreign assistance should go up by at least \$4 billion to \$5 billion annually to finance programs that promote modernization and economic opportunity in the Islamic countries of the Middle East and Central and South Asia.[1]

Yet, the authors did not limit the recommended aid to developing economy, but suggested also 'supporting nascent institutions of civil society; promoting pluralism of information and opinions … and creating modern educational systems that give young people in Muslim societies the tools they need to flourish in a world where global connections become ever more important' (ibid.).

In view of this broad consensus, Alan Krueger, an economist from Princeton University, and I investigated whether there is a causal link between poverty, education and terrorism (Krueger and Malečková 2002, 2003).[2] Our research concentrated primarily (though not exclusively) on international terrorism and incidents of political violence that involve citizens or the territory of more than one country. Specifically, we analysed the determinants of participation in militant activities in the Middle East and public opinion polls on the strength of support for attacks against Israeli targets in the West Bank and the Gaza Strip. We also looked at cross-country data on the connection between economic conditions on the national level and the occurrence of terrorism by individuals from various countries.

This chapter focuses on the hypothesis about poverty as a root cause of terrorism. It describes two types of research that can be carried out when studying the causes of terrorism. The first type concentrates on micro-forces, the individuals' social backgrounds as a potential motivation for joining and supporting militant or terrorist movements, and the second type considers the broader societal conditions that could influence participation in terrorist acts. The combination of these two approaches should provide some insights into the question about the economic motivation of terrorism.

Social background of the participants

It is often emphasized that various types of terrorism differ substantially and so do their causes. Many question both the possibility and the utility of any attempts to create a 'profile' of the terrorist because terrorists represent the population from which they are drawn and its diversity. Yet, scholars have studied the social background and other characteristics of the perpetrators of various types of terrorist acts in different settings, from Europe through the Middle East and Asia to Latin America.

In their influential research, Russell and Miller (1978) were able to create profiles of 350 individuals active in groups operating from Latin America to Europe, and Japan to Turkey. They found that over two-thirds of arrested terrorists 'came from the middle or upper classes in their respective nations or areas' (Russell and Miller 1978: 54). Their work has been criticized for generalizations based on comparisons of terrorist groups in various regions. Their conclusions could be challenged also from the temporal perspective; in other words, do the terrorists of the 1990s or the early twenty-first century resemble those of the 1960s and 1970s studied by Russell and Miller? Another concern is that Russell and Miller's sample was drawn from news accounts, and likely over-represented the leaders of terrorist movements. However, their work still provides not only useful information, but also a good example of a comparative approach to the study of terrorism across countries.

A 1999 report on the sociology and psychology of terrorism prepared by the Federal Research Division of the Library of Congress for the US Central Intelligence Agency agrees with Russell and Miller in that 'the occupations of terrorist recruits have varied widely' and that 'terrorists come from middle-class families', but the report limits this characterization to terrorists in the most developed countries (Hudson 1999). According to the author, 'European and Japanese terrorists are more likely the products of affluence and higher education than of poverty'. Except for Latin America, 'terrorists in much of the developing world tend to be drawn from the lower sections of society. The rank and file of Arab terrorist organizations include substantial numbers of poor people, many of them homeless refugees' (ibid.). The report also states that the only professions that are over-represented among the terrorists are students and the unemployed. Little evidence was provided to buttress the claim that terrorists in Third World countries were more impoverished than their countrymen, however.

Our findings, as well as studies by other scholars (Sageman 2004), challenge the report's division between the developed world and the less developed world. In particular, the poverty paradigm does not seem to prevail among the Middle East extremist groups.

Lebanon-based Hezbollah with its Shia Muslim membership is an example of a religious-political movement devoted to various types of activities, including education, health care and politics. In order to achieve its goals – to end Israeli occupation of Lebanon and to establish a Shi'ite state in Lebanon, inspired by Iran – Hezbollah used both political and illegal means, such as taking Western hostages and carrying out suicide bombings. Krueger and I compared the social characteristics of 129 members of Hezbollah's militant wing who died in action in the 1980s and early 1990s (Hurvitz 1998)[3] with the general Lebanese population from which they were drawn.[4] The comparison indicated that the Hezbollah militants did not come from the most impoverished groups of the population. Poverty rate is 28 per cent for the deceased members of the Hezbollah's militant wing and 33 per cent for the Lebanese population. The difference is not statistically significant if the members of Hezbollah are compared with the Lebanese population as a whole. However, if the comparison is limited to the regions from which Hezbollah militants were mostly drawn (i.e. districts with a higher proportion of Shia population and Beirut) the difference becomes statistically significant. In this sample, our statistical analysis revealed that poverty has a rather strong negative effect on the likelihood that someone will become a Hezbollah fighter, or, to put it differently, a 30 percentage point reduction in poverty is associated with a 15 per cent increase in participation in Hezbollah (Krueger and Malečková 2002).

The results are not qualitatively different for other militant groups in the Middle East. For example, Berrebi compared biographical information on 285 militants from the Palestinian Islamic Jihad and Hamas with the Palestinian population of roughly the same age. He also focused on the social backgrounds of the extremists from these two groups. Between 1987 and 2002, neither the perpetrators of violence against Israeli targets in general nor the suicide bombers in particular came from more impoverished families than the population as a whole. In a sample of 48 suicide bombers, the poverty rate is less than half of the poverty rate of the Palestinian population of the same age. Moreover, the suicide bombers were much more highly educated than the general population (Berrebi 2003).

In the past, Arab, and particularly Arab Muslim organizations, were believed to reject women's participation in militant activities. Yet, there have always been some organizations that used women as perpetrators of violent acts. Leaving aside the German terrorist groups of the 1970s, which seem to have been more 'egalitarian' regarding the sex of their members, even the Popular Front for the Liberation of Palestine had a woman, Leila Khalid, among its leaders. Usually, though, women are assigned only support roles in terrorist organizations (Russell and Miller 1978: 49–50; Galvin 1983: 30–1).

Since the outbreak of the latest Intifada there have been repeated suicide attacks against Israel carried out by women. The Intifada had strong support among women and many women were inspired to join militant groups. Some Muslim religious leaders and the leaders of Palestinian resistance organizations gave legitimacy to the inclusion of women in the fight against Israel. Some of the women who carried out suicide attacks against Israel were considered, or felt themselves, marginalized (e.g. divorced women), others were educated women with respected professions or college-enrolled women on their way to respected careers.

And yet another example, from the other side of the Middle Eastern conflict: the biographies of 27 members of the Jewish Underground, which killed a couple of dozen and injured nearly 200 Palestinians in the early 1980s, provide information on their social backgrounds. Nothing suggests that the Jewish extremists came from economically disadvantaged groups; they included army officers, scholars, students, engineers, a land dealer and a computer programmer (Segal 1988: viii–xii).

Although these findings are limited to one region, they provide little support for the view that those who live in poverty are disproportionately drawn to participate in terrorist activities.

Where do terrorists come from?

One of the major criticisms of the inference that poverty is not a root cause of terrorism because terrorists are less likely to come from impoverished backgrounds than their non-terrorist countrymen is that terrorists may act out of concern for their poor countrymen or other disadvantaged groups of population, not out of their own personal desperation. For example, one scholarly report claims, 'Well-off young people, particularly in the United States, West Europe and Japan, have been attracted to political radicalism out of a profound sense of guilt over the plight of the world's largely poor population' (Hudson 1999). Yet, little data exist to date to support or disprove such a view.

There are several, far from perfect, ways by which to address this issue; for example to compare various countries where terrorist attacks occurred or did not occur. Todd Sandler and Walter Enders used a data set of international terrorist acts, *International terrorism: attributes of terrorist events* (ITERATE), recorded according to the country where international terrorist acts took place (Sandler and Enders 2004). An alternative route that Krueger and I pursued was to follow the country of origin of the perpetrators of major international terrorist events. In particular, we created a data set on the country of origin of the terrorists from the US Department of State's annual description of significant international terrorist incidents. The international terrorist event is defined in the description as a terrorist attack involving citizens or the territory of more than one country. Although this data set has some shortcomings (e.g. it does not include smaller incidents), it can be used in order to estimate whether international terrorists tend to come from rich or poor countries.

When the number of terrorists originating from each country is related to characteristics of the country such as the GDP per capita, literacy rates, prevailing religion, religious and ethnic fractionalization, and political and civil freedoms, one should get an idea about the characteristics of the countries that produce most terrorists. The variable that is most consistently associated with the number of terrorists is population: larger countries tend to have more terrorists. In a simple model that omits other factors it also appears that poorer countries have more international terrorists. However, when one controls for various variables in order to see if income is a cause or stands for something else, GDP per capita is unrelated to the number of terrorists from a country. Most importantly, controlling the extent of civil liberties in a country renders the effect of GDP per capita statistically insignificant and of minor importance (Krueger and Malečková 2003).

The prevailing religion in a country, measures of religious and ethnic fractionalization, and illiteracy in general, or the male and female illiteracy rate separately, do not seem to have any effect on participation in international terrorism. The proportion of religious believers has a positive impact on the extent of international terrorist acts that arise from members of a country. However, this is the case with any of the major religious groups: Buddhism, Christianity, Hinduism and Islam. We do not find that citizens of countries with a larger share of their population affiliated with any of the major religious faiths are more or less likely to be involved with international terrorism. None of the religions has a monopoly on terrorism.

Public opinion and support for terrorism

Terrorism does not occur in a vacuum. Public support can be viewed as a relevant condition for the lasting appeal of political violence and its perpetuation. Some scholars emphasize that social support differs according to the type of terrorist movement. While social-revolutionary (e.g. anarchist) groups can hardly hope for much public approbation, nationalist-separatist groups can rely on substantial support among the broader population of the same ethnic group (Hudson 1999). The latter could be applied to various Middle Eastern movements as well.

Public support may also affect the process of joining a militant or terrorist group. New members often come from public sympathizers of the group. They may be radicalized by personal encounters with violence on the part of the official state representatives against extremists. This was the case with many Palestinians, men and women. Women, in particular, are reported to join militant groups such as ETA and the IRA from the ranks of sympathizers and passive supporters. They are motivated by their political commitment as well as by their sensitivity to the sufferings of the imprisoned or injured terrorists (Galvin 1983: 23–4).

Public opinion polls can provide information on which segments of the population support terrorist or militant activities. A survey among both Catholics and Protestants in Ulster in 1968 showed that extreme views concerning the solution to the problem of Northern Ireland were more widespread among the poorer (53 per cent) than among the more affluent (42 per cent) Protestants, while income did not make a substantial difference for the views of the Catholic respondents (Rose 1971, 1975).[5] These results concern a situation before the escalation of violence in Ireland and leave open the question of whether and how the support changed in the following years. Other settings, such as the Middle East, are even more relevant in the context of this chapter.

The Palestinian Center for Policy and Survey Research, based in Ramallah, conducted several public opinion polls among the Palestinian population concerning their attitudes towards the relations with Israel and violence as a solution of these relations. The survey of 1,357 Palestinian adults (over 18) in the West Bank and Gaza from December 2001 is particularly interesting because it includes questions about the attacks of September 11 and views about attacks on Israeli targets in their aftermath. It is important to note, however, that the public opinion poll took place in the middle of a rather tense period in the Middle East and in international relations in general. Later surveys conducted by the Center showed somewhat different results, including higher support for a mutual cessation of violence. Views expressed in a public opinion poll at that specific point in time also have to be distinguished from active support for, and participation in, violent attacks against Israel or terrorist activities worldwide.

According to the 2001 survey, the support for armed attacks against Israeli targets by the Palestinian population ranges from 73.9 per cent among the unemployed to 86.7 per cent among the merchants, farmers and professionals and to 89.7 per cent among students. Most Palestinians believed that 'armed attacks against Israeli civilians inside Israel so far have achieved Palestinian rights in a way that negotiations could not' (Krueger and Malečková 2002).

At the same time, however, such attacks were generally not interpreted by the Palestinian public as terrorism. When asked, 'In your opinion, are there any circumstances under which you would justify the use of terrorism to achieve political goals?', only 34.6 per cent of craftsmen, labourers and employees, 41 per cent of students and 43.3 per cent of merchants, farmers and professionals answered 'yes or definitely yes', while 48.3–58 per cent of the Palestinians answered a clear 'no'.

It is worth noting that with education the support for attacks against Israeli targets increases, but so does also the disagreement with the attacks. Palestinians with lower education had less clear views on the issues of the survey. Interestingly, the unemployed were less likely to report 'no opinion' than employed Palestinians.

Breaking the data down by occupational status also yields remarkable patterns. According to the 2001 public opinion poll, support for armed attacks against Israeli targets was strongest among students, and among farmers, merchants and professionals. The same groups supported most intensively (95.7 per cent of students and 94.2 per cent of merchants, farmers and professionals) attacks against Israeli soldiers in the West Bank and the Gaza Strip and agreed that there were some circumstances under which they would justify the use of terrorism to achieve political goals. In contrast, the unemployed were less likely to support armed attacks against Israeli targets (73.9 per cent) and against Israeli soldiers in the West Bank and the Gaza Strip (89.9 per cent). These results are particularly interesting.

The survey also shows that the women who carried out suicide attacks against Israeli targets were not merely manipulated dupes. It is noteworthy that housewives' responses were quite similar to those of the general public. Eighty two per cent of housewives supported armed attacks against Israeli targets (compared to 73.9 per cent of the unemployed and 80.8 per cent of the labourers, craftsmen and employees) and 91.3 per cent among the housewives supported the attacks against Israeli soldiers in the West Bank and the Gaza Strip (compared to 89.9 per cent of the unemployed and 93.4 per cent of the labourers, craftsmen and employees).

A new direction for investigation

Leaving aside those who believe that various manifestations of terrorism are so different that there is no sense in analysing them as one phenomenon, there are two approaches to the study of terrorism. The first one reflects a belief that, despite all the differences, there is something that connects all or most of the heterogeneous cases of terrorism and thus it is possible to find the common characteristics of the terrorists or the 'root cause' of terrorism (e.g. in poverty). The second approach limits the common features and causes to a group of terrorist incidents, whether a 'type' of terrorism, a wave of terrorism typical of a certain period in time, domestic versus international incidents or political violence in either the developed or the developing world.

Thus, the Report of the Library of Congress, criticizing the work of Russell and Miller (which emphasized that terrorists come from the middle classes) as dated, mentions that:

> Increasingly, terrorist groups are recruiting members who possess a high degree of intellectualism and idealism, are highly educated, and are well trained in a legitimate profession. However, this may not necessarily be the case with the younger, lower ranks of large guerrilla/terrorist organizations in less-developed countries, such as the FARC, the PKK, the LTTE, and Arab groups, as well as with some of the leaders of these groups.
>
> (Hudson 1999)

The members of the latter organizations are recruited largely from poor people, according to the Report.

Our research suggests that at least in some regions outside the Western world, namely the Middle East, terrorists are also predominantly drawn from the ranks of the middle and upper income classes. Marc Sageman, who studied 172 participants of the militant movement led by al-Qaeda, also shows that the activists do not come prevailingly from the most impoverished and ignorant segments of the population (Sageman 2004).

In fact, international terrorist organizations may prefer highly educated individuals with established careers and special skills to poor, unsophisticated and uneducated people, even for suicide bombings. The more educated, experienced and qualified individuals better fit into a foreign and strange environment, and thus have a better chance of success. It is likely that, in the future, international terrorists who threaten economically developed countries will belong largely to the ranks of the relatively well off and highly educated, and will include women.

Our research dealt particularly with the Middle East and with international incidents and thus it does not exclude variations in different contexts or regarding domestic terrorist acts. An aspect worth mentioning is the relationship between terrorism and civil war. While it remains unclear whether countries undergoing civil wars are more likely to create conditions that enable or provoke (international) terrorism, poverty is often quoted among the 'root causes' of civil wars. Thus James Fearon and David Laitin, who studied the occurrence of violent civil conflicts around the world for the period 1945 to 1999, rank poverty, which 'marks financially and bureaucratically weak states and also favors rebel recruitment', among the most relevant conditions that promote the onset of civil wars (Fearon and Laitin 2003: 75). Paul Collier, concentrating on the period between 1965 and 1999, emphasizes the difference between civil war and international wars, and shows that lack of democracy, inequality, and ethnic and religious divisions have no systematic effect on the occurrence of civil wars. In contrast, such economic conditions as low national income or dependence upon primary commodity exports are significant predictors of civil wars (Collier 2001: 143–61).

Of course, the connection between economic conditions and civil wars does not mean that a similar relationship exists between poverty and terrorism. Interestingly, Claude Welch's study of political violence in China, India, Kenya and Zaire in the nineteenth and twentieth centuries suggests that economic conditions and social inequality may have facilitated, but not directly caused the rebellions. 'Political acts such as rebellion require political explanations. It is in the weakness of governments that rebellion arises…' (Welch 1980: 335). Nevertheless, the above-mentioned works on economic causes of civil wars can serve as examples of cross-country analyses also for the study of the relationship between national income and the incidence of international terrorist acts.

Cross-country analysis studying terrorism as a phenomenon with potential common features should yield some insights in the question of the 'root causes' of international terrorism. Once we allow for the fact that poor countries tend to have fewer civil liberties, poverty does not appear to be a predictor of the number of international terrorists coming from a country (Krueger and Malečková 2003).

In our cross-country analysis comparing the number of terrorists originating from individual countries, apart from population, the only variable that was consistently associated with the number of terrorists was the Freedom House Index of political rights and civil liberties. Civil liberties are defined by the Freedom House organization as the 'freedom to develop views, institutions, and personal autonomy without interference from the state'. At a given level of income, the countries that lack civil liberties tend to be more likely to produce international terrorists (ibid.). If the opportunities for political involvement are limited, terrorism may appear to extremists as the only viable means of communication or influence.

This finding is in agreement with the understanding of terrorism as mainly an answer to political complaints and of terrorists as motivated by political involvement and belief in a political cause, rather than by economic considerations. Just as political participation is much more typical of people who are wealthy enough to concern themselves with more than mere economic subsistence while the impoverished are less likely to vote, the poor are also less likely to become engaged in terrorist organizations.

However, this does not explain why 'civil liberties' should matter more than 'political freedoms', another Freedom House variable that we tried for predicting participation in terrorism. Further research should develop these preliminary findings, check them in other quantitative comparative frameworks and analyse the qualitative aspects of 'civil liberties' as well.

Conclusions

The increasing agreement among scholars that no single root cause of terrorism exists (and their doubt about the very question of root causes) does not mean that it is necessary to give up searching for causal explanations of terrorist incidents. Poverty and lack of opportunity still occupy a prominent place among the potential causes of terrorist acts, not only in politicians' speeches, but also in scholarly works.

The two modes of empirical research described in this chapter come to the same conclusion about the connection between poverty and (international) terrorism. The first approach introduced here was a micro-level analysis studying both the individual's characteristics for participation in militant movements and the support for these movements. It concentrated on one region, the Middle East. This research suggests that neither the participants nor the adherents of militant activities in the Middle East are recruited predominantly from the poor.

The second approach, the cross-country analysis of the relationship between economic conditions in various countries and the number of international terrorists originating from these countries, shows that poverty on the national level does not predict the number of terrorist attacks carried out by individuals coming from a country. It also suggests that there is no other single common cause of terrorism, such as religion, though there may be some conditions under which terrorism becomes more likely. These conditions seem to be political, rather than economic. According to the cross-country analysis, a lack of civil liberties is a relevant factor in creating such conditions.

In our research, the evidence on both the individual and the national level indicated that there is no direct connection between poverty and terrorism, at least in the case of international terrorist activities. The perpetrators of international terrorism are more likely to be drawn from the middle and upper classes than from impoverished families. Yet, there is no need for similar qualifications, a well-to-do background and education, in various local settings and militant groups, which may be more likely to choose their foot soldiers and support personnel from among the poor, unskilled and uneducated. Therefore, the stereotype of a poor and illiterate terrorist should not be simply replaced by another stereotype: of an educated representative of the middle or upper classes.

However, even if poverty is not a root cause of terrorism, it is a cause of much suffering around the world, and this should be enough reason to pursue policies to eradicate it.

Notes

1   Sokolsky and McMillan (2002).
2   This chapter is based on the research in these papers.
3   We obtained the data on the members of Hezbollah who died in action from the biographies gathered by Eli Hurvitz that included the individuals' age at death, highest level of school attended, poverty status, region of residence and marital status. It should be noted that the Hezbollah fighters died while engaged in activities that cannot always be considered terrorist.
4   These data are from the Lebanese Population and Housing Survey in 1996 conducted by the Administration Centrale de la Statistique.
5   I am grateful to Christina Paxson for bringing this survey to my attention.

Bibliography

Atran, S. (2003) 'Genesis of suicide terrorism', *Science*, **299**, 1534–9.
Berrebi, C. (2003) 'Evidence about the link between education, poverty and terrorism among Palestinians', Princeton University Industrial Relations Section Working Paper No.477.
Black, I. and Morris, B. (1991) *Israel's Secret Wars: The Untold History of Israeli Intelligence*. London: Hamish Hamilton.
Collier, P. (2001) 'Economic causes of civil conflict and their implications for policy', in Crocker, C.A., Hampson, F.O. and Aall, P. (eds) *Turbulent Peace: The Challenges of Managing International Conflict*. Washington, DC: USIP, pp. 143–61.
Fearon, J.D. and Laitin, D.D. (2003) 'Ethnicity, insurgency, and civil war', *American Political Science Review*, **97**, 75–90.
Friedman, R.I. (1992) *Zealots for Zion: Inside Israel's West Bank Settlement Movement*. New York: Random House.
Galvin, D.M. (1983) 'The female terrorist: a socio-psychological perspective', *Behavioral Sciences & the Law*, **1**, 19–32.
Hudson, R.A. (1999) 'The sociology and psychology of terrorism: Who becomes a terrorist and why?', a report prepared under an interagency agreement by the *Federal Research Division, Library of Congress*, http://www.loc.gov/rr/frd
Hurvitz, E. (1998) 'The military wing of Hezbollah: a social profile', unpublished Master's thesis, Tel Aviv University.
Jai, J.J. (2001) 'Getting at the roots of terrorism', *The Christian Science Monitor*, December 10.
Krueger, A.B. and Malečková, J. (2002) 'Education, poverty, political violence and terrorism: Is there a causal connection?', NBER Working Paper 9074.

Krueger, A.B. and Malečková, J. (2003) 'Education, poverty and terrorism: Is there a causal connection?', *Journal of Economic Perspectives*, **17**, 119–44.

Neff, D. (1999) 'Jewish terrorists try to assassinate three Palestinian mayors', *Washington Report on Middle East Affairs*, **18**, June, 87–8.

Rose, R. (1971) *Governing Without Consensus: An Irish Perspective*. Boston: Beacon Press.

Rose, R. (1975) *Northern Ireland Loyalty Study*. Michigan: Inter-University Consortium for Political Research, Study No.7237.

Russell, C.A. and Miller, B.H. (1978) 'Profile of a Terrorist', in Elliott, J.D. and Gibson, L.K. (eds) *Contemporary Terrorism: Selected Readings*. Gaithersburg: International Association of Chiefs of Police, pp. 81–95; Reprinted in Freedman, L.Z. and Alexander, Y. (eds) (1983) *Perspectives on Terrorism*. Wilmington: Scholarly Resources, Inc., pp. 45–60.

Sageman, M. (2004) *Understanding Terror Networks*. Philadelphia: University of Pennsylvania Press.

Sandler, T. and Enders, W. (2004) 'An economic perspective on transnational terrorism', *European Journal of Political Economy*, **20**(2), June, 301–16.

Segal, H. (1988) *Dear Brothers: The West Bank Jewish Underground*. Woodmere, NY: Beit-Shamai Publications Inc.

Sokolsky, R. and McMillan, J. (2002) 'Foreign aid in our own defense', Op-ed, *The New York Times*, February 12.

Tyson, L. (2001) 'It's time to step up the global war on poverty', *Business Week*, 3 December.

Welch, C.E. (1980) *Anatomy of Rebellion*. Albany: State University Press of New York.

4 The social and psychological characteristics of terrorism and terrorists

John Horgan[1]

The history of terrorism teaches us many things. One valuable lesson is that those who employ terrorism as well as those affected by it are capable of holding a number of seemingly incongruous and ambiguous views about the nature of terrorism, and political violence more generally. It is important to acknowledge the implications of this for our understanding of terrorism particularly if we are to help psychological perspectives on terrorism move beyond their still pre-paradigmatic nature. Upon closer inspection, it is not difficult to see how the strategy of terrorism is littered with paradoxes. Terrorists seek to establish a captive audience through the propagation of terrible deeds, while simultaneously erecting barriers between them and their intended audience as a result of what they have just done. Similar paradoxes are found in the actions of those who are tasked with responding to the terrorist. We may well be aware of how certain responses to terrorism increase support for the terrorist, yet we find it inhuman and absurd to resist engaging terrorists in ways other than those we assume are deserving of the acts of cowards. It is naturally easier to attempt to prevent future instances of some action by immediately punishing it than it is to try to find some other way of perhaps redirecting that behaviour, or what underpins it (i.e. the expected consequences of engaging in that behaviour) elsewhere. The idea may appear unusual because by implication then we admittedly already know how, in several ways, we probably should not respond to terrorism. The issue then becomes not 'How do we fight terrorism?', but 'Why aren't we doing it in ways we all seem to agree on as being appropriate?'.

An uncomfortable realization we are going to have to accept sooner or later is that terrorism is no longer incomprehensible or mysterious, yet the ways in which we pose questions relating to the psychology of the terrorist obscure this. That realization is obscured further because we rarely appreciate that analyses of terrorism have an unerring tendency to mix fact and fiction in varying quantities.[2] It is partly from this realization, and from a sense of frustration due to the continuation and expansion of forms of insurgent political violence that the issue of there being a 'root cause' to terrorism arises.

The notion that a homogeneous factor (or unique set of attributes) contributes to the emergence of terrorism is attractive for many reasons; in terms of understanding terrorism, we could easily then dilute what is in reality an exceptionally complex process into a more discrete and manageable problem. I would argue that it is somewhat misleading, if not naive, to assume that we can remove the grievances of terrorists in an attempt to prevent terrorism from occurring. The uncritical acceptance of such an assumption represents a fundamental misconception about the nature of terrorism (in particular its use as a strategy to influence the political process) as well as what creates and sustains it. The realities of responding to terrorism might be more appropriately grounded in, for example, avoiding the consequences that sustain terrorism by encouraging developments to engage the terrorism process in different, more flexible, ways.

Expressing such a sentiment about terrorist grievances in this way may appear negative, and to some will seem consistent with heavy-handed approaches to the problem. However, this should not be the case, and it is not unless we pay close attention to the language and psychology of terrorist movements that we appreciate why such sentiments are not necessarily negative at all. The grievances of most terrorist groups, we should remember, may well be virtual, imaginary or historical (each or all of which are invoked as a means of interpreting and working through current events), self-serving, and often susceptible to change between the onset of terrorist violence and various stages of its subsequent development.[3] (Terrorist behaviour most certainly involves callousness, arrogance, barbarity, injury and death, but the reality of terrorism in today's world is that political movements that use terrorism skilfully manipulate events, and their media coverage, to create for their existing or potential audiences deliberate and often sophisticated impressions and interpretations serving their own particular purposes.) Moreover, and particularly since the 1990s, the continued expansion of religious terrorism, single-issue terrorism, and organized crime-related terrorism as well as other expanding 'grey areas'[4] relate to exploitative ideologies that in reality pose immense stumbling blocks if the notion of addressing grievances is seen as a way forward in tackling terrorism. One outcome of recognizing this is that in any case, and it may appear contradictory, we are often not realistically in a position to address terrorist grievances per se until the terrorist campaign has developed. Only subsequently might we be able to seek to address grievances within a mutually beneficial framework, regardless of the reality assumed or represented by the terrorist group or its enemy.

There are further important issues to recognize in attempting to develop a conceptual framework for understanding terrorism within which meaningful psychological perspectives might develop. (Organized terrorist-directed political violence is usually part of a much more complex set of activities related to the attainment of a social or political goal, and accordingly what we see or hear about terrorism is always one small (albeit the most public via its dramatic impact) element of a wider and ultimately, more complex array of activities (both in terms of, for instance, a specific incident itself and its broader political significance)) Terrorism may often be well organized, it may be technically adept and it can have sophisticated political ends as many of the larger and well-known movements such as the Islamic Jihad, Hamas, the Provisional IRA and al-Qaeda show. A valuable lesson to learn from the ongoing 'War on Terrorism' is that it is wrong for us to uncritically attribute such qualities to all terrorist groups at all times. In fact, this is an important theme in analyses of terrorism that relate both to pure and applied research especially, as well as policy concerns which might relate to some form of threat assessment and the management of the security problems posed by terrorist groups. The capacities, abilities and presumed intentions of terrorist organizations (as well as what terrorism can and does realistically achieve: indeed what perhaps it should be allowed to achieve) should neither be over- nor underestimated, but examined critically using what intellectual, conceptual and other tools we have at our disposal. This is a principle we must value, that the tendency for uncritical analyses has not infrequently happened to give much ground for the trenchant criticism against many contributors to terrorism research. The nature and extent of how terrorism has been used has undergone radical evolution even since the 1990s. International terrorists are now truly borderless and flexible in ways most of us only appreciate following successful terrorist operations (e.g. a bombing), and this poses major challenges to responses to terrorism. Yet, we must always strive to tackle the problem (at whatever level is adopted) with perspective and experience.

However, we must be realistic in attempting to build on this. An uncomfortable reality is that we are currently nowhere near an agreed understanding of terrorism, let alone a proper formulation of the questions that might emerge from any one perspective (in this case, a psychological one). As academics, we might sometimes be guilty of presupposing the existence of a certain level of thinking (at a political level) about terrorism, but part of the problem is that we cannot agree on its nature (that the perceived essence of terrorism may be constantly changing is an important feature of this), and ironically our responses to it are often such that we only engage in and sustain the problems we are discussing.

The notion of a 'root cause', and perhaps by implication, a 'root response', needs careful clarification, because the implications of not doing so are dangerous and potentially misleading as far as the systematic formulation of strategic responses to terrorism are concerned. An example might be useful to illustrate this. An account of the social and psychological characteristics of terrorists and terrorism might relate to any or all of the following empirical factors, each of which would have a unique preventative implication:

- why people want to become involved in a group that engages in terrorist violence;
- how people become involved;
- what roles or tasks they fulfil once a member;
- how and why they move within and through the terrorist organization;
- how the individual both 'assimilates' the shared values and norms of the group, and how he/she then 'accommodates' to engagement qualities not previously considered or expected prior to membership (and why different members 'assimilate' and 'accommodate' at varying rates, as well as whether or not this relates to some individual qualities as opposed to post-recruitment processes experienced at individual levels);
- how the members engage in specific acts of violence;
- why and how they affect other members (and are themselves influenced by others) at various stages of their own and others' involvement;

- why they ultimately want to, or have to, leave the organization;
- how they ultimately want to, or have to, leave the organization.

A critical conceptual point to note, and one that is simultaneously vital in formulating responses, is that the issues these questions address (a) may not be necessarily related to each other, and (b) answering one may not necessarily reflect upon another. For example, answering questions about why people may wish to become involved in terrorism may have little bearing on what they do as terrorists. Similarly, answering questions about what keeps people involved with a terrorist organization may have surprisingly little if any bearing on what subsequently sees them disengaging from the organization.

Again, it is possible that when we ask 'What are the root causes of terrorism?' we may in fact be trying to force the answer to all of these 'routes to, through, and away from terrorism' and other questions in some singular explanation.[5] We ought to clearly realize then that if we do not ask the right questions, we most certainly will not arrive at meaningful answers, regardless of the perspective we take in trying to approach the problem in the first place. We can realize that the question 'How do we prevent terrorism?' is as complex as 'What causes it?'. The relevance of making these distinctions is not an academic exercise, but I believe represents the defining quality of the need to see terrorism not as a social movement, or a homogeneous threat deriving from some homogeneous origin, but as a process which is susceptible to, and limited by, among other things, strategic and psychological factors. Thinking about terrorism as a process of course reflects its complexity, but thinking in this way can also help us to prioritize the questions we need to answer, and better focus policy decisions and resource allocation, which after all, should reflect the reality of any response.

Another concern that simultaneously relates to finding root causes as well as to how psychological approaches to terrorism have developed over the years is one of perspective, the relationship between perspective and evidence, and how this matters in a more practical sense for our efforts at understanding terrorism. Reich (1990) warned about the limitations of the perspectives we adopt in considering terrorist behaviour. A danger, he stressed, is in allowing any one individual perspective to be pushed beyond its own explanatory power. This problem has long been evident in many approaches to terrorism. However, since the events of 11 September 2001, we have seen a promising resurgence of empirical data-driven research[6] that may have more hopeful long-term benefits for our understanding. Such efforts must be actively encouraged as the only answer to settling disputes about how best to understand and respond to terrorism is to regard rigour and evidence as the most important qualities of our research.

Although there are signs that we are beginning to critically examine our perspectives on terrorism, problems of perspective remain a reflection of the complex bases of terrorist behaviour. Another obvious significant ongoing challenge is to understand how the broader social problems relate to smaller, individual ones. On the one hand, we have an array of socio-political issues that would seem in some way to be relevant to the creation of conflict within and between societies and groups. On the other, we have smaller individual qualities that drive action, the relevance of which we frequently misinterpret, often through needless interdisciplinary tensions and unfortunate representations of different perspectives. Individual qualities in the process of terrorism are important: given the extent of the conditions assumed to generate conflict, why is it still that so few people engage in terrorism? (Perhaps as important, we rarely ask the opposing empirical question, 'Why is it that so many do not engage in terrorism?'. Posing the problem in this way generates quite different issues for the kind of analysis we undertake.) The answer to questions like this will vary enormously depending on what level and range of activity we are willing to classify as terrorism, but we can identify three possible starting points or assertions which authors have used (sometimes implicitly) to help clarify answers to problems of this kind.

- That the person who engages in terrorism is different or special (this argument becomes heightened when we limit our perception of 'terrorist behaviour' to planting bombs or engaging in other acts of violence).
- That the label 'terrorism' is misleading, and skews our perception of the problem. This has nothing to do with arguments about the perceived legitimacy of armed resistance by an insurgent group or any similar 'moral' argument, but relates to the conceptual point made above: if we broaden our thinking on the concept, then 'terrorism' encompasses more activity and more people.[7]
- We don't really know (but still assume) that a core 'causal' factor in terrorism lies in the connection between the broader conditions and individual perceptions of those conditions; an area that might be understood with reference to the qualities of ideological control.[8]

An over-reliance (although constantly changing in nature) on the first assertion has led to attempts to identify common features (often in terms of presumed inner or mental qualities) of people who engage in political violence.[9] Such inner qualities are assumed to play a significant role in predisposing a supposed 'type' of person towards political violence as well as causing terrorism altogether. The notion of a terrorist profile may be administratively attractive (even seductive, since it enables us to simplify an enormously complicated process into misleading and simplistic answers),[10] but it is unhelpful.[11] Many of the personal traits or characteristics we attempt to identify as belonging to the terrorist are neither specific to the terrorist nor serve to distinguish one type of terrorist from another. Neither are the routes into and through terrorism distinct in a psychological sense from other kinds of social movements nor are such features homogenous between terrorist movements (we often forget that terrorism represents a limited, albeit public and dramatic, element of much broader activity in some of the larger extremist movements). Indeed many of the psychological attributes presumed unique to terrorists are implicitly suggested and interpreted as social or psychological deficiencies. I will not engage in this discussion here, but such accounts present us with neat, plausible ways of reducing what is in reality a set of idiosyncratic circumstances and events that shape individual attitudes and behaviours;[12] in so doing, they serve to confuse and limit understanding. There are no a-priori qualities of the terrorist that enable us to predict the likelihood of risk of involvement and engagement (which is, after all, the true scientific test of such profiles) in any particular person or social group that is valid or reliable over a meaningful period of time.

We may, however, achieve a greater understanding of the relevance of individual qualities when we consider the second assertion above (namely the label 'terrorism' and its implications for our analyses of the problem). A recent example that might help us consider this point is that Donald Rumsfeld, the US Defense Secretary reminded us that a 'new vocabulary' would emerge from the 'War on Terrorism'[13] and the Bush administration's doctrine of pre-emption. It would be dangerous to overlook how the use of such language impacts on the identification of terrorism and the terrorist. This is an enormously important issue that has the potential to both singularly skew, or improve, our understanding of the process of terrorism.

The point is worth considering further. The relationship between the terrorist and his/her environment is central to understanding the relevance of agreeing in our analysis on 'who or what a terrorist is', and this has been repeatedly exposed since the events of September 11. Again this is not so much a question about the legitimacy of the label 'terrorist' per se, but has more to do with an issue of both the scope and management of the problem. In the days after the al-Qaeda atrocities, President Bush made a series of then significant speeches in preparation for the Administration's attempts at solidifying American and world opinion towards their impending campaign. A critical warning, repeated in several speeches within the same week by the President, was that: 'anybody who houses a terrorist, encourages terrorism will be held accountable' (Office of the Press Secretary 2001a), 'we're talking about those who fed them, those who house them, those who harbor terrorists' (Office of the Press Secretary 2001b), 'it is a different type of battle … a different type of battlefield' (Office of the Press Secretary 2001a), 'if you harbor a terrorist, if you aid a terrorist, if you hide terrorists, you're just as guilty as the terrorists' (Office of the Press Secretary 2001c).

Given the intense public fallout from political negotiations at the time, both in the USA and Great Britain, one might argue that at the heart of such sentiments is the assumption that there is no legitimacy to some kinds of protest or dissent. Equally, however, it reveals a change in what might be thought of as 'terrorist behaviour', broadening our perceptions of who the terrorists are and what it is they do.[14] In one way, this does lend support for the need to consider a model of *violence within the political process* as a more viable way of understanding the relationship between non-state terrorism and the actions of the state in response to, or as a provocation to non-state actors. It represents, however, a stark contrast with the first assertion we considered. In ways perhaps unintended from the expected consequences of the Bush speeches, the question 'What is a terrorist?' has been focused and clarified, and the goals of counter-terrorism have become much more pointed, both in the time leading up to and beyond the 'War on Terrorism' and the war on Iraq. Indeed, President Bush's comments in those speeches lead us to the identification of some distinctive goals we might tentatively consider in why we want to identify (or attempt to identify) the root causes of terrorism at all:

- the suppression of violent political dissent; after all, this is a clear message that has come from both the preparations for and engagement with both the 'War on Terrorism' as well as the intervention in Iraq; or
- the control or management of violence; or
- understanding the broader processes.

There is no reason why these objectives cannot or could not coexist, but the distinctions are important. If the overall goal in discussions of terrorism is one of prevention, then the starting point is an acceptance that, deriving from the foregoing analytical principles, prevention can only be understood in terms of what position and time in the terrorism process we are facing. For the same reason that the head-counting of captured or killed terrorists tells us relatively little about the progress of a broad counter-insurgency campaign, shooting terrorists, infringing basic human rights, or corrupting the democratic process will not work because it only feeds into and engages with the processes inherent in political violence by sustaining the legitimization of the imperative strategy of terrorism at all junctures.

Efforts at viewing terrorism as a process might help develop our understanding of psychological approaches to terrorism. Some approaches have been developed, and one of the more detailed recent ones is grounded in a behavioural approach (Taylor and Horgan 2002), drawing on approaches to understanding other forms of illegal activity (significantly, where the preoccupations about finding root causes have traditionally led to failure to manage and control the problem). It is not possible in this chapter to fully discuss this model, but perhaps the most significant features to emphasize are that:

- we already have clear and unambiguous ways of identifying focus points of dangerousness and risk assessment for involvement in terrorism;
- we can appreciate and understand the significance of problematic cognitions as a factor in the escalation of engagement with terrorism (an argument which must not be confused with issues to do with attempts at establishing the presence of 'personality traits' or other presumed essential qualities of terrorists);
- we can also already establish the nature of the relationship between 'relevant offending behaviour' (i.e. engagement with violent terrorist activity) and other forms of both illegal and legal political activity.

A process-based approach is valuable for many other reasons, although I do not believe we have fully considered the broader social and political implications of such an approach. By taking a process perspective, we can see in social and psychological terms how disparities in profiles, individual backgrounds and routes into terrorism can become focused against and resistant to the consequences of responses to terrorism (which, from the terrorist perspective, is a vital psychological quality of such organizations in times of threats from external sources). It is important to realize that a process-grounded social psychological model of terrorism need not seek to invalidate case histories of terrorists, but its true value may be that it allows us to see how different people, with different backgrounds, and each with distinct routes into and through the terrorist movement, engage with the process in different ways. In practical terms, it can help us both to draw distinctions between phases of the process and to develop clearer policy focuses. The potential significance of this analytical framework should not be underestimated in terms of its potential to contribute to policy.

Until we arrive at clearer prioritization of our expected outcomes in understanding and responding to terrorism, continued conceptual confusion about the phases of engagement with terrorism contributes to the narrow policy measures aimed at undermining it. The benefits of comparing the phases of terrorist engagement as similar to engagement in criminal behaviour have been described by Taylor (1988) (i.e. in recognizing that the influences on decisions to become, remain and disengage from terrorist activity are not necessarily similar), and these must be explored further. However, the relevance of recognizing this aspect of the process is in itself often still lost when considered from a broader perspective.

I will conclude this chapter by highlighting some further issues I believe will continue to negatively affect our analyses. Another reality of terrorism (and another perhaps unintended feature of President Bush's speeches) is the recognition that it is neither a military nor a police problem in essence. At its core, terrorism has throughout history remained, and will continue to remain, a problem of civil society. Terrorism exists within and between societies, often most visibly through its claimed 'representation' (be it real or imagined) for specific communities. We may be familiar with the notion that terrorists are not markedly different from the members of the communities they claim to represent, but the reverse is naturally also true. This highlights the need for an analysis of the social factors that sustain support for a terrorist group, and in particular the apparent contradictions that underpin terrorist support. Paramount among these is the fact that although a community represented by the terrorist may abhor or reject individual atrocities, they may remain supportive of the terrorist campaign in a broader sense. If there is any more obvious reason why a doctrine of military pre-emption or extra-legal moves against suspected terrorists are laden with serious risk in light of these realities and how they relate to sustaining the terrorism process, then it would be worth identifying.

One final consequence to highlight the effort to identify relevant psychological processes in the development of terrorism is the realization that terrorism, like other forms of deviant behaviour, can have its roots in mundane, non-deviant behaviours. The argument has been made in detail that one of the most important aspects of terrorist psychology is in understanding the effectiveness and limitations of ideological control over behaviour (Taylor and Horgan 2002). It is an argument that is often difficult and unsettling to grasp, and to some this point leads to the unfortunate assumption that this in some way legitimizes political violence. It does not, nor should we allow it to, but despite how we often dismiss it in our analyses, it appears that this may well be the defining attribute that will ultimately, and despite the long-term benefits of such an approach, lead to the idea of a terrorism process becoming unacceptable to our political leaders.

Notes

1   I am grateful to Max Taylor for discussion on some of the concepts presented here, and to Lorraine Bowman for comments on an early draft. Responsibility for what is presented here rests with me, the author.
2   Although given the political fallout in Britain and the USA arising from the nature of the intelligence reports that supposedly contributed to the decisions to invade Iraq in 2003, this may be rapidly changing.
3   The Provisional IRA in Northern Ireland being a prime example.
4   See Raufer (2000)
5   And even at that, we need to distinguish how and why an individual becomes part of an *existing* terrorist group from that person who becomes part of an effort aimed at creating a *new* terrorist group.
6   About a dozen articles have emerged in the last 12 months. For a very recent example of first-hand research see Post, Sprinzak and Denny (2000).
7   Although the point may seem obvious it is worth restating that the activities that immediately merit the label 'terrorism' are typically the most dramatic and obvious acts of what we might in some cases describe as social movements. Certainly the point becomes clearer when we consider the extensive range of activities engaged in by some of the larger groupings such as the Republican movement in Northern Ireland, or Hamas. In some ways, to define such movements by focusing on the most illegal and abhorrent of their activities is not in itself inappropriate, but it can skew our analysis. This is important when considering the factors that contribute to and sustain individual engagement in terrorist violence for individuals who may have previously engaged in the organization in other ways (not necessarily illegal).
8   See Taylor and Horgan (2002)
9   For reviews see Horgan (2003a), Crenshaw (1986) and Silke (1988).
10   See Taylor (1988).
11   For an overview see Horgan *et al.* (2003).
12   For detailed discussions see Horgan (2003b) and other chapters in Silke (2003).
13   See Shultz and Vogt (2003).
14   A mirrored implication is a changing perception about the identification and role of civilians in conflict, from the point of view of terrorist groups. Al-Qaeda statements post-11 September stressed that civilians are not innocents because they elected and sustained the US government: this is what makes them guilty and necessary targets. Rarely do terrorists make such a link explicitly, regardless of how groups in the past justified or explained civilian casualties (usually as by-products of, or casualties in, a war, but rarely deliberately targeted in such a systematic manner). The relevance of this point to the present discussion relates to the broadening of an already blurred category within the process.

Bibliography

Crenshaw, M. (1986) 'The Psychology of Political Terrorism', in Hermann, M.G. (ed.) *Political Psychology: Contemporary Problems and Issues.* London: Josey-Bass, pp. 379–413.
Horgan, J. (2003a) 'The Search for the Terrorist Personality', in Silke, A. (ed.) *Terrorists, Victims, Society: Psychological Perspectives on Terrorism and its Consequences.* London: Wiley, pp. 3–27.
Horgan, J. (2003b) 'Leaving Terrorism Behind', in Silke, A. (ed.) *Terrorism, Victims, Society: Psychological Perspectives on Terrorism and its Consequences.* London: Wiley.
Horgan, J., O'Sullivan, D. and Hammond, S. (2003) 'Offender profiling: a critical perspective', *The Irish Journal of Psychology*, **24**(1–2), 1–21.
Office of the Press Secretary (2001a) *President building worldwide campaign against terrorism.* Remarks made by President Bush and President Megawati of Indonesia at a 'photo opportunity', The White House Oval Office, 19 September.
Office of the Press Secretary (2001b) *President urges readiness and patience.* Remarks by

President Bush, Secretary of State Colin Powell and Attorney General John Ashcroft, Camp David, Thurmont MD, 15 September.

Office of the Press Secretary (2001c) *International campaign against terror grows*. Remarks made by President Bush and Prime Minister Koizumi of Japan at a 'photo opportunity', The White House Colonnade, 25 September.

Post, J.M., Sprinzak, E. and Denny, L.M. (2003). 'The terrorists in their own words: interviews with 35 incarcerated Middle Eastern terrorists', *Terrorism and Political Violence*, **15**(1), 171–84.

Raufer, X. (2000) 'New World Disorder, New Terrorisms: New Threats for Europe and the Western World' in Taylor, M. and Horgan, J. (eds) *The Future of Terrorism*. London: Frank Cass and Co., pp. 30–51.

Reich, W. (ed.) (1990) *Origins of Terrorism: Psychologies, Ideologies, Theologies, States of Mind*. Washington DC: Woodrow Wilson Center Press.

Shultz, R.H. and Vogt. A. (2003) 'It's war! Fighting post-11 September global terrorism through a doctrine of preemption', *Terrorism and Political Violence*, **15**, 1–30.

Silke, A. (1988) 'Cheshire cat logic: the recurring theme of terrorist abnormality in psychological research', *Psychology, Crime and Law*, **4**, 51–69.

Silke, A. (ed.) (2003) *Terrorism, Victims, Society: Psychological Perspectives on Terrorism and its Consequences*. London: Wiley.

Taylor, M. (1988) *The Terrorist*. London: Brassey's.

Taylor, M. and Horgan, J. (2002) 'The psychological and behavioural bases of Islamic fundamentalism', *Terrorism and Political Violence*, **13**, 37–71.

5   The socio-cultural underpinnings of terrorist psychology

When hatred is bred in the bone

Jerrold M. Post

The spectrum of terrorism

There is a broad spectrum of terrorist groups and organizations, each of which has a different psychology, motivation and decision-making structure. Indeed, one should not speak of terrorist psychology in the singular, but rather of terrorist psychologies. Figure 5.1, which is a modified version of Schmid's well-known typology (see Chapter 18),[1] depicts the many categories of terrorist types. In the top tier, I differentiate political terrorism from criminal and pathological terrorism. Studies of political terrorist psychology do not reveal severe psychiatric pathology (Post 1993). In fact, political terrorist groups do not permit emotionally disturbed individuals to join as they represent a security risk. Seriously disturbed individuals tend to act alone.

   Considering the diversity of causes to which terrorists are committed, the uniformity of their rhetoric is striking: polarizing and absolutist, it is a rhetoric of 'us versus them'. It is rhetoric without nuance, without shades of grey. 'They', the

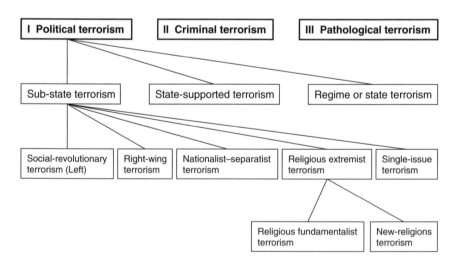

Figure 5.1 Modified version of Schmid's typology of terrorism.

establishment, are the source of all evil in vivid contrast to 'us', the freedom fighters, consumed by righteous rage. And, if 'they' are the source of 'our' problems, it follows ineluctably in the special psycho-logic of the terrorist, that 'they' must be destroyed. It is the only just and moral thing to do. Once one accepts the basic premises, the logical reasoning is flawless.

What accounts for the uniformity of the terrorists' polarizing absolutist rhetoric? My own comparative research on the psychology of terrorists does not reveal major psychopathology, agreeing with the finding of Crenshaw (1990): 'the outstanding common characteristic of terrorists is their normality'. Similarly, in a review of *The Social Psychology of Terrorist Groups*, McCauley and Segal (1987) conclude that 'the best documented generalization is negative; terrorists do not show any striking psychopathology'.

Nor does a comparative study reveal a particular psychological type, a particular personality constellation, a uniform terrorist mind. But while there is a diversity of personalities attracted to the path of terrorism, an examination of memoirs, court records, and, on rare occasions, interviews, suggests that individuals with particular personality traits and personality tendencies are drawn disproportionately to terrorist careers; in particular, frustrated individuals, who tend to externalize, seeking an external cause for their difficulties. Unable to face their own inadequacies, the individuals with this personality style need a target to blame and attack for their own inner weakness, inadequacies and lack of success. Such individuals find the polarizing absolutist rhetoric of terrorism extremely attractive: 'it's not us – it's them'. 'They are the cause of our problems' provides a psychologically satisfying explanation for what has gone wrong in their lives. And a great deal has gone wrong in the lives of individuals who are drawn to the path of terrorism.

To summarize the foregoing, terrorists as individuals for the most part do not demonstrate serious psychopathology. While there is no one personality type, it is the impression that there is a disproportionate representation among terrorists of individuals who are aggressive and action-oriented and place greater than normal reliance on the psychological mechanisms of externalization and splitting. There is suggestive data indicating that many terrorists come from the margins of society and have not been particularly successful in their personal, educational and vocational lives. The combination of the personal feelings of inadequacy with the reliance on the psychological mechanisms of externalization and splitting makes especially attractive a group of like-minded individuals whose credo is 'It's not us – it's them. They are the cause of our problems. And it therefore is not only not immoral to strike out at them – it becomes a moral obligation'. Terrorism is not a consequence of individual psychological abnormality. Rather it is a consequence of group or organizational pathology that provides a sense-making explanation to the youth drawn to these groups.

In the middle tier of Figure 5.1, state terrorism refers to the state turning its resources (i.e. police, judiciary, military, secret police, etc.) against its own citizenry to suppress dissent, as exemplified by the 'dirty wars' in Argentina. When Saddam Hussein used nerve gas against his own Kurdish citizens, this was an example of state CBW (chemical and biological weapon) terrorism. State-supported terrorism is of major concern to the

USA. Currently on the list annually distributed by the US Department of State are Iran, Iraq, Libya, Sudan, North Korea and Cuba. In these situations, when states are acting through terrorist groups, fearing retaliation, the decision making of the state leadership will be a significant constraint upon the group acting under their influence or control.

In the lower tier, a diverse group of sub-state terrorist groups is specified: social-revolutionary terrorism, nationalist-separatist terrorism, right-wing terrorism, religious extremist terrorism, subsuming both religious fundamentalist terrorism and terrorism perpetrated by non-traditional religious groups (such as Aum Shinrikyo), and single issue terrorism.

Social-revolutionaries

Social-revolutionary terrorism, also known as terrorism of the Left, includes those acts perpetrated by groups seeking to overthrow the capitalist economic and social order. Social-revolutionary groups are typified by the European 'fighting communist organizations' active throughout the 1970s and 1980s (e.g. the Red Army Faction in Germany and the *Brigate Rosse* in Italy). Social-revolutionary terrorist groups have experienced a significant decline over the last two decades, paralleling the collapse of communism in Europe and the end of the Cold War.

Nationalist-separatists

Nationalist-separatist terrorism, also known as ethno-nationalist terrorism, includes those groups fighting to establish a new political order or state based on ethnic dominance or homogeneity. The Irish Republican Army, the Liberation Tigers of Tamil Eelam (LTTE) of Sri Lanka, the Basque Fatherland and Liberty (ETA) in Spain, and radical secular Palestinian groups such as Fatah, the Abu Nidal Organization and the Palestinian Front for the Liberation of Palestine-General Command (PFLP-GC) are prominent examples. Nationalist-separatist terrorists are usually attempting to garner international sympathy for their cause and to coerce the dominant group. Thus ETA is attempting to pressure Spain to yield to its demands for an independent Basque state. These causes of the nationalist-separatist terrorist groups and organizations are particularly intractable, for the bitterness and resentment against the dominant ethnic group have been conveyed from generation to generation (Post 1993). Hatred has been 'bred in the bone'. In these organizations, the young revolutionaries are often extolled as heroes within their communities, for their mission reflects their people's cause. Among the incarcerated Palestinian terrorists that my research group have been interviewing, with support from the Smith-Richardson Foundation, the regularity with which Palestinian youth chose to enter these groups was striking. The responses of the interview subjects indicated, 'Everyone was joining. Everyone was doing it. It was the thing to do'. They have heard the bitterness of their parents and grandparents in the coffee houses in Jordan and the occupied territories about the economic injustices they have suffered. Youths drawn to the path of the IRA heard similar bitter stories in the pubs of Northern Ireland.

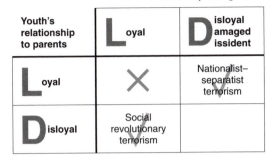

Figure 5.2 Generational pathways to terrorism.

As reflected in Figure 5.2, the generational dynamics of these nationalist-separatist terrorists are the very opposite of the social-revolutionary terrorists discussed earlier. They are carrying on the mission of their parents and grandparents who have been damaged by, or are disloyal to, the regime. They are loyal to families that are disloyal to the regime. Their acts of terrorism are acts of vengeance against the regime that damaged their families. This is in vivid contrast to the social-revolutionary terrorists who are rebelling against the generation of their parents who are loyal to the regime. They are disloyal to the generation of their families that is loyal to the regime. Their acts of terrorism are acts of revenge against the generation of their family, which they hold responsible for their failures in this world.

The modern era of terrorism is usually dated to the early 1970s, represented by the iconic images of the radical Palestinian terrorist group seizure of the Israeli Olympic village at the 1972 Munich Olympics. This event captured an immense international television audience and demonstrated powerfully the amplifying effect of the electronic media in the Information Age. In the beginning of the modern era, these two groups (the social-revolutionary terrorists and the nationalist-separatist terrorists) were responsible for the large majority of terrorist acts. They were attempting to call the attention of the West to their cause, and regularly claimed responsibility for their acts.

Religious fundamentalist terrorism

In the 1970s and 1980s, most of the acts of terrorism were perpetrated by nationalist-separatist and social-revolutionary terrorists, who wished to call attention to their cause and accordingly would regularly claim responsibility for their acts. They were seeking to influence the West and the establishment. But in the following decades, no responsibility has been claimed for more than 40 per cent of terrorist acts. I believe this is because of the increasing frequency of terrorist acts by radical religious extremist terrorists. They are not trying to influence the West. Rather the radical Islamist terrorists are trying to expel the secular modernizing West. And they do not need recognition by having their name identified in a *New York Times* headline or in a story on CNN. They are 'killing in the name of God' and don't need official notice; after all, God knows.

Traditional groups include Islamic, Jewish, Christian and Sikh radical fundamentalist extremists. In contrast to social-revolutionary and nationalist-separatist terrorists, for religious fundamentalist extremist groups, the decision-making role of the pre-eminent leader is of central importance. For these true believers, the radical cleric is seen as the authentic interpreter of God's word, not only eliminating any ambivalence about killing, but endowing the destruction of the defined enemy with sacred significance.

The radical cleric, whether ayatollah, rabbi or priest, has used sacred text to justify killing in the name of God. Ayatollah Khomeini employed a radical interpretation of the Qur'an to provide the ideological foundation for his Islamic revolution, and selected verses to justify terrorist extremity, such as 'And slay them where ye catch them, and turn them out from where they have turned you out ... Such is the reward of those who suppress the faith' (2: 190–3). In a radio broadcast on 5 June 1983, Khomeini exhorted his followers, 'With humility toward God and relying on the power of Islam, they should cut the cruel hands of the oppressors and world-devouring plunderers, especially the United States, from the region'. To those who died fighting this holy cause, Khomeini assured a higher place in paradise. In inciting his followers during the Iran–Iraq war, he rhetorically asked, 'Why don't you recite the sura of killing? Why should you always recite the sura of mercy? Don't forget that killing is also a form of mercy'. He and his clerical followers regularly found justification for their acts of violence in the Qur'anic suras calling for the shedding of blood (Robins and Post 1997: 153–4).

These organizations are hierarchical in structure; the radical cleric provides interpretation of the religious text justifying violence, which is uncritically accepted by his 'true believer' followers, so there is no ambivalence concerning use of violence, which is religiously commanded. These groups are accordingly particularly dangerous, for they are not constrained by Western reaction, indeed they often wish to expel secular modernizing influences. They have shown a willingness to perpetrate acts of mass casualty terrorism, as exemplified by the bombings of Khobar Towers in Saudi Arabia, the US embassies in Kenya and Tanzania, the USS Cole, and, on a scale never seen before, the coordinated attacks on the World Trade Center in New York and the Pentagon in Washington, DC. Osama bin Laden, responsible for these events has actively discussed the use of weapons of mass destruction in public interviews.

While not a religious authority, Osama bin Laden is known for his piety, and has been granted the title emir. Like Khomeini, Osama bin Laden regularly cites verses from the Qur'an to justify his acts of terror and extreme violence, employing many of the same verses earlier cited by Khomeini. Consider this extract from the February 1998 fatwa:

In compliance with God's order, we issue the following fatwa to all Muslims:
The ruling to kill the Americans and their allies – civilians and military – is an individual duty for every Muslim who can do it in any country in which it is possible to do it, in order to liberate the al-Aqsa Mosque and the holy mosque [Mecca] from their grip, and in order for their armies to move out of all the lands

of Islam, defeated and unable to threaten any Muslim. This is in accordance with the words of Almighty God, 'and fight the pagans all together as they fight you all together', and 'fight them until there is no more tumult or oppression, and there prevail justice and faith in God'.

We – with God's help – call on every Muslim who believes in God and wishes to be rewarded to comply with God's order to kill the Americans and plunder their money wherever and whenever they find it.

Jihad Against Jews and Crusaders, World Islamic Front Statement

Note it is not Osama bin Laden who is ordering his followers to kill Americans. It is God! Osama bin Laden is the messenger, relaying the commands of God, which are justified with verses from the Qur'an.

But as the events of September 11 make clear, for the al-Qaeda organization, there is no constraint against mass casualty terrorism. And it is the willingness, indeed the goal to take as many casualties as possible that is the dynamic of the 'true believers' of the al-Qaeda group under the destructive charismatic leadership of Osama bin Laden that places this group at high risk to move into the area of CBRN (chemical, biological, radiological, nuclear) terrorism. They have already crossed the threshold of mass casualties using conventional terrorism, demonstrating a willingness to perpetrate super-terrorism.

Al-Qaeda, Hamas, Hezbollah and the Islamic Jihad all have found an abundance of recruits, eager to join these Islamic fundamentalist terrorist organizations. For them, like the youth drawn to the path of nationalist-separatist terrorism, hatred has been 'bred in the bone'.

These two groups (nationalist-separatist terrorists and Islamist religious fundamentalist terrorists) represent the major threats to contemporary society and will be the focus of the remainder of this chapter. I will use the words of terrorists themselves as examples to allow the reader to enter their minds, drawing on material from the research project involving semi-structured interviews with 35 incarcerated radical Palestinian terrorists, both radical Islamist terrorists from Hamas, Islamic Jihad, and Hezbollah, and secular terrorists from Fatah and the Palestinian Front for the Liberation of Palestine, as well as interviews conducted with an Abu Nidal terrorist and al-Qaeda terrorists in connection with federal trials. It should be emphasized that (1) the terrorists were incarcerated, and (2) the quotes are from terrorists who agreed to be interviewed. While offering valuable insights into the psychology of these terrorists, these quotations should not be taken as representing the psychology of all terrorists for the interview subjects assuredly cannot be taken as a statistically representative sample.

Nationalist-separatist secular Palestinian terrorism

The cauldron of life experiences of an Abu Nidal terrorist

In 1997, I had the opportunity and challenge of assisting the Department of Justice as an expert on terrorist psychology at the trial in Federal Court in Washington DC of Mohammad Rezaq, an Abu Nidal terrorist who played a leading role in the skyjacking of an Egypt Air passenger jet in which more than fifty lost their lives in the skyjacking and the subsequent SWAT team attack on the hijacked plane in Malta.

The defendant epitomized the life and psychology of the nationalist-separatist terrorist. He assuredly did not believe that what he was doing was wrong. From boyhood, Rezaq had been socialized to be a heroic revolutionary fighting for the Palestinian nation. Demonstrating the generational transmission of hatred, his case can be considered emblematic of many from the ranks of ethnic/nationalist terrorist groups, from Northern Ireland to Palestine, from Armenia to the Basque region of Spain.

In 1948, when the subject's mother was eight years old, as a consequence of the 1948 Arab–Israeli war, her family were forced to flee their home in Jaffa in Israel. They left for the West Bank, where Rezaq was raised. In 1967, when Rezaq was eight, the family fled their pleasant West Bank existence during the 1967 war, ending up in a crowded Palestinian refugee camp in Jordan. Her mother told him bitterly that this was the second time this had happened to her.

At the camp he went to a school funded by the UN and was taught by a member of Fatah whom he came to idolize. At the time Arafat's stature as a heroic freedom fighter was celebrated in the camps. He was taught that the only way to become a man was to join the revolution and take back the lands stolen from his parents and grandparents. He first joined Fatah after going AWOL from the Jordanian Army. When he first participated in a terrorist action, he felt at last he was doing what he should do. He left Fatah after becoming disillusioned with Arafat's leadership and ended up in the most violent secular Palestinian terrorist group, the Abu Nidal organization. When he ultimately was assigned a command role in the skyjacking of an Egypt Air airliner, he felt he was at last fulfilling his destiny. He was taking a bold action to help his people. He was a soldier for the revolution and all actions that led to major loss of life were seen as required by his role as a soldier for the cause.

Interview extracts

While most Fatah members reported that their families had good social standing, their status and experience as refugees were paramount in their development of self-identity.

> I belong to the generation of occupation. My family are refugees from the 1967 war. The war and my refugee status were the seminal events that formed my political consciousness, and provided the incentive for doing all I could to help regain our legitimate rights in our occupied country.

For the secular terrorists, enlistment was a natural step. And it led to enhanced social status.

> Enlistment was for me the natural and done thing … in a way, it can be compared to a young Israeli from a nationalist Zionist family who wants to fulfil himself through army service.

> My motivation in joining Fatah was both ideological and personal. It was a question of self-fulfilment, of honour and a feeling of independence … the goal of every young Palestinian was to be a fighter.

> After recruitment, my social status was greatly enhanced. I got a lot of respect from my acquaintances, and from the young people in the village.

In addition to causing as many casualties as possible, armed action provided a sense of control or power for Palestinians in a society that had stripped them of it. Inflicting pain on the enemy was paramount in the early days of the Fatah movement.

> I regarded armed actions to be essential, it is the very basis of my organization and I am sure that was the case in the other Palestinian organizations. An armed action proclaims that I am here, I exist, I am strong, I am in control, I am in the field, I am on the map. An armed action against soldiers was the most admired … the armed actions and their results were a major tool for penetrating the public consciousness.

> The various armed actions (stabbing collaborators, martyrdom operations, attacks on Israeli soldiers) all had different ratings. An armed action that caused casualties was rated highly and seen to be of great importance. An armed action without casualties was not rated. No distinction was made between armed actions on soldiers or on civilians; the main thing was the amount of blood. The aim was to cause as much carnage as possible.

Islamist fundamentalist terrorism

Interview with a Tanzanian embassy bomber

In the spring and summer of 2001, I had the opportunity of interviewing at length one of the defendants in the al-Qaeda bombing of the US embassy in Tanzania. Raised on Zanzibar off the coast of Tanzania, he was eight years old when his father died. He was then educated in a *madrasa*, where he was taught to never question what you are told by learned authorities. When he was the equivalent of a junior in high school his brother directed him to leave school and help him in his grocery store in Dar es Salaam. There he was miserable – alone, friendless, isolated – except for his attendance at the Friday prayer services at the mosque, where he learned from the imam that they were all members of the *umma*, the community of observant Muslims, and had an obligation to help Muslims wherever they were being persecuted. He was shown videos of Muslim mass graves in Bosnia and the Serbian military, of the bodies of Muslim women and children in Chechnya and the Russian military. He became inspired and vowed to become a soldier for Allah. But he was informed, I infer by a spotter from al-Qaeda, that he could not do this without obtaining training. So, using his own funds, he went to Pakistan and then on to a bin Laden training camp in Afghanistan, where he was taught weapons and explosives handling in the mornings and had four hours of ideological training each afternoon. After seven months, when he could not join the struggle in Bosnia or Chechnya, although offered the opportunity to fight in Kashmir, he returned to Dar es Salaam, where he again pursued his menial existence as a grocery clerk, frustrated at his inability to pursue jihad. Three years later he was called in the middle of the night and asked, 'Do you want to do a jihad job?' and without further inquiry, he accepted. What had been a positive motivation to help suffering Muslims gradually was bent to his participating in this act of mass casualty terrorism.

Interview extracts

The mosque was consistently cited as the place where most members were initially introduced to the Palestinian–Israeli conflict, including members of the secular groups. Many of the secular members report that while activism within the community was most influential in their decision to join, their first introduction to the cause was at the mosque or in another religious setting. Authority figures from the mosque are prominent in all conversations with group members, and most dramatically for members of the Islamist organizations. The introduction to authority and unquestioning obedience to Allah and authority is instilled at a young age and continues to be evident in the individual members subservience to the larger organization. This preconditioning of unquestioning acceptance of authority seems to be most evident among the members of the Islamist groups such as Hamas and Islamic Jihad.

> I came from a religious family, which used to observe all the Islamic traditions. My initial political awareness came during the prayers at the mosque. That's where I also was asked to join religious classes. In the context of these studies, the sheikh used to inject some historical background in which he would tell us how we were effectively evicted from Palestine.

> The sheikh also used to explain to us the significance of the fact that there was an IDF (Israeli Defense Force) military outpost in the heart of the camp. He compared it to a cancer in the human body, which was threatening its very existence.

> At the age of 16 I developed an interest in religion. I was exposed to the Moslem brotherhood and I began to pray in a mosque and to study Islam. The Qur'an and my religious studies were the tools that shaped my political consciousness. The mosque and the religious clerics in my village provided the focal point of my social life.

Community support was important to the families of the fighters as well:

> Families of terrorists who were wounded, killed or captured enjoyed a great deal of economic aid and attention. And that strengthened popular support for the attacks.

Perpetrators of armed attacks were seen as heroes, their families got a great deal of material assistance, including the construction of new homes to replace those destroyed by the Israeli authorities as punishment for terrorist acts.

The emir blesses all actions:

Major actions become the subject of sermons in the mosque, glorifying the attack and the attackers.

Joining Hamas or Fatah increased social standing:

Recruits were treated with great respect. A youngster who belonged to Hamas or Fatah was regarded more highly than one who didn't belong to a group, and got better treatment than unaffiliated kids.

Anyone who didn't enlist during that period (*intifada*) would have been ostracized.

View of armed attacks

Armed attacks are viewed as essential to the operation of the organization. There is no question about the necessity of these types of attacks to the success of the cause.

You have to understand that armed attacks are an integral part of the organization's struggle against the Zionist occupier. There is no other way to redeem the land of Palestine and expel the occupier. Our goals can only be achieved through force, but force is the means, not the end. History shows that without force it will be impossible to achieve independence. Those who carry out the attacks are doing Allah's work …

The more an attack hurts the enemy, the more important it is. That is the measure. The mass killings, especially the martyrdom operations, were the biggest threat to the Israeli public and so most effort was devoted to these. The extent of the damage and the number of casualties are of primary importance.

The justification of suicide bombings

The Islamist terrorists in particular provided the religious basis for what the West has called suicide terrorism as the most valued technique of jihad, distinguishing this from suicide, which is proscribed in the Qur'an. One in fact became quite angry when the term was used in our question, angrily exclaiming:

This is not suicide. Suicide is selfish, it is weak, it is mentally disturbed. This is *istishhad* (martyrdom or self sacrifice in the service of Allah).

Several of the Islamist terrorist commanders interviewed called the suicide bombers 'holy warriors who were carrying out the highest level of jihad'.

> A martyrdom operation is the highest level of jihad, and highlights the depth of our faith. The bombers are holy fighters who carry out one of the more important articles of faith.
>
> (Hassan Salame)[2]

> It is attacks when their member gives his life that earn the most respect and elevate the bombers to the highest possible level of martyrdom.

Sense of remorse, no moral red lines

> When it came to moral considerations, we believed in the justice of our cause and in our leaders ... I don't recall ever being troubled by moral questions.

> In a jihad, there are no red lines.

But the Palestinian suicide bombers differ significantly from the suicidal hijackers of 9/11. While the following description has been shifting, for the most part the suicide bombers of Hamas and Islamic jihad are 17–22 years old, unmarried, uneducated, unemployed. Unformed youth, they have been told by their recruiters that they face bleak prospects but can do something significant with their lives, that by becoming a *shaheed*, they will enter the hall of martyrs, bringing prestige and monetary rewards to their families.

In contrast, the suicidal hijackers of 9/11 were older (28–33 years old) and a number of the 19 hijackers were well educated and came from comfortable middle-class Saudi and Egyptian families. These are fully formed adults who have subordinated their individuality to the destructive charismatic leadership of bin Laden.

While many drawn to the path of religious fundamentalist terrorism are poor and uneducated, for some of these terrorists there are suggestive similarities to the generational dynamics of the social-revolutionary terrorists. Osama bin Laden himself is the most striking example of these generational dynamics. He is the seventeenth of 25 sons of a multi-billionaire Saudi construction magnate, whose financial empire and wealth came from a special relationship with the Saudi royal family. When he railed at the corruption of the Saudi royal family and their lack of fidelity to Islam in permitting the American military to establish a base on holy Saudi land, he was striking out at the source of his family wealth, leading not only to his being expelled from Saudi Arabia, but also severely damaging his family, who also turned against him.

Fusion of the individual and the group

Once recruited, there is a clear fusing of individual identity and group identity, particularly among the more radical elements of each organization. This is true both for the

Islamist terrorists of Hamas and Islamic Jihad as well as for those of al-Qaeda. Many of the interviewees reported growing up or living in a repressed or limited socio-economic status. Their ability to work was regulated, the ability to travel freely was severely restricted and there was a general impression that they were denied the opportunity to advance economically. There was a common theme of having been 'unjustly evicted' from their land, of being relegated to refugee status or living in refugee camps in a land that was once considered theirs. Many of the interviewees expressed an almost fatalistic view of the Palestinian–Israeli relationship and a sense of despair or bleakness about the future under Israeli rule. Few of the interviewees were able to identify personal goals that were separate from those of the organization to which they belonged. The appeal of al-Qaeda is to alienated youth; often feeling they are blocked in societies where there is no real possibility of advancement.

There is a heightened sense of the heroic associated with fallen group members and the community supports and rallies around families of the fallen or incarcerated. Most interviewees reported not only enhanced social status for the families of fallen or incarcerated members, but financial and material support from the organization and community for these families as well. 'Success' within the community is defined as fighting for 'the cause': liberation and religious freedom are the values that define success, not necessarily academic or economic accomplishment. As the young men adopt this view of success, their own self-image then becomes more intimately intertwined with the success of the organization. With no other means to achieve status and 'success', the organization's success becomes central to individual identity and provides a 'reason for living'. Again, while this dynamic emerged clearly for the youth of Islamic Jihad and Hamas, it is also probably a strong characteristic of those attracted to the path of radical Islam elsewhere.

The subordination of individual identity to collective identity is found across all organizations regardless of ideological affiliation. As individual identity succumbs to the organization, there is no room for individuality – individual ideas, individual identity and individual decision making – while at the same time self-perceived success becomes more and more linked to the organization. Individual self-worth is again intimately tied to the 'value' or prominence of the group, therefore each individual has a vested interest in ensuring not only the success of the organization, but to increase its prominence and exposure. The more prominent and more important (and often the more violent) a group is the greater the prestige that is then projected onto group members. This creates a cycle where group members have a direct need to increase the power and prestige of the group through increasingly dramatic and violent operations.

As the individual and group fuse, the more personal the struggle becomes for the group members. There is a symbiotic relationship created between the individual need to belong to a group, the need to ensure success of the group, and an enhanced desire to be an increasingly active part of the group. There is a personalization of the struggle, with an inability to distinguish between personal goals and those of the organization; they are one and the same. In their discussion of armed action and other actions taken, the success or failure of the group's action is personal: if the group succeeded, then as an individual they succeeded; if the group failed, they failed. Pride and shame as expressed by the individual are reflections of group actions, not individual actions, feelings or experiences. There is an overarching sense of the collective that consumes the individual. This fusion with the group seems to provide the necessary justification for their actions and absolution, or loss of responsibility, to the individual: if the group says it's OK, then it's OK. If the authority figure orders an action, then the action is justified. Guilt or remorse by the individual is not tolerated because the organization does not express it. Again this is intensified among Islamist groups who feel they have a moral obligation to the cause and a religiously sanctioned justification for their actions.

Most interestingly and illustrative of this concept of individual and group fusion is the perception or characterization of 'the enemy'. While there are slight differences between the secular and Islamist groups in the exact definition of the enemy, the overall experience in defining the enemy is remarkably similar. The Islamist groups are fighting for a pure Islamic state. Many interviewees cite Iran as an example of the type of state they would like to create. While the secular groups have a type of constraint by the nature of their view of the struggle, the Islamist groups have no such restraint. There is no concern about alienating any 'earthly' population, as the only 'audience' they are seeking to satisfy is Allah. With their direction coming in the form of *fatwas* (religious edicts) and sanctioned by religious clerics and other figures, the identification of the enemy is clear and simple for these Islamist groups: whether it is Israel or the USA, it is anyone who is opposed to their worldview.

Terrorist psychology: implications for a counter-terrorist strategy

If these conclusions concerning the individual, group and organizational psychology of political terrorism are valid, what are the implications for anti-terrorist policy? (It is interesting to observe how passionately arguments are waged concerning counter-terrorist policies given the relative lack of reliable understanding of terrorist psychology.) This emphasizes that this is no mere academic exercise, for after all, policies designed to deter terrorists from their acts of terrorism should be based on an understanding of 'what makes terrorists tick'.

Since terrorisms differ in their structure and dynamics, counter-terrorist policies should be appropriately tailored. As a general rule, the smaller and more autonomous the group, the more counterproductive is external force. When the autonomous cell comes under external threat, the external danger has the consequence of reducing internal divisiveness and uniting the group against the outside enemy. The survival of the group is paramount because of the sense of identity it provides. Terrorists whose only sense of significance comes from being terrorists cannot be forced to give up terrorism, for to do so would be to lose their very reason for being. To the contrary, for such individuals violent societal counter-reactions reaffirm their core belief that 'it's us against them and they are out to destroy us'. A tiny band of insignificant individuals has been transformed into a major opponent of society, making their 'fantasy war', to use Ferracuti's (1983) apt term, a reality. One can indeed make the case that left to their own devices these inherently unstable groups will self-destruct.

Similarly, for terrorist organizations for which violence is defined as the only legitimate tactic for achieving their espoused goals, outside threat and a policy of reactive retaliation cannot intimidate the organizational leadership into committing organizational suicide and ceasing to exist. For that is what ceasing committing acts of political violence would be if those acts were the sole self-definition.

For complex organizations dedicated to a cause, such as Basque separatism, where an illegal terrorist wing operates in parallel with a legal political wing as elements of a larger loosely integrated organization, the dynamics, and the policy implications, are again different. In such circumstances, if the overall organizational goals (in this case Basque separatism) are threatened by societal reactions to terrorism, one can make a case that internal organizational constraints can operate to constrain the terrorist wing. However, insofar as the terrorist group is not fully under political control, this is a matter of influence and partial constraint, for as has been noted earlier, ETA has its own internal dynamics and continues to thrive despite the significant degree of separatism already achieved.

For state-supported and directed terrorist groups, the terrorist group is in effect a paramilitary unit under central governmental control. In this situation, the individual, group and organizational psychological considerations discussed thus far are not especially relevant. The target of the anti-terrorist policy in this circumstance is not the group per se but the chief of state and the government of the sponsoring state. Since the survival of the state and national interests are the primary values, there is a rational case to be made that retaliatory policies can have a deterring effect, at least in the short term. But even in this circumstance, to watch the children in the camps in the aftermath of bombing attacks shaking their fists in rage suggests such tactics are contributing to rising generations of terrorists.

Just as political terrorism is the product of generational forces, so too it is here for generations to come. When hatred is bred in the bone, and passed from generation to generation, it does not yield easily to peace talks. There is no short-range solution to the problem of terrorism. Once an individual is in the pressure cooker of the terrorist group, it is extremely difficult to influence him. In the long run, the most effective anti-terrorist policy is one that inhibits potential recruits from joining in the first place, for once an individual is in the grip of the terrorist group the power of the group and organizational psychology will increasingly dominate his psychology.

Political terrorism is not only a product of psychological forces, its central strategy is psychological. For political terrorism is, at base, a particularly vicious species of psychological warfare. It is violence as communication. Up until now, the terrorists have had a virtual monopoly on the weapon of the television camera as they manipulate their target audience through the media. Countering the terrorists' highly effective media-oriented strategy through more effective dissemination of information and public education must be key elements of a proactive programme.

As important as it is to inhibit potential terrorists from joining, so too it is important to facilitate terrorists leaving. The powerful hold of the group has been described in detail. By creating pathways out of terrorism, that grip can be reduced. Amnesty programmes modelled on the highly effective programme of the Italian government can usefully contribute to that goal.

And reducing support for the group, both in its immediate societal surroundings and in the nation at large, are further long-range programmes to foster.

Terrorists perpetuate their organizations by shaping the perceptions of future generations of terrorists. Manipulating a reactive media, they demonstrate their power and significance and define the legitimacy of their cause. To counter them, effective education and dissemination of objective information are required.

One does not counter psychological warfare with smart bombs and missiles, although they can certainly play a useful role in a military campaign against harbouring states. One counters psychological warfare with psychological warfare. In the long run, the most effective ways of countering terrorism is to:

- *Inhibit potential terrorists from joining the group:* Security alone cannot accomplish this. Alienated youths must be able to envisage a future within the system that promises redress of long-standing economic and social inequity and come to believe that political activism can lead to their finding a pathway to these goals. Otherwise, striking out violently in despair will continue to seem like the only course available.
- *Produce dissension within the group:* The groups are virtual hothouses of tensions and rivalries. Active measures are required to magnify these tensions and pressures.
- *Facilitate exit from the group:* Once a terrorist has become a member of a group and committed terrorist acts, he/she is a wanted criminal with seemingly 'no way out'. Yet, as noted above, with the *pentiti* programme in Italy, a similar programme in the Basque region, and the so-called 'super-grass' programme in Northern Ireland, where reduced sentences or amnesty are offered for cooperation with the authorities (in effect a 'protected witness' programme, including for the Basque region plastic surgery and resettlement in Latin America), this can not only ease exit but also can produce dissension within the group as well.
- *Reduce support for the group:* This is particularly important, as important as inhibiting potential recruits from joining in the first place which indeed contributes to this goal. Thus the group or organization must be marginalized, its leader delegitimized. Osama bin Laden at the present is a romantic hero to many alienated youths in the Islamic world; his organization, al-Qaeda, a highly attractive option to consider. An effective strategic communication programme will increasingly marginalize al-Qaeda as an aberrant extremist group that is contrary to mainstream Islam, and will depict bin Laden not as a heroic figure, but as a self-consumed individual whose extreme actions damage all of Islam and the future of aspiring Muslim youths.

All of these goals are components of a strategic communication process that must be a central component of our anti-terrorist policy. This is not a policy that will swiftly end terrorism, but a process that must be put in place. Just as many of the attitudes that have made the path of terrorism attractive to alienated youths have taken root over decades, it will require decades to reduce the attractiveness of terrorism for those who have been raised in a climate dominated by hopelessness and despair, with hatred bred in the bone, so that extremism and violence have increasingly come to be seen as the only course.

Notes

1   Alex P. Schmid's typology is displayed in Figure 18.1. My version has expanded the category *Religious extremist terrorism* with two subtypes: *Religious fundamentalist terrorism* and *New religions terrorism*.
2   Hassan Salame was responsible for the wave of suicide bombings in Israel in 1996 which killed 46 people. He is now serving 46 consecutive life sentences.

Bibliography

Crenshaw, M. (1990) 'The Logic of Terrorist Behavior as Product of Strategic Choice', in Reich, W. (ed.) *Origins of Terrorism: Psychologies, Ideologies, Theologies, States of Mind*. Cambridge: Cambridge University Press, pp. 7–24.

Ferracuti, F. (1983) 'Psychiatric aspects of Italian left-wing and right-wing terrorism', paper presented to the 7th World Congress on Psychiatry, Vienna, July.

McCauley, C.R. and Segal, E. (1987) 'Social Psychology of Terrorist Groups', in Hendricks, C. (ed.) Group Processes and and Intergroup Relations, vol. 9 of the *Annual Review of Social and Personality Psychology*. Beverley Hills, CA: Sage.

Post, J. (1993) 'Terrorist Psycho-logic: Terrorist Behavior as a Product of Psychological Forces' in Reich, W. (ed.) *Origins of Terrorism: Psychologies, Ideologies, Theologies, States of Mind*. Cambridge: Cambridge University Press.

Robins, R. and Post. J. (1997) *Political Paranoia: The Psychopolitics of Hatred*. New Haven, CT: Yale University Press.

ʊ Social, organizational and psychological factors in suicide terrorism

Ariel Merari

Introduction

For many people suicide attacks are the symbol of terrorism. More than any other form of terrorism these attacks demonstrate terrorists' determination and devotion, to the extent of killing themselves for their cause. The vigour of this resolve is frightening and, as it is probably intended to do, instils the impression that people who are willing to sacrifice themselves cannot be stopped and their cause is bound to win. Suicide attacks have also been more lethal than other forms of terrorism. The attacks of 11 September 2001 in the USA caused nearly 10 times more fatalities than any previous terrorist attack in history. In Israel, suicide attacks in the course of the Palestinian *intifada* have constituted less than one per cent of the total number of terrorist attacks, but resulted in 51 per cent of the Israeli fatalities. The lethality of suicide attacks may explain the increasing attractiveness of this method for terrorist groups. Robert Pape (2003), for example, has attributed the proliferation of suicide attacks to their apparent effectiveness, arguing that campaigns of suicide terrorism have often succeeded in gaining at least partial concessions from the targeted governments.

Suicide terrorism is proliferating. Systematic use of suicide attacks by terrorist groups started in the early 1980s, but more than 50 per cent of the attacks have taken place since 2000. The growth is not only in the frequency of attacks, but also in their geographical spread and the number of groups involved. In the period of 1981–99, suicide attacks took place in seven countries (Lebanon, Sri Lanka, Israel, Turkey, Yemen, Kenya and Tanzania), whereas in the period of 2000 to March 2004 suicide attacks have occurred in 18 countries (Israel, Sri Lanka, the USA, Russia, Afghanistan, Pakistan, Morocco, Tunisia, Saudi Arabia, Yemen, Indonesia, Philippines, Kashmir, Iraq, Kenya, Turkey, Spain, and China). The problem is, therefore, growing rapidly.

Suicide terrorism has been mostly explained as being a result of religious fanaticism. Other explanations viewed suicide terrorism as a result of personality characteristics (Stein 2003), poverty and ignorance (Weinberg *et al.* 2003), psychological trauma (Sarraj 2002), and revenge for personal suffering or for the loss of a family member (Joshi 2000; Margalit 2003). These explanations, however, have relied on indirect or secondary data and are, therefore, conjectural or speculative. This chapter examines these explanations in light of empirical data that has been gathered on suicide terrorists, mainly in Israel.

Some of the misconceptions of suicide terrorism have their roots in erroneous definitions of this phenomenon. Some of the writers, for example, have regarded as suicide terrorism also acts in which the perpetrator carried out the attack knowing that death was highly likely, but did not actually happen (Atran 2003). This inclusion is problematic because of several reasons. First, although many of the perpetrators of these attacks, which Margalit calls 'no escape attacks', have indeed been killed, some of them survived after being caught or even managed to escape despite the meagre chance. Second, it is practically impossible to determine the precise subjective or objective likelihood of being killed in a given action. Soldiers in the First World War who climbed out of the trenches to charge against machine gun and artillery fire and were killed by the thousands, had a very high chance of getting killed. The likelihood of death for a British or French soldier in the battle of the Somme was probably no less than the chance of a Palestinian terrorist who fires an automatic weapon at Israeli inhabitants of a West Bank settlement. Even if we agreed that there is no meaningful difference between a perceived sure death and a subjective 90 per cent chance of being killed, there is no way of determining the actual or subjective likelihood of dying in action. And, most importantly, presumably, there is a fundamental psychological difference between the act of self-immolation and the situation of being killed by others. The difference is not only in the perceived certainty of dying in the case of suicide and the chance, however meagre, of surviving enemy's fire, but in the mental state that allows a person to destroy himself/herself by his/her own hands.

It is therefore necessary to define this form of behaviour at the outset of this chapter. A suicide terrorist attack is a situation in which a person intentionally kills himself (or herself) for the purpose of killing others, in the service of a political or ideological goal. This definition excludes situations in which the person does not know that his/her action would result in certain death, as has occasionally happened when an explosive charge that a person was carrying was detonated from a distance by remote control operated by another person, so as to make it look like a suicide attack, although the courier of the device was unaware of this plan (Merari 1990). A definition such as that offered by Ganor (2000), which reads 'operational method in which the very act of the attack is dependent upon the death of the perpetrator' does not exclude these false suicide cases.[1]

The purpose of this chapter is to explain the phenomenon of suicide terrorism. Following a description of the history of this phenomenon and its temporal and geographical scope, the chapter portrays the personal characteristics of suicide bombers, as gleaned from interviews with the families of completed suicides and with would-be suicides that failed to complete their mission. The paper then examines the question to what extent can general theories of suicide account for this particular form of self-immolation, reaching the conclusion that suicide terrorism is *sui generis* in the sense that existing theories of suicide fall short of explaining it. On the basis of empirical evidence, the chapter then proposes an explanation, which focuses on social pressure and commitment to the group as main factors. Having reached the conclusion that suicide terrorism is a group rather than an individual phenomenon, the paper examines the question of what factors lead a terrorist group to embark on a campaign of suicide attacks. The paper concludes with suggested avenues for coping with suicide terrorism.

History and incidence

Some authors have suggested that the practice of suicide terrorism can be traced in history to ancient groups such as the Jewish Sicarii (first century AD) and the Assassins (Hashishiyun), who operated in the eleventh to thirteenth centuries AD. However, bearing in mind the nature of suicide attacks as defined here, this claim is erroneous because of the absence of the element of self-immolation. Both the Sicarii and the Assassins killed their opponents by dagger. They took a very high risk of being caught and executed in the process, but they never killed themselves. In that, they are not different from many terrorists in the course of the nineteenth and twentieth centuries, who took extremely high risks in carrying out their attacks, including nineteenth-century anarchists, early-twentieth-century Russian social revolutionaries, as well as Latin American and Middle Eastern terrorists in the second half of the twentieth century.

Genuine suicide attacks in a military context took place in the Second World War, most notably by the Japanese kamikazes. In these cases soldiers did kill themselves on purpose so as to kill enemy fighters. These actions, however, were done in the framework of a military unit rather than by members of a terrorist group.[2] Conceivably, as explained below, the psychological process involved in the making of a military suicide unit is somewhat different from the process of making an individual suicide terrorist. Nevertheless, the processes involved in suicide attacks (i.e. involving self-killing) by an insurgent organization that operates in military formations in the framework of a guerrilla struggle, are probably quite similar to those that drove the Japanese kamikazes. So far, the only insurgent group that has used suicide attacks in the setting of a unit's battle against enemy soldiers has been the Tamil Tigers.

Apparently, the first terrorist suicide attack took place in Beirut on 15 December 1981. On that date a suicide driver reportedly drove an explosives-laden car into the Iraqi embassy, killing himself as well as 61 other persons and injuring more than 100.[3] Iraq claimed that the attack was carried out by the Iranian and Syrian intelligence services. The use of suicide attacks as a systematic tactic, however, began only in 1983. On 18 April that year, a truck containing a large amount of explosives crashed against the American embassy in Beirut, killing 80 and wounding 142. More attacks followed: On 23 October, the US Marines' barracks and the French paratroopers' headquarters were concurrently attacked by car bombs driven by suicides. The attack on the Marines' barracks resulted in 276 dead (including 243 Marines and 33 Lebanese civilians) and the attack on the French paratroopers caused 58 deaths. On 4 November 1983, a suicide driver crashed a car laden with explosives into the Israeli Government Building in the city of Tyre in South Lebanon, killing 88 and wounding 69. Another suicide attack in 1983 against an American embassy took place in Kuwait on 12 December.

Whereas the initial attacks were done by militant Islamic groups (which later formed Hezbollah), more groups adopted this mode of terrorism. By 1986 it became clear that most of the suicide attacks in Lebanon had been perpetrated by secular groups, most of them pro-Syrian, such as the Syrian Socialist National Party (SSNP), the Syrian Ba'ath Party, the Lebanese Ba'ath Party, and even the Communist Party. Most, if not all, of the secular groups' attacks were prepared by Syrian intelligence agents, who recruited the suicides, trained them and provided the explosive charges. Most of the suicide attacks in Lebanon were directed against military personnel: American and French soldiers of the Multi-National Force in 1983, and Israeli and South Lebanese Army soldiers thereafter. Two attacks targeted the American Embassy, and a couple of attacks targeted political parties in Lebanon.

In 1987, following the Lebanese example, the Tamil Tigers for the Liberation of Eelam (LTTE) adopted the tactic of suicide attacks. Until the ceasefire agreement on 23 February 2002, this organization carried out more than 170 suicide attacks, exceeding any other single group around the globe (Gunaratna 2000; Schweitzer 2001). The great majority of the attacks were directed against the Sri Lankan army and navy. Several attacks targeted politicians.

The number of suicide attacks carried out by Palestinian groups is about as large as the number of such attacks perpetrated by the LTTE. The first Palestinian suicide attack took place in April 1993. As of 1 May 2004, the total number of Palestinian suicide attacks reached 176. Of these, 78 attacks have been carried out by Hamas. The Palestinian Islamic Jihad (PIJ) carried out 44 attacks. Two other groups adopted this tactic in the Second Intifada: Fatah (under the name of al-Aqsa Martyrs' Brigades) carried out 34 attacks, and the Popular Front for the Liberation of Palestine (PFLP) carried out eight. Most of the attacks targeted random Israeli civilians, in public places (public transportation, shopping malls and coffee shops), but some were directed against Israeli soldiers.

The Kurdistan Workers' Party (PKK) was responsible for 15 suicide attacks, starting from June 1996. Until it declared a ceasefire in July 1999, this group carried out 15 suicide attacks, most of them by women. The targets were mostly Turkish police and military personnel.

Al-Qaeda started using suicide attacks in August 1998, simultaneously targeting the American embassies in Kenya and Tanzania. The combined number of casualties of these attacks reached 301 dead and 5000 wounded. In October 2000, al-Qaeda carried out a suicide attack on an American ship, the USS Cole, off the coast of Yemen. Seventeen seamen were killed and 39 wounded. On 11 September 2001, the group carried out the largest terrorist attack of all times: the crashing of hijacked planes on the World Trade Center and the Pentagon, which resulted in more than 3,000 fatalities. After the American occupation of Afghanistan and the demise of the Taliban regime, suicide terrorist attacks by anti-American, militant Islamic groups continued around the world. Although the precise organizational affiliation of the perpetrating groups with al-Qaeda has not been quite clear in most cases, the ideological affinity is beyond doubt. Suicide attacks inspired by anti-Western and/or anti-Jewish sentiments have been carried out in Tunisia, Morocco, Turkey, Iraq, Saudi Arabia, Yemen, Indonesia and Kenya.

Chechen rebels have carried out at least 16 suicide attacks, starting from 7 June 2000. Existing evidence suggests that the adoption of suicide attacks as a main mode of operation has been due to al-Qaeda's inspiration (Paz 2000).

In Iraq, suicide attacks started on a large scale soon after the US occupation. Similarly to other countries where suicide attacks have been used by terrorist groups, this form of attack has by far caused more casualties than any other mode of terrorist operation. Most of the attacks have, apparently been carried out by Salafiya Jihadiyya, an al-Qaeda affiliated group led by Mus'ab al-Zarqawi, although some of them have also been attributed to two other militant fundamentalist Islamic groups, Ansar al-Islam and Ansar al-Sunna, as well as to followers of Saddam Hussein.

Strategic consequences

Suicide attacks have proved to be a highly effective terrorist tactic. This statement seems self-evident in the wake of the 11 September 2001 al-Qaeda attacks in the USA. Yet, both before and after that crucial date in modern history this terrorist mode of operation has had far reaching strategic consequences. In the 1980s, a multi-national force, composed of American, French and Italian soldiers, was sent to Lebanon to ensure the pacification of the country and the institution of an independent government following the Israeli invasion of 1982. Suicide attacks against the Force (as well as against the US embassy) were the direct cause of the participating countries' decision to withdraw from Lebanon, leaving that country to the mercy of Syrian influence. No doubt, this move has had a significant effect on Lebanese politics in subsequent years.

Suicide attacks carried out by Hamas and the Palestinian Islamic Jihad (PIJ) after the Oslo agreement of 1993 have also had a momentous impact on the Israeli–Palestinian peace process and, as a secondary consequence, on Israel's relations with the Arab world in general. While the peace process was going on, Hamas and the PIJ tried to abort it by carrying out numerous suicide attacks against civilians in Israel's main cities. Large segments in the Israeli public interpreted these attacks as an indication that the Palestinian Authority under Yasser Arafat's leadership is doing nothing to stop anti-Israeli terrorism and that the Palestinians do not genuinely want peace. In the electoral campaign of early 1996, the incumbent Labour Party Prime Minister, Shimon Peres, was initially leading by about 20 percentage points. Yet, following a series of suicide attacks in Jerusalem and Tel Aviv, right-wing candidate Benjamin Netanyahu closed the gap and defeated Peres by a small margin. The ensuing policy change virtually froze the peace process for a long time. Thus, suicide attacks have been a main factor in bringing about a confidence-destruction process that continues at this time.

Following the American occupation, Iraq has been the leading country for the number of suicide attacks: 51 attacks which caused about 700 fatalities by the end of March 2004 (Atran 2004). While it is too early to assess at this fluid stage the impact of these attacks on the future of Iraq in particular and on the American War on Terrorism and the US political-strategic stature in general, it seems likely that they will have a considerable effect.

The profile of suicide terrorists

Psychological data on suicide terrorists of most groups has not been published. Since 1983 I have collected data on suicide terrorism around the globe from a variety of sources, using mainly media reports that included demographic and biographical details of suicides, sometimes based on interviews with the suicides' families. Valuable information was gained from interviews with jailed would-be suicides. Particularly useful as a basis for psychological autopsy was a systematic set of data on 34 of the 36 suicide Palestinian terrorists in the period of 1993–8.[4] These data were based on interviews with family members (parents and siblings) of the suicides. Other data included interviews with persons who attempted to carry out suicide attacks but failed, and with Hamas and Palestinian Islamic Jihad (PIJ) trainers of suicide bombers. Data on suicide terrorists in Israel after 1998 and on suicide attackers in Lebanon in the period of 1983–9 (almost all suicide attacks in Lebanon took place within this time frame) are mainly based on media sources and include some demographic characteristics, as well as on interviews with jailed would-be suicides. These data, supplemented by information on other groups, are summarized below.

Demographic characteristics

- *Age:* The mean age of the Lebanese suicide bombers was 21, and the age range was 16–28. The mean age of the Palestinian suicides prior to the Second Intifada was 22, with a range of 18–38. The age range of the Palestinian suicides in the Second (current) Intifada has been somewhat broader (17–53), but the average remained the same at 22. The age of LTTE suicides is younger, most of them under 15, as a matter of the organization's policy (Joshi 2000).
- *Marital status:* Data for the Lebanese sample are lacking, but clearly almost all of the suicides were single. In the Palestinian sample, 91 per cent were single. The fact that almost all suicides have been single may suggest that single persons are more willing to volunteer for suicide missions. However, in the Palestinian case, it has also been the policy of the organizations to refrain from recruiting married persons for such missions.
- *Gender:* In the Lebanese case, 84 per cent of the suicides were males (all the females were sent by secular groups). All of the Palestinian suicides prior to the Second Intifada were males. This, however, was a result of the fact that until recently, the Palestinian organizations that used suicide attacks were religious groups, which objected to the use of women in combat missions. During the Second Intifada the secular groups of Fatah and the Popular Front for the Liberation of Palestine (PFLP) also espoused suicide attacks. These groups used women as well as men for suicide missions. It is also noteworthy that left-wing Turkish and Kurdish groups, as well as the Tamil Tigers, have used women as often as men for suicide attacks. In the LTTE there is a special women suicide unit, called 'Birds of Freedom' (Joshi 2000), and women have comprised about 40 per cent of the terrorist suicides. Of the 15 suicide attacks dispatched by the Workers' Party of Kurdistan (PKK), 11 were carried out by women (Ergil 2001). Thus, the greater number of male suicides in the Lebanese and Palestinian cases only reflects the preference of religious Islamic groups.
- *Socio-economic status:* Reliable data are only available for the Palestinian sample. In general, contrary to some claims that poverty has been a major factor in the

inclination to embark on a suicide mission, the economic status of the Palestinian suicides' families is about the same as a cross-section of the Palestinian society in the Occupied Territories. The education level of the suicides at the time of their suicidal attack was also a close representation of Palestinian society; 88 per cent of the suicides had a full high-school training or higher.

Other potentially relevant factors

- *Religion:* Suicide attacks in Lebanon were initially carried out by the radical Shi'ite groups, which eventually formed Hezbollah. For this reason the phenomenon of suicide terrorism, especially the Middle Eastern brand, has been associated in public perception with religious fanaticism. This notion also permeated academic writings. However, by 1986 it became clear that nearly two-thirds of the suicide attacks in Lebanon were carried out by secular groups (Merari 1990). The conclusion that religious fanaticism is neither necessary nor a sufficient factor in suicide terrorist attacks gains further support from the fact that several non-religious groups have resorted to this tactic. Thus, the Tamil Tigers (LTTE), is composed of Hindus, and motivated by nationalist-separatist sentiments rather than by religious fanaticism. Suicide attacks have also been carried out by Marxist (and therefore clearly non-religious) groups such as the Kurdish PKK and the Turkish Revolutionary People's Liberation Front.
- *Revenge for personal suffering:* Some observers have suggested that the suicides have been motivated by the wish to take revenge on the enemy for suffering that they had personally undergone (Joshi 2000; Fisk 2001). Whereas this explanation is clearly incorrect in the case of the September 11 attackers, it may still be true with regard to suicide attacks in most other places, such as Lebanon, Israel, Turkey and Sri Lanka. This question was directly examined in the study of the Palestinian 1993–8 suicides. In that study, the suicides' families were asked about events that could, presumably, provide a reason for a personal grudge. These included the killing of a close family member by Israeli forces, killing of a friend, wounding or beating of the suicide in clashes with Israeli soldiers, and arrest of the suicide. Analysis of the results suggests that a personal grudge has not been a necessary factor, and apparently not even a major factor in creating the wish to embark on a suicide mission, although it presumably was a contributing factor in some of the cases.

Personality factors and psychopathology

In none of the cases did interviews with would-be suicides, or parents and siblings' descriptions of the suicide's personality and behaviour (for complete suicides) suggest the existence of clear symptoms of psychopathology. Furthermore, the descriptions did not reveal a common personality type for all or most of the suicides. About one-third of the cases, however, revealed suicidal tendencies, although they did not display the main recognized risk factors for suicide, namely, clinical depression, alcoholism or drug abuse, and a record of suicide attempts (see, for example, World Health Organization 1993; Jacobs *et al.* 1999).

Furthermore, existing sociological and psychological theories of suicide seem to be inappropriate for explaining suicidal terrorism. A full survey of the compatibility of suicide theories with the phenomenon of terrorist suicide is beyond the scope of this chapter and I shall therefore address this issue rather succinctly. Of the sociological theories, the closest to explaining this phenomenon seems to be Durkheim's concept of altruistic suicide, more specifically, his subcategory of 'optional' altruistic suicide (Durkheim 1951). Optional altruistic suicides are cases in which suicide is considered a merit by society but is not obligatory, such as the Japanese samurai custom of seppuku (or hara-kiri). However, the suitability of Durkheim's concept to the phenomenon of terrorist suicide is questionable on several grounds. Durkheim used the concept of altruistic suicide to characterize societies, not individuals. He explained the differences in suicide rates of various societies by the attributes of these societies. He inferred the motivation for committing suicide from the characteristics of the society to which the suicides belonged. Thus, he regarded suicides in the military as 'altruistic' because of the characteristics that he attributed to the army, such as obedience and sense of duty. He related to altruistic suicide as a stable rather than a situational characteristic of the society in question. Altruistic suicide characterizes societies that are highly 'integrated', in Durkheim's terms, that is very cohesive and, therefore, exert much influence on their members. Hence, to apply Durkheim's concept of altruistic suicide to the phenomenon of terrorist suicide is to attribute these suicides to the traits of the societies (a religious group, an ethnic community, a caste or a social organization such as the army) in which they occur. Terrorist suicide, however, has taken place in very diverse societies. In addition to Lebanese Shi'ites, Lebanese Sunnis, secular Lebanese, Palestinians, Egyptians, Armenians, Marxist Kurds, and Tamil Hindus, suicide for a political cause has also been committed by communist Germans, Catholic Irish, and Protestant Americans (John Wilkes Booth, who assassinated President Lincoln, committed suicide after the murder). It can be argued that the important factor is not the larger social unit (the ethnic group, religious group or nation) but the micro-society of a terrorist group itself that provides the social milieu amenable to generating self-sacrificial suicide, in accordance with Durkheim's altruistic variety. They are highly cohesive, rigorous, create rules of conduct and behaviour ethics that members are expected to abide and live by. Yet, the great majority of the terrorist groups, regardless of their structure, have not resorted to suicide attacks at all. Furthermore, there is no evidence that terrorist groups, which maintain a particularly strict discipline and a tight structure, have resorted to suicide tactics more than the looser groups. On the contrary: among the Palestinian groups, the Popular Front for the Liberation of Palestine (PFLP) has a much tighter structure and discipline than Hamas. Yet, the PFLP has only generated a few suicide attacks whereas Hamas has carried out many.

Psychological theories of suicide cannot readily explain the phenomenon of terrorist suicide either. Psychoanalytic theories view suicide as a result of an 'unconscious identification of the self with another person who is both loved and hated. Thus it becomes possible to treat oneself, or some part of oneself (typically one's disavowed body) as an alien and an enemy' (Maltsberger 1999: 73). While my study did not provide tools for examining the suicides' unconscious processes, no external supportive evidence of this theoretical explanation of suicide was found either. But these theories would find it hard to explain the waves of suicide terrorism in the Lebanese, Palestinian and Sri Lankan cases, as well as the episodes of cluster suicides, such as the 11 September 2001 attacks in the USA, the Irish hunger strikers in 1981, and the cases of Palestinian suicide attacks in duo or trio.

One of the most influential theories on suicide is that of Shneidman. Whereas psychoanalytical theories have basically viewed suicide as aggression (directed internally), Shneidman emphasizes the element of despair. In his view, the wish to commit suicide is almost always caused by intense psychological pain, which is generated by frustrated psychological needs. Suicide is committed by persons who view it as the best way to stop the pain. The prevailing emotion of suicides is the feeling of hopelessness-helplessness (Shneidman 1985, 1999). Farber (1968) also underscored the role of hopelessness in generating the wish to commit suicide. The greater the feeling of hope, the less the likelihood of suicide. Hope is the perceived ability to influence the world, and to be satisfied by the world. Farber's concept of hope, however, relates to the individual's expected ability to function within his own social milieu, rather than to a general communal situation, such as being under occupation. Lester and Lester (1971: 45) noted in this regard that suicidal people tend to see not only the present but also the future as bleak, expecting to be socially isolated in the future. With regard to terrorist suicide, however, whereas it can be argued that at least in some cases the suicide attacks are motivated by despair at the national or community level, despair that is associated with frustrated national needs, there is no evidence that the persons who carried out the suicide attacks suffered from despair at the individual level. The profile of the suicide in none of the cases studied resembled a typical suicide candidate, as described in the literature. The young persons who eventually committed suicide had no record of earlier attempts of self-immolation, were not in strife with their family and friends, and most of them expressed no feelings of being fed up with life. In the suicides' notes and last messages the act of self-destruction was presented as a form of struggle rather than as an escape. There was no sense of helplessness-hopelessness. On the contrary, the suicide was an act of projecting power rather than expressing weakness. Although in a significant number of the cases the suicide expressed interest in paradise and admiration for martyrdom, only a few talked openly about their personal wish to commit an act of martyrdom. With all due caution, it seems that most terrorist suicides in the Palestinian sample were not 'suicidal' in the usual psychological sense.

The key to understanding terrorist suicide should, therefore, be sought in a realm other than personality disorders and suicidality.

Terrorist groups as suicide production lines

An important clue to understanding the phenomenon of terrorist suicide can be gained from the hunger strike of ten IRA and INLA members in Belfast's Maze prison in 1981 (Beresford 1994; O'Malley 1990). Ten Irish nationalists, led by Bobby Sands, starved themselves to death when their demand to be recognized as political (rather than common criminal) prisoners was rejected by the British government. Although this event does not qualify as an act of suicidal terrorism because the hunger strikers did not kill anyone but themselves, it was an act of self-destruction for a political cause and, as such, can teach us much about the psychological mechanisms involved in suicide terrorism. Self-starvation is an extremely demanding way to die, much more difficult than the instantaneous death caused by a self-inflicted explosion: it took the hunger strikers from 50 to more than 70 days to die. During that time mothers, fiancées and priests begged the strikers to stop their self-destruction. Moreover, the hunger strikers were Catholics, for whom suicide was a mortal sin. The force that led them to continue their strike to the very end, ignoring all these pressures, must have been very strong. What was this force that sustained their determination? The assumption that all ten were suicidal persons, who happened to be in jail at the same time, is rather implausible. It is also unlikely that they were motivated by religious fanaticism and the promise of a place in paradise. The only way to understand this frightening demonstration of human readiness for self-sacrifice is to look at the influence of the group on its individual members. The chain suicide was a product of a group contract that one could not break. The group pressure in that situation was as strong as the group pressure that led hundreds of thousands of soldiers in the First World War to charge against enemy machine-gun fire and artillery to almost sure death. And, it was even stronger once the first hunger striker died. From that point on, the contract to die could not be broken any more, because the person who could release the next in line from their commitment was already dead.

A more comprehensive picture of the process of making suicide bombers was gained from data collected on Palestinian suicide terrorists, including interviews with trainers for such missions and surviving would-be suicides. The findings of these data are supported by circumstantial evidence from suicide terrorism in other countries. The data suggested that there are three main elements in the preparation of a suicide bomber by an organization, namely, indoctrination, group commitment and a personal pledge. These elements are described below.

- *Indoctrination:* Throughout the preparation for a suicide mission, the candidate is subjected to indoctrination by authoritative persons in the group. Although the candidate is, presumably, convinced from the start in the justification of the cause for which he/she is willing to die, the indoctrination is intended to further strengthen the motivation and to keep it from dwindling. Indoctrination in the religious Palestinian groups (Hamas and PIJ) included nationalist themes (Palestinian humiliation by Israel, stories of Arab glory in the days of Mohammad and the Caliphate, examples of acts of heroism during the Islamic wars), and religious themes (the act of self-sacrifice is Allah's will, and description of the rewards guaranteed for *shaheeds* (martyrs) in paradise).
- *Group commitment:* The mutual commitment of candidates for suicide operations to carry out the self-sacrificial attack is a very powerful motivation to stick to the mission despite hesitations and second thoughts. The chain suicide of the Irish hunger strikers in 1981 is an example of this social contract that is extremely hard

to break (Merari 1990). In Hamas and the PIJ, the preparation for suicide attacks is often done in cells, consisting of three to five volunteers. These cells are characterized in the organization as 'martyrdom cells' (*khaliya istishhadiya*), to differentiate them from ordinary 'military cells' (*khaliya askariya*). Members of these cells are mutually committed to each other in this kind of an unbreakable social contract. In the LTTE, male and female suicides are trained in special units, called 'Black Tigers' and 'Birds of Freedom', respectively. Presumably, they are also bonded in a social contract to commit the suicidal mission. In fact, the power of a group commitment and inability to break it was also the basis of the willingness of Japanese pilots in the Second World War to fly on kamikaze missions. Last letters of kamikazes to their families, written shortly before they took off for their last flight, indicated that while some of them went on their suicidal attack enthusiastically, others regarded it as a duty that they could not evade. Presumably, the group commitment element was also influential in the 9/11 attacks in the USA.

- *Personal pledge:* Many Middle Eastern groups adopted a routine of releasing to the media a videotape shortly after a suicide attack. These tapes are also usually presented by the organization to the suicide's family, after the operation, as a farewell message. Typically, in this tape, the suicide is seen, rifle in hand (and, in Islamic groups, a Qur'an in the other hand), declaring his intention to go on the suicide mission. This act is not only meant for propaganda. It is primarily a ceremony intended to establish an irrevocable personal commitment of the candidate to carry out the suicide attack. This ritual constitutes a point of no return. Having committed himself in front of a television camera (the candidate is also asked at that time to write farewell letters to his family and friends, which are kept by the group alongside with the videotape for release after the completion of the suicide mission), the candidate cannot possibly turn back on his promise. In fact, in both Hamas and the PIJ, from that point the candidate is formally referred to as 'the living martyr' (*al-shaheed al-hai*). This title is often used by the candidates themselves in the opening sentence of the video statement, which routinely starts with 'I am [the candidate's name], the living martyr … '. At this stage, the candidate is, presumably, in a mental state of a living dead, and has already resigned from life.

Public support

The magnitude of public support for suicide operations seems to affect both the terrorist group's willingness to use this tactic and the number of volunteers for suicide missions. Most, if not all, terrorist groups that have used suicide attacks are not indifferent to the opinions and attitudes of what they view as their constituency: the population whose interests they claim to serve and from which they recruit their members. In choosing tactics and targets, the group tends to act within the boundaries of its constituency's approval. During the last six months of 1995, for example, Hamas refrained from carrying out suicide attacks, because its leadership realized that such actions would not be supported by the Palestinian population at that time and would thus have had an adverse effect on the organization's popularity. In the Palestinian case, public support for terrorist attacks against Israel in general and for suicide attacks in particular has waxed and waned since the Oslo agreement of 1993, ranging from as low as 20 per cent support in May 1996 to more than 70 per cent in May 2002 (Center for Palestine Research and Studies 2000; Jerusalem Media and Communication Centre 2002; Palestinian Center for Policy and Survey Research 2002). The great increase in the frequency of suicide attacks during the Second Intifada (the 'al-Aqsa Intifada') reflects the greater willingness of Palestinian youth to volunteer to, or to be recruited for, what is generally regarded in the community as acts of ultimate patriotism and heroism. Songs praising the *shaheeds* are the greatest hits, the walls in the streets and alleys of Palestinian towns in the West Bank and the Gaza Strip are covered with graffiti applauding them, and their actions are mimicked in children's games. In this atmosphere, not only the terrorist groups see a public licence to continue the suicide attacks, they also have a constant flow of youngsters ready to become human bombs. The role of the preparation of the suicide candidate as described in the previous section, is to make sure that the youngster who, because of social pressure, said 'yes' to an offer to become a *shaheed*, or even the enthusiastic volunteer, would not have second thoughts and change his mind.

The importance of public attitude notwithstanding, it should be emphasized that so far there has not been even a single case of a person who carried out a true terrorist suicide attack (i.e. intentionally killing himself/herself while killing others for a political cause) on his or her own whim. In all cases it was an organization that decided to use this tactic, chose the target and the time, prepared the explosive charge, and arranged the logistics necessary for getting the human bomb to the target.

Which groups use suicide attacks?

Although the use of suicide terrorism is spreading, only a minority of the active terrorist groups around the globe have so far resorted to this tactic. An important question is, therefore, whether these groups have common characteristics that could be identified as factors that have influenced their decision to use suicide attacks. Table 6.1 lists the groups that have used suicide attacks, the cause of their struggle and the period in which they have operated.

Most of the groups that have used suicide terrorism are militant Islamic organizations. Since 1983, 30 groups have carried out suicide attacks. Seventeen of these groups could be characterized as militant Islamic, 11 as non-religious nationalist/ethnic, and two as radical Left wing. These characterizations, however, may be somewhat misleading, as some of the Islamic groups were also ethnic-nationalist. Arguably, the main motivation of at least some of these groups is nationalist rather than Islamic.

This is certainly true for the Palestinian Hamas and Islamic Jihad, the Chechen rebels, and perhaps also for the Kashmiri groups Lashkar i-Toiba and Jeish e-Muhammad.

The share of Islamic groups in suicide terrorism has grown dramatically in recent years. Of the 23 groups that used suicide terrorism before 11 September 2001, only 10 (43 per cent) were Islamic groups, whereas of the 17 groups that have used suicide attacks after 9/11, 13 (76 per cent) are Islamic. These facts clearly show that, at least under the present circumstances, the characteristic of militant Islamism is a significant contributing factor in determining a group's proclivity to use suicide attacks, although it is neither a necessary nor a sufficient factor. However, the importance of the Islamic factor has still to be explained. As noted above, some authors have attributed the use of suicide attacks by Islamic groups to Islamic traditions and practices, as well as to cultural traits of Islamic societies in general and Arab societies in particular. This view fails to account for the fact that not all Islamic groups have resorted to suicide attacks, and those that did have done it over a limited period of time. This fact suggests that the political context, as perceived by the group, may be more important than the group's religious and cultural background.

Under what circumstances does a group, Islamic or not, decide to resort to suicide attacks? Asking members to kill themselves is an extreme step, which is contradictory to basic psychological tendencies. For this reason, it is logical to expect that only under extreme circumstances would a group be willing to resort to this extreme way of fighting. Extreme circumstances are situations in which, by the group's perception, its main cause or its organizational existence are in grave danger.

This logical hypothesis seems to be supported by empirical facts in some, but not all cases. Hamas, for example, started using suicide attacks in 1993, at the beginning of the Israeli–Palestinian peace negotiations. The peace process was perceived by Hamas as an existential threat, both because it antagonized the very basis of Hamas ideology, but also because it was perceived as a danger to the organizational existence of the group under PLO control. The LTTE started using suicide attacks in 1987, at a time when the group was in retreat under the blows of the Sri Lankan army (Gunaratna 2000). Likewise, the Kurdish PKK decided to use suicide attacks at a time when the group was in distress, suffering heavy blows from the Turkish army, which resulted in a deteriorated morale among the group's fighters. The group intensified the use of suicide attacks after the capture of its leader, Abdullah Ocalan (Ergil 2001; Schweitzer 2001). A back-to-the wall situation has also been a major factor in the decision of some other groups to resort to suicide attacks, for example the Chechen rebels and the Turkish DHKP-C. The latter group staged a couple of suicide attacks at a time when a mass-hunger strike to death of its members in Turkish prison (an act of desperation in itself) failed to achieve any effect on the Turkish authorities.

At odds with these groups, however, the context of suicide attacks carried out by several other groups, notably al-Qaeda and its satellite groups in Indonesia, Saudi Arabia, Morocco, Tunisia and Turkey, cannot be described as a back-to-the-wall situation. Al-Qaeda was not under a devastating American offensive when it decided to carry out the suicide attacks in 1998, 2000 and September 2001. And, despite the American 'War on Terrorism', nor did al-Qaeda's affiliated groups in Muslim countries, such as Turkey and Indonesia, face a threatening turn of events, at least in their local habitats, that prompted them to resort to the most extreme measures in their power. Possibly, the use of suicide attacks by these groups reflects the fact that this terrorist method has become fashionable and a routine trademark of militant Islamic groups. This fashion has set a new standard of operation that obliges these groups.

Fashion alone, however, is apparently insufficient to sustain a massive campaign of suicide terrorism. All the groups that have carried out a large number of suicide attacks

Table 6.1 Nationality and motivation of groups that have used suicide attacks

Group	Nationality	Motivation	Period
Hezbollah[a]	Arab–Lebanese	Islamic, sectarian-ethnic	1983–99
al-Amal	Arab–Lebanese	Ethnic	1984–97
SSNP[b]	Arab–Lebanese	Nationalist	1985–7
Ba'ath	Arab–Lebanese	Nationalist, socialist	1985–6
SNO[c]	Arab–Lebanese	Nationalist	1985
Lebanese Communist Party	Arab–Lebanese	Nationalist, communist	1985
Egypt-Arabism	Arab–Egyptian	Nationalist	1987
PFLP	Arab–Palestinian	Nationalist	1989–2004
PFLP–GC	Arab–Palestinian	Nationalist	1988
Hamas	Arab–Palestinian	Nationalist, Islamic	1983–2004
Palestinian Islamic Jihad	Arab–Palestinian	Nationalist, Islamic	1993–2004
Fatah	Arab–Palestinian	Nationalist	2001–4
Gama'ah al-Islamiyya	Egyptian	Islamic	1993–5
al-Jihad	Egyptian	Islamic	1995
Chechen rebels	Chechen	Islamic-nationalist	2000–4
GIA	Arab-Algerian	Islamic	1995
Lashkar e-Toiba	Kashmiri	Islamic	1999–2004
Lashkar i-Jhangvi	Pakistani	Islamic	2003–4
Jeish e-Muhammad	Kashmiri	Islamic	2000–3
Harkat-ul Mujahideen al-Alami (Harkat ul-Ansar)	Pakistani	Islamic	2002
al-Qaeda	International	Islamic	1998–2004
Ansar al-Islam	Iraqi–Kurdish	Islamic	2003–4
Ansar al-Sunna	Iraqi–Kurdish	Islamic	2003–4
Salafia Jihadiyya[d]	Jordanian–Gulf	Islamic	2003–4
PKK	Kurdish	Nationalist	1996–9
DHKP-C	Turkish	Socialist	2001–3
TIKKO[e]	Turkish	Socialist	1999
Hizb ut-Tahrir	Uzbekistani	Islamic	2004
LTTE	Tamil	Ethnic-separatist	1987–2003
Jama'ah Islamiyya	Indonesian	Islamic	2002–3

a   Including constituent groups.
b   The Syrian Social Nationalist Party (a Lebanese group).
c   The Socialist Nasserite Organization (a Lebanese group).
d   A group affiliated with al-Qaeda, led by Ahmad al-Khalayla, also known as Abu Mus'ab al-Zarkawi.
e   The Turkish Peasants and Workers Liberation Army.

over a long period of time, notably the Palestinian groups, LTTE, the PKK and the Chechen rebels, have indeed felt an existential threat to their cause, the survival of their organization, or both. It therefore seems that in a group's decision to use suicide attacks, cultural background and ideology play a less important role than perceived necessity.

Coping with suicide terrorism

What can be done to prevent suicide terrorism? Three levels of counter-action should be addressed: physical defensive measures; deterring the group; and influencing the opinions and attitudes of the terrorists' constituency. In the context of this chapter I shall only address briefly the deterrence and public opinion aspects.

- *Deterring individual suicides:* A major difficulty in coping with suicide terrorism is the problem of deterring people who are willing to die. In a search of punishments that may deter suicides, it has been suggested that even a person who is ready to sacrifice himself would not want his loved ones to suffer. Indeed, so far the terrorist suicides in the Palestinian and Lebanese arenas could be sure that their families would be rewarded socially and materially rather than be punished. However, the idea of punishing the relatives of suicide terrorists is morally and legally problematic and is likely to prove politically counter-productive.

- *Deterring groups:* Because suicide terrorism is a group rather than an individual endeavour, effort to deter this tactic must be mainly directed at the groups that use it, rather than at the individuals that carry it out. While some individuals may be suicidal or at least willing to sacrifice themselves for a cause, all organizations, with the exception of some irrational cults, ascribe the highest importance to their continued survival and are, therefore, deterrable. A credible threat of severe punishment that implies the demise of the group would, presumably, deter that group from using suicide attacks (or any other mode of struggle defined by the deterrer as intolerable and therefore punishable behaviour). I believe that bin Laden would not have carried out the 9/11 attacks had he known that they would lead to the destruction of his organization and the Taliban regime that hosted it. It should be emphasized, however, that for achieving an effective deterrent, the threatened punishment must be both extremely severe and highly credible. When he carried out the 9/11 attacks, bin Laden regarded the US counter-threats as neither severe nor credible (bin Laden 1996).

- *Influencing the terrorist group's constituency:* Both the terrorist group's policy and the number of volunteers for suicide missions are influenced by the attitude of the population that the group claims to represent. Arguably, changing the attitudes of this population has the best long-range effect on the use of suicide attacks by the group.

Notes

1   This definition was adopted by some other writers, for example Weinberg *et al.* (2003).
2   For the purpose of this chapter, I use the US Department of State's definition of terrorism: 'The term *terrorism* means premeditated, politically motivated violence perpetrated against noncombatant targets by subnational groups or clandestine agents, usually intended to influence an audience' (US Department of State 2000).
3   The attack was carried out in the context of the Iran–Iraq war (see Mickolus *et al.* 1989; webref 2005).
4   My thanks are due to Ms Nasra Hassan who conducted the interviews.

Bibliography

Atran, S. (2003) 'Genesis of suicide terrorism', *Science*, **299**, 1534–9.

Atran, S. (2004) 'Mishandling suicide terrorism', *The Washington Quarterly*, **27**(3), 67–90.

Beresford, D. (1994) *Ten Men Dead*. London: Harper Collins.

bin Laden, O. (1996) 'Declaration of war against the Americans occupying the Land of the Two Holy Places', 23 August.

Center for Palestine Research and Studies (2000) http://www.cprs-palestine.org

Durkheim, E. (1951) *Suicide: A Study in Sociology*. New York: The Free Press.

Ergil, D. (2001) 'Suicide Terrorism in Turkey', in Ganor, B. (ed.) *Countering Suicide Terrorism: An International Conference*, The International Policy Institute for Counter-Terrorism at the Interdisciplinary Center, Herzliya, Israel, pp. 105–28.

Farber, M.L. (1968) *Theory of Suicide*. New York: Funk and Wagnalls.

Fisk, R. (2001) 'What drives a bomber to kill the innocent child?' *The Independent*, 11 August.

Ganor, B. (2000) 'Suicide terrorism: An overview', The International Policy Institute for Counter-Terrorism at the Interdisciplinary Center, Herzliya, Israel, http://www.ict.org.il

Gunaratna, R. (2000) 'The LTTE and suicide terrorism', *Frontline*, **17**(3), 5–8 February, http://www.flonnet.com/fl1703/17031060.htm

Hoffman, B. (1998) *Inside Terrorism*. London: Victor Gollancz.

Israeli, R. (1997) 'Islamikaze and their significance', *Terrorism and Political Violence*, **9**(3), 96–121.

Jacobs, D.G., Brewer, M. and Klein-Benheim, M. (1999) 'Suicide Assessment: An Overview and Recommended Protocol', in Jacobs, D.G. (ed.) *The Harvard Medical School Guide to Suicide Assessment and Intervention*. San Francisco, CA: Jossey-Bass, pp. 3–39.

Jerusalem Media and Communication Centre (JMCC) (2002) http://www.jmcc.org

Joshi, C.L. (2000) 'Sri Lanka: suicide bombers', *Far Eastern Economic Review*, 1 June.

Lester, G. and Lester, D. (1971) *Suicide*. Englewood Cliffs, NJ: Prentice Hall.

Maltsberger, J.T. (1999) 'The Psychodynamic Understanding of Suicide', in Jacobs, D.G. (ed.) *The Harvard Medical School Guide to Suicide Assessment and Intervention*. San Francisco, CA: Jossey-Bass, pp. 72–82.

Margalit, A. (2003) 'The suicide bombers', *The New York Review of Books*, 16 January, http://www.nybooks.com/articles.15979

Merari, A. (1990) 'The Readiness to Kill and Die: Suicidal Terrorism in the Middle East', in Reich, W. (ed.) *Origins of Terrorism: Psychologies, Ideologies, Theologies, States of Mind*. Cambridge: Cambridge University Press, pp. 192–207.

Mickolus, E., Sandler, T. and Murdock, J.M. (1989) *International Terrorism in the 1980s: A Chronology of Events, Vol. 1*. Ames, IA: Iowa State University Press, pp. 233–4. Also http://www.wordspy.com/words/suicidebomber.asp

O'Malley, P. (1990) *Biting at the Grave*. Boston, MA: Beacon Press.

Palestinian Center for Policy & Survey Research (PSR) (2002) http://www.pcpsr.org

Pape, R. (2003) 'The strategic logic of suicide terrorism', *American Political Science Review*, **97**(3), 343–61.

Paz, R. (2000) 'Suicide terrorist operations in Chechnya', *ICT Commentary*, http://www.ict.org.il

Post, J. (2001) *Killing in the name of God: Osama bin Laden and radical Islam*, A presentation at the New York Academy of Medicine, 30 October. Also http://www.theapm.org/cont/posttext.html

Sarraj, E. (2002) 'Suicide bombers: dignity, despair, and the need for hope', *Journal of Palestine Studies*, 1 June, 71–6.

Schweitzer, Y. (2001) 'Suicide Terrorism: Development and Characteristics', in Ganor, B. (ed.) *Countering Suicide Terrorism: An International Conference*, The International Policy Institute for Counter-Terrorism at the Interdisciplinary Center, Herzliya, Israel, pp. 75–85.

Shneidman, E.S. (1985) *Definition of Suicide*. New York: Wiley.

Shneidman, E.S. (1999) 'Perturbation and Lethality', in Jacobs, D.G. (ed.) *The Harvard Medical School Guide to Suicide Assessment and Intervention*. San Francisco, CA: Jossey-Bass, pp. 83–97.

Stein, R. (2003) 'Evil as Love and as Liberation: The Mind of a Suicidal Religious Terrorist', in Moss, D. (ed.) *Hating in the First Person Plural: Psychoanalytic Essays on Racism, Homophobia, Misogyny and Terror*. New York: Other Press.

Taylor, M. (1988) *The Terrorist*. London: Brassey's Defence Publishers.

US Department of State (2000) *Patterns of global terrorism 1999*, Department of State Publication 10687, April.

Weinberg, L., Pedhazur, A. and Canetti-Nisim, D. (2003) 'The social and religious characteristics of suicide bombers and their victims with some additional comments about the Israeli public's reaction', *Terrorism and Political Violence*, **15**(3), 139–53.

World Health Organization (WHO) (1993) *Guidelines for the primary prevention of mental, neurological and psychosocial disorders, 4. Suicide*, Geneva, Division of Mental Health, World Health Organization (publication No. WHO/MNH/MND/93.24).

7 Palestinian resistance and 'suicide bombing'

Causes and consequences

Hisham H. Ahmed

Introduction

Since 28 September 2000, the Palestinian–Israeli conflict has taken a new turn. A qualitatively more dramatic phase has characterized relations between the Israeli occupation authorities and the Palestinian people in the West Bank and the Gaza Strip. Needless to say that tensions have reached a watershed and the calamity of the situation has become almost unprecedented.

Triggered by Ariel Sharon's calculated, provocative violation of the Muslims' Aqsa Mosque, the people of Palestine launched the Aqsa Intifada in reaction to Israeli measures of widespread killings, mass arrests, large-scale confiscation of lands and increased house demolitions. It was also in response to the crippling of the Palestinian economy and chokehold on ordinary people's lives at the numerous Israeli 'checkpoints' during the arduous seven-year-old political process known as the Oslo Accords. Certainly, as the 'resolution of the plot' of dashed expectations and hopes was marked by the failing Camp David talks during the summer of 2000, all that was needed to stir an already volatile environment was just a trigger. To embarrass his political rival at the time, Prime Minister Ehud Barak, and in an attempt to win the hearts and the minds of the Israeli public by highlighting his courage and bravery, Sharon took the perfectly calculated step which would allow him to dominate the Israeli political arena since then, and which would impact on political, psychological, military and other developments.

Psychologically, as a result of Sharon's injurious provocation, the dream of peace by Israeli and Palestinian societies was shattered. Politically, the Oslo Accords, as well as consequent Palestinian–Israeli agreements, were put on hold and/or scrapped, as Sharon publicly declared on more than one occasion and especially after he assumed office. Those Palestinian forces who strived for conciliation were completely overwhelmed by the daily oppressive confrontation with Israeli occupation forces and policies. Even the idea of negotiations, within Palestinian society, was outmanoeuvred by the determination to put an end to the occupation, not in the least by a variety of different resistance operations. Certainly, Islamic groups, most notably Hamas and Islamic Jihad, have manipulated the failure of the Oslo Peace process to advance their agenda and to discredit the Palestinian Authority.

Palestinians were no longer content with symbolic expressions of protest through stone throwing, as was the case during the 1987 six-year-old Intifada, and more importantly here, as was the case during the first few weeks of the Aqsa Intifada. With intensified Israeli policies of targeted assassination, brutalizing reoccupation, mass incarceration and starvation, Palestinians apparently were no longer willing to be the only recipients of death and terror. Hence, more Israelis were killed and injured, especially under Sharon's rule, than at any previous stage of the conflict. The ratio of Israelis killed compared to Palestinians was narrowed dramatically, to reach 1:3 during Sharon's rule, compared to 1:10 under Barak and 1:15 under Benjamin Netanyahu.

By and large, the terms of the game were profoundly changed, and new modes of conduct were introduced: Israeli troops reoccupied all of the 'Occupied Territories' and the remnants of Palestinian hopes for coexistence were crushed. Of course, the logic of cause-and-effect relationship with regard to events and consequences notwithstanding, the argument of which came first, 'the chicken or the egg', only further muddied the discourse on the Palestinian–Israeli conflict. The reinstitutionalization of the Israeli occupation regime; the lack of realization of 'legitimate' Palestinian hopes and ambitions and the continued denial of Palestinian national rights established a new more worrisome era, dominated by the proliferation of random killing by one side and 'suicide bombing' by the other. Inevitably, there was more death, destruction and suffering.

Why did Palestinians rely heavily (but, certainly, not exclusively) on 'suicide bombing' operations against Israelis during the course of the Aqsa Intifada? Why and how was this form of resistance adopted by secular resistance groups, such as the Aqsa Martyrs Brigades of Fatah and the Abu Ali Mustafa Brigades of the Popular Front for the Liberation of Palestine, after it had previously been the monopoly of Islamic religious resistance groups, namely Hamas and the Islamic Jihad? What factors could lead a young Palestinian woman/man to explode her/himself against Israeli targets? Why is there strong Palestinian public support for 'suicide bombing' operations in spite of worldwide media condemnation of such attacks? And finally, how do Palestinians view themselves being perceived as 'suicidal' and/or 'homicidal'?

A multiplicity of factors stand at the heart of this complex phenomenon in Palestinian society that are conceptual, military, psychological, social, religious and political in nature. A careful consideration of the mindset and the rationale surrounding the carrying out of such attacks necessitates a deeper than the surface examination of the interplay between the dominant overall internal and external culture. Undoubtedly, no one is believed to assume that such operations are genetically innate to Palestinian society or that they are a monopoly of Islamic and Arab culture. Were they as such, 'real' solutions would perhaps be easier to introduce to such critical issues.

Operational definitions

Conceptually, it is rare to think of a phase in the history of the Palestinian–Israeli conflict where Palestinian resistance against the Israeli occupation has not been associated with terrorism, especially by Israel and its supporters in the West. The terms 'terrorist' and 'terrorism' have almost always been associated with Palestinians and their struggle. Since the founding of the Palestine Liberation Organization in 1964, it has had to contend with its label as a 'terrorist' organization for almost 30 years. In the West, a blanket judgement was passed on nearly every form of PLO activity as an act of terror. The 'battle of concepts and ideas' in the Palestinian–Israeli conflict was a fundamental part of the process to discredit the Palestinian drive for freedom, independence, statehood and self-determination. The Palestinian people under occupation had (and continue) to reckon with their dehumanization and demonization no less than they had to withstand their dispossession, loss of dignity, homelessness and oppression. Even as the unarmed Palestinians relied exclusively on peaceful means of protest and resistance against the Israeli occupation throughout the 1987 Intifada, little progress was achieved as far as the exercise of their national rights is concerned. In broad terms, Palestinians continued to be viewed as the main obstacle to peace in the region by Israel and its supporters in the West as late as the failure of the Camp David talks in the summer of 2000. In essence, the battle waged on the Palestinians from the start of the conflict was moral as well as material in nature. Its overarching objective has been to legitimize the subjugation of Palestinians by systematically 'blaming the victim' for the fate it is worthy of receiving.[1]

Therefore, the compelling label of Palestinian 'bombing operations' as 'suicidal' and/or 'homicidal' acts of terrorism is to be understood in that context. Particularly as the conflict became more intense and bloodier in the last few years, the compulsion for the dismissal of reasoning phenomena, acts and events apparently grew in strength. Although both Palestinian and Israeli societies respectively reached a stage of 'mutual vulnerability' during the Aqsa Intifada, albeit with material and human losses having been substantially greater in the former rather than the latter, the conventional wisdom in the West continues to propagate the idea that Palestinians (under occupation) rather than Israelis (the occupiers) are the root cause for the absence of peace and stability, and hence, for terrorism. 'Suicide bombing' operations are used as the tool for enhancing this prevalent notion. In the process, concepts, meanings, dynamics and resolutions have been convoluted, only setting the stage for further deepening rifts and profound hatred. Peace in the Middle East seems to be untenable more than at any other stage in the past: Palestinians are viewed as ruthless, merciless and uncivilized 'suicidal' killers more than in any previous period. 'Suicide bombing' in Palestinian society, however, does not reflect a culture of death, but a despair of occupation. As the renowned Palestinian poet, Mahmoud Darwish, stresses, 'We have to understand, not justify, what gives rise to this tragedy ... Palestinian people are in love with life. If we give them hope, a political solution, they'll stop killing themselves'.[2]

Are acts of resistance, in which Palestinians explode themselves against Israelis, indeed acts of suicide as the predominantly held portrayal insistently suggests? Obviously, proponents, many analysts and observers view such acts otherwise. When questioned while in his prison cell by the former Israeli Defence Minister, Benjamin Ben-Eliezer about the reasons behind his attempt 'to commit suicide' before he was captured, Rasan Stiti, vehemently rejected the notion, 'No, that's not it. That's not right. I didn't go to commit suicide. I went to die a martyr's death … I learned how important it is to be a *shaheed*.[3] A leading Palestinian lawyer, Jonathan Kuttab,[4] questions whether 'suicide' should always be viewed as 'a *terrorist* tactic that should be outlawed by the international community'. He reasons (2003), 'if the target of the attack is clearly military and not civilian, the willingness of the fighter to die or take a 100 per cent risk of fatality (while strange to the Western mind) is not prohibited under current international laws'. Kuttab reminds us,

> … unfortunately, all war and armed struggle involves high risks of fatality both to the perpetrators and their enemies. This includes the perpetrator taking the supreme sacrifice in an effort to inflict maximum casualties on his enemies and as a method for drawing attention to his cause.

A 'martyrdom operation', as it is articulated in the Palestinian lexicon, is considered 'the loftiest objective' a Palestinian can pursue in the national struggle against Israeli occupation (Levy-Barzilai 2002). 'It must be a great feeling to be able to do that,' thinks Neda Taweel, sister of the 'suicide-bomber' Diya Taweel (Baker 2001).

A 'suicide bomber' is considered a *shaheed* (a martyr). The concept of martyrdom (*istishhad*) in Islam is, of course, in diametrical contradiction to suicide (*intihar*), that is taking one's life because of mental disturbance or illness. An individual commits suicide when 'the balance of the mind is disturbed'. As Bassam Jarrar, director of Al Noon Center for Qur'anic Studies in Ramallah stresses (Baker 2001), martyrdom is 'the denial of the self for the benefit of the whole'. And for him, 'this is the epitome of human qualities'. While 'anyone who commits suicide cannot do anything good for himself or his country', Diya's sister explains (Baker 2001). He who commits suicide is 'someone who is sick, not someone who can sacrifice his life for others,' she concludes. In fact, 'the recruiters [of would-be martyrs] are scrupulous in turning away those whose motives would "taint" a mission, such as people in debt or with a history of mental instability – those seeking a glorious exit to an ignominious life' (Goldenberg 2002a).

Islam strictly forbids suicide and considers it an unforgivable, sinful act:

> O ye who believe … do not kill yourselves … If any do that in rancour and injustice, soon shall We cast him into the Fire.
>
> (Qur'an (Surah Al Nisaa) Chapter 4: The women, v.29)

The Qur'an does not consider martyrs to be dead. Rather,

> … they are alive who are cared for by God.
>
> (Qur'an (Surah Al Baqarah) Chapter 2: The cow, v.154)

'It is usually the enemy who calls them suicide bombers,' says Bassam Jarrar (Baker 2001). The leading Islamist authority, Sheikh Yusuf al-Qaradawi, differentiates between 'suicide' and martyrdom:

Attacks on enemies are not suicide operations but 'heroic martyrdom operations' in which the kamikazes act not out of hopelessness and despair but are driven by an overwhelming desire to cast terror and fear into the hearts of the oppressors.

(Pipes 2001)[5]

Qaradawi's definition, although using different terms and stemming from a vastly different ideological orientation, is corroborated by the politically motivated definitions of such attacks by 'experts'. The Israeli terrorism expert, Yoram Schweitzer (2000), views 'a suicide terror attack' as a 'politically motivated violent attack perpetrated by a self-aware individual (or individuals) who actively and purposely causes his own death through blowing himself up along with his chosen target'. Isn't this the readiness to sacrifice one's life in the process of destroying or attempting to destroy a target to advance a political goal?

Therefore, it follows that what is considered an act of suicide by some is viewed as a form of self-sacrifice for a noble ideal and/or cause, that is martyrdom, by others. Any self-respecting society views its selfless heroes with the utmost degree of idealization. This is certainly applicable to Western as well as to Eastern civilizations. In fact, 'suicide was of comparatively rare occurrence' in traditional Muslim society, as Franz Rosenthal points out (Pipes 2001). 'Suicide' attacks, though, date far back to ancient times when they were employed by the Jewish Sicairii and the Islamic Hashishiyun (Schweitzer 2000). 'Self-sacrifice is a way of legitimizing a cause, inspiring imitation, and promising individual glory,' according to Martha Crenshaw of Wesleyan University (Pipes 2001). British regiments fighting in France during the First World War 'are covered with commemorations to men who supposedly "laid down their lives" or "gave their lives" for their country' (Fisk 2001). During the Second World War, Japanese resistance dramatically introduced kamikaze missions where fighter pilots would blow themselves up on impact with enemy ships (Baker 2001; Pipes 1986). In recent times, such forms of self-sacrifice against military targets and/or personnel are called guerrilla warfare and those who engage in them are deemed freedom fighters.

In Palestinian society, self-sacrificial attacks against Israelis started in 1994, only after the extremist physician-settler Dr Baruch Goldstein massacred (under the observation and supervision of the Israeli army) 29 Palestinian worshippers while they were kneeling in prayer at dawn in the Ibrahimi Mosque in Hebron during the Muslims' holy month of Ramadan. Hamas retaliated by sending one of its attackers on a 'bombing operation' against an Israeli target in Afula. Subsequently, Islamic Palestinian resistance groups engaged in 'suicide bombing attacks', but rather on a limited, infrequent basis until the start of the Aqsa Intifada in late September 2000. Then, no longer were such attacks confined to Islamic religious groups. Secularists have also adopted this tactic in their resistance activities against an increasingly entrenched Israeli occupation. In other words, this tactic has acquired more prevalence and popularity in Palestinian resistance, to the extent that it has greatly characterized Palestinian–Israeli relations in recent years.

Military considerations

The asymmetrical balance of power between Israelis and Palestinians in favour of the former may have been the cause as well as the result of the ineptness of the Arab regional political system. The role of the Arab state in providing for the welfare of its citizens has continued to dwindle, giving rise to the prominence of non-state actors (groups and organizations). In the case of the Palestinians, the inability of the Palestinian political body, that is the PLO/PNA, to deliver the promised peace of the Oslo Accords has deepened frustration and despair among the people on the one hand, and has created the compulsion to consider alternatives other than negotiations on the other. The pressure cooker the occupation regime has established in the West Bank and the Gaza Strip only helped define the nature and dynamics of such alternatives. Encouraged by the successful Lebanese model of popular resistance to drive the Israeli occupation out of South Lebanon in May 2000 against the failure of the formal state to achieve this objective, Palestinians in the occupied territories have aspired to arrive at a strategic 'balance of terror' with their rival, especially in the absence and the seeming impossibility of a strategic 'balance of power'. The advantage of the 'balance of terror' compared to a 'balance of power', as Mahmoud El-Maraghi (2001) posits, is that it 'does not provide for equality or the interaction of peers'.

As Israel enjoys a distinct regional superpower status, Palestinians are left with bitter options: either to give in to Israel's military superiority or to resist. Of course, regular warfare is unthinkable, for Israeli air-, land- and sea-power superiority is not challengeable. The Israeli army possesses the means and the know-how to inflict (as it actually does) irreparable damage on Palestinians: the sheer thought of a head-on collision with one of the world's best equipped armies is certainly irrational, if not suicidal. The outcome is, undoubtedly, predestined and the conclusion is a for gone one. Symbolic resistance through stone throwing did not seem to be a viable, satisfactory option. The odds seemed very high. For the twenty-year-old electrical engineering student at Bir Zeit University, Diya Taweel, resistance was not a stone thrown at a powerful military machine, as his sister recalls from discussions with him. For Diya, it had to be much more:

> Once I asked him if he threw rocks. He said he didn't because there was no point. He said if you go to throw a rock you are committing suicide because a rock doesn't do anything. If you want to face their guns, you have to have something better than a rock.
>
> (Neda Taweel (Baker 2001))

What would be 'better than a rock'? Searching for an easier-to-make and easier-to-use, cheaper, effective, almost risk-free and precise weapon was dictated by the need to reciprocate the volatility of advanced fighter jets and helicopters and tanks.[6] Although categorized as collateral damage, the Israeli killing and wounding of thousands of Palestinian civilians on an ongoing basis has ruptured the moral deterrent of resorting to 'suicide bombing attacks' against Israelis, including civilians.[7] This compromised morality is in great part the product of the realization that all Israelis are army reservists, if not actually serving in the regular army: military service is mandatory. This psycho-military compulsion is compounded by the fact that

> the Palestinians had suffered so many civilian casualties since the Intifada began that Palestinians found joy in any suffering inflicted on their enemy. There was a feeling that 'they should suffer too'; which is exactly how Air Marshal Sir Arthur Harris explained his area-bombing policy against German civilians.
>
> (Fisk 2001)

Also important to note here is that most Israeli seemingly-civilian sites are not devoid of military presence, since Israel is one of the most militarized states in the world. Government-owned buses are used for transporting army soldiers and it is hard to think of any location that does not have military and/or security personnel present (Carlson 2002). Indeed, Suzanne Goldenberg of *The Guardian* makes the same point in her observations about 'suicide bombing', except that the cause and effect seem to be reversed:

> This is a conflict that has been fought without rules. On one side stands an army of volunteers, ready to kill and be killed, intent on inflicting the maximum [...] casualties. They can strike anywhere, at any time ... On the other side stands a regional superpower which unleashed F-16s and Apache helicopters, gunboats and tanks against Palestinian refugee camps and towns, and assassinated leading activists.
>
> (Goldenberg 2002b)

In essence,

> If it is considered moral and justifiable for the Israeli army to kill over 19 Palestinian civilians, including many children, and destroy their houses on top of their heads just to kill a wanted Palestinian activist, why is it not OK for Palestinians to go after settlers and soldiers while other Israelis stay indifferent as we are getting slaughtered on a daily basis?

> We do not have highly-advanced weaponry with which to face a regular army. All we are in control of are our bodies. We do not like or want to die. But if this is what it takes to terrorize them as they brutalize us all the time, why not do it?
>
> (Palestinian youth)[8]

This is the same logic Dr Ramadan Abdallah Shallah, secretary-general of the Palestinian Islamic Jihad, uses to explain the rationale behind using 'body bombers' against Israeli targets:

Our enemy possesses the most sophisticated weapons in the world and its army is trained to a very high standard ... We have nothing with which to repel killing and thuggery against us except the weapon of martyrdom. It is easy and costs us only our lives. Human bombs cannot be defeated, not even by nuclear bombs.

(Sprinzak 2000)

The words of the Palestinian young man and the analysis made by Shallah are echoed by none other than Ted Turner, vice-chairman of AOL Time Warner, the parent company of CNN. In an exclusive interview with *The Guardian*, Turner highlighted the impact of the asymmetrical military structure of Palestinian resistance: 'The Palestinians are fighting with human suicide bombers, that's all they have. The Israelis [...] they've got one of the most powerful military machines in the world. The Palestinians have nothing'(Burkeman and Beaumont 2002).

Of course, the military underpinnings behind martyrdom operations stem from a number of interrelated sets of factors. It is strongly believed that the reputed Israeli intelligence service can have less control over Palestinian resistance relying on 'suicide attacks'. The details of planning and execution are gone with the attacker. No escape plan is required. 'Unlike other operations that can be better contained by the Israeli army, these operations make the Israeli citizen feel that the danger is close to him,' as Bassam Jarrar put it (Baker 2001). For Jarrar, this kind of attack also aims to achieve a variety of objectives. First, the feeling of fear they generate negatively influences Jewish immigration, which is usually done at the expense of Palestinian land and people who have to make room for the new immigrants: 'Anyone thinking of immigrating to Israel will think twice' (ibid.). And second, fear will also make the Israeli economy suffer: 'Anyone considering investing in Israel will think again and anyone who is considering leaving the country will think even harder' (ibid.).

Thus, while inflicting damage, such 'smart' or 'intelligent' human bombs which have a human guidance system are considered 'the most accurate missile: the bomber can pick exactly where to stand'.[9] For example, 'Hamas uses these tactics and means of struggle,' according to Abdulaziz Al Ranteesi, a Hamas leader in Gaza, 'because it lacks F-16s, Apaches, tanks and missiles, and so we use any means that we have [...] because we are under occupation and are weak' (Goldenberg 2002a).[10] It is also believed that 'this kind of operation really hits the Israelis where it hurts,' as Anwar Ayam, the brother of a 'suicide bomber' from Tulkarem, put it. Moreover, such attacks 'will destroy their economy [and] cause [...] more casualties than any other type of operation' (Goldenberg 2002a). Not only that, but this tactic 'will destroy their [Israeli] social life. They are scared and nervous, and it will force them to leave the country because they are afraid' (ibid.).

For its part, the association of Palestinian religious scholars lent its backing to 'martyrdom operations' on several grounds. First, they are legitimate because they 'destroy the enemy and put fear in the hearts of the enemy, provoke the enemy, shake the foundations of its establishment and make it think of leaving Palestine' (ibid.). Secondly, they are expected to 'reduce the numbers of Jewish immigrants to Palestine, and [...] will make them [Israel] suffer financially' (ibid.).

In addition, it is also believed that such attacks are expected to generate the maximum amount of publicity for the Palestinian cause: 'The relatively high number of casualties guaranteed in such attacks, which are usually carried out in crowded areas, ensures full media coverage' (Schweitzer 2000).[11] A 'suicide attack' also serves as a weapon of retaliation and deterrence. Above all, it is intended to have a 'profound negative impact on the Israeli public's sense of personal security,' as it 'is aimed at causing devastating physical damage, through which it inflicts profound fear and anxiety' (ibid.). Furthermore, such attacks are used 'to instil a feeling of helplessness in the [targeted] population' and to make them conclude 'they have no way of protecting themselves against such attacks'. Accordingly, 'these feelings strike a blow to public morale, creating fear and panic' (ibid.). In other words,

> What the Palestinian suicide bombers are doing with these acts is telling the Israelis that we can reach anywhere. We are there. As long as you don't recognize us and don't want us to have a state, Israel can claim that it's establishing security, but they must also know that we can reach them anywhere. This is what the Palestinian suicide bombers are demonstrating by their actions. Israelis will not have security as long as they don't want to give us our state.
> (Nura Karmi (2003), Coordinator of Women's Programmes for Sabeel, the Ecumenical Liberation Theology Center, Jerusalem)

Psychological motivations

The fact is unmistakable and the message comes over loud and clear: a deep sense of injustice beyond the stage of profound frustration and despair stands at the heart of the issue. The Palestinian drive for freedom has been hampered by Israeli occupation atrocities. Resorting to 'body bombing' signifies failure of other attempted tactics, to the same extent that it reflects the immensity of pain and feeling of demoralization that engulfs Palestinian society. Israeli repression has, indeed, created a strange state of mind in Palestinian society: as a result of this abnormal environment, the psyche of many Palestinians has been scarred. Wherever and whenever you look around in Palestinian society, you are bound to see and feel innumerable cases of severe individual and collective anguish created by the occupation. The lack of normalcy of life can be seen on the streets torn up by army 'chokepoints'; in the demolished homes; in the burnt and destroyed farmland; and on the faces of children whose childhood has been stripped away due to deprivation and hopelessness. The profundity of frustration a Palestinian feels is bound to have mobilized a variety of psychological motives for resisting the Israeli occupation and all of its institutions and components, be they material or human.

Almost every Palestinian young man has suffered severe hardship at the hands of the Israeli occupation, such as arrest, beatings, injury and deportation. 'Every Palestinian, without exception, has felt the suffocating strangle of Israeli military control on their life' (Baker 2001). Diya Taweel, for example, could have been impacted by the view of the Psagot settlement at the hilltops of Ramallah, as he was able to see it brightly lit from his house every night. Alternatively, it could have been his daily encounters with the many roadblocks on his way to Bir Zeit University or the friends he saw wounded or imprisoned that triggered his desire for revenge (ibid.).

However, the story of Arin Ahmed, a would-be bomber, is even more telling. During her conversation with the Israeli former minister of defence, Ben-Eliezer, she unequivocally states that her motive for considering a 'body attack' on Israelis was not military or religious in nature. Rather, it was exclusively personal: 'I was in distress. I was depressed … You [Israelis] killed my friend. We were friends for a year and a half' (Levy-Barzalai 2002).

Most experts feel that there is a common denominator among 'suicide bombers', that is the lack of a horizon, a lack of hope, that they are people who had lost faith in life. 'Certainly, there is misery. Certainly, there is frustration. Certainly, they feel hopelessness' (ibid.). This already bad situation for Palestinians is usually exacerbated by Israeli army military operations that 'become a hothouse that produces more and more new suicide bombers'. Such operations 'kindle the frustration, hatred and despair and are the incubator for the terror to come' (ibid.).

For Ted Turner of CNN, 'poverty and desperation are the root cause of Palestinian suicide bombings' (Burkeman and Beaumont 2002). For Robert Fisk of *The Independent*, 'suicide bombings' are the product of societal instability generated by conditions of anguish: 'What happens when the balance of a whole society's mind has been disturbed?' he wonders. Illustrating the point, Fisk describes his own feelings as he was experiencing Palestinian misery:

> Walking through the wreckage of the Sabra and Chatila Palestinian refugee camps in Beirut … the same camps in which up to 2,000 civilians were massacred in 1982 and for which, on page 103 of its report, the Israeli Kahan Commission held Ariel Sharon 'personally responsible' – I could only wonder at the stability of the survivors who still lived there amid the concrete huts and the garbage and the football-sized rats. If I lived here, I remember thinking, I would commit suicide.
>
> (Fisk 2001)

For him, therefore,

> When a society is dispossessed, when the injustices thrust upon it appear insoluble, when the 'enemy' is all-powerful, when one's own people are bestialized as insects, cockroaches, 'two-legged beasts', then the mind moves beyond reason.
>
> (ibid.)

Thus, as Fisk stresses, 'the suicide bomber was the logical product of a people who have been crushed, dispossessed, tortured and killed in terrible numbers'.

The daily conditions of Palestinians living under occupation are bound to create immense anger, bitterness and hatred. The sights of Palestinian children being killed,[12] women and children going hungry,[13] a civilian population being brutalized (Aloni 2003), and constant curfews (Levy 2002) are enough to create dozens of new 'suicide bombers'.

Iyad Sarraj, a psychiatrist who heads the Gaza Community Mental Health Project, and who studied the bombers, and the would-be bombers who crossed his path, concludes that the motive behind 'suicide bombing' is rooted in trauma: injury to a father or brother in the First Intifada, or the death of a friend or even a distant relation in the present upheavals. To clarify this, he states that 'in every case of suicide bombing, there is a personal tragedy or a trauma'. More specifically, 'the people doing the suicide bombing today are the children of the First Intifada and they have witnessed or suffered personal trauma in one form or another that is humiliating' (Goldenberg 2002b). Sarraj succinctly sums up the psychological dynamics behind 'body bombings' as follows:

> The Palestinians have been driven to a state of hopelessness and despair, the kind of despair that comes from a situation that keeps getting worse, a despair where living becomes no different from dying. Desperation is a very powerful force – it is not only negative, but it can propel people to actions or solutions that would have previously been unthinkable. [...] The rapid Israeli military deployment and its immediate shoot-to-kill policy have deepened the sense of victimization, helplessness and exposure of the Palestinian masses. [...] Suicide bombing is an act of ultimate despair, a horrific reaction to extremely inhuman conditions in a seriously damaged environment of hopelessness. Suicide bombing is the ultimate cry for help.
>
> (Sarraj 2003)

For Shafiq Masalha, a clinical psychologist and lecturer at the Tel Aviv and Hebrew Universities, who conducted research on the dreams of Palestinian children between the ages of 10 and 11, there is an abnormally high percentage, 15 per cent, who dream of becoming martyrs, which indicates 'that ... life is very difficult, to the point that children are starting to think of death', and 'that a certain image has been drawn in people's minds that the martyr will enjoy a wonderful life in heaven'. For Masalha, this becomes 'especially true because there is such a great difference between reality and what they are "promised" ' (Baker 2001).[14]

Istish-hadiyyin ('suicide bombers') are by and large motivated by sights of hurt they have witnessed. Therefore, most of them are moved to act by their sweeping desire to take revenge. The continuation of Israeli brutalities serves as a fierce provocation for many Palestinian youngsters to expend their life of hopelessness and despair for the sake of their society. Most of the *Istish-hadiyyin* tend to be young, aged 18–27, unemployed, poor and witnesses of torture and/or death at the hands of Israeli soldiers. As the will of the *shaheed*, Hisham Ismail Abd-El Rahman Hamed (who blew himself up in November 1994, killing three Israeli soldiers and wounding two Israelis) shows, the feeling of hurt is always present. 'Dear family and friends! I write this will with tears in my eyes and sadness in my heart. I want to tell you that I am leaving ... because ... this ... is by all means more important than staying alive on this earth'.[15] The will of another *shaheed*, Salah Abed El Hamid Shaker, who blew himself up with another *shaheed* at Beit Lid on January 1995, killing 18 Israelis and wounding 36, is even more illustrative: 'I am going to take revenge upon the ... enemies of humanity'.[16] Ariel Merari, a psychologist at Tel Aviv University has depicted 'that intense struggles produce several types of people with the potential willingness to sacrifice themselves for a cause'. An attacker might be concerned with 'imitating the glorious acts of others, responding to a perception of enormous humiliation and distress, [and with] avenging the murder of comrades and relatives' (Sprinzak 2000).

The story of Ayat Al-Akhrass is particularly poignant. A young 18-year-old girl from Deheisheh refugee camp near Bethlehem blew herself up on 29 March 2002, killing two and injuring 28 Israelis in the process. Ayat did not seem to suffer personal disturbances from the brutally harsh conditions of life in the refugee camp. Spectacularly beautiful, she was top in her class and engaged to be married. But the cruel living conditions in her family's one-room home[17] in the camp and the ongoing sights of Palestinians, especially children, brutalized by the Israeli army triggered her desire to take revenge and to send a deep outcry to the inept Arab army generals, as her will demonstrates: 'Do view my martyrdom as an attempt to embarrass you and to break the silence that engulfs you while our people are being slaughtered'.[18] Indeed, her action was a testimony to how some young Palestinians barely beginning their lives react to conditions and circumstances around them. Ayat represents a great loss to Palestinian society, to no less an extent that she did to the lives she lost with her. She was as bright as a young lady of her age might like to be. She left home on a Friday morning to go to school for makeup classes lost because of the curfews. Not even her would-be husband could tell. She knew exactly what she was doing: As the story goes, she warned some Palestinian women at the site of her bombing to leave immediately so that they would not be hurt. Her story resonated loudly and widely in the Arab world. Desperation is certainly to blame, not personal though, but national and political.

Religious dynamics or orientalist fabrications

In Islam, a *shaheed* is promised paradise with all its glories and attractions. Certainly, martyrs are assigned a special status in that they are not considered dead but alive, even if they are not seen (Qur'an (Surah Al Baqarah) Chapter 2: The cow, v.154). In the struggle (jihad), a Muslim aspires for one of the two: victory or martyrdom. To become a *shaheed*, therefore, is a particularly noble achievement. It demonstrates closeness to God and selflessness of behaviour. Moreover, a *shaheed* is one who is glorified and idealized: he/she symbolizes personal sacrifice for the collective good.

However, at no point in the Qur'an is there any mention of the reductionist conception of the virgins in paradise (the legendary reward for martyrs): 70 or 72 loving virgins, the notion is no less than stereotypical and delegitimizing. Of course,

Islam as a religion serves as a very strong driving force behind the conviction of its believers to act for the sake of God. The struggle over Palestine is not devoid of holy values and the sanctity of holy places. Yet, if we were to assume that it is this fabricated notion of virgins which drives a Palestinian to go on a 'suicide bombing' mission, what would we say of non-Muslims who do the like: Palestinians, Kurds, or Tamils? What do we say of Palestinian secularists who resort to 'martyrdom operations' in their resistance against the Israeli occupation? Indeed, 'there are rewards, certain enticements', as Bassam Jarrar explains. The most important rewards, however, are spiritual in nature: 'Although the spiritual reward is the most bountiful, more "simple" people are lured by the physical rewards of martyrdom, or what they believe them to be' (Baker 2001).

For most *shaheeds*, or would-be *shaheeds*,

> Life here is just a pathway to life in the next world. The loss of life here is not such a big thing. Here it's just preparation. The next world is the true life, for the holy ones who are worthy of reaching there.
>
> (Levy-Barzalai 2002)

Hassan Nasrallah of Hezbollah views the rewards a *shaheed* seeks in psycho-religious terms. Explaining how one considers becoming a *shaheed*, Nasrallah says:

> Imagine you are in a sauna. It is very hot but you know that in the next room there is air conditioning, an armchair, classical music and a cocktail. So you pass easily into the next room. That is how I would explain the mind of the martyr to a Westerner.
>
> (Fisk 2001)

Ranteesi of Hamas emphasizes that 'it is not just for paradise, or the virgins, but because we are under occupation and are weak' (Goldenberg 2002a). Among other things, this led Suzanne Goldenberg to conclude that

> religious indoctrination is no longer central to the preparation of the bombers – especially for secular groups such as the al-Aqsa Martyrs' Brigades and the Popular Front for the Liberation of Palestine. But the iron fist of Ariel Sharon – the incursions into West Bank towns and refugee camps by Israeli armour and helicopter gunships, the mass arrests and lengthy curfews – has only increased the determination of those who would embrace martyrdom.
>
> (Goldenberg 2002a)

In fact,

> it has no longer become a far-fetched conclusion that Sharon, by virtue of his reckless assault on Palestinians, has created a societal factory of suicide bombers,

100 Hisham H. Ahmed

not only among Muslims, but also among Palestinian Christians, hitherto unaccustomed to consider resorting to such measures.

(Ahmed 2003)

Islam is no more than a mobilizing ideology to indoctrinate believers into not accepting oppression and subjugation. Undoubtedly, it is the fact that life under occupation is intolerable and unbearable which leads Palestinian youngsters to sacrifice their bodies and their targets to draw attention to the Palestinian cause.

Conclusion

The phenomenon of 'martyrdom operations' or 'suicide bombings' certainly deserves the utmost care and concern. Palestinian society suffers no less by such operations than the targeted Israeli population. The best, most courageous young men and women are the ones whose lives are expended. No rewards and/or status can compensate for the loss of life. The more military operations the Israelis conduct in the occupied territories, it has been amply demonstrated by experience, the more 'human bombs' are mobilized in Palestinian society.

Those who become *shaheeds* are sanctified by religion, idealized by society and assigned the rank of heroes. Upon one's martyrdom, a wedding-like celebration is usually held. Families do not receive condolences but congratulations, perhaps to boost the morale of the family after the loss. Pain and the sense of honour converge in a most unique way. The occupation authorities impose collective punishment on Palestinians to deter would-be 'bombers' from pursuing their operations. The Israeli army, in addition to launching repeated military operations, engages in demolishing houses of 'suicide bombers' in an attempt to halt future attacks. The occupation has also conducted deportations of families of Palestinians engaging in resistance. Other punitive measures have been undertaken against Palestinians in an effort to put an end to such a phenomenon, but to no avail. The record is voluminous regarding the causal relationship between Israeli occupation measures and Palestinian reactions. The cycle of violence is vicious, indeed.

In fact, it is no exaggeration to suggest that the occupation regime, especially since Ariel Sharon came to power, has become the greatest deterrent to Palestinian and Israeli security alike. Sharon himself admitted to his cabinet that the Israeli occupation was not a good thing.[19] The solution does not lie in increasing military preponderance and ferocity: rather, it is definitely political in nature. For as long as a people are deprived of the most basic of their rights, the chances remain high for further deterioration. Hope primarily resides in the Israeli public's perception that their security is organically connected to Palestinian security and exercise of national rights. Desperation needs to be replaced with a hopeful outlook on life. A positive vision for the future needs to take over.

Notes

1 For a more detailed analysis see Said and Hitchens (1988).
2 See Maya Jaggi (2002).
3 For a first-hand understanding of how a proponent of martyrdom operations thinks and feels, see the content of the conversations Benjamin Ben-Eliezer, the former Israeli Defence Minister, had with two Palestinian 'suicide-bombing' candidates, Arin Ahmed and Rasan Stili, as he visited them in their prison (Levy-Barzilai 2002).
4 Jonathan Kuttab is an attorney working in Jerusalem. He is a member of the New York, Israeli and Palestinian Bar associations and is extremely active in human rights issues.
5 See also Lexington Area Muslim Network (2000).
6 For a discussion of the advantages of guerrilla warfare over conventional war see Sprinzak (2000).
7 The Gaza Community Mental Health Programme (2003) cites 2,292 Palestinians killed, 22,437 injuries, over 3,100 homes destroyed, 227,995 trees uprooted and almost 100,000 dunums of Palestinian land confiscated or razed by Israeli forces and/or settlers since the beginning of the Aqsa Intifada.
8 An extract from an interview conducted by the author in March 2003. The name of the interviewee is kept anonymous for security reasons at his request.
9 See the comments made by Major General Eival Gilady, Chief of Strategic Planning for the Israeli Army in Goldenberg (2002a).
10 For more on Ranteesi's views see also Paz (2003).
11 See also Crenshaw (2003).
12 As of 28 February 2003, at least 415 Palestinian children under 18 have been killed (American Educational Trust, Americans for Middle East Understanding, Black Voices for Peace, and Jews for Peace in Palestine and Israel 2003). See also Levy (2003).
13 Almost 25 per cent of Palestinian children are suffering from acute or chronic malnutrition for purely man-made reasons, and nursing and pregnant women are consuming 15–20 per cent fewer calories than before the start of the Intifada. Peter Hansen, the Commissioner General of the UN Relief and Works Agency (UNRWA) has stated that the consequent anaemia, low folic acid intake and lack or proteins threaten women's health and the normal development of their children (Hansen 2003).
14 See also Masalha (2003).
15 *Maariv*, 13 November 1994, p.15, cited in Ganor (2000).
16 *Maariv*, 23 January 1995, cited in Ganor (2000).
17 Her one-room house was so small that the Israeli army engineers did not deem her home worthy of demolition as was their usual policy for resistance activists.
18 Her will was frequently broadcast on al-Jazeera television and many other networks.
19 'Sharon said continued Israeli rule over 3.5 million Palestinians is "bad for us and them".' *The Christian Science Monitor*, 27 May 2003.

Bibliography

Ahmed, H. (2003) 'Ariel Sharon and the fate of local, regional and international peace', *Palestine–Israel Journal*, **10**(1), 93–8.
Aloni, S. (2003) 'Murder of a population under cover of righteousness', *Ha'aretz*, 6 March.
American Educational Trust, Americans for Middle East Understanding, Black Voices for Peace, and Jews for Peace in Palestine and Israel (2003) *Remember these children*, a joint report, 27 March.
Baker, J. (2001) 'When they go to die', *Palestinian Report*, 18 July.
Burkeman, O. and Beaumont, P. (2002) 'CNN chief accuses Israel of terror', *The Guardian*, 18 June.
Carlson, C.E. (2002) *Smart bombs versus intelligent bombs: the suicide bomb hocus*, a lecture presented at Colorado State University, 8 December: Hold These Truths Ltd.

Crenshaw, M. (2003) ' "New" versus "old" terrorism', *Palestine–Israel Journal*, **10**(1), 48–53.

El-Maraghi, M. (2001) 'Poised in fear', *Al Ahram Weekly*, 5–11 July.

Fisk, R. (2001) 'What drives a bomber to kill the innocent child?', *The Independent*, 11 August.

Ganor, B. (2000) *Suicide terrorism: an overview*, lecture, The Israeli International Policy Center for Counter-Terrorism, 15 February.

Gaza Community Mental Health Programme (2003) *Intifada report 28 September 2000–14 April 2003.*

Goldenberg, S. (2002a) 'The men behind the suicide bombers: every death is the product of a well-oiled killing machine', *The Guardian*, 12 June.

Goldenberg, S. (2002b) 'A mission to murder: inside the minds of suicide bombers', *The Guardian*, 11 June.

Hansen, P. (2003) 'Hungry in Gaza', *The Guardian*, 5 March.

Jaggi, M. (2002) 'The profile: Mahmoud Darwish', *The Guardian*, 8 June.

Karmi, N. (2003) 'Violence and its alternatives', a roundtable discussion held 4 March 2003, *Palestine–Israel Journal*, **10**(1), 71–84.

Kuttab, J. (2003) 'Victim terrorism', *Palestine–Israel Journal*, **10**(1), 23–7.

Levy, G. (2002) 'A million people under curfew', *Ha'aretz*, 30 June.

Levy, G. (2003) 'The 411th child', *Ha'aretz*, 11 April.

Levy-Barzalai, V. (2002) 'A near death experience', *Ha'aretz*, 20 June.

Lexington Area Muslim Network (2000) *Fatwas on suicide bombs*, Lexington@leb.net, 29 November.

Masalha, S. (2003) 'Children and violent conflict: a look at the inner world of Palestinian children via their dreams', *Palestine–Israel Journal*, **10**(1), 62–70.

Paz, R. (2003) 'Ranteesi versus the United States: new policy of a new leader of Hamas?', *Occasional Papers*, **1**(5), (GLORIA) Center for Global Research in International Affairs, April.

Pipes, D. (1986) 'The scourge of suicide terrorism', *National Interest*, Summer.

Pipes, D. (2001) 'The (suicide) jihad menace', *Jerusalem Post*, 27 July.

Said, E.W. and Hitchens, C. (eds) (1988) *Blaming the Victims: Spurious Scholarship and the Palestinian Question.* New York: Verso.

Sarraj, I. (2003) 'On violence and resistance', *Palestine–Israel Journal*, **10**(1), 36–40.

Schweitzer, Y. (2000) *Suicide terrorism: development and characteristics*, a lecture presented at the International Conference on Countering Suicide Terrorism at ICT, Herzliya, Israel, 21 February.

Sprinzak, E. (2000) 'Rational fanatics', *Foreign Policy*, September/October.

8   Roots of terrorism in the Middle East

Internal pressures and international constraints

Abdullah Yousef Sahar Mohammad

Introduction

Arguably, one of the major developments in the 'new world order' since the collapse of the Soviet Union has been the escalation of the phenomenon of terrorism. This does not imply that the world was free from terrorism before that period, but the subject was neither addressed nor recognized as such a major phenomenon in the international system as other major issues were during the cold war era. Yet, despite international efforts by states, institutions and academics, terrorism has still not been firmly defined. In addition, there are several demanding questions that need to be carefully considered, such as the following:

- What is terrorism?
- Who is the terrorist?
- What is the difference between terrorists and freedom fighters?
- What can be said about state-sponsored terrorism?

Without investigating these critical questions it will be very difficult to reach any concrete results regarding the roots of terrorism. Therefore, theoretical and operational borders between what is considered terrorism and what is not form the basis for identifying the causes of this phenomenon. This ambiguity as to the definition of terrorism, which overshadows the notion of terrorism, may contribute to different types of violence in the name of fighting or reacting to terrorism by the conflicting parties. The 'general practice of violence' has become the generator of the terrorism cycle in many regions, particularly in the Middle East.

How to explain terrorism in the Middle East is the prime concern of this chapter. Other related accompanying questions will be raised, such as:

- What are the main roots of terrorism in the Middle East?
- Are the roots of terrorism related only to the regional political environment or are they also linked to the international domain?
- Why is there an increase in terrorism in this area?
- How might terrorism be minimized?

Explaining terrorism in the Middle East

Various scholars have developed integrated but contending approaches to explaining terrorism in the Middle East. 'Terrorology' has become a popular field for many reasons. Besides being an academic field of study, this science has become an area of political propaganda and an ideological battlefield. In his work 'International Terrorism: Image and Reality' (1991), Noam Chomsky has indicated two approaches to the study of terrorism. The first is the literal approach, where the research is carried out seriously and objectively. The other is the propagandistic approach in which the notion of terrorism is addressed on the bases of political and ideological interests. Unfortunately, the most popular literature on terrorism adopts the propagandistic approach. Edward Herman and Gerry O'Sullivan have discussed this problem in a systematic way in their pioneering research 'Terrorism as Ideology and Cultural Industry' (1991). Their research indicates that of 32 of the leading recognized experts on terrorism, 31 fall into either the category of moderate establishment or right-wing establishment. Moreover, both the moderate establishment and the right-wing establishment adopt the 'patriotic model'. In their words, this model is one

> in which all virtues are ascribed to oneself and one's friends and clients, all villainy is attached to the enemy. It reiterates a litany of myths and fabrications which have been built up to justify Western interests and policy.
>
> (Herman and O'Sullivan 1991: 44)

In the same regard, some Middle Eastern scholars point to the contaminating effect of the penetration of the Middle East by the West as the sole cause of terrorism (Abdulmahdi 1992; Alsamak 1992; Aljahmani 1998). Many of these scholars view the US policies in the Middle East as the main cause of terrorism in and of the area (Saleh 2003). Other scholars have suggested a combination of factors as the primary root causes of terrorism in the Middle East. The literature that deals with the causes of terrorism is fragmented over a broad and unorganized scheme, as detailed in the following sections.

The political approach

Many works within this camp have related the causes of terrorism to both international and internal politics. Fikri Abdulmahdi (1992) suggests that the major factors behind terrorism are the conflict between the West and East during the cold war era, the Israeli occupation of Arab lands, savage Middle Eastern security intelligence forces, and the policing methods of dictatorial regimes in the Middle East. Yasseen Al Saleh (2003) also sees these as major factors. According to Al Saleh, the dearth of democracy in Arab states in combination with the collaboration between the US government and many regimes in the Middle East prevent certain opposition groups from expressing themselves. In effect, they have no say, political or otherwise, in the running of their countries. As a result, they turn to suicide attacks as a weapon of last resort, and religion for divine validation. Thus, terrorism has become a heroic means of influence for some of the banned political opposition groups. The inequality, oppression and injustice perpetrated in this region are also diagnosed as major causative factors resulting in the resort to terrorism (Alakra 1993).

The socio-economic approach

The deterioration of socio-economic conditions in many Middle Eastern societies has contributed in many ways to the eruption of terrorism. For Abdunaser Hariz (1996), terrorism is a result of economic and social deprivation. While their countries are full of economic potential and resources, many Middle Eastern youths and well-educated citizens are left without either jobs or any of the other prerequisites of a satisfactory life. The perceived inequities of the capitalist system are also seen as a main instigator of the terrorist actions carried out by some groups. Najeeb Alshami (2002) pointed out that economic corruption is manifested by both the internal economic elites and by international capitalist powers. The collaboration among the capitalists around the world is not above suspicion in accelerating poverty and other social-economic malaises of the Arab world. Other scholars, such as Ahmad Abualroos (2001), sum up the causes of terrorism in several interrelated ways. Economic conditions, a political vacuum, a high rate of illiteracy, the collapse of the family system, and religious fanaticism are all related to the phenomenon of extremism: the vehicle of terrorists on the road to their destiny.

The psycho-sociological approach

Many theories have been developed within this approach. Some scholars view terrorism as the outcome of psychological defects at the personal level. Others see it as inherited in-group thought which then leads on to the adoption of terrorism as a collective action. At the personal level, scholars such as Khalil Fazil (1991) and Ehud Sprinzak (1998) pay attention more to the psychological reasoning behind terrorist actions carried out by certain individuals. Fazil relates what he sees as this psychological defect to the personal disorder inherited from a deprived and aggravated environment. Sprinzak, on the other hand, focuses on the case of the radical group *The Weathermen* which bombed a police monument in Chicago in 1969. In his analysis, radicals typically go through several stages of radicalization in relation to the political order before they become terrorists. He describes the stages as 'crisis of confidence', 'conflict of legitimacy' and 'crisis of legitimacy'. Furthermore, the terrorist's action is mainly 'a product of a profound delegitimization that a large number of people undergo in relation to the established social and political order' (p.85). It is worth noting that terrorists find themselves opposed by stronger forces which, by means of the law, prohibit direct confrontation.

Despite his lack of enthusiasm in reaching any firm findings regarding personality factors of terrorists, particularly among those who committed suicide, Ariel Merari (1998) thinks that a broken family background is acceptable as at least a partial explanation for acts of terrorism. Jerrold Post (1998) argues that the logic of the individuals involved in terrorism is grounded in their psychology and reflected in their rhetoric. Their particular logic, according to Post, is utilized as a justification for their violent acts (p.25).

Islamic extremism

In the work of many traditional and neo-orientalist scholars, such as Daniel Pipes (1983), Bernard Lewis (1993) and Raphael Israeli (1993, 2000), we find that the idea of an international Islamic threat against Western democracies is a given. One of Israeli's books, *Fundamentalist Islam and Israel* (1993), preaches, in essence, that the Islamists believe in violence as an acceptable means to a political end. Islamists, in his view, are not merely opposed to Israel or certain of the Arab regimes, but against any and all who do not conform to their narrow-minded ideology (pp. 25–46). Therefore, these Islamists are a threat not just to Middle Eastern powers, but also to Western democracies (pp. 199–201). His recommendation to those Western states, such as Great Britain and Germany, that have given political asylum to many Islamic groups, is to be wary of Muslim communities because they will, sooner or later, seek autonomy (pp. 183–4). Another work by Israeli, published seven years later, 'Western democracies and Islamic fundamentalist violence', has little more to add to his previous work other than to add the caveat to all Western democracies that it is not just Islamic groups but also Middle Eastern regimes that 'will turn against the West' (2000: 172).

Despite the fact that some radical Islamic organizations pose a real threat to any perceived as 'other', it seems that this aggressiveness is not exclusively Islamic, but can be seen in the narrow-minded and antagonistic behaviour of many fanatical groups (including Christians, Jews and Hindus) against whoever holds views that differ from theirs. Unfortunately, the current thinking of some concerning the nature of Islamic movements is seriously flawed. This is particularly true of the perspective of adherents to the orientalist school, who have a strong influence on the nature of the literature and teaching of Islam to be seen in the West. Although this is not the place to expound on this ontological problem, it is worth mentioning that this flawed perception of the true nature of Islamic movements is infiltrating the theorizing and understanding of terrorism by many intellectuals as well as governmental apparatus in the West. This in turn causes great damage to the efforts of those involved in the battle against terrorism. Indeed, it is far from the truth to say that Islamic groups represent one ideological orientation. In fact they are in disagreement over a wide spectrum of issues, including the legitimacy of violence as a political tool, relations with the existing regimes in the Middle East and the West, and even whether it is permissible to be involved in politics at all. However, despite such ideological fragmentation among the Islamists, they are fully united on the one issue of opposition to Israeli occupation of parts of the Islamic Holy Land. It is this very unity of purpose among the Islamists that refutes all attempts by such as Raphael Israeli to pigeonhole them as mere practitioners of violence and intolerance.[1]

The multidimensional cause-effect methodology

The above review of some of the approaches to the study of terrorism leaves us with a mixture of both conviction and doubt. Accepting their holistic, disjointed or one-dimensional arguments would be difficult. In his articulate study, 'The Discipline of Terrorology', Alexander George (1991: 92) wrote:

> Terrorology is intellectually sterile, if not bankrupt, because the construct of 'terrorism' employed by terrorologists was not developed in response to honest puzzlement about the real world, but rather in response to ideological pressure.

I would go further and maintain that the field of terrorism is contaminated by what Noam Chomsky (1991) describes as a propagandistic approach, construing the concept of terrorism as a weapon to be exploited in the service of those who would maintain the prevailing system of power.

It is on that assumption that the argument of this study will be based. As indicated earlier, terrorism is a subject preoccupied with value judgements and political interests. For many scholars, it is very difficult to remain objective, particularly when their lives have been overshadowed by the actions and reactions of terrorists. This study attempts to apply 'a multidimensional cause–effect methodology' in order to address the topic under study in a dynamic fashion rather than as a static model.

Within the framework of this multidimensional, cause–effect methodology, the causes of terrorism in the Middle East will be studied through four main independent variables (Table 8.1): socio-economic, literacy, democratic and extremism.

The economic indicators of Middle Eastern economies (particularly the Arab states) vary greatly. Although the economies of the United Arab Emirates and Kuwait produce some of the highest national incomes in the world, the economies of the majority of Arab countries, such as Sudan, Yemen and the occupied territories (West Bank and Gaza), are best classified as feeble. The average annual per capita income for Kuwait is $22,500, for the UAE $17,700, Sudan $940, Yemen $750 and the occupied territories $2050. The unemployment rate also varies among the Arab states. Unemployment rates are low in the Gulf states: Kuwait 1.8 per cent, UAE 2.6 per cent, Oman 2.9 per cent, Bahrain 3.1 per cent, Qatar 5.1 per cent and Saudi Arabia 6 per cent. In contrast, a very high rate of unemployment persists in some Arab countries: Algeria 34 per cent, Libya 30 per cent, Yemen 30 per cent and Sudan 30 per cent. In others, the unemployment rate ranges from 25 per cent in Jordan to 11.8 per cent in Egypt. (See Table 8.2.)

Regardless of their level of economic well-being, all Arab societies experience a certain degree of social and economic injustice. In the vast majority of these countries, a feeling of inequality is felt among the general population. Even in the richest countries, such as Kuwait, there is a general perception of economic inequality whereby a large portion of the national wealth is believed to be enjoyed by a small elite at the

Table 8.1 The multidimensional cause–effect methodology

Independent variables	Intervening variables	Dependent variable
1 Socio-economic	1 Perceived American political bias and double standards	
	2 Israeli occupation and politics in Palestine	
		Terrorism in the Middle East
2 Literacy rate		
3 Democratic		
4 Extremism		

expense of the majority. However, those who have committed terrorist actions in Kuwait have never based the justification for their actions upon economic factors of any kind. In fact, all terrorist incidents that have taken place in Kuwait, thus far, have been related to issues of foreign policy, such as American involvement in Iraq. Similarly, most, or perhaps all, terrorism in Saudi Arabia and Egypt can be directly linked to those countries' foreign policies rather than local economic issues. Hence, it is untrue to suggest that terrorism is a result of economic factors. It is also doubtful whether economic factors are directly related to the causes of terrorism on the regional level. This flies in the face of the view of America, as propounded in its proposals for the Greater Middle East, that in order to tackle terrorism we must first deal with economic factors. Similarly, Anatol Lieven (2001), in his work on the roots of terrorism, has stated that economic factors are the main causative agents of international terrorism. Developing the economies of Middle Eastern countries may be desirable as an end in itself. However, it is doubtful that any such economic development will solve any serious political problems, particularly those related to the continuing occupation of Arab lands in defiance of countless United Nations resolutions, and the feeling of oppression and victimization experienced by the Islamic nation (*Ummah*) as a direct result of America's backing of the Israeli occupation. It is this very targeting of the *Ummah*, the historically united Islamic entity, which has delivered the people of the region into the arms of the Islamists. If the West fails to understand this elemental truth, we can only look forward to a future of greater terrorism.

The level of literacy varies greatly from one Arab country to another. The highest rate of illiteracy, 62 per cent, is found in Yemen, while the lowest, 13.6 per cent, pertains in Jordan (see Table 8.2). Compared with the levels of illiteracy in the Middle East twenty or thirty years ago, the current level of literacy is a great improvement. Despite that progress, terrorism has grown. How can one explain this seeming contradiction? It is possible that a higher level of literacy reinforces people's awareness of the surrounding political ills, especially in frustrating economic and social conditions. As a consequence, they become more aggressive and, since open criticism is outlawed by the dominant political regimes, this aggression must be expressed through

Table 8.2 Socio-economic dimensions in Middle Eastern societies

Country	Age 0–14 (%)	Age 15–40 (%)	Age 40 and above (%)	Unemployment (%)	Literacy (%)	Per capita income ($)
Kuwait	29.36	68.32	2.32	1.8	78.6	22,500
Saudi Arabia	43	54	3	6	62.8	10,500
UAE	30	68	2	2.6	79.2	17,700
Bahrain	29.2	67.7	3.1	3.1	85.2	15,900
Qatar	26	71	3	5.1	79.4	17,000
Oman	41	57	2	2.9	80	8,000
Egypt	35	61	4	11.8	51.4	3,000
Syria	39.3	57.5	3.2	20	70.8	3,200
Lebanon	28	66	6	18	86.4	5,000
Yemen	47	49	4	30	38	750
Tunisia	30	64	6	16.5	66.7	5,500
Morocco	35	60	5	19	43.7	3,600
Palestine	45	52	3	14.5	—	2,050
Libya	36	60	4	30	76.2	7,900
Jordan	38	59	3	25	86.6	3,500
Algeria	34	62	4	34	61.6	5,600
Sudan	45	53	2	30	46.1	940
Iraq	41.1	55.9	3	60	58	2,500

underground means. Still, this classic explanation does not fully explain the contradiction of rising levels of education and concurrent rises in levels of terrorism. This contradiction is further compounded by the fact that Middle Eastern-related terrorist acts take place in many countries, including democratic states with a reasonable welfare system, such as the USA, and in less democratic countries with a higher per capita income, such as Kuwait. In view of this, a more explicatory and problem-solving method is required to explain terrorism.

Despite some slow-paced progress in democratization, most Arab countries lack open political systems. According to Keith Jaggers and Robert Gurr (1995), when employing a Polity III criterion that measures democracy, the Arab countries are far behind in the process of democratization. By utilizing Jaggers and Gurr's measurement, Lebanon is the highest-ranked state in terms of democracy, scoring four on a ten-point scale. The other Arab countries ranged between zero and one on the above-mentioned scale (Alqasem 1999). Fragmented democratization processes are in progress in some countries, such as Qatar and Bahrain. A relaxation of political restrictions in countries such as Kuwait and Jordan is under way. However, political pluralism, a free press, political tolerance and other facets of democratic life are still lacking. It is worth noting that these small measures toward democratization in Kuwait and Jordan have not minimized terrorist incidents. Taking this phenomenon at its face value, one might argue, erroneously, that democratization leads to further terrorist activities. Is it possible, theoretically, to argue that there is a direct correlation between the lack of democracy and greater terrorism, while at the same time arguing that increased democratization does not lead to a reduction in terrorism? This question will be dealt with later in this chapter.

Extremism has spread across most countries in the Middle East. It is true that religious extremism is the most conspicuous form, but other forms of extremism are also emerging in the region: secular extremism as practised by the government in Tunisia and the military elite in Turkey; racism against minorities, such as Kurds and ethnic Iranians in Iraq; and schismatic extremism, as experienced by Shi'ite Muslims in some Gulf countries. Religious extremism did not start in the 1980s, as many scholars have presumed. It emerged following the 1967 defeat of the Arab regimes by the Israelis and the resultant occupation of a large portion of Arab territories and, more importantly, the destruction of the Arab dream of pan-nationalism. The 1967 defeat of some Arab states by Israel was not simply military, but also an ideological defeat of secular nationalism as a mobilizing force. This defeat allowed the 'Islamic Alternative', as propagated by the opponents of Jamal Abdul Nasser, the Muslim Brethren (the Ikhwan Al Muslmeen Movement), in Egypt, and King Faisal in Saudi Arabia.

Islam as a political force became more appealing to the common man, as well as to some of the existing Arab governments, after the incineration of The Dome of the Rock, the third holiest site for Muslims, in Jerusalem on 22 August 1969. As the occupying power, Israeli forces were held responsible by many Arabs and Muslims for the conflagration at the Holy Mosque. This incident became the catalyst for the rise to dominance of Islamic discourse over the hitherto prevailing secular and nationalistic doctrines.

Since the mid-1970s, Islamic groups have become deeply involved in the internal political arena and gained popular support in a defective political and economic environment. In addition, the external political inadequacy of the existing political regimes has resulted in their being undermined. As the existing political regimes are unable to respond successfully to the problem of daily political realities, these organizations have become a political alternative for the frustrated majority. Thus, Islamic groups, through the use of religious rhetoric, have become increasingly popular and pose a real challenge to many governments in the region. Due to the undemocratic nature of most, if not all, Middle Eastern countries, clashes between the two parties (the Islamic groups and the governments) have swept away the possibility of any other political alternative. Consequently, violence and terrorism have arisen as outlets for political views. In addition, the Islamic groups have offered an acceptable explanation of military and political defeats by utilizing irrefutable religious principles. Islamic movements were able to employ Qur'anic verses to interpret reality and deliver answers to many critical questions, such as how it was that Israel could defeat Muslims despite being heavily outranked in terms of population and natural resources. According to the Islamists, the answer is very simple: 'We Muslims departed from the path of the true followers of Allah'. In the Muslim holy book, the Qur'an, there are many verses calling on the faithful to adhere to the will of Allah. In return they are assured of his blessing and support. An example of such verses is Verse 7, Mohammad: 'Ye who believe if ye will aid (the cause of) God, He will aid you and plant your feet firmly'. Within the vast majority of Muslim societies, this tenet of Islam has become unchallengeable; it allows the promise of another reality to believers, especially welcome in the midst of the breakdown of traditional secular and nationalist support systems.[2]

At the same time, the Islamic groups have boosted their credibility with the public through successful armed confrontation against two of the world's most sophisticated military machines: the Red Army of the Soviet Union in Afghanistan and the Israeli forces in south Lebanon. By combining the previously-mentioned interpretation of political realities with the military victories against Israel and the Soviet Union, Islamic movements have generated not just more support for their socio-political ideology, but also increasing patronage for their tactical methods, including the use of violence, as a means of liberation from both internal pressures and external constraints.

The Israeli defeat of the Arabs in 1967 and the burning of the Holy Mosque in 1969 were both events that were seen to have occurred under and, by implication, as a result of a secular form of government. By contrast, the defeat of both the Russians in Afghanistan and the Israelis in south Lebanon was seen as a direct result of the power of the emerging Islamic movement. The effect of these historical events on the Arab psyche cannot be underestimated. On the one hand, they served to generate a uniquely honest self-critique of the deficiencies, and subsequent defeats, that secularism and nationalism had brought to bear on the Arab nation. And, on the other hand, they indicated a viable alternative route along the path of Islamic ideology. Therefore, Islam has been operationalized as an episodic discourse to diagnose and treat the political, economic and social defects of the Middle East. In the beginning, this tendency was accepted or, at least, tolerated by most Arab governments. However, it was not long before several demands for reform by many Islamic groups were rejected by the mostly secular-dominated elites; clashes between the upper and the lower echelons (the non-official civil Islamic societies) broke out. An unbridgeable cleavage ensued between state-sponsored Islamic institutions and a public Islamic *Weltanschauung* assumed by many charismatic Islamic groups. Furthermore, clashes between the two parties intensified in the 1980s, on the heels of the Islamic revolution in Iran.

The revolution in Iran has fired the ambitions of many Muslim groups to carry out their programme of change through radical means. Consequently, many Middle Eastern governments have become very sensitive about Islamic activists becoming involved in politics. In the absence of any legitimate and accepted arena of rational political dialogue, extremist views have coloured the actions of all parties involved. Given this assessment, it is uncertain whether extremism is an independent cause of the recent terrorism or if it is an effect of accumulated historical events punctuating the episodes of interference by forces from without and exasperation with forces from within.

On the basis of the above argument, it seems that terrorist incidents occur in almost all the Arab states regardless of their levels of societal dissatisfaction, economic injustice, political liberalization or extremism. The real puzzle, therefore, is whether one can exclude these variables from a causal correlation with terrorism. Is it possible to suggest that there is no relation between these variables and terrorism and go against the conventional assumption as addressed above? Could it be possible that these variables sometimes cause paradoxical outcomes, depending on space and time, or is there another explanation?

By utilizing a multidimensional cause-effect methodology, two possible and compatible explanations may be obtained. The first is based upon a conventional correlation between independent and dependent variables, in addition to the intervening variables. Basically, this explanation involves the four previously mentioned variables (socio-economic, literacy, democratic, extremism). However, it assumes that their effect on the dependent variable (terrorism) is inextricably linked with intervening variables.

Two intervening variables are assumed (see Table 8.1). The first intervening variable is the perceived American bias toward Israel and the double standard of American policy toward Arab states. The second is the occupation of Arab territories and the policies pursued by successive Israeli governments. In as far as political activists recognize these variables, their response is either violently for or against the USA, Israel and collaborating Arab governments. Regardless of whether this presumption of American, Israeli and/or collaborating Arab governments' responsibility is real or imagined, it plays a significant role in the Islamic activists' 'rationalization' of their violent acts.

For these activists, violence becomes a rational choice based on an assessment of the other possible options, or lack of same. Furthermore, such a rationalization is made not merely on the basis of materialistic calculations, but is also founded on divine gains. It is worth mentioning that it is not religion alone that dictates the formula of rationality; there are also other factors. The absence of other means of expression, the imbalance in direct confrontations, and the wish to maintain mutual deterrents are significant factors in rationalizing violent acts against adversaries. The other may see it as an irrational act, but after careful assessment of the procedural accounting of gains and losses as compared with the other possible alternatives, the violent option outweighs other realistic alternatives as recognized by the committers. Martha Crenshaw, in her study 'The Logic of Terrorism: Terrorism Behaviour as a Product of Strategic Choice' (1998: 11), has stated:

> … terrorism is often the last in a sequence of choices. It represents the outcome of a learning process. Experience in opposition provides radicals with information about the potential consequences of their choices. Terrorism is likely to be a reasonably informed choice among available alternatives, some tried unsuccessfully.

The second explanation, compatible with the first, is summarized in the *Intensification of the Zero-Sum Terrorism Cycle* (IZSTC) model (see Figure 8.1). The more the

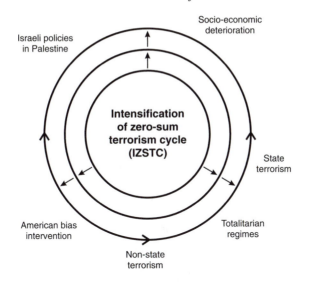

Figure 8.1 Intensification of zero-sum terrorism cycle (IZSTC).

opposing parties engage each other in conflict, the more the cycle of violence is, thus, perpetuated. This tit-for-tat type of engagement can only result in a deepening spiral of violence. In this model, all variables (independent, intervening and dependent) reproduce themselves in an intensified cycle. This cycle of terror is characterized by the following:

1   All parties engage in the dilemma of a zero-sum game that does not permit openings for negotiations or a settlement in which a win–win scenario is possible. In this situation, any gain by any party is necessarily a loss for the other. Therefore, an exchange of violence is the only existing option for all involved. Ultimately, they employ the same argument to justify their violent actions aimed at minimizing the other's power. Indeed, some Arab countries, the USA, Israel and some Islamic groups will all ultimately resort to the same instruments of death. Whether they rationalize their killing of others by utilizing 'consequentialism' or 'deontology' justifications, states and non-state actors fall in the same category of ruthlessness, illegality and immorality.[3]

2   A rhetoric of blame is used to justify retaliation against the other(s). Rhetoric is also used as a mobilizing machine that justifies the violation of international laws and civil liberties, particularly by states. Unfortunately, democratic states such as the USA have implemented policies and adopted laws that jeopardize civil liberties and human rights. Influenced by domestic lobbyists (Lieven 2001), one-sided traditionalists and neo-orientalists associated with right-wing politicians, and by the heat of 11 September 2001, the USA government has pursued the same policy against terrorism as Israel, which is best described by Pedahzur and Ranstorp (2001) as an implementation of the 'war model' instead of the 'criminal

justice model' to counter terrorism.[4] Thus, many in the Islamic world consider these violations of democratic codes as clear contradiction of the liberalism preached by Western politicians in general and the American government in particular. This perception of American political behaviour has caused a great deterioration in the public perception of the validity of democratization in many Islamic countries. In turn, adopting the 'war model' in the battle against terrorism has played into the hands of many Islamic movements, particularly the more radical ones, whose aim is to portray the West as hypocritical and ready to employ double standards when it suits their interests.

3   As the cycle of violence escalates, retaliation is designed to deliver greater impact than the action committed by the opponent. In other words, retaliation is vengeance that should inflict more damage to the challenger(s) than the opponent's prior action. Over time, these tit-for-tat actions lead to ever more technologically advanced and dangerous methods of deterrence and retaliation, particularly when highly organized Islamic organizations that cannot consent to defeat at the hands of 'unbelievers' are involved. Feeling overwhelmed by technological and organizational advances of states which rely also on the 'war model', might lead certain Islamic organizations to seek non-conventional weapons to use as a deterrent in confronting their foes. In the event of such a catastrophe, we must expect the worst. Therefore, the Israeli policy of assassination targeting Hamas figures such as Sheikh Ahmad Yasseen and Abdulaziz Al Ranteesi cannot be expected to bring about an end to the Palestinian struggle against Israel. Rather, it will bring about a further escalation of the cycle of violence which will spill over not just into the region but will also pull in all countries involved or associated with the endorsement of Sharon's zero-sum game policies.

4   As this situation continues, casualties increase and the distance between the rivals is widened. Therefore, possible chances for negotiations become very limited. That leaves the opposing parties with a diminishing opportunity for a compromise exit. Furthermore, this scenario will probably develop into an open-ended situation in which more complications will surface in an already ghastly political environment.

5   With the zero-sum game mentality in control of political direction, the cycle of reciprocal terror will further escalate as time passes. Furthermore, the tempo of events will increase and more losses for the contestants can be anticipated over the long term. That is especially true in the case of Sharon's 'war model' policy's aim of ending violence between Palestinians and Israelis, and avoiding the ensuing causalities and deaths. More than three years after his visit to the courtyard of the Dome of the Rock, and despite his promises to put an end to the 'Palestinian violence' within a year, Sharon is unable to either end the Intifada or minimize its ramifications.

6   Causes and effects become intermingled. It will be very difficult even for neutral parties to judge who is right and who is wrong. Mediation will be a very complicated task in which international arbitrators (states or organizations) may easily be rejected by any side. Hence, any benign international intervention is jeopardized, which, alas, may pave the way for perpetual conflict.

7   Through this cycle, terrorism is committed not only by non-state actors, but also by states; this produces further complications. Terrorism, thus, becomes unsolved mystery. It is very clear that many states have committed terrorism, without, however, ever being held responsible. The following are just four examples of forgiven and forgotten state terrorism:

- The Israeli hijacking of a civilian aircraft operated by Syrian airlines in 1954 to negotiate the freeing of alleged spies caught by the Syrian authorities.
- The shooting down an Egyptian-owned civilian plane in 1956 by Israeli forces and the subsequent deaths of 16 innocent people because Israeli intelligence thought that Colonel Abdul-Hakeem Amer, the Egyptian defence minister, was on board.
- The genocide of 69 farmers in Qebia town in 1950 by an Israeli military unit of which Ariel Sharon was in charge.
- The current policy of demolition of houses and killing of innocent people in the occupied territories because Israeli forces want to assassinate a suspected terrorist or to punish some who are alleged to have given help.

The above are just a few examples that give an insight into how it is that non-governmental Islamic organizations, particularly in the Middle East, can justify their illegal and immoral actions to the public and find sympathy and support. It is very obvious that some people in Gaza, the West Bank and in some Arab capitals, who celebrated the tragedy in America on 11 September 2001, have been at the receiving end of the double standards with regards to terrorism as employed by Israel and the USA in the Middle East. The killing of innocent people or the demolition of their houses is acceptable neither to democracy or Islam. Alas, it appears that in reality a Machiavellian paradigm is the real generator of actual behaviour that overshadows the political restraints and moral order of Islam and liberal democratic values.

8   Due to a broad spectrum of violence, terrorism is more likely to be globalized. The extended capability of all contenders generalizes the contemporary practice of terror as it is happening in the core and in the periphery. This may be expected to produce structural conflict as supporters of the main challengers become polarized. In such a scenario, the next international configuration will be coloured by a bandwagoning alliance among states and non-state actors.[5] This kind of alliance responds only to circumstantial and short-term interests rather than to substantial and strategic issues related to perpetual peace.

9   Radicalization overwhelms rationalization. Indeed, rationality is now at the service of radicalism. This course will definitely lead to further victimization and the loss of innocent lives.

10   It is anticipated that the clash of civilizations will be intensified and extended to the moderate elements in many societies. Thus, cultural dogmatism increasingly overwhelms tolerance and openness as the cycle of violence and terrorism escalates.

Seeking an exit

The Middle Eastern countries need to be engaged in systematic progressive change if conflict, violence and terrorism are to vanish. However, responsibility also rests on the American side. The US government has played a significant role in Middle Eastern politics. Unfortunately, that role has become more supportive of Israel at the expense of the Arab nations. The recent developments in the region following the Iraqi invasion of Kuwait, the collapse of Soviet Union power and the demolition of the Iraqi regime have raised serious challenges to all parties, particularly the USA. As a superpower and the major actor, it is always held liable by the other actors when political defects emerge.

To end this human misery, bilateral and multilateral efforts have to be reinforced, especially by the leading industrialized nations such as Japan and the more powerful European states. With their political and economic qualifications, they can deliver substantial help to the Middle Eastern nations as well as exerting a certain degree of pressure on America and Israel to adopt a more moderate position in regard to the Arab–Israeli conflict. Finally, it is very important to recognize that the mentality of militarism in zero-sum game theory has no future in the region. Instead, a win–win game scenario based on economic cooperation and interdependence must pertain. Otherwise, war, fanaticism and the hegemony of the few will continue to deny to the majority a just peace and collective security.

Notes

1   For more discussion on the internationalization of the Islamic threat see Mohammad and Al-Abdullah (2002).
2   See Hussain (1988: 75–100) for a brief discussion on Islamic views of confrontation adopted by main Islamic figures such as Hassan al-Bana, Sayyid Qutb, Abdul Salam Farag, Ayatollah Khomeini, Ali Shariati, and Sayyid Muhammad Hussein Fadlallah. In addition see Beinin and Stork (1997) for a comprehensive view of contemporary political Islam. Also see Ruedy (1996), particularly Chapter 2, in which a balanced discussion is introduced regarding Islamic conceptualizations of temporary political issues.
3   Garrett O'Boyle defines 'consequentialism' justifications as '... the doctrine that says that the right act [in] any given situation is the one that will produce the best overall outcome in terms of the identified end – is often regarded by its critics as a reformation of the rude concept of the "end justifying the means"' (p.25). 'Deontology', in O'Boyle's words, 'refers to a moral system in which states of affairs or actions are judged only, or primarily, by their accordance with a preordained set of moral rules and codes. Religiously (*sic*) based morality is an example' (p.26). For more details of this argument see Boyle (2002).
4   In their study, 'A tertiary model for countering terrorism in liberal democracies: the case of Israel', Pedahzur and Ranstorp (2001) identified both models as the following: 'In the "war" model, a stronger emphasis is placed on the actual restraint of terror than on the maintenance of liberal democratic rights, whereas in the "criminal justice model", the preservation of democratic principles is a fundamental premise in the fight against terror, even at the expense of a reduced effectiveness of counter-terrorist measures' (p.2).
5   For more elaboration on bandwagoning alliance see Schweller (1994: 72–107) and Walt (1987).

Bibliography

Abdulmahdi, F. (1992) *Explosions and Terrorism* (Almutafajerat Wa Elerhab). Cairo: Dar al Ma'aref (in Arabic).

Abu Alroos, A. (2001) *Terrorism, Extremism and International Violence* (Alerhab Wa Tatref Wa Onf Aldawli). Alexandria: Almaktab Aljame'e Alhadeeth (in Arabic).

Alakra, O. (1993) *The Political Terrorism* (Alerhab Alseyasi). Beirut: Dar Altalea'a Lilteba'a Walnasher (in Arabic).

Ali, A.Y. (ND) *The Glorious Qur'an: Translation and Commentary.* Beirut: Dar Al Feker.

Aljahmani, T. (1998) *The Concept of Terrorism* (Mafhoom Alerhab). Damascus: Dar Huran Lilteba'a Walnasher Waltawzee'a' (in Arabic).

Alqasem, S. (1999) *Democracy and War in the Middle East, 1945–89* (Aldemocratiah Wa Alharb fi Alsharq Alawsat Khelal Alfatra ma bin 1945–89), Strategic Studies (Derasat Estratigia). Abu Dhabi: The Emirates Strategic Center No. (27).

Alsamak, M. (1992) *Terrorism and Political Violence* (al erhab Wa Onf Alseyasi). Beirut: Alsharika Alalamia liltiba'a Wanashir (in Arabic).

Alshami, N. (2002) 'The causes and motivation of economic terrorism' (Dawaf'a alerhab Aleghtesadi Wa Asbabah), *AlBayan Newspaper* (United Arab Emirates), 7-6-2002 (in Arabic).

Beinin, J. and Stork, J. (eds) (1997) *Political Islam: Essays from Middle East Report.* Los Angeles: University of California Press.

Chomsky, N. (1991) 'International Terrorism: Image and Reality', in George, A. (ed.) *Western State Terrorism.* New York: Routledge.

Crenshaw, M. (1998) 'The Logic of Terrorism: Terrorism Behavior as a Product of Strategic Choice', in Laqueur, W. (ed.) *Origins of Terrorism.* Washington, DC: Woodrow Wilson Center Press.

Fazil, K. (1991) *The Psychology of Political Terrorism* (Saykologeiat Alerhab Alseyasi). Cairo: Dar Altebaa' Almotamaiza (in Arabic).

George, A. (1991) 'The Discipline of Terrorology', in George, A. (ed.) *Western State Terrorism.* New York: Routledge.

Hariz, A. (1996) *The Political Terrorism: An Analytical Study* (Alerhab Alseyasi: Drasa Tahlilih). Cairo: Madboli Press (in Arabic).

Herman, E. and O'Sullivan, G. (1991) 'Terrorism as Ideology and Cultural Industry', in George, A. (ed.) *Western State Terrorism.* New York: Routledge.

Hussain, A. (1988) *Political Terrorism and the State in the Middle East.* London and New York: Mansell Publishing.

Israeli, R. (1993) 'Fundamentalist Islam and Israel', *The Jerusalem Center for Public Affairs.* New York: Lanham.

Israeli, R. (2000) 'Western democracies and Islamic fundamentalist violence', *Terrorism and Political Violence,* **12**(3 and 4), 160–73.

Jagger, K. and Gurr, T.R. (1995) 'Tracking democracy's third wave with Polity III data', *Journal of Peace Research,* **32**(4), 469–82.

Lewis, B. (1993) 'Islam and liberal democracy', *The Atlantic Monthly,* February, 89–94.

Lieven, A. (2001) 'The roots of terrorism and a strategy against it', *Prospect Magazine,* **68**, October.

Merari, A. (1998) 'The Readiness to Kill and Die: Suicidal Terrorism in the Middle East', in Laqueur, W. (ed.) *Origins of Terrorism.* Washington, DC: Woodrow Wilson Center Press.

Mohammad, A. and Al-Abdullah, H. (2002) 'The internationalization of political Islamic threat to the New World Order: a revised image', *American Journal of Islamic Social Sciences*, **19**(1), 51–71.

O'Boyle, G. (2002) 'Theories of justification and political violence: examples from four groups', *Terrorism and Political Violence*, **14**(2), 23–46.

Pedahzur, A. and Ranstorp, M. (2001) 'A tertiary model for countering terrorism in liberal democracies: the case of Israel', *Terrorism and Political Violence*, **13**(2), 1–26.

Pipes, D. (1983) *In the Path of God: Islam and Political Power*. New York: Basic Books.

Post, J. (1998) 'Terrorism Psycho-logic: Terrorist Behavior as a Product of Psychological Forces', in Laqueur, W. (ed.) *Origins of Terrorism*. Washington, DC: Woodrow Wilson Center Press.

Ruedy, J. (ed.) (1996) *Islamism and Secularism in North Africa*. New York: St Martin's Press.

Saleh, Y. (2003) 'Authority, terrorism and Islam' (Sulta Wa Erhab Wa Islam), *The Journal of Literature* (Majalat Aladab), January 2003, Beirut (in Arabic).

Schweller, R.L. (1994) 'Bandwagoning for profit: Bringing the revisionist state back', *International Security*, **19**, Summer, 72–107.

Sprinzak, E. (1998) 'The Psychopolitical Formation of Extreme-Left Terrorism in a Democracy: The Case of The Weathermen', in Laqueur, W. (ed.) *Origins of Terrorism*. Washington, DC: Woodrow Wilson Center Press.

Walt, S. M. (1987) *The Origins of Alliances*. Ithaca, NY: Cornell University Press.

9 Nationalist separatism and terrorism in comparative perspective

Fernando Reinares

Nationalist movements often include political organizations seeking the separation of a certain territory and its society from the state or states to which these both formally belong. Far from often, however, can independentism or irredentism be associated to the use of violence and terrorism. Actually, contemporary nationalist movements vary greatly not only as to the extent of support enjoyed within their populations of reference but also with respect to the scope and intensity of their separatist aims. Moreover, in only some of the cases where demands for distinctive or unified statehood prevail has terrorism been adopted by nationalist insurgents. Thus, there is no direct causal nor unavoidable connection between separatist nationalism as expression of political discontent, socio-economic grievances or identity claims and terrorist violence. Contrary to what is frequently taken for granted not only outside academic circles but even among scholars, nationalist separatism does not in itself explain nationalist separatism terrorism. There has to be something else in between an ideology and its corresponding mass mobilizations, on the one hand, and violence to achieve certain political objectives, on the other.

Therefore it seems important enough to explore structural and situational variables which intervene in making terrorism a more than probable choice by collective actors endorsing nationalist separatist aspirations. This chapter aims precisely at summarizing major socio-economic, cultural and political preconditions which increase the likelihood for terrorist organizations to be formed out of a broader nationalist sector. Additionally, precipitants observed in the actual option for terrorism by separatist insurgents are also described and discussed, as well as factors explaining variations in the duration and consequences of terrorist campaigns once finally initiated. In this sense, the causes of nationalist separatist terrorism, like internal dynamics and external constraints affecting independentist or irredentist terrorist organizations, would be expected analytically to coincide with those held most relevant when enquiring into the etiology of the terrorist phenomenon and the evolution of terrorist organizations in general. Adopting a middle-range perspective and deriving arguments from a comparative approach, this essay on nationalist separatism and terrorism focuses mainly on cases observed since the late 1960s in Western industrial societies, though noticing its immediate antecedents and current diffusion prospects across the world.

Nationalist separatism and terrorist organizations

As already mentioned, it is not uncommon for nationalist movements to pursue separatism, even if the emphasis on such aspirations may oscillate over time. This goal is sometimes equated to the creation of a new sovereign state based on the collectivity defined as a nation and the geographical space inhabited by them. Nationalist separatism is then equivalent to independentism. However, separatist aspirations may also refer to the subsequent merging of a given land and its population with an already existing state. Nationalist separatism is then referred to as irredentism. By definition, both independentism and irredentism imply a lack of state legitimacy among those who adhere to these political objectives. Sometimes they constitute a very small proportion of the people pertaining to a given minority, while at other times they constitute a rather large percentage. This questioning of the adequacy and legitimacy of an existing state and its institutions may be due to such diverse and not necessarily overlapping factors as pre-modern reminiscences embedded in the political culture, objective socio-economic and cultural discrimination, a generalized perception of inefficient performance by central administration agencies or recurrent repression by the ruling majority, just to mention those perhaps more salient ones.

Independentist and irredentist political organizations sometimes try to advance their alleged ends by means of violence. Collective violence may then include terrorism. What makes terrorism a distinctive form of violence? There are three basic traits which combined allow us to distinguish terrorism from other types of violent social interaction (Reinares 1998: 13–45, 2003a). Firstly, an act of violence is to be considered as terrorist when its psychical effects within a certain population or social aggregate, in terms of widespread emotional reactions such as fear and anxiety, are likely to condition attitudes and behaviour in a determined direction, and are out of proportion with respect to its actual or potential material consequences, in terms of physical damage inflicted to people and things. Secondly, for that violence to have such impact it must be systematic and rather unpredictable, usually directed against targets selected because of their symbolic relevance within a prevailing cultural frame and in a given institutional context. Thirdly, the harming of such targets is used to convey messages and threats that make terrorism a mechanism of both communication and social control.

Terrorism can thus be practised by different actors and with an ample variety of purposes. Terrorism becomes political when it intends to affect the distribution of power and social cohesion within a given state jurisdiction or in a wider, international scenario. Therefore, terrorism practised with the intention to achieve nationalist separatist objectives of an independentist or irredentist nature is political. Terrorism acquires an insurgent character if it attempts to change the established political order and a vigilante disposition when used in order to preserve existing relations of power and social arrangements. Almost by definition, nationalist separatist terrorism corresponds to insurgent terrorism. Thus conceptualized, terrorism can be incorporated either on a tactical or strategic basis, that is, as part of a much broader repertoire of violence or as the predominant method adopted by separatist insurgents. Actually, terrorist organizations, that is small armed clandestine groups specialized in the practice of terrorism, can be and are actually found among the actors present in a given nationalist movement sector. Indeed, the wave of contemporary terrorism initiated during the late 1960s and nowadays probably in its late stages taken as a whole, was to a large extent protagonized by terrorist organizations formed as radicalized expressions of their respective nationalist movements.

Social structures and economic complexities associated to modernization, including sophisticated networks of transportation and communication which create vulnerabilities but also facilitate mobility and provide access to publicity, become permissive preconditions for terrorism (Crenshaw 1981: 381–2; Targ 1988). Most probably, this is why terrorist organizations espousing nationalist separatist aims emerged or acted, since the late 1960s, mainly in Western industrial and highly urbanized societies. The best known examples are those of the provisional IRA (Irish Republican Army) in the United Kingdom and ETA (*Euskadi ta Askatasuna*, Basque Homeland and Freedom) in Spain. The former killed nearly 2,000 people until the late 1990s, whereas fatalities produced by the latter amount to 800 during the same period of time. Other significant cases include the FLNC (*Fronte di Liberazione Naziunale di a Corsica*, National Liberation Front of Corsica) in France, the FLQ (*Front de Libération du Québec*, Liberation Front of Quebec) in Canada, and both the Puerto Rican FALN (*Fuerzas Armadas de Liberación Nacional*, Armed Forces of the National Liberation) as well as *Macheteros* in the United States of America. The overall lethality of these terrorist organizations has ranged between one and several dozen people killed, thus far from the previous figures. Many more, but less relevant cases, both in terms of fatalities and the period during which such armed underground groups were active, have also been noticed in these countries as well as other states for the past four decades.

Worldwide diffusion of nationalist separatist terrorism

The model of terrorist organizations observed in advanced industrial societies has been closely approached later on by irredentist armed groups particularly active throughout the 1980s in economically and politically less developed environment, although they were also responsible for episodes of transnationalized terrorism in Western modernized countries. The PKK (*Patiya Karkeren Kurdestan*, Kurdish Workers' Party), for instance, conducted a terrorist campaign since the mid-1980s, mainly in the south-eastern region of Turkey with the alleged purpose of establishing an independent Kurdistan, comprising also territories across the border in other countries such as Iraq. By the early 1990s, their militants numbered a few thousand and had killed nearly 10,000 people. Though they eventually adopted a more conventional guerrilla style repertoire of violence, tactical use of terrorism persisted over time. Another relevant example is found among the various shadowy Sikh separatist groups, which turned to insurgent terrorism in Punjab, in the north-west of India. From the early 1980s until well into the following decade, their diffuse terrorist activities, practised by around 4,000 armed activists in the context of a broader violent conflict between religious communities, resulted in nearly 12,000 fatalities while aiming at the establishment of an independent Khalistan. The Abu Sayyaf Group, with a membership of no more than 330 Muslim radicals who exert no territorial control, was formed at the end of the 1980s and is also known for its basic reliance upon terrorism as a means to achieve the goal of an independent Islamic theocratic state in Mindanao, in the southern Philippines. Actually, these last two cases illustrate how separatist aspirations may be framed in fanatical religious terms.

Nevertheless, a good number of other independentist or irredentist organizations have systematically resorted to terrorism as an auxiliary method of violent action inside and outside industrialized countries. South Moluccan extremists, as a matter of fact, perpetrated acts of terrorism in the Netherlands during the 1970s, no doubt benefiting from the aforementioned facilities common to open and modern societies. Moreover, that form of violence has later been diffused worldwide in the context of violent nationalist conflicts, as a result of both emulation and adaptive behaviour of certain armed groups to stalemate situations or asymmetry regarding their antagonists, a trend also likely to be facilitated by the ongoing process of globalization. Tactical resort to terrorism has been noticed, for instance, among radicalized factions of separatist insurgent movements in places as diverse as Sri Lanka and countries across south-east Asia. For example, an armed secessionist group, the LTTE (Liberation Tigers of Tamil Eelam), has regularly complemented guerrilla warfare with terrorist actions since the late 1970s, against Singhalese civilians and state security officers, but especially during the 1990s in Colombo and other urban areas, in pursuit of an independent socialist state comprising the northern and eastern island provinces.

Following the breakdown or reconfiguration of former communist regimes, terrorist violence became noticeable in the context of bloody civil wars being fought in the peripheries of the Russian Federation and former Yugoslavia. As to the former, the UÇK (*Ushtrie Çilimtare e Kosovës*, Kosovo Liberation Army) was an armed organization created around 1995 in exile by insurgency diaspora entrepreneurs but with the long-term aim of uniting in a common state all Albanians, including not only the ones living in Kosovo but also those of Macedonia, Montenegro and southern Serbia, with currently existing Albania. However, the irredentist group was disarmed and dismantled in September 1999 by international peace-keeping forces sent to the area, but not before it had launched a number of terrorist attacks against Serbian people and interests in Kosovo, and grew from no more than 200 members to a guerrilla movement involving several thousand fighters. Interestingly enough, this violent antagonism stimulated nationalist separatist terrorism in nearby countries. In Russia, the surge of terrorism throughout the 1990s is related to an armed internal conflict in and around Chechnya. Drive for independence also coupled in this case with Islamic fundamentalism, following federal military intervention in the region in 1994. Since the end of that decade, devastating bomb attacks against civilian targets, perpetrated by Chechen rebels who in addition were Muslim extremists, have been taking place in cities such as Moscow and Grozny.

Antecedents for the wave of nationalist separatist terrorism experienced in a number of Western European and North American countries since the late 1960s, a cycle which diminished greatly as the century closed, can be found in some notorious insurrections against colonial rule that followed the Second World War. Actually, the political outcomes of this anticolonial wave of terrorism stimulated a subsequent one, this time somewhat combined with new Left radicalism. However, those past achievements proved illusory for independentist or irredentist terrorist organizations active throughout the last four decades, since some of them have been particularly durable but none succeeded (Rapoport 2004: 56). Nevertheless, examples such as the *Irgun Zvai Leumi* (National Military Organization) in Palestine around the mid-1940s, the EOKA (*Ethniki Organosis Kyprion Agoniston*, National Organization of Cypriot Fighters) in Cyprus and the FLN (*Front de Libération Nationale*, National Liberation Front) in Algeria (the last two a decade later), demonstrated that urban terrorist campaigns could be successful in undermining the prestige and control of existing authorities. They mobilized support within and beyond the immediate geographical confines of violent conflict, and ultimately achieved sovereign statehood and similar political objectives. From then on, terrorism deployed in populated cities by clandestine organizations comprising no more than a few hundred members or by larger armed groups composed of thousands of militants, was to be perceived as an effective means to transform hitherto local conflicts into international issues (Hoffman 1998: 45–65).

Ideologies, politics and nationalist separatist terrorism

Are some nationalist doctrines more likely to justify and even promote independentist or irredentist terrorism than others? May opportunity structures for terrorism denote significant variations depending on the characteristics of different political regimes? In an attempt to answer the first of these two questions, it is worth remembering that many scholars commonly divide nationalisms into two types, namely ethnic and civic, based on the content of their public demands and their criteria for including people in what is defined as national collectivity (Greenfeld 1992; Brubaker 1992). Ethnic nationalisms usually emphasize common race, culture, language, religion, shared historical experiences or kinship myths. As a result, primordial attributes tend to determine inclusion or exclusion from the imagined national community and shape the envisioned polity. Civic nationalisms, by contrast, base their appeals on distinctive political traditions, institutions and values. Belonging depends above all upon political loyalty and is typically acquired through birth or long-term residence in a given national territory.

It may plausibly be assumed that those nationalist ideologies closer to the civic type tend towards moderation and inclusiveness. Accordingly, they are particularly congruent with the foundations of open and pluralistic polities, though not necessarily bound to be peaceful. Constitutional patriotism, for instance, would correspond to what is conceptualized as civic nationalism. However, nationalist doctrines resembling the ethnic version usually adopt an exclusionary character and would therefore be prone to violent confrontation with the excluded aggregate inside or outside a given country. Whereas civic nationalism would emphasize the protection of individual rights and public liberties, ethnic nationalism concedes priority to the claims of presumed aggregate demands, to the point of justifying or tolerating human rights violations insofar as these shared aspirations are advanced. Ethnic nationalism resembles in this sense the somewhat earlier and more classical notion of integral nationalism, opposed during the nineteenth century to that of liberal nationalism, to the extent that the former was thought of as linked to a closed society in which the individual counted for less than the national collectivity (Hayes 1931).

Surely not by accident, most of the contemporary terrorist organizations espousing independentist or irredentist goals have been inspired by ethnic nationalisms turned into ideologies of violence. Ethnic nationalism has provided exclusionary attitudes and dichotomic beliefs to those who engaged in the most deadly and enduring separatist terrorist campaigns since the late 1960s, largely carried out in the context of democratic regimes. The trajectories of the IRA and ETA in relation to original Irish and Basque nationalism respectively, or even that of the FLNC with respect to Corsican nationalism, illustrate this assertion. Ethnic nationalism, coupled with secular doctrines or religious creeds, also underlines the most relevant cases of independentist and irredentist terrorist campaigns conducted in semiperipheral regions of the world, as mentioned earlier. Conversely, nationalist ideologies of predominantly discernible civic contents, such as Quebecois or Catalan nationalism, provide rather different panoramas. For instance, mainstream parties and pressure groups within the latter nationalist movement quickly reacted against the kidnappings and bombings perpetrated in the mid-1980s by a minuscule and ephemeral separatist underground organization called *Terra Lliure* (Free Land), so as to prevent terrorism from becoming normalized. The FLQ did not last long as the terrorist organization was severely contested by leaders and followers of moderate nationalist parties. It should be needless to specify all those other cases of civic nationalism which simply did not produce separatist terrorist violence.

Ethnic nationalism often incorporates traditions of violence which may indeed operate as societal and cultural facilitators for terrorism. That is, myths, legends, customs or habits that sanction the use of violence against political adversaries, such as, for instance, a given government or a rival out-group, so as to make those means appear morally and politically justifiable. Ireland provides once again a good example, because of the tradition of physical force dating from, at least, the nineteenth century, which offered historical inspiration and partial excuses for terrorism practised much more recently by the Provisional IRA in Northern Ireland (Alter 1982; Townshend 1983). Basque nationalism also portrays its population of reference as bellicose men who fiercely resisted whatever attempts were made throughout centuries and even millennia at invading or conquering the territories they inhabited. Basque separatist terrorists thus tended to see themselves as contemporary *gudaris*, or, translated from the vernacular, indigenous or autochthonous warriors who continue the same rebellious and uncommitted disposition of their ancestors. This kind of legacy, as well as the perception of previous national liberation struggles successfully fought around the world, provide good basis for utilitarian motivations that some young people may rely upon when deciding to join a terrorist organization such as ETA or the IRA (Reinares 2001; Alonso 2003).

As to the political opportunity structures for terrorism in general and nationalist separatist terrorism in particular, those are thought much more conducive under authoritarian regimes and liberal democracies than in the context of totalitarian dictatorships (Wilkinson 1986; Reinares 1998: 58–68). The latter type of political systems, totalitarian polities, offer little if any opportunity structure not only for violent but for peaceful dissent as well. Preconditions for the radicalization of political and particularly nationalist protest into terrorism, as well as the practice of terrorist violence itself, are considered the more likely under authoritarian regimes, where paths to the legal expression of opposition are very restricted or simply blocked; but where official repression also tends to be largely inefficient. As a result, direct and permissive causes then coincide (Crenshaw 1981: 384). ETA, as a matter of fact, was formed as a terrorist organization during the 1960s, as the Francoist dictatorship entered into a period of crisis and liberalization (Reinares 1996). However, its violence escalated dramatically as the country underwent a transition from authoritarian rule and nationalist conflicts entered a period of resolution. Actually, democratic transitions from authoritarian or totalitarian rule often create fertile conditions for exclusionary nationalism and violent ethnic conflict, including terrorist campaigns (Snyder 2000: 37–9).

Furthermore, elaborating from an analytical and empirical distinction proposed in a comparative study on basic types of contemporary liberal democracies (Lijphart 1999), it can be argued that those closer to what is described as a consensual model seem to have been far less affected by terrorism, including nationalist separatist terrorism, than those other polities approaching the majoritarian type, where the incidence of independentist or irredentist terrorist violence has been very limited. This varying vulnerability, as to what the political opportunity structure is concerned, can be explained in terms of differential institutional ability to regulate nationalist conflicts before they may eventually radicalize, more or less rapidly, to the point of becoming violent and thus provide ground for the formation of clandestine political organizations specialized in terrorist activities. Likewise, it could be stated that consensual democracies tend to be much better adapted to formulate and implement not only timely but also efficient policies when needed to deal with a sudden, unexpected eventual outbreak of insurgent terrorism, as in the form of independentist or separatist terrorism.

From ethno-nationalist mobilization to insurgent terrorism

Separatist grievances manifested within an identifiable collectivity or minority part of a larger population are not in themselves a necessary and, at the same time, sufficient cause for terrorism, though probabilities increase in those instances where ethnic nationalism is highly influential and political opportunity structures initially permissive to disruptive violence. Moreover, the basis for shared discontent prompting independentist or irredentist terrorism varies greatly from one case to the other. Sometimes, separatist terrorism emerges out of a social segment suffering from economic disadvantages with respect to other racial, territorial, linguistic or religious segments within the same state boundaries. However, nationalist terrorist campaigns have been and are also launched by extremists belonging to minorities enjoying rather privileged welfare standards when compared to other people in the same region or country. That is to say, there is no clear link between economic indicators and nationalist separatist terrorism (Hewitt 2001: 28–9). Furthermore, the issue in question can as easily be one of secular or religious identity, cultural elements banned or simply perceived as threatened and discriminated among those who consider themselves aggrieved. Discontent translated into nationalist separatist violence may actually be real or fancied, though defined as real and thus real in its consequences.

The fact is, however, that peaceful nationalist mobilizations of one or the other kind tend to precede the actual formation of terrorist organizations endorsing independentist or irredentist goals. For instance, their emergence may be linked to the forced or unforced fall of a nationalist protest cycle. Should this be the case, overreaction by legal authorities in response to conventional social protest conducted by nationalist organizations (like coercion against public expressions of independentist and irredentist discontent on the part of unofficial adversarial groups) can stimulate retaliatory violence in the form of insurgent terrorism. In other words, critical incidents may become a major variable in providing emotional as well as rational motivations to engage in terrorist activities. Protestant vigilante violence that met the basically Catholic civil rights movement in Northern Ireland during the late 1960s, as well as unexpected repression by the British armed forces and security agencies since the early 1970s, prompted the Provisional IRA to terrorist retaliation and produced a transfer of legitimacy among the affected population (White 1993). Republican and Loyalist armed organizations engaged from then on in a process of sectarian terrorism lasting for three decades.

More typically, though, terrorism is adopted by weakened nationalist separatist organizations as a tactical innovation in their repertoire of disruptive collective action. These political organizations may prove unable to reach influential stances through conventional procedures, see themselves affected by time constraints in order to benefit from changing opportunity structures or have been expelled from relevant public decision-making processes, in this last case, either as a result of state coercion or simply open pluralistic competition, electoral processes for instance. As it has been suggested with respect to the FLQ in Quebec, decisions first to use violent means of action early during the 1960s and then to escalate terrorist activities at the very end of that same decade resulted not only from difficulties encountered by moderate separatist associations in integrating their radical factions but also from a generalized perception among activists, belonging to the fringes, of being ignored by both institutions and major actors, or treated as an insignificant entity precisely when changes in the distribution of power and influence were taking place in society at large (Breton 1972).

Indeed, the occurrence of separatist terrorism can sometimes be linked with a decline in electoral mobilization supporting nationalist parties. For instance, a sharp decline in the Puerto Rican independentist vote around the early 1960s was followed shortly afterwards by a campaign of separatist terrorism perpetrated by the FALN until the late 1970s and then by *Macheteros* until about the mid-1980s. However, it is worth emphasizing that, in the context of democratic polities, the decision to opt for terrorism or maintain a terrorist campaign is commonly made by radical separatists irrespective of the electoral strength of nationalism as a whole. There are several cases where nationalism has been successful in electoral terms but the actual occurrence of separatist terrorism shows important variations from one country to another, and those cases where neither an evident relationship exists between a comparatively low nationalist vote and the frequency of separatist terrorism experienced. In other words, no obvious relationship has been found between nationalist separatist vote and separatist terrorism (Hewitt 2001: 29–30).

What, then, would be the purpose of terrorism when finally adopted in pursuit of separatist nationalist goals? What circumstances and calculations often lead to the formation of a terrorist organization in pursuit of independentist or irredentist aspirations? As it may well be deduced from some of the illustrations and examples offered above, terrorism may be used with the proximate intention of gaining recognition or attention. A method, for instance, to compensate the shortage of members and other resources with some spectaculars carried out by just a few activists. Resorting to terrorism may also be a procedure to violently differentiate a given group from similar others within a multi-organizational and highly competitive nationalist sector, particularly when the contention for power intensifies. Finally, it can become a method to advertise independentist or irredentist demands, either because these find no significant support in the public opinion or because such goals have become marginalized by the electorate. Hoping to gain international recognition, the Popular Front for the Liberation of Palestine (PFLP), as well as other similar nationalist groups, decided to perpetrate acts of terrorism mainly in Western European countries since the late 1960s and through the 1970s. Nowadays, interdependency seems to encourage transnational terrorist activities aiming at separatist goals and even the networking of ethno-nationalist terrorist organizations.

On the maintenance of nationalist separatist terrorism

Unless there is some kind of active sponsorship or passive assistance coming from outside the existing state boundaries, the persistence of any terrorist organization tends to be highly contingent upon the amount of popular support or social tolerance mobilized among its population of reference. Certainly, the IRA benefited from foreign aid provided from descendants of Irish immigrants living in the USA or even from Libya. ETA found sanctuary in the southwest of France and training facilities in the past from Algeria and armed groups within the Palestinian Liberation Organization. And the Puerto Rican FALN enjoyed the sympathy of Cuban authorities. Nevertheless, terrorist organizations aiming at nationalist separatist goals develop calculated mobilization strategies in order to achieve support or tolerance within their population of reference. Actually, they engage in a struggle over legitimacy, trying to create and institutionalize a subculture of violence (Burton 1978; Gal Or 1991; Laitin 1995; Llera 2003). The success of these mobilization strategies is strongly determined by state responses to terrorism. As with colonial powers during the 1940s and 1950s, industrialized societies ruled by authoritarian regimes are more likely to unwillingly favour the terrorist organizations in that struggle over legitimacy. Functioning liberal democracies, where both the rule of law and the strength of civil society are present, tend to prevent governmental reactions from being disproportionate and therefore counter-productive.

Is there any relationship between the persistence of independentist or irredentist terrorist organizations and the social class to which their members and constituents mainly belong? A comparative study on the origins and evolution of violent nationalist conflicts in some Western industrialized societies found that educated activists from the middle classes often prevail among those who initiate separatist terrorism. However, the expansion and continuity of such violence were actually determined by the extent to which young males extracted from lower strata of society became hegemonic within an armed clandestine organization and working-class people were a majority among its supporters (Waldmann 1989). This has been the case of lasting ethno-nationalist terrorist organizations such as the ETA in the Basque Country and the IRA in Northern Ireland, contrary to, for instance, the FLQ in Quebec or Terra Lliure in Catalonia. The same research provided no confirmation whatsoever for a hypothesis, often taken for granted in the social science literature, according to which nationalist conflicts are more likely to produce violence and terrorism when cleavages accumulate, so that the adversary group defined within a minority along ethnic and cultural lines is at the same time the privileged one in social and economic terms.

It is commonly assumed that terrorist organizations or armed groups systematically practising acts of terrorism tend to follow a logic of self-maintenance (Crenshaw 1985; Porta 1995). Terrorism ceases to be a means to achieve nationalist ends and becomes an end in itself, both a way of life and a lifestyle for the terrorists. This logic usually implies important changes in the victimization patterns adopted by insurgent separatists. When organizational continuity is highly dependent upon active support or passive tolerance from the population of reference, but popular sympathy or acquiescence subsides, people from the same ethnic or religious group of those who practice terrorism become targets themselves. Since the mid-1990s, for example, as it became clear for ETA leaders that the terrorist organization was in a stage of decline and facing widespread criticism from within their surrounding population, Basque moderate nationalists and, above all, non-nationalist citizens became a priority target for separatist violence (Reinares 2003b). Likewise, following the prospects for conflict resolution derived from a period of political initiatives and negotiations between central authorities and regional leaders, Sikh radical separatists changed their victimization patterns to such an extent that it cannot be explained solely by factional rivalries (Wallace 1995: 400). During the first half of the 1980s, the large majority of those killed in Punjab by fundamentalist separatists were Hindus, whereas in the second half an overwhelming proportion of people assassinated were Sikhs.

All this, no doubt, has important implications for governmental initiatives aiming at peaceful regulation of underlying social and political antagonisms. The more a terrorist organization becomes relatively successful in achieving a significant degree of resource mobilization, the less effective would be, at least in the short term, whatever processes of conflict regulation are eventually designed and implemented by democratic institutions to settle a nationalist separatist dispute which had turned violent.

Evidence demonstrates that in the middle and long term, political reforms adopted in the framework of representative institutions and by legitimate authorities are expected to satisfy or at least accommodate nationalist demands, thus facilitating the decline and even disappearance of terrorist organizations active in the pursuit of separatist goals. Democratic governments, however, must make decisions necessarily taking into account the plurality of collective identities and political allegiances already existing among those citizens affected. Such plurality may well limit the scope of nationalist separatist achievements and make it impossible to meet the usually radical expectations of independentist or irredentist terrorist organizations.

Bibliography

Alonso, R. (2003) *Matar por Irlanda: el IRA y la Lucha Armada*. Madrid: Alianza Editorial.

Alter, P. (1982) 'Traditions of Violence in the Irish National Movement', in Mommsen, W.J. and Hirschfeld, G. (eds), *Social Protest, Violence and Terror in Nineteenth- and Twentieth-century Europe*. London: St Martin's Press, pp. 137–54.

Bilge, N. (1995) 'The nature of PKK terrorism in Turkey', *Studies in Conflict and Terrorism*, **18**, 17–37.

Breton, R. (1972) 'The socio-political dynamics of the October events', *Canadian Review of Sociology and Anthropology*, **9**(1), 33–56.

Brubaker, R. (1992) *Citizenship and Nationhood in France and Germany*. Cambridge, MA: Harvard University Press.

Burton, F. (1978) *The Politics of Legitimacy: Struggles in a Belfast Community*. London: Routledge and Kegan Paul.

Chalk, P. (2001) 'Separatism and south-east Asia: the Islamic factor in southern Thailand, Mindanao and Aceh', *Studies in Conflict and Terrorism*, **24**, 241–69.

Crenshaw, M. (1981) 'The causes of terrorism', *Comparative Politics*, **13**, 379–99.

Crenshaw, M. (1985) 'An organizational approach to the analysis of political terrorism', *Orbis*, **29**, 465–89.

Crenshaw, M. (1995) 'Thoughts on Relating Terrorism to Historical Contexts', in Crenshaw, M. (ed.) *Terrorism in Context*. University Park: Pennsylvania University Press, pp. 3–24.

Fusi, J.P. (2003) *La Patria Lejana: El Nacionalismo en el Siglo XX*. Madrid: Taurus.

Gal Or, N. (1991) *Tolerating Terrorism in the West*. London and New York: Routledge.

German, T.C. (2003) *Russia's Chechen War*. London and New York: RoutledgeCurzon.

Gil, J. (1991) *La Corse entre la Liberté et la Terreur*. Paris: La Différence.

Gow, J. (2003) *The Serbian Project and its Adversaries*. London: Hurst and Company.

Greenfeld, L. (1992) *Nationalism: Five Roads to Modernity*. Cambridge, MA: Harvard University Press.

Hayes, C.J.H. (1931) *The Historical Evolution of Modern Nationalism*. New York: Richard Smith.

Hewitt, C. (2001) 'Separatism, irredentism and terrorism: a comparative survey, 1945–2000', in A. P. Schmid (ed.), *Countering Terrorism through International Cooperation*. Milano: International Scientific and Professional Advisory Board, United Nations Crime Prevention and Criminal Justice Program, pp. 25–37.

Hoffman, B. (1998) *Inside Terrorism*. London: Victor Gollancz.

Joshi, M. (1996) 'On the razor's edge: the Liberation Tigers of Tamil Eelam', *Studies in Conflict and Terrorism*, **19**(1), 19–42.

Kola, P. (2003) *The Search for Greater Albania*. London: Hurst and Company.

Laitin, D. (1995) 'National revivals and violence', *Archives Européennes de Sociologie*, **36**, 3–43.

Lijphart, A. (1999) *Patterns of Democracy: Government Forms and Performance in Thirty-six Countries*. New Haven, CT: Yale University Press.

Llera, F.J. 'La Red Terrorista: Subcultura de la Violencia y Nacionalismo en Euskadi', in Robles, A. (ed.) *La Sangre de las Naciones: Identidades Nacionales y Violencia Política*. Granada: Universidad de Granada, pp. 265–96.

Porta, D.D. (1995) *Social Movements, Political Violence and the State: A Comparative Analysis of Italy and Germany*. Cambridge: Cambridge University Press.

Ramsay, R. (1983) *The Corsican Time Bomb*. Manchester: Manchester University Press.

Rapoport, D. (2004), 'The Four Waves of Modern Terrorism', in Cronin, A.K. and Ludes, J.M. (eds) *Attacking Terrorism: Elements of a Grand Strategy*. Washington, DC: Georgetown University Press, pp. 46–73.

Reinares, F. (1995) 'Orígenes y efectos de la violencia independentista en el proceso político puertorriqueño', *América Latina Hoy*, **10**, 171–88.

Reinares, F. (1996) 'The political conditioning of collective violence: regime change and insurgent terrorism in Spain', *Research on Democracy and Society*, **3**, 297–396.

Reinares, F. (1998) *Terrorismo y Antiterrorismo*. Barcelona: Ediciones Paidós.

Reinares, F. (2001) *Patriotas de la Muerte. Quiénes han Militado en ETA y por qué*. Madrid: Taurus.

Reinares, F. (2003a) 'Terrorism', in Heitmeyer, W. and Hagan, J. (eds) *International Handbook of Violence Research*. The Hague: Kluwer Academic Publishers, pp. 390–405.

Reinares, F. (2003b) 'Democratization and State Responses to Protracted Terrorism in Spain', in Leeuwen, M.V. (ed.) *Confronting Terrorism: European Experiences, Threat Perceptions and Policies*. The Hague: Kluwer Law International, pp. 57–70.

Samaranayake, G. (1997) 'Political violence in Sri Lanka: a diagnostic approach', *Terrorism and Political Violence*, **9**(2), 99–119.

Snyder, J. (2000) *From Voting to Violence: Democratization and Nationalist Conflict*. New York: Norton and Company.

Tan, A. (2000) 'Armed Muslim separatist rebellion in south-east Asia: persistence, prospects and implications', *Studies in Conflict and Terrorism*, **23**, 267–88.

Targ, H.R. (1988) 'Societal Structure and Revolutionary Terrorism: A Preliminary Investigation', in Stohl, M. (ed.) *The Politics of Terrorism*. New York and Basel: Marcel Dekker, pp. 119–43.

Townshend, C. (1983) *Political Violence in Ireland: Government and Resistance Since 1848*. Oxford: Clarendon Press.

Waldmann, P. (1989) *Ethnischer Radikalismus. Ursachen und Folgen gewaltsamer Minderheitenkonflikte*. Opladen: Westdeutscher Verlag.

Wallace, P. (1995) 'Political Violence and Terrorism in India: The Crisis of Identity', in Crenshaw, M. (ed.) *Terrorism in Context*. University Park: Pennsylvania State University Press, pp. 352–409.

White, R. (1993) *Provisional Irish Republicans: An Oral and Interpretive History*. Westport, CO: Greenwood Press.

Wilkinson, P. (1986) *Terrorism and the Liberal State* (2nd ed.). Basingstoke, Hampshire: Macmillan.

10 Root causes of terrorism?

A case study of the Tamil insurgency and the LTTE

Shri D.R. Kaarthikeyan

Is the study of the root causes of terrorism really useful?

If terrorism has to be combated effectively, a study of the root causes is a requisite precondition. A candid understanding and acknowledgement of deep-rooted sentiments that have provided an effective platform for the launch and growth of an armed struggle that has translated itself into terrorism would be the first step towards combating terrorism. Identifying the root causes and acknowledging the presence of such factors help establish the much-required rapport with the masses behind any terrorist group. Addressing the root causes comes only secondary as in all probability it might be a Herculean and sometimes even an impossible task to reverse the course of history that has given birth to these root causes.

In most developing countries, the state of governance leaves much to be desired. Just grievances are ignored and the situation is left to deteriorate to such abysmal levels after which brute force is the only viable option available to quell the armed rebellion. At this stage, even an acknowledgement of the presence of root causes and a sincere beginning to address such causes can weaken the terrorists' case and bring in popular support for counter-terror operations.

The study of the root causes of any terrorist movement is absolutely necessary, as identifying and totally removing them should, at least in principle, end terrorism. Of course, it may be close to impossible to identify each and every root cause and to remove all of them, but the effort should be towards that ideal. As the root causes are identified and removed, the *raison d'être* for the birth, sustenance and growth of terrorism is removed. To that extent, the rooting out of terrorism becomes possible.

Of course, there will always be some with grievances, either imaginary or impossible to redress by any government, who continue to indulge in senseless acts of violence and destruction. The aim should be to identify and address the genuine causes in a pragmatic manner instead of boxing oneself in by setting a utopian goal of removing them altogether. This has to be explained appropriately by the state to all concerned so that the public at large are not misled by terrorists, who may magnify out of proportion minor, or manufacture imaginary, grievances.

Sri Lanka is home to one of the longest surviving ethnic crises in the world, with more than 60,000 people killed on both sides. The Tamils in Sri Lanka wanted an end to their discrimination. The Liberation Tigers of Tamil Eelam's (the LTTE or Tamil Tigers) answer to their plea was a separate homeland.

When the legitimate and reasonable demands of the moderate Tamil leaders, led by the Federal Party, the Tamil United Liberation Front (TULF) and other organizations, through the democratic process inside and outside the parliament did not evoke any positive response from the Sinhala-majority dominated Sri Lankan government, several Tamil groups of youth took to arms. The LTTE, the most ruthless militant group, eliminated moderate Tamil political leadership as well as other militant groups such as TELO, EROS and EPRLF and became the most dominant Tamil militant group. Today, the LTTE is the major dominant force claiming to represent the interests of the Sri Lankan Tamils.

While practically all other rival militant groups and moderate Tamil parties having either been silenced by elimination or won over by intimidation, it cannot be said, even today, that it is solely the LTTE which represents all the aspirations and hopes of all Sri Lankan Tamils. All the same, the LTTE does represent a considerable majority of the Sri Lankan Tamil population inside and outside of Sri Lanka.

The Sri Lankan Tamil situation is so complex that we need to consider a large number of isolated and interconnected causes and influences that have resulted in the present complex situation today. Born out of discrimination, bred under oppression and strengthened through orchestrated state violence, the LTTE remains one of the longest insurgencies in contemporary politics. It commenced fighting for a separate homeland and still continues to do so, unlike many similar outfits that have adapted their goals to suit political developments. There are various causes that have made the LTTE what it is now, but for want of space it is possible to discuss only a few.

Structural causes

According to the Sri Lanka Central Bank Survey in 1981/82, there was no disparity in the per capita incomes of the Sinhalese and Sri Lankan Tamils, which stood at approximately LKR1,184 and LKR1,189, respectively. However, the plight of the Indian Tamils working there was pathetic at about LKR 519 (Sivarajah 1992). With regard to employment, Sri Lankan Tamils in the Ceylon Civil Service was 13.1 per cent in 1981; it had been 24.7 per cent in 1948. The percentage of unemployed educated Tamil youths was more than any other community in the country (Wriggins 1960). While 48.9 per cent of Tamil students entered universities in 1969, this dropped to only 22.1 per cent in 1983. This was a result of the system of 'standardization' introduced in 1972 that mandated Tamil students to obtain a higher aggregate of marks than their Sinhalese counterparts to gain admission. This discrimination in education took its toll on employment as well. Additionally, the government indulged in a number of measures to alter the demography of the Tamil-dominated areas that resulted in Sinhalese settling in Tamil areas. The Tamils protested against this policy, which they termed 'colonization' in the Veliyoa area. In the Triconmalee district, the percentage of the Tamil populace decreased from 40.2 in 1946 to 33.6 in 1981 owing to these demographic alterations. This too brought far-reaching consequences.

It must be pointed out here that these causes were not the result of a natural handicap that was left unaddressed, but a deliberate, forced, and state planned impediment to place the Tamils at a distinct disadvantage.

Motivational causes

A list of motivational causes seems endless. Only a few are documented here to show the crucial developments that resulted in the rise of Tamil militancy: primarily the rise of the LTTE.

In June 1956, S.W.R.D. Bandaranaike, who had formed the government after winning the elections with the promise that he would make Sinhala the only official language within 24 hours of being voted to power, introduced the 'Sinhala Only' bill. On 5 June 1956, Tamils led by Chelvanayakam's Federal Party organized protest, in which a Sinhala mob injured many of them. This was followed by violence in Batticaloa and Gal Oya in which 'between 20 and 200 persons were killed, depending on which side was doing the tallying' (Wriggins 1960). According to James Manor (1990), 'scores of Tamils, certainly well over one hundred, were massacred and hundreds more were driven into hiding'. Incidents such as these resulted in the formation of an underground Tamil group called Pulip Padai (Army of Tigers) in 1961, which faded away by 1965.

The adoption of a new republican constitution in 1972 became the 'the critical starting point' which resulted in the growth of Tamil separatism (de Silva 1998). Sri Lanka was declared a republic, Sinhala received constitutional status as the official language and Buddhism became the state religion. This was a big blow to the Tamils, who, having taken full advantage of the education the British had introduced, held more state jobs; the 'Sinhala Only' legislation adversely affected this position. The upward mobility of those who already had jobs was also jeopardized. As indicated earlier, the government also introduced a 'standardization' system for admission to institutions of higher learning, under which Tamil students had to score more marks than their Sinhalese counterparts. Up to this time, admission to higher courses in science, medicine and engineering were taken by Tamil students on merit in numbers disproportionate to their population. This system now came under attack.

By disenfranchising the Indian Tamils working there, the numerical strength of the Tamil was made to appear less than half of what it was; by projecting Sinhala as the only official language, Tamil culture was suppressed; through resettlement, demographic changes were engineered in Tamil-majority areas to further weaken the Tamils numerically; by giving special status to Buddhism, the religion of the Tamils (Hinduism) was obscured; by constitutionally re-emphasizing the unitary character of the government, moderate demands for federalism were foreclosed; and by 'standardization', the future of the younger generation of the Tamils was damned. The Tamils realized that they had been reduced to second-rate citizens in the land of their birth and decided to fight back.

One of the earliest militant groups, the *Tamil Eelam Liberation Organization* (TELO), emerged in 1971. It was followed in 1972 by the formation of the Tamil

New Tigers led by 18-year-old Velupillai Prabhakaran. On 5 May 1976 he renamed his organization the *Liberation Tigers of Tamil Eelam* (LTTE). Many other militant outfits soon mushroomed.

The Tamil political parties attempted to secure recognition of some of the Tamil demands at the same time as the growth of the militant groups. With successive Sinhalese governments belittling and ignoring the demands expressed though peaceful and democratic means, the voice and clout of the militants grew among the Tamil population. Though several militant groups espousing the same cause were operating, the LTTE emerged the most powerful not only because of their rigid policy of 'no compromise' on their initial goal of a separate homeland for the Tamils, but also because of their systematic annihilation of other rival groups to emerge as the sole representatives of the Tamils. If and when the Sri Lankan government decided to accede to the demands of the Tamils, it would be on LTTE's terms, as is being witnessed today.

The LTTE's pre-eminence amongst other militant groups is largely due to its leadership, headed by Prabhakaran. He is a demi-god to his cadres who would willingly lay down their life for him. His ruthlessness and military genius have been crucial motivating factors within the LTTE.

Trigger causes

Events in 1983 catapulted the struggle for a separate homeland to new levels, which has not only triggered the growth of militancy but sustained it as well.

A significant event that took place in that year was the death, under tragic circumstances, of the man responsible for managing the LTTE when Prabhakaran was in Tamil Nadu (India) following the promulgation of the Prevention of Terrorism Act in 1979. This man was Seelan and his death triggered 'a chain reaction', which altered the 'course of Tamil militancy' (Narayan Swamy 1994). In July 1983, the LTTE attacked an army patrol, code named 'Four Four Bravo', near Tinneveli, killing 13 Sri Lankan soldiers (Ratnatunga 1988). The massacre, the delay in transporting the bodies from Jaffna to Colombo, and the Sinhala media 'added fuel to the mounting grief and rage' (Tambiah 1996). It sparked off another bloody anti-Tamil pogrom in Colombo and other major towns claiming hundreds of Tamil lives; over 3,000 Tamils were reported to be killed. More than 18,000 Tamil homes were destroyed and over 150,000 Tamils became refugees in their own country.[1] The violence was organized 'by gangs which were obviously trained and who operated with military precision'. Their targets were the economic bases of the Tamils in Colombo and their homes (Dissanayake 1983). President Jayewardene had no words of sympathy for the Tamils.

The 1983 riots changed the Tamil militant movement in Sri Lanka in many aspects. Several factors were responsible for the changes: the anti-Tamil violence and the 1983 riots; the vigorous drive for recruitment by the LTTE; the generation of Tamil migrants; and the willingness of the Tamil population to join the militant movements. According to William McGowan (1992):

Tamil rebel groups launched intensive recruitment drives in the refugee camps of Southern India and in Tamil areas under Sinhalese military occupation in the north and the east. Issues such as national self-determination, university admissions and equity in land settlement paled before the basic desire for vengeance and the quest for safety in an independent Tamil State. Thousands joined the movement.

The 1983 riots also made the Tamil community ignore the social differences that existed among them. The deployment of armed forces against the militant in the north and east 'brought the Tamil youth together irrespective of both educational levels and social differences (Sivathamby 1989). In short, it became a potent mobilizing factor.

Sustaining and facilitating causes

It would not be surprising to note that the fuelling causes (globalization and modernization) behind many terrorist groups are also the pillars on which LTTE stands tall. The LTTE was enterprising to the extent that it not only thrived because of these factors, but it also managed to establish successful international business operations that generated funds and ensured a constant supply of arms and ammunitions for its fight against the Sri Lankan Army. Eighty to ninety per cent of the LTTE's money comes from its international dealings that range from collection from the diaspora to illegal activities.

The Sri Lankan Tamil diaspora in Switzerland, Canada, Australia, the UK, the USA and the Scandinavian countries is one source of funds for the LTTE. That apart, there is regular diversion of donations made to non-profit cultural bodies for rehabilitation or related activities in Sri Lanka (Chalk 2000). According to one report, collection of money from Tamil expatriate sources is insignificant when compared to the money accruing from narcotics (Williamson and de Silva 1998). One of the key links to the LTTE's international infrastructure is its own shipping business, with at least ten freighters, equipped with sophisticated radar and satellite communication systems, that carry legitimate cargo about 95 per cent of their time. The shipping business is absolutely crucial for the LTTE in carting sophisticated weaponry from all over the world to its war against the Sri Lankan government.

The LTTE has fully utilized technology to its advantage, sometimes even one step ahead of what the Sri Lankan State could manage: the first rocket-propelled grenade launcher was recovered from a LTTE camp. Similarly, night-vision glasses were used for the first time in the Sri Lankan battlefield by the LTTE. The LTTE, at the forefront of insurgent technological innovation, has gained mastery in the use of dual technology. The LTTE purchased (before the Sri Lankan military) Global Positioning Satellite systems to accurately target its projectiles. The LTTE have also used a land-based satellite system to communicate with its overseas cadres.

As mentioned earlier, the factors listed above do not constitute the totality of causes that have triggered and sustained the LTTE. It is but a modest attempt to highlight the overall trends that have influenced the growth of the organization.

Countering terrorism: the Sri Lankan response

The government's response, though not letting up on the demands posed by the Tamils, has been 'vacillating and full of contradictions'. Soon after the 1977 general elections, violence between the Sinhala and Tamil communities peaked resulting in the deployment of the police and the military. Curfews were established in some areas. This was followed by the promulgation of the Prevention of Terrorism Act in 1978 that gave sweeping powers to the law enforcement agencies. Soon after, in 1978, the government introduced certain concessions to the Tamils, including a declaration of Tamil as a national language. In 1979, legislation for the formation of District Development Councils was introduced. However, in 1981, following the death of two policemen at an election meeting in Jaffna, police who were brought in from other parts of Sri Lanka went on a rampage by burning the marketplace, the office of the Tamil newspaper *Eelanadu* and the priceless Jaffna Public Library. Jostled between bouts of communal violence for the next two years, 2,000 Tamils were killed and 200,000 were rendered homeless. In 1984, the government made an unsuccessful attempt at peace through the talks held in Thimpu (Bhutan) with India as the mediator. Before the Indo–Sri Lankan Agreement could finally be signed in 1987, Sri Lanka almost doubled its security forces and the LTTE increased the intensity of its attacks. Ever since, the government's attempts at dialogue interspersed with military offensives have not yielded any result.

Even before the Indian Peace Keeping Force (IPKF) left the island, the Sri Lankan government led by Premadasa held secret talks with the LTTE. It has been reported that the Sri Lankan government even provided arms to the LTTE to fight against the IPKF. After the IPKF left the island, the government held peace talks with the LTTE, but these broke down in 1990. The LTTE's main demand of returning Jaffna was not acceptable to the Premadasa government. When the talks failed, the LTTE began the next round of war: Eelam War II. It captured Jaffna in 1991 and the fight between the two forces continued until Chandrika Kumaratunge came to power in 1994.

Chandrika announced new proposals that included devolution of power to Tamil areas; merger of the north and east, where the Tamils were the majority and a major role for the LTTE in the government formed at the provincial level. A new peace process was initiated between the government and the LTTE. The talks however broke down again, leading to Eelam War III.

The Sri Lankan Army captured Jaffna in 1996 and restricted the LTTE to the Vanni region. From 1996 to 1998 the Sri Lankan Army had the upper hand, but after that lost the initiative to the LTTE. In 2000, the LTTE captured the crucial Elephant Pass, and ever since there has been a military stalemate.

The government changed after the 2001 elections. The new government led by Ranil Wickremesinghe has initiated a new round of peace talks with the LTTE. There were at least three significant breakthroughs during these peace talks, including an agreement on humanitarian measures, a disarmament process and, more significantly, the LTTE's readiness, in principle, for a federal structure.

The JVP (Janata Vimukti Peramuna) is a party which is neither Left nor Right, but incorporates all features. Ever since its first uprising was put down with the assistance from India in 1971, it has had a grudge against India. This grudge formed the main reason for the renewal of its violence when the IPKF was undertaking operations in Sri Lanka after the 1987 Indo–Sri Lanka Accord. The pressure from the JVP was crucial to Premadasa in asking the IPKF to leave. In fact Premadasa used the JVP pressure as an excuse to call for the removal of the IPKF. When Premadasa started cleaning up the JVP cadres, it was alleged that the JVP had a pact with the LTTE in fighting Premadasa. JVP was ultimately put down ruthlessly by Premadasa.

The JVP is now no longer considered to be an underground organization and has been contesting elections since 1994. Though it won only one seat in the 1994 elections, it applied pressure against any concession to the Tamils. JVP in principle is against even any federal solutions to the Tamil insurgency. It won 16 seats in the 2001 elections; its pressure on the streets against the Ranil-led peace process with the LTTE came in handy for President Chandrika to dismiss the government and call for fresh elections.

Chandrika's SLFP and JVP formed a pre-poll alliance to form the United People's Freedom Alliance in the March 2004 elections in Sri Lanka. If they were to form the government, much would depend on how much pressure the JVP and the Buddhist Sangha could exert in finding a permanent solution to the Tamil problem.

9/11 and after

In many ways the events of 11 September 2001 have altered the security discourse in the international system, and changed the structure of this system itself. In the post-cold war era the state began to lose its pre-eminence as being the principal actor in the structure of international security. Globalization, regionalization and economic liberalization had diluted the state's sphere of influence and replaced it with transnational institutions and supranational organizations. However, 9/11 has given a boost to the waning power of the state. The state, as an entity, became more powerful; its actions against terrorism, even when disproportionate to the acts of terror, are unquestioned. Most governments in South Asia have adopted a more militaristic approach towards handling the issue of insurgency and terrorism. The only positive development in South Asia on the terrorism front, post-9/11, is the international pressure that persuaded the Sri Lankan government and the LTTE to initiate their dialogue under the aegis of Norway. This has happened because the cataclysmic events of 9/11 have successfully delegitimized armed violence and narrowed down the operational space of many terrorist organizations operating on the platform of self-determination and freedom struggle. Unfortunately, the 'War against Terror' has been contextualized to the extent that it has remained as a tool only against those the USA wishes to target and not all groups. As a result, the fear of reprimand that coerced the LTTE to sit down with the Sri Lankan government is fast waning. The current setback in the peace talks is just a manifestation of this realization.

What next?

After years of conflict, can it be confidently said that the Tamils still want a separate homeland? Or would they be satisfied with appropriate measures that safeguard their rights? If the Tamils are willing to settle for something less, would the LTTE permit them to? And if a separate homeland is provided, what next? Would the oppression, rigidity and partiality of the Sinhala state be replaced with that of the LTTE?

To sum up, the LTTE has reached its current strength and stature because of the following factors:

- The discriminatory policies and practices of the Sri Lankan State against the linguistic and religious Tamil minority.
- The Sri Lankan government's continued insensitivity and indifference to the just and legitimate demands of the Tamil minority.
- Suppression by use of force by the Sri Lankan State of the democratic aspirations and legitimate demands of the minority Tamils in the earlier stages.
- Indifference, tolerance (and later even incitement and encouragement) by the State to violence perpetrated against the minority Tamils by the majority Sinhalese.
- The emergence of a firm, unyielding and ruthless leadership of the LTTE.
- The highest motivation on the part of any number of LTTE cadres to willingly die for the cause by undertaking suicide missions.
- The sympathy and support, moral and material, from the large Sri Lankan Tamil diaspora in many parts of the world.
- An inconsistent counter-terror policy of the state.
- Support from many quarters by way of arms and equipment and moral support to the LTTE in its insurgency.
- Lack of seriousness and sincerity on the part of both the parties during various peace initiatives.

What are the options before the Sri Lankan government?

Option A

Give up on peace talks, continue with the military option, suppress or subjugate the rebels and make efforts to govern the Tamil areas in a democratic manner through moderate Tamil leaders.

The military option has not worked during the last two decades. There has been large-scale killing on both sides. There has been equally large-scale desertion from the Sri Lankan Army. The economy is in shambles. A will to fight to the finish is lacking on the part of the Sri Lankan military apparatus. The LTTE is also facing a shortage of recruits of ideal fighting age, due to large-scale migration to many parts of the world and thousands having been killed in the ethnic conflict with Sri Lankan forces and in the conflict with the IPKF. The recent, and the first ever, open challenge to the unquestioned supremacy of the leadership of Prabhakaran by Karuna (alias Vinayagamurthy Muralidharan) is going to be an important turning point not only for the LTTE but also the Sri Lankan peace process in particular.

Will this lead to what William Zartman calls a 'mutually hurting stalemate'? Clearly neither side can alter the status quo dramatically either politically or militarily. Besides, the status quo clearly is hurting both the parties. Will both the parties come to the negotiation table and engage in a sustained and systematic process? There is lingering mutual suspicion about the sincerity on both sides. The LTTE has used the peace talks in the past to reinvigorate itself and fight back; whereas the government faltered mainly due to internal domestic compulsions.

Option B

> Continue peace talks, accommodate the LTTE's more reasonable demands and go in for a genuine democratic federal governmental apparatus.

This seems to be the only option which is capable of success and which will benefit both the parties. Only this will put an end to the indiscriminate killing and destruction which has already claimed over 60,000 lives.

Peace negotiations, by their very nature, are tedious, long and time-consuming. It is bound to be more so in the case of Sri Lanka and LTTE, both of which carry a complicated history of embitterment.

Death and destruction on both sides for over two decades has created enormous bitterness, enmity, mutual mistrust and suspicion. Much more efforts and greater sincerity is called for on the part of both the parties. The only consideration for the Sri Lankan government should be to maintain the integrity of the nation and a democratic structure. The goal of the LTTE should be to obtain a federal system in which the Tamils in the North and the East should be free to elect the government of their choice to preserve their own language, culture and to fully realize their economic, social and political potential.

Notes

1 The 1983 anti-Tamil riots went through two phases. The first was spontaneous and took place in the immediate aftermath of the slain soldiers' bodies being brought to the cemetery. The second was very organized.

Bibliography

Chalk, P. (2000) 'Liberation Tigers of Tamil Eelam', *Commentary*, 77, 17 March, http://www.csis-scrs.gc.ca/eng/comment/com77_e.html

de Silva, K.M. (1998) *Reaping the Whirlwind: Ethnic Conflict: Ethnic Politics in Sri Lanka*. New Delhi: Penguin Books, p.155.

Dissanayake, T.D.S.A. (1983) *The agony of Sri Lanka*. Colombo: Swastika, p.80.

McGowan, W. (1992) *Only Man is Vile: The Tragedy of Sri Lanka*. New York: Farrar, Straus and Giroux, p.182.

Manor, J. (1990) *The Expedient Utopian: Bandaranaike and Ceylon*. Cambridge: Cambridge University Press.

Narayan Swamy, M.R. (1994) *Tigers of Lanka: From Boys to Guerrillas*. Delhi: Konark Publishers, p.89.

Ratnatunga, S. (1988) *Politics of Terrorism: The Sri Lanka Experience*. Belconnen, Australia: International Fellowship for Social and Economic Development, pp. 4–5.

Sivarajah, A. (1992) 'The Rise of Militancy in Tamil Politics', in Jayasekera, P.V.J. (ed.) *Security Dilemma of a Small State*. Institute for International Studies (Peradeniya Sri Lanka), New Delhi: South Asian Publishers, pp. 120–45.

Sivathamby, K. (1989) 'Community, Identity and Militarization in Sri Lanka: Tamil Militants', in Wignaraja, P. and Hussain, A. (eds) *The Challenge in South Asia: Democracy, Development and Regional Cooperation*. New Delhi: Sage Publications, pp. 254–5.

Tambiah, S.J. (1996) *Levelling Crowds: Ethno-nationalist Conflicts and Collective Violence in South Asia*. New Delhi: Vistaar Publications, p.95.

Williamson, H. and de Silva, M. (1998) 'To catch a Tiger', *The Island*, 25 May.

Wriggins, H.W (1960) *Ceylon: Dilemmas of a New Nation*. Princeton, NJ: Princeton University Press, p.261.

11 Right-wing terrorism

Wilhelm Heitmeyer

Problems of definition

The problems of research into terrorism begin with the definition of the concept and thus with the classification of violent activities and their goals. Moreover, the analyses of the process through which these activities can escalate into a certain form of violence, namely terror, pose a special problem. Accordingly, both the definitional framework and the analysis of the processes affect the assumptions about possible explanations for the roots of terror.

Right-wing terrorism, moreover, is exceedingly difficult to analyse and its development out of right-wing extremism is especially problematical. Another important consideration is whether or not theories of right-wing extremism can be used to interpret this radicalization process.

If, in searching for an initial definition, one follows Peter Waldmann's attempt, this has consequences for the further analysis of this particular field of research, namely right-wing terror. Waldmann's definition runs as follows:

> Terrorism refers to systematically planned, shocking acts of violence directed from underground against a political order. They are designed to produce a general sense of insecurity and fear, but also sympathy and support.
>
> (Waldmann 2002: 11)

This definition is tied up closely with the use of violence and the impact of shock. As much as it may be useful to have a clearly defined conceptual base, the question remains as to whether all terrorist activities can be accounted for in this way. Victor Walter has developed a wider concept that includes a number of process elements:

> Regardless of its political orientation, the first element of the terror process, in a logical as well as chronical [*sic*] sense, is the specific act or threat of violence, which induces a general psychic act for fear, which in turn produces typical patterns of reactive behaviour.
>
> (Walter 1969: 7)

This highlights two aspects. Firstly, the threat potential is a decisive element of the definitional framework and, secondly, there is a clear reference to what has to be explained, namely, the political interaction processes.

In summary, right-wing terrorism is a product of political interaction and the radicalization of other forms of threat-based right-wing attitudes and behaviour, such as opportunity-dependent violence by (youth) gangs, subcultural violence (such as that of skinhead groups), organized party-political Right extremist violence, and religiously oriented right-wing extremist group violence.

A problem of numerical strength

In most cases, we have only estimates of the numerical strength of these groups and their membership in various countries. One reason for this is that some groups have no formal membership arrangements. Another is that their activities are largely secretive. In any case, numbers and membership allow only indirect conclusions regarding the quality and frequency of violence. The German example demonstrates this. At the end of 2000, there were 144 right-wing extremist organizations or groups with an estimated membership of 51,000 (Bundesministerium des Innern/Bundesministerium der Justiz 2001: 280). While the Bundesamt für Verfassungsschutz (German Federal Office for the Protection of the Constitution) considered that the estimated numbers had been falling slightly, the potential numbers of pro-violence right-wing extremists had risen steadily from 6,200 in 1995 to 9,700 in 2000 (2001: 3). Between 1990 and 2000, these groups' members became younger, more militant, more violent, and more action-oriented (ibid.: 26). Similar trends on the potentially violent side of right-wing

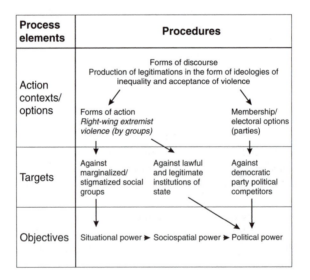

Figure 11.1 Overall context, options, targets, and objectives of right-wing extremism.
Source: Heitmeyer 2003, p.402.

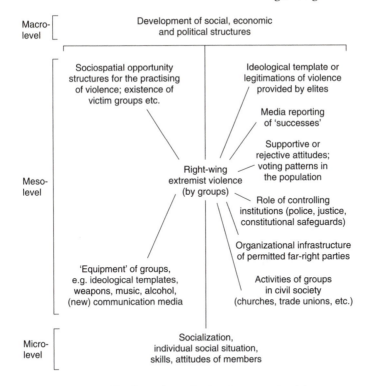

Figure 11.2 Structural model for the analysis of right-wing extremist violence.
Source: Heitmeyer 2003, p.405.

extremism have also been reported in other countries. In Sweden, the hard core of right-wing extremism is estimated to number some 500 individuals, and the development of a terrorist variant is no longer ruled out, whereas there were still no indications of anything of this kind in Germany at the beginning of 2002. In the USA, reporting the number of groups and their membership is posing similar problems, with the consequent uncertainty of whether these figures are rising or falling.

Analytical framework

We need to be aware of the specific political allure of the right-wing approach. Figure 11.1 shows a survey of the political spectrum and provides a summary of the action contexts to be taken into account, as well as the available options, targets and objectives of right-wing extremism.

Additionally, we have to stress the need for a structural model to analyse the dynamics of right-wing extremist violence which may escalate into right-wing terrorism (see Figure. 11.2).

The definitional element of a convincing 'threat potentials' (in Walter's concept) makes it possible for terrorist groups to exert permanent pressure on certain targeted groups, that is, to 'terrorize' them in an unspectacular way such that members of the particular targeted group must, at any time (and now also in any place) expect to become victims of terror. In this sense, terror means that the victims experience a 'loss of control' over their own lives.

I would therefore like to propose that the definitional framework, which primarily focuses on the spectacular act, and which can also be objectively identified, be extended to include the subjective side of the victims' groups in order to concentrate more on the political interactions. This also means looking at terror not only as an act, but seeing it as a process that is apt to change discourses, everyday life and public order in a society.

If a central criterion of terror consists in placing people in a permanent state of fear so that they must expect an attack at any time, then the attacks by groups of right-wing youths should be included in the analysis. They use terrorist means, thereby severely limiting the freedom of movement of others. Certain urban neighbourhoods or locations are turned into 'zones of fear'. This is achieved by the simple numerical superiority of those who sometimes threaten and sometimes use violence against their victims who are clearly at a disadvantage. However, what distinguishes these groups from classical terrorist formations is that they do not act covertly and for this reason rarely use firearms or explosives.

In these specific cases it is therefore important that, firstly, there should be no over- or underreaction by the police and the judiciary. What is required is a credible probability of sanctions, which, however, do not destroy the chances of a normal career open to all citizens. Secondly, such groups must not get the impression that they are the 'executors' of a tacitly consenting population or segment thereof. Thirdly, the political elite bear responsibility, on the one hand, for ensuring that topics marked by group-focused enmity are kept off the agenda, and, on the other hand, they must ensure that there is no breakdown in communication with such groups, as this would quickly lead to the formation of conspiracy theories which play an important role in right-wing camps.

Conspiracy theories are of central importance to the escalation process and the transition from right-wing extremism to terrorism. This is because, on the one hand, enemies can be constructed everywhere, and on the other, because perpetrators develop their own role as executors of a silent majority.

The analysis of right-wing extremism should thus include the wider range of manifestations that fall within its boundaries. Terrorism is never static, but is driven by a dynamic of radicalization that develops successively, and in which several groups of actors of a state or civil society become involved before the variants of right-wing extremism in a more narrow sense eventually emerge.

Right-wing terror: forms of manifestation

Looking at the four basic categories that terrorism draws on, namely social-revolutionary, ethnic-nationalistic, religious and vigilantist (Waldmann 1998), ethnic-nationalistic terror occupies a central position. At the same time, other forms of terror that draw on these categories, or combinations and collaborations between terror groups of different ideologies, must not be overlooked. In the USA, in particular, there are right-wing organizations which are hostile to the government and pursue both ethnic-nationalistic and religious aims, and also practise vigilantism (for instance, when they break into abortion clinics and kill medical personnel). This also applies to the Boeremag organization in South Africa whose terror is primarily directed against infrastructure so as to incite the black population to riots against whites. This organization traditionally mixes white supremacist Afrikaner politics with Christian fundamentalism. Their core idea is that white Afrikaners are God's chosen people, and they are to bring forth the light of Christian civilization.

Such mixed ideologies, in particular, make explanations difficult, because terror groups can so easily adapt their legitimization strategies to changing conditions. Another difficulty is that political interests are combined with deep-seated religious beliefs, which often induces groups to hermetically seal themselves off from outside influences.

Manifestations of right-wing terrorist activities vary greatly. They include, for instance, Triple A in Argentina in the 1970s (Waldmann 2002: 12), Vitt Ariskt Motstånd (VAM) in Sweden in the early 1990s (Bjørgo 1997: 146ff.), the activities of Timothy McVeigh and his attack in Oklahoma City in 1995, as well as the bomb attack at the Munich Oktoberfest in 1980.

In Europe, right-wing terrorism was particularly widespread in Italy in the 1980s. The Bologna bombing (1980) was an example. Apart from the neo-fascist groups, such as *Ordine Nuovo*, there were the NAR (*Nuclei Armati Revoluzionari*), which became infamous for their indiscriminate bombings aimed at public institutions, public transport and schools (Laqueur 1987: 334). What distinguished the Italian groups from most other terrorist groups was their anti-communist background (Weinberg 1995) and their attempts to bring about a strong state by a campaign of bombings, a 'strategy of tension', (i.e. causing chaos, panic and fear). The situation became especially controversial because of the involvement of actors from the political establishment.

Right-wing extremist violence or terrorism is mostly carried out by representatives of the ethnic majority population against weaker minorities. But, on the other hand, we have to observe the violence of ethnic minorities against the dominant ethnic group, such as Basque or Palestinian nationalist terrorism. Some forms of ethnic-national liberation terrorism also have dimensions of ethnic cleansing that relate them to right-wing extremists. Right-wing ideas may have had an increasing influence among 'national liberation movements' during the last decade or two, compared with the more Marxist revolutionary ideas that inspired national liberation movements in the 1960s and 1970s.

Concerning right-wing terrorism in Europe and Latin America, there are obvious differences. In Europe the groups were small and their attacks were directed against foreigners and the democratic system in general. In South and Central America the right-wing terror in the 1970s was much more comprehensive. The central aim was to stabilize the dictatorships.

This leads us to the conclusion that different explanations are needed. In the current situation of right-wing terror, most violence committed by conspiratorial groups or individual perpetrators is directed against those considered 'unequal' (that is, groups of aliens or those who are weak), against political opponents (such as trade unionists, journalists, etc.), and also against the state and its representatives. Targeted groups vary according to ideological orientations. While target definitions in the USA rely on the ideological element of ZOG (the Zionist Occupation Government), in the European variants, such as VAM in Sweden, this is only the case if the they are directly emulating a US group. The aim is to challenge those in power by means of 'bombing' but without actually presenting any concrete ambitions for power. As a rule, these are weak groups making a strong impact through a centrally placed shock effect: a communication strategy to take hold of, and occupy, people's minds.

Sprinzak (1995) has attempted a typification. It is historically based and includes a wide range of variants. However, there is room for discussion as to whether all the forms mentioned (i.e. revolutionary terrorism, reactive terrorism, vigilante terrorism, racist terrorism, millenarian terrorism and youth counter-culture terrorism) should be subsumed under the concept of 'terror'.

Much more interesting as critical 'terrorism' types are the constellations resulting from political interactions. In the European situation we can ascertain four related ideas:

- A violent form of right-wing extremism is more likely to develop where there is no political representation through political parties or channelling mechanisms in the form of electoral success at national level. This applies to groups in Sweden, the United Kingdom and Germany, and to some militias in the USA.
- Right-wing extremist violence can exist or develop without electoral successes for the far Right, but can never survive without xenophobic and right-wing population moods and attitudes among the population.
- The greater the level of violence perpetrated by right-wing extremist groups, the lower is the political weight attached to legitimate power-sharing.
- Political marginalization of right-wing extremist parties and groups produces variable results. In some cases it leads to fragmentation of the extreme Right, while in others it may lead to radicalization, which manifests itself in political murders, incitements to murder on the Internet, and the procurement of arms. These must all be considered preliminaries to right-wing terrorism.

These constellations offer some opportunities for societal and political intervention in order to avoid any escalation processes.

Escalation: the dynamics of violence

Escalation depends on the political interaction processes which include four essential elements: the socialization of the perpetrators, the organization of the groups and their ideology, and the opportunity structure.

The development of the escalation process also depends on the intervention of the several institutions, groups and actors illustrated in Figure 11.2.

One form of escalation is micro-social. Within a limited context of interaction, violence intensifies to the point where victims are killed. In other words, acts of violence 'run out of control', and the targets of the attacks are individually 'dehumanized'. In the meso-social variant, by contrast, the escalation spills over onto the attacked group through the agency of labelling media (Brosius and Esser 1995) or the exceeding of thresholds.

Group 'equipment' plays an important part in the practice/prevention or escalation/ de-escalation of violence. The availability of alcohol and/or music (e.g. skinhead concerts) and rituals, all increase internal cohesion and provide functionalizable trigger factors to release the potential for violence. The new communications media provide improved opportunities for organization, mobilization and mobility, and the possibility of international networking (e.g. in the case of skinheads, 'Blood and Honour').

In the social and political environment, the greatest contribution made by right-wing extremist parties is the potential for organizational support. A society's elite also contribute to the legitimization of an ideology of inequality by the way in which they 'grade' or value immigrants (e.g. as 'useful' or 'useless') and so build up the potential encouragement of violent action.

Media reports of particular right-wing events, especially of 'successes', also always serve to disseminate the positions of the elite and confirm the status of the groups as a factor to be taken seriously, which in turn may be propitious for escalation. In Germany in 1992/93, for example, reports in the mass media covering tragic arson attacks on asylum seekers' hostels were rapidly followed by an increased number of similar attacks (Koopmans 1996: 205).

The patterns of attitudes and overt contrasting positions among the population determine the extent to which the groups derive potential motivation from them. Problems are caused by feedback and booster effects provided by some sectors of the population, for example in connection with conflicts over asylum seekers. They play a part in escalation and mobilization when the violent groups can see themselves as acting (as a 'national vanguard') on behalf of silent groups among the population. Ultimately, the density of control exercised by government institutions is of central importance to the use of violence.

The theory of 'split delegitimization' in relation to the escalation of the use of right-wing extremist violence is relevant to the case of the USA. It is also, to some extent, relevant to Sweden, particularly because here central targets include not just alien groups, as is usually the case in Europe, but the state as well. Sprinzak's general theory (1995) on how radicalization turns into terrorism identifies three levels. The first level, a crisis of confidence, is followed by the second, a radicalization in the form of a conflict of legitimacy, in which the political system is called into question (e.g. because of 'Zionist infiltration'). On the third level, the crisis of legitimacy broadens to include every individual associated with the system, extending beyond depersonalization and dehumanization to include actual violence against such persons, which can now be justified as a blow struck against the hated system. According to Sprinzak, some forms of right-wing (or 'particularistic') terrorism represent a special variety of this radicalization process, as the enemy is not seen as constituted by one enemy but rather by two enemy categories: a 'foreign' enemy (e.g. immigrants or ethnic minorities) which allegedly seeks to destroy one's own community or race, and the 'traitors', (i.e. the 'system' which aids and protects the foreign enemy). In the imagery of ZOG, politicians, bureaucrats, the police, the media, intellectuals and anti-racists are all considered to be treacherous collaborators abetting the Jews in taking control of our society.

An important factor in this process is the role played by the state because both underreaction and overreaction may well accelerate the process of radicalization (Neidhardt 1989). Underreaction can imply 'encouragement', while, on the other hand, excessive repression may escalate into anger and hatred, especially when the repression lacks consistency (Gurr 1969: 473) where ideally the culprits would be prosecuted and the innocent spared.

Escalation is aggravated, moreover, by breakdowns in communication. Especially when horrific acts of violence occur, the moral postulates within a society are both (re)activated and, as a rule, raised to a higher level to clearly dissociate it from the motives of terrorist groups and demonstrate its superiority. But this may also explain why escalation occurs. The higher the moral standards invoked, the smaller the chances of communication aimed at integrating the underlying conflicts into processes marked by lower levels of violence. It is therefore a matter of concern that religious categories are (again) becoming factors guiding the governmental policies of liberal democracies. The reason is that the underlying conflicts are no longer being interpreted as issues of 'more or less', but as simple 'either-or' conflicts (Hirschman 1994), leading to corresponding types of behaviour by the state or terrorist groups.

Explanatory approaches

There is general agreement that there can be no unified theory explaining terrorism (Reinares 2003). For this reason the survey of theories and hypotheses by Lia and Skjølberg (2000), for example, is commendable for its description of the broad spectrum of existing theories. On the other hand, this survey is also problematic because it tries to cover terrorism in general and, by way of its overview, unintentionally generalizes the diversity of terrorism. Variants with their specific target groups, recruiting groups, mobilization potentials, national traditions, etc. are lost in the process. A suitable approach would be first to clearly present the specifics of a variety of terrorism and then confront them with existing theories.

What are the specific characteristics of right-wing terrorist violence? As mentioned above, its basic and most common form is the ethnic-nationalistic variant. This requires an explanation as to why this variant has developed, a variant which is not driven by social inequality, such as in the case with terrorism conducted by the Left. Instead, the variant of inequality, in the sense of unequal worth of groups of aliens whose protection by the state is an assumed threat to one's own group, has become central.

The core ideological patterns display a contradictory and thus explosive structure: there are fantasies of superiority vis-à-vis aliens and, at the same time, feelings of inferiority vis-à-vis 'relevant others', that is, toward groups similar to one's own ethnic group or toward other social groups. These feelings are marked by self-elevation on the one hand and devaluation, or even dehumanization, of enemy groups, mostly of different ethnic origin, on the other, and are frequently accompanied by militaristic vocabulary.

To develop the contours of a theory of right-wing terror, a distinction should be made between preconditions and precipitants (Bjørgo 2003). But in explaining terror, at least of the spectacular type, we face a structural problem. It is true that multilevel concepts on the macro-level (namely, societal developments) and their explanatory potential regarding the origin and spread of ideologies can be linked to individual factors at the micro-level and then combined with analyses at the meso-level of collective violent actions in order to explain politicization and potential escalation. This would be a viable approach to the preconditions.

But it is the precipitants which are decisive in triggering concrete acts of terrorism. This confronts us with the central problem of contingency. No systematic explanations can be offered, nor predictions made. As far as the preconditions are concerned, we favour a framework combining the approaches of social psychology, subculture theory and modernization theory, and include concepts of politico-cultural research.

Modernization theory approaches take as their starting point the processes of social change and their individual, social and political repercussions in terms of problems of integration and disintegration (Heitmeyer 1994; Anhut and Heitmeyer 2000; Albrecht 2003: 636ff.). This approach provides an explanation of the conditions that cause individuals or groups to regard it (because of structural access problems, uncertainties and collapse of recognition) as 'necessary and appropriate' to perceive the options offered by the far Right as attractive explanations of their own situations and so turn to right-wing extremist groups.

The disintegration approach provides a 'theory-organizing' framework to explain the manifestations. With regard to the origins of ideologies of inequality and acceptance of violence, the approach adopts socialization theory arguments on the micro-level, by citing early injuries to recognition, which determine the quest for security and superiority and combine high levels of anomie and insecurity with authoritarian reflexes.

Concerning the socialization of perpetrators from right-wing extremist groups, the results of the research differ. While specific configurations of stress are regularly cited in German studies, Hamm (1993: 114), for example, does not identify any particular family problems in his study of American skinheads. He does not regard the family experience as a significant predictor of right-wing violence or terrorism.

Studies of perpetrators suggest certain common characteristics (Bjørgo 1998; Merkl 1997; Lööw 1995; Willems *et al.* 1993; Heitmeyer and Müller 1995). The age structure in Europe is in the 16–26 bracket, although the average age is far higher in cases such as the American militia and in national liberation movements.

For the stage of politicization, which is linked to losses of confidence in the political system, the assumption of a politico-cultural approach (including an assumption of delegitimization) is applied (Sprinzak 1995). Since compensation for (perceived or experienced) threats to status is important at this stage, damage to integration and recognition makes it natural that violence-prone ingroup/outgroup distinctions (in the sense of the social identity theory) should become sharper and, as a result, groups and communities with a high level of internal integration (in accordance with assumptions of subculture theory) become more important.

The escalation stage, in the light of the framework approach, is linked to potentially recognition-enhancing opportunities to demonstrate (new) power in violent situations or with regard to certain territories, which are most likely to be pursued by groups that are successful in creating clear scapegoats for their own situation or scenarios of threat that act as triggers of violence. Conflict theory can be applied here. To what extent individuals indulge in such escalations depends on numerous factors (such as reference group orientation, comparative processes, etc.) which can be introduced, in particular, by social-psychological approaches.

The example of the Oklahoma City bombing serves to illustrate the interplay of the following factors:

- On the level of society, there is the deep economic crisis of the heartland, which affects a large number of small farms (whereas modern types of farming have been successful). So we can assume that there exists a relative deprivation which can explain the hatred toward the state, which does not intervene.
- The surrounding farming province had gradually become a distressed region, making it a likely hotbed for the conspiracy theories of certain groups against the state. In US political culture such conspiracy theories can be easily activated and are supported not only by the likes of Timothy McVeigh. Social destruction as a socialization experience and the rigid disciplinary system of the army were the central elements in the individual biography and the weapons-linked occupation of the perpetrator. Mentally, he lived in the world of *The Turner Diaries*, the novel about an attack on the FBI and a racial war against the 'system'.

These are elements of the preconditions for the process of radicalization in the Oklahoma City case, while the revenge on the government for its attack on a sect in Waco and the shooting by federal agents of a right-wing rebel at Ruby Ridge, can be assumed to have been among the main precipitants, or 'trigger causes'.

The Oklahoma City bombing is also an example of how societal framing functions. Psychopathological theories, which do not make any great contribution to explaining political interaction processes, are revalued in order to decrease the public's perception of the potential threat emanating from terrorist groups and to obscure problematic societal developments. As a result, complex processes are evaded; groups involved in such incidents can be kept out of the public eye, and the death penalty can be more easily imposed on individual perpetrators.

Assumptions about future trends

It can be assumed that political terrorism will increase worldwide in the form of inexpensive 'low-intensive wars'. In view of the technical means, it is likely that, in general, there will be a growing 'loss of control' for both governmental institutions and victim groups, leading in turn to an increase in security apparatus or even a high-security state. This will hardly be successful, however, for a security paradox is at hand. This means that, while more and more advanced security agencies are being set up, new gaps in security also emerge, leading to an anxiety spiral in society. This, in turn, contributes to the success and stabilization of terrorist action, because minds remain 'occupied' and authoritarian societal developments cannot be ruled out.

The right-wing variant of terror is likely to pose a threat in particular to those societies that are undergoing 'transition', such as South Africa, which is changing from an apartheid regime to a democratic society, or societies possessing a 'basic stock of equipment' in the form of conspiracy theories, a weapons scene, religious groups plying their views, and social deprivation. The USA must be counted among these societies (Dees and Corcorau 1996; Stern 1996; Kaplan and Weinberg 1998). On the other hand Pedahzur (2001) shows in his comparative analysis of the US, German and Israeli responses that a strong civil society in the USA may prevent a serious development.

Instances of cooperation can be expected, at least between some of the terror variants. This is especially true of right-wing and Islamic terror because both have a common enemy – 'World Jewry' – and both subscribe to conspiracy theories. Kaplan and Weinberg (1998: 73) foresee developments in the USA characterized by a 'radical holy war' and increasingly autonomous small groups that are extensively armed. The fight against right-wing terror should be much easier, relatively speaking, since their leading cadres are not particularly intellectual. Moreover, right-wing extremism tends to be more centred on worldly ideologies and interests. Recruitment to these groups depends on a person's radical views. Islamic terrorists, on the other hand, attach greater weight to religious expectations of salvation (through 'Holy War') and recruitment functions via ethnic affiliation, ensuring the groups' internal cohesion and exclusivity, and thus making them far more dangerous.

Bibliography

Albrecht, G. (2003) 'Sociological Approaches to Individual Violence and their Empirical Evaluation', in Heitmeyer, W. and Hagan, J. (eds) *International Handbook of Violence Research*. Dordrecht/Boston/London: Kluwer Academic Publishers.

Anhut, R. and Heitmeyer, W. (2000) 'Desintegration, Konflikte und Ethnisierung', in Heitmeyer, W. and Anhut, R. (eds) *Bedrohte Stadtgesellschaft. Soziale Desintegrationsprozesse und ethnisch-kulturelle Konfliktkonstellationen*. Weinheim/Munich: Juventa.

Bjørgo, T. (1997) *Racist and Right-wing Violence in Scandinavia: Patterns, Perpetrators and Responses*. Oslo: Tano Aschehoug.

Bjørgo, T. (1998) 'Entry, Bridge-burning, and Exit Options: What Happens to Young People Who Join Racist Groups – And Want to Leave?' in Kaplan, J. And Bjørgo, T. (eds) *Nation and Race: The Developing Euro-American Racist Subculture*. Boston: Northeastern University Press.

Bjørgo, T. (2003) *Root causes to terrorism*, Introduction to international expert meeting in Oslo 9–11 June 2003, unpublished working paper.

Brosius, H.-B. and Esser, F. (1995) *Eskalation durch Berichterstattung? Massenmedien und fremdenfeindliche Gewalt*. Opladen: Westdeutscher Verlag.

Bundesministerium des Innern/Bundesministerium der Justiz (2001) *Erster Periodischer Sicherheitsbericht*, Berlin.

Bundesamt für Verfassungsschutz (2001) *Ein Jahrzehnt rechtsextremistischer Politik: Strukturdaten, Ideologie, Agitation, Perspektiven 1990–2000*, Köln.

Dees, M. and Corcorau, J. (1996) *Gathering Storm: America's Militia Threat*. New York: Harper Collins Publishers.

Gurr, T. (1969) 'A Comparative Study of Civil Strife', in Graham, H.D. and Gurr, T. (eds) *Violence in America: Historical and Comparative Perspectives, Vol. 1*. Washington DC: US Gov. Print. Off., pp. 473ff.

Hamm, M.S. (1993) *American Skinheads: The Criminology and Control of Hate Crime*. Westport, CT: Praeger.

Heitmeyer, W. (1994) 'Das Desintegrationstheorem', in Heitmeyer, W. (ed.) *Das Gewaltdilemma*. Frankfurt: Suhrkamp.

Heitmeyer, W. and Müller, J. (1995) *Fremdenfeindliche Gewalt junger Menschen: Biographische Hintergründe, soziale Situationskontexte und die Bedeutung strafrechtlicher Sanktionen*. Bonn: Forum Verlag.

Heitmeyer, W. (2003) 'Right-wing Extremist Violence', in Heitmeyer, W. and Hagan, J. (eds) *International Handbook of Violence Research*. Dordrecht/Boston/London: Kluwer Academic Publishers, pp. 399–436.

Hirschman, A.O. (1994) 'Wieviel Gemeinsinn braucht die liberale Gesellschaft?', *Leviathan*, **22**(2), 293–304.

Kaplan, J. and Weinberg, L. (1998) *The Emergence of a Euro–American Radical Right*. New Brunswick/New Jersey/London: Rutge University Press.

Koopmans, R. (1996) 'Explaining the rise of racist and right violence in Western Europe: Grievances or opportunities?', *European Journal of Political Research*, **30**, 185–216.

Laqueur, W. (1987) *Terrorism*. Frankfurt am Main: Ullstein.

Lia, B. and Skjølberg, K.H.-W. (2000) *Why Terrorism Occurs: A Survey of Theories and Hypotheses on the Causes of Terrorism*. Norway: Kjeller (FFI/Rapport – 2000/02769), also available at http://www.nupi.no/IPS/filestore/02769.pdf

Lööw, H. (1995) 'Racist Violence and Criminal Behaviour in Sweden: Myths and Reality', in Bjørgo, T. (ed.) *Terror from the Extreme Right*. London: Frank Cass, pp. 116–61.

Merkl, P.H. (1997) 'Why Are They So Strong Now?', in Merkl, P.H. and Weinberg, L. (eds) *The Revival of Right-wing Extremism in the 1990s*. London: Frank Cass, pp. 17–46.

Neidhardt, F. (1989) 'Gewalt und Gegengewalt: Steigt die Gewaltbereitschaft zu Gewaltaktionen mit zunehmender Kontrolle und Repression?', in Heitmeyer, W., Moller, K. and Sunker, H. (eds) *Jugend-Staat-Gewalt*. Weinheim/Munich: Juventa, pp. 233–43.

Pedahzur, A. (2001) 'Struggling with the challenges of right-wing extremism and terrorism within democratic boundaries: a comparative analysis', *Studies in Conflict & Terrorism*, **24**, 339–59.

Reinares, F. (2003) 'Terrorism', in Heitmeyer, W. and Hagan, J. (eds) *International Handbook of Violence Research*. Dordrecht/Boston/London: Kluwer Academic Publishers, pp. 309–21.

Sprinzak, E. (1995) 'Right-wing Terrorism in a Comparative Perspective: The Case of Split Delegitimization', in Bjørgo, T. (ed.) *Terror from the Extreme Right*. London: Frank Cass, pp. 17–43.

Stern, K.S. (1996) *A Force Upon the Plain: The American Militia Movement and the Politics of Hate*. New York: Simon & Schuster.

Waldmann, P. (1998) *Terrorismus: Provokation der Macht.* Munich: Gerling.

Waldmann, P. (2002) 'Terrorismus als weltweites Phänomen: Eine Einführung', in Frank, H. and Hirschmann, K. (eds) *Die weltweite Gefahr: Terrorismus als internationale Herausforderung.* Berlin: Berlin Verlag, pp. 11–26.

Walter, V. (1969) *Terror and Resistance: A Study of Political Violence.* New York: Oxford University Press.

Weinberg, L. (1995) 'Italian Neo-fascist Terrorism: A Comparative Perspective', in Bjørgo, T. (ed.) *Terror from the Extreme Right.* London: Frank Cass, pp. 221–38.

Willems, H., Eckert, R. and Würtz, S. (1993) *Fremdenfeindliche Gewalt: Einstellungen, Täter, Konflikteskalation.* Opladen: Leske & Budrich.

12 Social-revolutionary terrorism in Latin America and Europe

Peter Waldmann

From the late 1950s to the 1990s, Latin America and Europe witnessed several series of guerrilla campaigns and terrorist attacks from left-wing extremists. About 25–30 groups of social-revolutionary terrorists were active during this period, most of them of limited scope and lacking major support in their respective societies, but some of them quite strong in terms of number of members and destructive power. Being considered in general more as a cause of trouble and annoyance than a serious challenge for the ruling class, in two cases (that of Cuba in 1959 and that of Nicaragua in 1979) they succeeded to overwhelm the government and to seize power.

I will explore four questions in this chapter. First I will ask whether a structural comparison between the two regions under consideration here, Europe and Latin America, is a promising path to discover 'root causes' of terrorism. The second section is focused on the terrorists themselves. Their social background and their actual social position are briefly examined in order to get an idea of their way of thinking and their motives to commit violent acts. In a further section I try to show that terrorism must be considered as one among several options to reach one's goal by violent means. As can be shown by comparing the European with the Latin American situation, the decision to employ terrorist violence depends less on deep-rooted 'causes' than on the social and geographic opportunity structures under which the violent groups have to operate. Finally, an overview of the long-term outcome of social-revolutionary terrorist and guerrilla movements will be given and the question will be raised if possibly there will be a revival of this kind of terrorism in the near future.

Structural comparisons – a promising path?

It seems rather tempting to compare the structural preconditions of the emergence of social-revolutionary movements in the second half of the last century in Europe and in Latin America, hoping that this might help to find out which causal factors were decisive. The remarkable structural differences between both regions, concerning, for instance, their class structure, the general level of poverty and regime stability, opens an especially promising path to limit the range of variables which produce left-wing terrorism.

For example there is no doubt that Europe was at that time a highly prosperous area, where the working class and the poor participated in the general growth of wealth, while Latin America, even if it made some progress in the process of modernization during this period, remained on the whole a widely underdeveloped region, whose characteristics were a widespread misery and a huge gap in the living conditions of the rich oligarchy and the bulk of the population. Nevertheless, both continents generated militant left-wing movements. Can we conclude then that the importance of poverty for the emergence of left-wing radicalism must be relativized?

Let me take another example. It is generally presumed that democratic regimes favour the formation of terrorist groups, offering them good chances on their territory by guaranteeing a series of individual and collective rights and by protecting the citizens against abuse of authority by the security forces. In fact the majority of the countries in which terrorist organizations emerged were, at least formally, democracies with freely elected political leaders. But there were also a few cases like Argentina and Brazil, which were governed by the military. The military dictatorship in these cases, far from deterring rebellious young people, was a further reason for them to take arms. Is it legitimate to conclude from these different political settings that the political regime in which a terrorist movement comes into being is of secondary importance?

I would not deny that structural considerations of the kind presented here, may have a certain value. They can help to eliminate those variables which are of no relevance at all for the phenomenon in question and give a first idea of what structural factors could play a role in explaining it. But there are at least three reasons which should warn us to not to overestimate structural variables and an analysis which strongly relies on them.

The first reason is that terrorist groups by their very nature and definition normally are groups of limited scope. For an underground organization it is crucial not to have too many members, since it otherwise risks infiltration by the secret services and to lose the control of its various branches. Often parallel groups exist, pursuing the same goals as the terrorist organization by other more or less pacific means (political parties or associations), but the main advantage of terrorism as a political weapon consists in being independent from support by larger groups. As it is the preferred tactic of relatively small groups, it remains doubtful to which point these groups represent the feelings and aspirations of broader segments of society, as a social class, a confessional or an ethnic group as a whole. Even if I do not want to go so far as Walter Laqueur did in an earlier book (1977), where he affirmed that terrorist groups may emerge in any society at any moment, it seems to me that often it is quite difficult to find a clear connection between how terrorists perceive a regime or a political and cultural situation and how the same situation is seen by those who are supposed to back them.

My second argument refers to the contagion effect of violence. It is of special relevance in as far as the relationship between left-wing terrorists on both sides of the Atlantic is concerned. It is well known that radical Marxists from Germany, Italy and France looked full of envy and admiration at the revolutionary experiments that took place in Cuba, Bolivia and Uruguay. The mere fact that most social-revolutionary terrorist groups arose at the same time, in the late 1960s and early 1970s, is a strong hint that imitation played a major role. If terrorism spreads like an epidemic across countries and continents, evidently it is of limited use trying to find out which are its structural causes. Even if these causes are missing, terrorism can develop as a consequence of its import from abroad.

Finally I would like to express my general doubts about the heuristic value of theories or conceptual models which try to explain terrorism by 'push factor' or 'driving forces' which make people act violently. Maybe there are forms of violence for which this model is appropriate, especially when a greater mass of people becomes excited, infuriated and finally vents its rage violently (urban riots, rebellious peasant movements). But it can by no means be generalized. It is easy to find situations in which violence is employed without anger or emotional excitement, just as a means to reach determined goals. Especially in the case of terrorist violence (violence committed by highly organized groups according to an elaborated design), it is advisable to abandon a model of 'push factors', replacing it by a 'strategic' model which emphasizes the rational element in the decisions taken by the relevant actors. That does not mean that structural factors become completely irrelevant in this context, but they are only to be taken into account in so far as they exercise, directly or indirectly, some influence on the mind-set and the perceptions of those who act violently: the terrorists.

The terrorists and their motives

From the preceding reflections the conclusion can be drawn that any serious effort to explore the determinants of terrorism should take as its starting point the terrorists themselves. Without enlarging our knowledge of their social background, their socialization and formation, their aims and ideas, there is little hope of understanding and combating terrorism.

As far as social-revolutionary terrorism is concerned, the empirical findings deliver a rather clear picture. In Latin America and in Europe most terrorists stem from the academic middle classes, partly also from a bourgeois milieu (significant exceptions are the Columbian FARC, partly also the *Brigate Rosse* from Italy). They were students, teachers, priests, journalists, higher clerks, etc. before joining the armed groups. This means they belong to the so-called intelligentsia. A relatively high percentage of the terrorists are women: most of them are still young, those who are more than 30 years old are an exception.

The middle-class origins of most members of social-revolutionary terrorist groups has two immediate consequences. First, it is evident that their personal situation has nothing to do with the needs and interests of the classes for which they are fighting. Coming from well-to-do social backgrounds and having grown up in comfortable conditions they pretend to defend the social interests of groups which they scarcely know and with whom they have not had much contact. In the second place, it is noteworthy that this kind of terrorism generally supposes a rupture with the generation of the parents. This seems to be quite a logical step if we take into account that in most of these cases the solidarity of the young man or woman with his/her own social class is substituted by its identification with another social class, that of the marginalized and the poor. The question raised in this context is why a young man or woman decides to change sides, which motives induce them to dedicate their energies to the radical transformation of a society in favour of the underprivileged and the poor.

Generally, these motives have not much to do with the real living conditions and aspirations of those whom the left-wing radicals pretend to defend and to liberate. On the contrary they are intimately related to the revolutionaries' own situation. My thesis is, in other words, that 'subjective' factors (rooted in frustrated career expectations, status problems, generation conflict, affinity to global ideological currents) offer a far better key to the violent behaviour of these groups and their members than do 'objective' factors (social misery and injustice, corrupt governments and so on).

Among the factors and processes which shape the mentality and contribute to the critical attitude of the left-wing radicals, the following are the most noteworthy:

- Processes of social change, which undermine stable patterns of behaviour, creating a general social climate of insecurity and rising expectations (e.g. in North Italy, Germany, Argentina). The consequences are frequently feelings of frustration among those whose exaggerated hopes of climbing up the social ladder were not fulfilled, as well as among the so-called losers in the modernization process.

- The sudden growth of those segments of the youth population who go to universities or colleges (e.g. in Argentina, Uruguay, Peru, Italy). This growth means that many young people coming from a non-academic social background begin to aspire to well paid professional positions. In some cases it means that they feel deceived because they are unable to comply with the high standards of academic institutions or because the academic labour market does not expand as quickly as the universities do. These young people no longer accept the social control of their parents which could have prevented them from joining a radical group.

- A generation conflict combined with some structural problem of the society in question (e.g. the national identity crisis in Germany and Italy, the legitimacy crisis in Argentina and Uruguay). Conflicts between older and younger generations are very common phenomena, but they only gain political relevance if they are additionally nourished by some hidden structural problems. It can be assumed that students and the youth in general are particularly sensitive to such latent tensions and contradictions and tend to transform them into open reproach against the older generation.

- Protest movements and a general mood of discontent and rebelliousness count also among the factors which often precede the founding of terrorist cells. Protest demonstrations may serve as a training ground for those determined to engage in a tighter confrontation with state authority. They open the possibility of attacking the security forces with unconventional means and methods, create new bonds of anti-state solidarity and have, last but not least, a strongly contagious effect on similar groups in other countries.

- The importance of some ideological foundation of political radicalism, which satisfies the intellectual ambitions of young academics, should not be underestimated either. The renaissance of Marxism in the 1960s, including as its Latin

American version the so-called 'Focus Theory' and the Maoism of the 'Shining Path' in Peru, fulfilled perfectly this function. Whether we can expect a revival of Marxism in the near future remains a question difficult to answer.

- Finally, left-wing terrorism depends on the existence of a self-appointed critical elite which feels responsible for shaping the future of society and curing its actual weaknesses, even in a radical way. If being a student in a country means nothing more than an investment into a higher income in the future, if young people exclusively pursue goals of personal satisfaction and happiness, the possibility of the emergence of a radical left-wing movement with messianic traits is significantly reduced.

The above-mentioned factors and processes help us to understand why in certain countries at a certain moment there was a general inclination of the academic youth and of intellectuals to join radical left-wing organizations. But they cannot, of course, explain why some of these young people (in most countries only a few) began to throw bombs and to kill innocent people while others did not. Nor do they answer the question why in some cases the violent campaign took the form of a guerrilla war, while in others it manifested itself in a series of terrorist attacks.

The strategic alternative: guerrilla warfare or terrorism

As already shown, terrorism cannot be isolated from other forms of violent behaviour, such as, for example, irregular protest movements. It must be analysed in the context of a general disposition of certain groups of young people to make use of violence in order to reach their goals, a disposition that can be expressed in various forms. What I'm especially interested in is the relationship between guerrilla warfare and terrorism. My thesis is that terrorism is often chosen as a strategic alternative to a guerrilla war because the latter is bound to a series of preconditions which do not exist.

Two of these conditions are especially important. First there must be a hinterland for this kind of warfare, consisting of hills and mountains, deep valleys or forests with difficult access where the rebels can hide themselves and to which they can retire when they feel threatened. A country consisting only of plains (such as Uruguay) provides little opportunity for the development of a guerrilla movement. The same holds true if a country, which originally offered good conditions for a guerrilla campaign, has developed an excellent communication network (road and rail) which permits the government to send its troops quickly to any zone threatened by rebellion. The second condition is a peasant population (rural workers, sharecroppers, squatters), sympathetic to the guerrilla fighters, providing them with information, with food and shelter and helping them as messengers. A completely uninhabited zone, even if geographically well suited for the guerrilla tactics of 'hit and run', is in this sense no more appropriate for this kind of warfare than the overcrowded suburbs of a big town. The reason is that in big towns any attack against representatives of the state inevitably also risks hitting innocents, thus alienating the broad population from the guerrillas who need its support as a fish needs water.

In contrast to guerrilla warfare, terrorism is a relatively 'economical' form of violence. It needs neither a special territory nor a broad base of sympathetic people and supporters. The main resources on which a terrorist campaign is based, arms or explosives and publicity, can be 'borrowed' from the enemy. The only thing absolutely crucial is a little group of highly motivated persons who are willing to risk their own lives and the lives of others.

Looking at these conditions it becomes clear why, during the last decades, Europe (with the exception of the Balkan region) did not have a single guerrilla campaign, but did see some waves of terrorist attacks, while in Latin America several guerrilla wars have taken place. Europe simply does not offer the necessary geographic and social conditions for a guerrilla campaign. In Europe the infrastructure for traffic and communication is so highly developed that no dissident group would have a serious chance in trying to infiltrate a remote region of a country and defend it against official security forces. Additionally, in Europe, the rural population constitutes only a small part of the whole population in most countries. Moreover, the living standard of European farmers is not comparable to that of the *campesinos* in Latin America; there would be little chance for rebellious movements to win them over.

There are two more arguments to support our assumption that the 'opportunity structure' is decisive for whether a guerrilla war is initiated or a campaign of terrorist attacks is planned. First, it seems symptomatic that terrorists rarely use the term 'terrorism' for what they do. They prefer to call themselves freedom fighters, guerilleros or revolutionaries. They see their violent attacks as a 'war of attrition' against an overmighty adversary. This means that generally they do not consider themselves as little conspiratorial groups but as the avant-garde of a vast movement.

The second argument reaches a conclusion of a similar kind. Several violent rebellious groups in Latin America began their 'careers' as guerrilla movements in the hinterland (e.g. in Bolivia, Argentina, Peru, Venezuela). Inspired by the success of the group around Castro in Cuba, they believed that similar favourable conditions were given in their own countries or could at least been created. When defeated by the military they went to the big cities to practise what, euphemistically, they called urban guerrilla war while in reality it was terrorism.

Success and failure

The factors that produce terrorism are not identical with those responsible for the persistence of the phenomenon over a longer span of time. In the beginning, the crucial factor is individual actors, their motives, goals, ambitions and frustrations. Once a terrorist group has been founded, it develops a life of its own: it stabilizes its structures, defends its interests, legitimizes its goals, organizes its activities and is not easy to destroy. The 'career' of social-revolutionary terrorist organisations offers good examples of this tendency of violent groups, once established, to persist in time and to defend successfully their existence.

Of course there were also some quite short-lived groups (e.g. *Action directe* in France, the group around Hugo Blanco in Peru in the 1960s, or the revolutionary focus founded and headed at the same time in Bolivia by Ernesto 'Che' Guevara). Generally, they belonged to the first, relatively inexperienced wave of terrorist or guerrilla fighters. Their quick annihilation by the security forces was mostly due to bad leadership, a false evaluation of the social situation and lack of solid preparation.

This changed in the 1970s and 1980s when a second wave of guerrilla and terrorist movements arose who had learned from the errors of their predecessors. They were better trained, had a more competent leadership, and had worked clandestinely for longer on the population before committing their first violent act. On the whole they represented a far more serious challenge to the political elite and the security forces of their respective countries than did the first generation of rebels. Even the Baader-Meinhof group in Germany, which never had more than a few hundred committed supporters at its disposal, was able to survive for more than two decades, committing from time to time highly sophisticated and dangerous attacks on leading personalities of the political, economic and administrative elite, before it disbanded voluntarily.

o There is no common denominator under which the 'career' of the two dozen of the more important social-revolutionary terrorist groups may be subsumed. Some of them were wiped out, others abandoned their revolutionary project voluntarily, thus disappearing definitely from the political landscape. This happened with the German RAF, the *Brigate Rosse* in Italy, the *Tupamaros* in Uruguay, the ERP and the *Montoneros* in Argentina, amongst others. On the other hand, there are also a few cases in which the rebels triumphed over the government and seized power. This was the case with Castro in Cuba, whose successful campaign against the Batista regime at the end of the 1950s initiated a series of similar attempts in Latin America to build up a guerrilla focus and to undermine formal authority structures. Twenty years later a similar situation occurred in Nicaragua. The *Sandinistas*, who had fought tenaciously without success against the Somoza regime over a long period, saw themselves suddenly backed by a large part of the population, especially the middle classes, so that they could overwhelm the government.

Many, maybe even most, of the terrorist and guerrilla groups, fall between these two poles: Even if they were able to attract the hopes and sympathies of a considerable part of the population and represented a serious challenge to the government at a certain moment, they could not transform their momentous political and military strength in an enduring power position. In the long run they were more a factor of annoyance and of periodic irritation for the forces of the establishment than a constant threat. After having been at the centre of public attention for some time, especially the media, which reported almost daily about them, they fell back into insignificance, reminding society by minor attacks from time to time that they had not yet abandoned their revolutionary plans.

An organization that does not fit into this general scheme is the Columbian FARC (to a lesser extent also the ELN of the same country). It differs from almost all the other groups in that its leaders were and are not intellectuals but farmers or ex-farmers. The FARC never got close to the point (and maybe its leaders even did not aspire to) where it could have defeated the security forces and seized power. However, for more than three decades, it continuously expanded its zones of influence and built up state-like structures and institutions within these zones. Actually, a line of informal partition can be drawn across Columbia between the official government on the one hand and the rebel forces on the other.

Prospects for the future

The predominant forms of terrorist violence are actually ethnic-nationalist terrorism and religious terrorism. Social-revolutionary terrorism seems to be of no global relevance anymore, its actual field of operation is limited to some Latin American countries such as Colombia, Peru and Mexico. Will this situation last or will we be confronted with a revival of left-wing violence in the near or far future?

Some indicators underscore this last mentioned possibility. One of the consequences of the worldwide-accepted doctrine of neo-liberalism has been that the gap between rich and poor classes on the national level, but also between prosperous and poor nations on a worldwide scale, has been continuously widening. Among the macro-regions, Latin America has the lowest scores for social justice and the highest scores as far as social inequality is concerned. Generally, a new kind of ruthlessness in social questions can be observed, a humiliating and degrading attitude towards those who have no qualified work and stay poor. Is this reopening of the social divide not an excellent breeding ground for left-wing radicalism?

A renaissance of militant anarchism or Marxism would not be surprising at all, but there are three arguments that make it improbable that this will happen in the near future. The first is that not enough time has passed since social-revolutionary movements were defeated and Marxist experiments thoroughly failed. The breakdown of long lasting socialist regimes has made it evident that this kind of system cannot compete with capitalism. Moreover, it has not yet been forgotten that most left-wing movements produced little benefit and caused much trouble, leading to real tragedies in some cases. For example in Argentina and in Uruguay, guerrilla and terrorist groups created a political chaos and legitimized the seizure of power by brutal military leaders who indiscriminately persecuted sympathizers of the terrorists and innocents. In Germany and in Italy, where the terrorist menace could be mastered by democratic means, there is a widespread conviction that this was a bloody utopian experiment, which should not be repeated. In the few cases in which Marxist rebels succeeded in taking over the government (Cuba and Nicaragua), their rule has a disillusioning if not deterring effect on most actual and potential followers.

The second reason why a reappearance of strong and militant social-revolutionary movements seems unlikely for the moment lies in the change of political and economic as well as ideological parameters over the last thirty years. While up to the 1970s the state was indisputably the most important actor on the international and the national stage, it later lost much of its competences and power. Neo-liberalism has induced a shift of responsibility from the collective level to the individual, transnational organizations and international treaties have been restricting more and more what originally were the sovereign rights of the state. These global changes had two main consequences for left-wing groups with revolutionary plans. These groups, as do all terrorist groups, need an enemy, an enemy with a clear profile and much power, who can be accused of being responsible for all the evils that they pretend to eliminate. If the state, for evident reasons, is nothing more than an agency of an international network of superior forces, whom shall they attack? On the other hand, the development of society by no means encourages the development of militant left-wing movements. Most individuals, being convinced that they have to take care of themselves and that they are the masters of their own happiness, see no reason to encourage or join an association which promises a radical power shift on the collective level. The transfer of hopes and energies from the public to the private sphere has weakened collective movements of all kinds. Even in Latin America, the classic continent of social discontent and unrest, protest demonstrations and movements have been replaced by individual deviant behaviour, criminality (especially theft and armed robbery) and anomie.

There is still a third argument which can be adduced against the imminent revival of social-revolutionary terrorism, at least in Europe and Latin America. As I explained in the second section, this kind of violence was especially exercised by academically trained people, by students and intellectuals who considered themselves to be the avant-garde and future elite of their countries. The profile of the average student has changed enormously in the last thirty years. The expansion of the universities and colleges in all Western countries and the inflationary growth of the student population have transformed academic youth into a group like any other which primarily defends its own corporate interests but no more feels responsible for the well-being of the community or the nation. In Latin America especially students and graduates from the universities have been submitted to a process of constant proletarianization. Many of them emigrated to richer countries to be able to work in their academic profession. Those who stayed in their countries were often forced to make their living in subordinate manual occupations. Being in an extremely vulnerable economic position, neither individually nor collectively they do possess the necessary strength to initiate a new protest cycle.

Bibliography

Allemann, F.R. (1974) *Macht und Ohnmacht der Guerrilla*. München: Piper.

Debray, R. *et al.* (1970) *Guerrilla in Lateinamerika: 11 Aufsätze zur Focustheorie*. Berlin: Wagenbach.

Lamberg, R.F. (1972) *Die Guerrilla in Lateinamerika, Theorie und Praxis eines Modells*. München.

Laqueur, W. (1977) *Terrorismus*. Kronberg: Athenäum.

Moyano, M.J. (1995) *Argentina's Lost Patrol: Armed Struggle 1969-1979*. New Haven/London: Yale University Press.

Münkler, H. (1980) 'Guerrillakrieg und Terrorismus', *Neue politische Literatur*, **25**(3), 299–326.

Münkler, H. (ed.) (1990) *Der Partisan. Theorie, Strategie, Gestalt*. Opladen: Westdeutscher Verlag.

Schmid, A.P. (1983) *Political Terrorism: A Research Guide to Concepts, Theories, Databases and Literature*. Amsterdam: North-Holland.

Waldmann, P. (1978) 'Ursachen der Guerrilla in Argentinien', *Jahrbuch für Geschichte von Staat, Wirtschaft und Gesellschaft in Lateinamerika*, **15**, 295–348.

Waldmann, P. (1983) 'Alte und neue Guerrilla in Lateinamerika – Folgen und Folgerungen aus der Revolution in Nicaragua', *Verfassung und Recht in Übersee*, **16**(4), 407–33.

Waldmann, P. (1986) 'Comparative Remarks on Guerrilla Movements in Argentina, Guatemala, Nicaragua und Uruguay', in Merkl, P. (ed.) *Political Violence and Terror: Motifs and Motivations*. Berkeley: University of California Press.

Waldmann, P. (1991) *Terrorismo y Guerrilla: un analisis comparativo de la violencia organizada en Europa y America Latina*, IRELA, Documento de Trabajo No. 32, Madrid.

Waldmann, P. (1992) 'Ethnic and Socio-revolutionary Terrorism: A Comparison of Structures', in Porta, D.D. (ed.) *Social Movements and Violence: Participation in Underground Organizations*, International Social Movement Research, Vol.4, pp. 237–57.

Waldmann, P. (1997) 'Cotidianización de la violencia: el ejemplo de Colombia', *en Analisis politico*, **32**, Sept./Dic., 34–50.

Waldmann, P. (2000) 'Gesellschaftliche Ungleichheit und gesellschaftliche Machtverhältnisse', in Hirsch-Weber, W. and Nolte, D. (eds) *Lateinamerika: ökonomische, soziale und politische Probleme im Zeitalter der Globalisierung*. Hamburg: Beiträge zur Lateinamerika-Forschung, Band 6, pp. 51–61.

Wunschik, T. (1997) *Baader-Meinhofs Kinder. Die zweite Generation der RAF*. Opladen: Westdeutscher Verlag.

13 The use of terrorism by organized crime

An Italian case study

Alison Jamieson

Introduction

In the decade that followed the fall of the Berlin Wall and the collapse of the Soviet Union, it was widely expected that the terrorist threat would diminish, together with the polarization of political ideologies that had inspired and at times directly funded various forms of terrorism. States that had supported terrorism for ideological motives during the cold war were less interested in the destabilization and political subversion of their rivals. The focus for law enforcement and intelligence services and sometimes even the armed forces in many countries was redirected to the operations of transnational organized crime and its primary source of profit, the illicit drugs trade. This new 'evil empire' was seen as an international security threat with the potential to destabilize governments and distort the mechanisms of the global economy. Profits were indeed considerable, especially in relation to the economies of the developing countries where much plant-based drug cultivation traditionally takes place, although they largely bypassed peasant farmers in favour of exporters and distributors to and in the industrialized consumer countries.

The high earnings to be made from the illicit trafficking of an increasingly broad range of goods and services, formerly associated with organized crime, inevitably attracted the interest of those terrorist groups which, deprived of state proxies and subsidies, were determined to fight on and required a new source of funds to do so. Some, like the *Sendero Luminoso* (Shining Light) in Peru, had been extorting 'revolutionary taxes' from coca growers and drug traffickers for years. But for several countries in Asia, Africa and the former East bloc (former pawns on the cold war chessboard) goods such as drugs, arms, illegal migrants and diamonds became a means of financial support for insurrection. 'Fighters turned felons' became a fast-growing criminal category, as was evident in Angola and Kosovo. In consequence, the 'ideological purity' of terrorism and the 'gangster capitalism' of organized crime began to overlap. Following 11 September 2001, the presence of al-Qaeda training camps and bases in Afghanistan, the source country for some 70 per cent of the world's illicit heroin supplies, blurred the distinction further. In fact, although the Taliban had imposed taxes on opium producers and exporters until they banned cultivation in 2001, there is scant evidence to link the wealth of Osama bin Laden and al-Qaeda to the Afghan drugs trade. Nonetheless the 'organized crime–terror nexus', a frequently coined epithet with sporadic but not infallible applicability, has crept into general usage by the international community.

Organized crime and terrorism should always be viewed as quite distinct phenomena in terms of motivation, operational tactics and ultimate objectives. It is important to distinguish between (a) the self-financing of terrorist groups by typical 'organized crime-type' activities, as described above, (b) pragmatic collaboration between terrorist and organized crime groups for mutually beneficial ends and (c) the use of terrorism by organized crime groups for political purposes. In the case of (b), one would need to understand both criminal paradigms in order to interpret the reasons for and expectations of any collaboration, and to estimate its likely durability and robustness.

Terrorism has no universally accepted definition, but according to Title 22 of the United States Code, Section 2656f(d), it can be described as

> premeditated, politically-motivated violence perpetrated against non-combatant targets by subnational groups or clandestine agents, usually intended to influence an audience.

The new United Nations Convention against Transnational Organized Crime, which entered into force in September 2003, defines an organized criminal group as

> a structured group of three or more persons, existing for a period of time and acting in concert with the aim of committing one or more serious crimes or offences [...] in order to obtain, directly or indirectly, a financial or other material benefit.

These definitions need some fleshing out.

With a few exceptions,[1] (some forms of terrorism have aimed at preserving the status quo), the terrorist is a revolutionary, with clear political objectives involving the overthrow of a government, and a set of articulated strategies to achieve them. Organized crime actors are inherently conservative: they tend to resist political upheaval and seek to establish conditions of order and stability that are more conducive to their ultimate goals of financial accumulation. Unlike terrorists, who project an 'ideal state' for which they are prepared to sacrifice their lives, organized crime sees no virtue in sacrifice, has no comparable sense of 'victory' or 'defeat', but operates according to a set of short- and medium-term goals to be realized with maximum profit and minimum risk.

In general, the organized criminal power system is not anti-state, but a parallel organizational model with its own legal and ethical rules, hierarchy of authority and military force. Rather than see the formal state disappear, organized crime seeks to maintain equilibrium between the public or institutional state and the privatized interests of the mafia state. Mafia-type organized crime groups need interlocutors (administrators, local and national politicians and other persons of influence) who can ensure a political climate favourable to their activities, and who are in a position to disburse economic resources and contracts from the public purse. In exchange, such organized crime groups may sometimes mobilize large quotas of votes on behalf of electoral candidates. Outside the political sphere, legitimate enterprises can benefit from mafia 'protection' while individuals, in public administration, the professions, police, judiciary or the private sector, may be corrupted by financial or other gifts, and threatened with the consequences of non-compliance with agreements made. Thus, unlike terrorists, whose *raison d'être* is direct confrontation with the state against which they practise violence, the survival of an organized crime group depends upon operating within the state, on the penetration by criminal actors of the legitimate political, economic and social spheres.

The degree to which organized crime succeeds in infiltrating state institutions will vary, and evolves over time, as Peter Lupsha (1996) has suggested. Organized crime often starts in a 'predatory' form, where criminal violence is most frequently used to gain and maintain dominance over territory and to create a monopoly of illicit force. Criminal gangs then utilize a 'window of opportunity' such as occurred in the USA with alcohol prohibition, to pass to a 'parasitic' stage where they develop a 'corruptive interaction with legitimate power sectors'. The 'symbiotic' stage is reached, according to Lupsha, when the host, the legitimate state, becomes dependent upon the parasite to sustain itself, that is, upon the monopolies and networks of organized crime. At this point the public interest is no longer represented because the typical tools of democratic control such as law, cannot be enforced.

For the reasons described above, great caution should be exercised in postulating any kind of stable alliance between organized crime and terrorism. Pragmatic, ad hoc agreements between criminal networks may exist on a temporary basis, for example to procure drugs or weapons, but the fundamental incompatibility of long-term objectives and means to achieve them suggests that the likelihood of a stable collaboration between the two types of violent organization will be low. However this has not prevented a form of 'learning curve' between them, and several examples exist where organized crime has adopted the terrorist strategy of violence against symbolic targets in order to influence political choices.

This chapter analyses the circumstances in which organized crime breaks out of the paradigm 'state within a state' to become 'anti-state', focusing particular attention on the use of terrorism by the Sicilian Mafia, *Cosa Nostra*, in the period 1992–3. It concludes by comparing the core characteristics of the Mafia with those of the Leftist terrorist group the *Brigate Rosse* (the Red Brigades).

Origins of *Cosa Nostra*

One cannot understand *Cosa Nostra* without knowing something of Sicily's history, which is one of invasion and occupation: Greek invaders in the eighth century BC were followed by Arabs, Normans, Germans, French and Spanish (with a brief interlude under the British) until unification in 1860. Sicilians learned to accommodate the occupier, showing superficial respect, at the same time remaining proud and contemptuous of their rulers. The Fascist period was experienced in much the same way.

The Mafia emerged in the mid-nineteenth century, not, as is commonly believed, the product of economic deprivation, but as the result of distorted state development; specifically as a result of the inability by central authorities to exercise a legitimate monopoly of the use of force over the periphery of the territories they ruled. Before and after Italian unification, absentee landlords of the large agricultural estates in Sicily needed estate factors and guards to supervise the work of peasant farmers and keep them in order, to combat banditry and collect taxes. The first mafiosi took on these functions and established themselves as surrogate authorities and as instruments of social control. This function was suspended during Fascism but resumed after the Allied invasion of Sicily, when Mafia members (the only civilians allowed to carry arms) were officially installed as mayors and law keepers all over Western Sicily as a reward for assistance given during the landings. The re-conferral of the right to use force against fellow citizens by and on behalf of the (acting) state authorities was an important factor in *Cosa Nostra*'s subsequent expansion.

Cosa Nostra has an 'ideology', understood as a socio-political programme or philosophy, which is shaped around the primary aims of profit and power, and is fully adapted to the modern world. But underneath the sophisticated exterior is an organizing framework that draws on profound elements of the Sicilian character: an inflexible values system based on honour, courage, obedience and silence. The exaggerated form in which these virtues are exalted may appear anachronistic, but it ensures the maintenance of discipline and legitimates the exercise of violence – such that the betrayal of an agreement, honour slighted, disregard for an order or for the rules of the organization provide justification for reprisal. The word *omertà* that translates as 'criminal silence' literally means 'the ability to be a man' and is considered a virtue by *Cosa Nostra* members.

Organized crime and terrorism

An analysis of the use of terrorism by organized crime would be incomplete without a brief mention of Colombia, for the recourse by the Medellin cartel to overt terrorist tactics is the best-known example of the practice. Attempts by courageous individuals within law enforcement, the judiciary and the political classes in Colombia to tighten or enforce laws against drug production and trafficking led to a series of targeted assassinations in the mid-1980s, which broadened at the end of the decade into a full-scale campaign of political terrorism. The focus for the campaign was Colombia's 1979 extradition treaty with the USA, under which drug traffickers could be sent to the USA for trial and subsequent imprisonment. In 1986 a Leftist guerrilla group backed by Medellin attacked the Palace of Justice in Bogotá, where the Supreme Court was evaluating the validity of the extradition treaty, killing around 100 people, including 11 judges. In 1989 the Liberal party presidential nominee, Luis Carlos Galan, a supporter of extradition, was assassinated for his electoral promises to apply the treaty and crack down on drug trafficking. The cartel responded by declaring 'absolute and total war' against the government between 1989 and 1993, in the course of which some 1,500 Colombians were killed. In this period terrorism effectively took over from organized crime as the organization attempted to murder and bomb its way to achieve political goals. In 1990 alone, 200 police officers were assassinated after Medellin leader Pablo Escobar offered a $4,000 reward for every one killed. On the orders of the *Extraditables* of Medellin, terrorist bombings and kidnappings of members of the Colombian elite became regular occurrences; in 1989 a civil airliner was blown up in midair with the loss of 110 lives. When the Supreme Court declared the 1979 treaty to be invalid, President Virgilio Barco responded by permitting extradition through administrative means. By March 1990 fifteen traffickers had been extradited to the USA, and a set of rigorous legal and law enforcement measures were in place. But the daily levels of daily violence had become intolerable for Colombian public opinion. The succeeding Gaviria and Samper governments exploited the rivalry between Medellin and its rival syndicate in Cali to capture or assassinate the Medellin leaders, and made legislative and judicial concessions in the form of lenient surrender terms and plea-bargaining legislation from which Cali members would benefit. The extradition of Colombian nationals was outlawed under the new 1991 constitution. By the mid-1990s the two main cartels were dismantled, but at great social and political cost.

The Sicilian Mafia has intervened in the Italian political process on many occasions but has never used terrorist tactics to quite such devastating effects as the Medellin cartel. However there are some similarities in the motivation for the recourse to terrorism. As in Colombia, profits from the drugs trade (in this case, heroin) enriched *Cosa Nostra* during the mid- and late-1970s. Massive capital accumulation made the Mafia bosses more arrogant with their political interlocutors and fearful of losing their dominant position in the marketplace. In the period 1979–82 it murdered two judges, three politicians, two police officers and the prefect (the highest national government representative on the island). Each had made a key discovery about Mafia operations and, possessing the courage to act on this knowledge, posed a direct threat to Mafia interests. In several cases the individuals worked alone or did not have the support of colleagues: Gaetano Costa, chief prosecutor in Palermo, had issued an arrest warrant for 55 Palermo heroin traffickers which his colleagues refused to sign; the Sicilian Communist party deputy, Pio La Torre, had drafted Italy's first incisive legislation on the investigation and seizure of assets of Mafia suspects; General Alberto Dalla Chiesa had perceived a new dynamic in the relations between the Catania and Palermo Mafia families and had requested sweeping new powers against *Cosa Nostra* such as he had successfully applied against left-wing terrorism. The murders were an attempt to unblock a situation when other means of intervention had proved either inefficient or impractical.

The tactic of targeted assassination practised by *Cosa Nostra* changed to pure terrorism just before Christmas 1984, when a bomb planted on a Naples–Milan overnight express train exploded as it travelled through a long tunnel near Florence, killing 16 and wounding 200. It was proved that the action had been ordered by *Cosa Nostra* and materially carried out by a Neapolitan group of Mafia hirelings with the aim of distracting the attention of police and judiciary from Sicily, where the testimonies of the first repentants (or *pentiti*) were leading to hundreds of arrests and the severe disruption of Mafia activities. It was 'disguised' as a right-wing bombing, such as had occurred at Bologna station in 1980, to throw investigators off the trail. At the subsequent trial the Florence court concluded,

> With the pre-Christmas massacre of 1984 the Mafia intended to fulfil a multiplicity of objectives, some of which can be attributed to its need, realized through the indiscriminate diffusion of terror, to weaken the democratic system of this country, to distract society's civil, political and judicial attention by false emergencies and thus to create that situation of uncertainty and disorientation within public authorities and of distrust of them by citizens which are the indispensable premises for the growth and consolidation of [Mafia] power.
>
> (Cipriani 1999)

It was the first instance in which the aggravating factor for terrorist crimes 'with the aim of subversion of the democratic order' had been applied to Mafia actions.

The car bomb campaign of 1993

Between May and July 1993, *Cosa Nostra* carried out five car bomb attacks in the cities of Florence, Milan and Rome. The first target was Maurizio Costanzo, Italy's most popular TV chat-show host, who escaped injury on the evening of 14 May when a parked car exploded as he was being driven away from the Rome theatre where he recorded his show. The second went off at 1 a.m. on 27 May outside a thirteenth-century building in Florence, home of Italy's oldest agricultural institute, and only yards from the Uffizi Gallery, which was damaged in the blast. The other three attacks occurred within minutes of each other around midnight on 27 July, damaging a cultural centre in Milan and two historic churches in central Rome. Altogether ten people died in the five attacks, including two children, and 95 were injured. Car bombs are not an infrequent technique used by *Cosa Nostra* to intimidate or kill, but in almost all other respects these were atypical actions:

- The mainland locations: *Cosa Nostra* was known to operate in Florence, Milan and Rome, but primarily in the financial and commercial sectors. Major acts of violence were almost always perpetrated in Sicily.
- With one exception, there was no deliberate intent to kill. The ten people who died were casual victims of circumstance.
- The choice of targets: only one was a physical person; the other four were buildings of cultural significance.

Precipitating factors

The car bomb attacks of 1993 are directly linked to the change of strategy decided on by *Cosa Nostra* one year before. This in turn must be set in context. The arrest and 'repentance' of Mafia boss Tommaso Buscetta in 1984 had set in motion a wave of arrests culminating in the 'maxi trial' of 1986–7, which put hundreds of Mafia members in prison, many of them with life sentences. The Italian judicial system has three stages, and only recognizes verdicts as definitive after a pronouncement by the Supreme Court, which comes several years after the original trial. From 1987 onwards, *Cosa Nostra* tried to sabotage proceedings by murdering or discrediting witnesses and putting pressure on politicians, lawyers and magistrates, but by the end of 1991 it became evident that these tactics were not succeeding. In January 1992 the Supreme Court ruled that the life sentences of 1987 were safe, rendering them definitive.

Other factors had convinced the Mafia that the post-war political generation had outlived its usefulness. Since 1989, the government presided over by Giulio Andreotti (his seventh) had introduced measures to protect the political and economic spheres against organized crime. With the end of the cold war, the exclusion pact that had kept the Italian Communist party from power was no longer tenable, and the advantages the Mafia had taken from its anti-communist stance had ceased. In February 1992 a series of corruption scandals known as *Tangentopoli* (or 'Bribesville') erupted. Among those incriminated were political figures and businessmen of national repute, some of whom were accused of making lucrative business arrangements with organized crime.

The murders began in March 1992. *Cosa Nostra* eliminated two former political intermediaries, Sicilian representatives of Andreotti's political faction. Ultimately it was Andreotti that the Mafia wished to punish, and it is likely that his non-election as head of state in May that year was due to his close friendship with one of the murdered men, Euro MP Salvo Lima. Andreotti's alleged Mafia connections came under scrutiny from this point onwards. Judges Giovanni Falcone and Paolo Borsellino were blown up in two bomb attacks in May and July in which Falcone's wife and eight bodyguards also died.

In June 1992 the Italian parliament passed a temporary package of emergency laws that was made permanent in August. The army was sent to Sicily to free up the police forces for the pursuit of organized crime. Mafia members who 'repented' were offered protection and reduced sentences, while the prison regime for Mafia bosses was made particularly severe. The legislation proved effective: hundreds of arrests were made and the number of state's witnesses rose from 58 in December 1992 to 388 by May the following year (Jamieson 1999).

The attribution of terrorism – the wider audience

Once investigators had discovered a common matrix behind the five car bomb attacks (confirmed by the method and timing of the actions and by forensic examination), the involvement of *Cosa Nostra* became evident: the source and mix of explosives in the devices was identical, and had been used in other Mafia actions. They were dubbed 'bombs of dialogue' because it became clear that their primary purpose was not to maintain equilibrium or prevent a change in the status quo but the opposite: to destabilize and intimidate the state, to weaken its will to combat organized crime and open up space for mediation with new interlocutors. The terrorist 'message' had several intended recipients:

- Parliament was to be punished for its anti-Mafia efforts.
- Public opinion would be frightened by the attacks and by the state's inability to prevent terrorism. A bomb explosion near the renowned Uffizi Gallery (perhaps the real target) would harm domestic and foreign tourism. In this context (it was later revealed) other actions had been discussed, such as blowing up the Leaning Tower of Pisa and strewing HIV-infected syringes on the beaches of the Adriatic coast.
- The bombings may have been planned to make public opinion more hostile towards southern Italy and to encourage the country's separation into three federations: the gain to the Mafia being that an autonomous South would be more permeable.
- Public opinion would certainly have been shocked by the murder of Costanzo, whose nightly shows attract millions of viewers. He had often criticized the Mafia on his TV shows, sufficient grounds in themselves to decree his murder. But he was also a director of one of three TV channels owned by business magnate Silvio Berlusconi, and some viewed this less as an attack on Costanzo than as a message to Berlusconi himself, who in 1993 was contemplating his entry into politics.
- The two attacks on churches in Rome were originally interpreted as a reprisal against Pope John Paul II, who had inveighed against the Mafia during a visit to Sicily in May 1993. It was later believed that ecclesiastical figures had been asked by *Cosa Nostra* to intervene to alleviate the harsh prison regime, and that the attacks were a response to the Church's non-intervention in this regard.

Theories still under investigation extend responsibility for instigating the car bomb campaign to non-Mafia actors, involving corrupt freemasonry, elements of the security services, and business interests damaged by the corruption scandals. Experts believe that the familiarity with the dynamics of terrorism and of mass-media communication, as well as the capacity to sound out and interpret political reaction were not the product of Mafia minds alone. Some form of 'integrated criminal power structure' was hypothesized, in which the converging interests of diverse sectors were represented.

It transpired that, in the second half of 1992, discussions were opened between *Cosa Nostra* and representatives of the Italian state, principally through the commander of the organized crime unit of the *carabinieri*. The aim on the one hand was to halt the murders and arrest top Mafia boss Totò Riina; on the other, *Cosa Nostra* hoped to have aspects of the anti-Mafia legislation modified. Officially no deals were done, and indeed the laws were not changed; however Riina was arrested in January 1993 in circumstances which remain unclear, and which were still under investigation. If the car bomb campaign had a specific 'trigger', it was probably Riina himself, who could have communicated the order through his lawyer, or by signals made during court appearances.

The reasons for the paradigm shift begin to emerge. *Cosa Nostra* made the transition 'state within a state' to 'anti-state' because the equilibrium that had been maintained throughout the post-war period had been broken. The cold war had provided an alibi for the creation and perpetuation of a power system in which the Mafia was a constituent element. The continuity of the same parties, party leaders and supporting bureaucracies, cemented in power by their anti-communist convictions, had led to a sense of invincibility that permeated ruling elites and Mafia alike. *Cosa Nostra* had resisted change for as long as possible, but when this became inevitable, the organization took pre-emptive action to hasten the end of the old order and to indicate its conditions for supporting the new.

Can comparisons be made with the terrorism of the Red Brigades?

This chapter began by discussing the different goals and modus operandi of terrorism and organized crime. It concludes with a brief indication of three areas where a closer comparison can be made between *Cosa Nostra* and *Brigate Rosse* (hereafter, the Red Brigades): the nature of group identity; the relationship to violence; tolerance and consensus.

Group identity

Group identity and the collective force of the group are essential concepts in analysing *Cosa Nostra* and the Red Brigades. They are what makes the 'whole' greater than the sum of its parts. In *Cosa Nostra* these elements can be summed up as the intimidation and subjugation of others by force or corruption, and the imposition of *omertà*. The Red Brigades also believed in the principle of collective intimidation, in the version, 'strike one to educate a hundred'. The exaggerated emphasis given to certain virtues by *Cosa Nostra* was mentioned earlier as providing a moral code for its actions; the Red Brigades also used self-justifying moralism to sanitize their conduct in their own eyes: brigadists paid themselves the wages of a metal mechanic in Fiat, and never robbed post offices because retired workers went there to draw their pensions and other benefits. One of the Red Brigades' founders has said that his greatest fear was of being arrested during a bank robbery and of being perceived as a common criminal acting for personal gain.[2] In this sense the type of violent action which terrorists engage in (and refrain from) is conditioned by ideological precepts.

Membership in the Red Brigades was a personal choice, but all actions were performed in the name of the proletariat and could only be of value within a group perspective. Membership of the group and the group's presumption to represent a wider constituency provided double protection against personal responsibility and guilt. One of the Red Brigades' ideologues described the importance of belonging to the group with reference to Sartre:

> I wanted to count as little as possible [...] to disappear into the function assigned to me [...] it was fundamental to accept and share everything [...] an effective re-appropriation of totality is only possible through the practice of the revolutionary group in action [...] life can only be called such if it violently breaks

the inertia of the structures of power. [...] Anyone who took part in the execution of a traitor was re-affirming the insuperability of the being-in-a-group as the limitation of his freedom and as his new birth, reaffirmed it in a bloody sacrifice which constituted the explicit recognition of the coercive right of all over each, and the threat of each to al'.

(Fenzi 1987: 63, 249 and 253)

A comparison can be made with the attraction experienced by a young male for the Calabrian mafia, the *'Ndrangheta*:

The mafia mentality is inside the young Calabrian inasmuch as it reproduces matriarchal Calabrian society in the cultural sense of belonging to the group, the friendship which becomes private, rather than public virtue. Because Calabrians have taken their identity from myth and folklore rather than from history, they live inside a cultural vacuum. Tradition without history produces a crisis of identity. The authoritarian image of the Calabrian father is deceptive for this reason. The father figure transmits only dogma and authoritarianism and is incapable of mediating change or patterns of socialization. He organizes reality according to rigid schemes with diametrically opposed extremes, and sees transformation and change as negative and dangerous. [...] Growing up in a region without history or identity produces melancholy, boredom and tension. The boredom of isolation is a typical existential condition of young Calabrians, and is quite separate from solitude. [...] The mafia organization creates a cultural identity behind which the whole existential condition is concealed; the absence of history, the idealization of tradition, authoritarian monism and the matriarchal family are all mirrored in the common identity of organized crime. Belonging to the group is not really such but an affective dependency that takes [an individual] from the family and replaces the maternal roles of care and control. It provides protection and reinforces identity but at the same time creates a dependency and an inability to go beyond. [...] Committing crimes within a criminal group fits with the existential condition because crimes have a purely contingent purpose. All [the individual] asks of the group is to do, and to obey.

(P. Gaeta 1997)[3]

Relationship to violence

The Red Brigades saw participation in violent acts as a cost. It could only be legitimized with reference to historical models of revolution or resistance in which the concept of the purifying bloodbath was axiomatic:

There were a whole series of cultural models which indicated that any major change in history had always passed through conflicts of the most violent type, between those defending the old social order and those wanting to impose the new. If you accept the premise of the inevitability of violence you accept that is a necessary price to pay, even though it has nothing to do with what will come afterwards.

(Faranda 1987)[4]

The cost of participation in acts of violence was reduced by a process of depersonalization, both of attacker and of victim. The attacker became a symbol of proletarian triumph over capitalism, the victim a hated symbol of oppression. A form of revolutionary hero worship evolved around revolutionary role models such as the Russian revolutionaries, Mao and Giap, Che Guevara, Carlos Marighella and the *Tupamaros*. Frantz Fanon's description of the liberating effect of violence was influential, as were the writings of black power activists such as George Jackson. Books by authors as diverse as Kerouac, T.E Lawrence and Robert Louis Stevenson had cult status.[5] The mythologization of violence permitted the simplification and mystification of reality: defeats could be portrayed as partial victories and 'action' justified existence.

Despite not recognizing the state's monopoly of the use of force, *Cosa Nostra* prefers to negotiate with its representatives rather than eliminate them. Violence is only used against institutional figures when essential aims cannot otherwise be achieved, as was seen above. However violence is considered indispensable as a means of enforcing the authority of the leadership over the cadres, or of one faction of the organization over another. Symbolism is present to a strong degree in language and gesture, but there is no ideological distancing from violence per se. *Cosa Nostra*'s relationship to violence is in fact strongly personalized, as are all its relationships in the economic or political sphere: relations with non-Mafia interlocutors are transposed into exchanges of favours which are fluid and dynamic, and capable of mutation over time (Catanzaro 1988).

Relationship with the outside world: tolerance and consensus

Terrorism and organized crime both need consensus in order to survive. *Cosa Nostra* never resorts to proselytism, but its wealth-generating activities and influence over economic and political spheres create a form of internal consensus within its own constituency. However terrorist organizations such as the Red Brigades must convince the hearts and minds of a broad external constituency if they are to be successful. For the first few years, until about 1973–4, the Red Brigades enjoyed a degree of support in Italian factories and universities and within the Milan intelligentsia, some of whom financed their activities. Their decision to break with the mass violence of the extra-parliamentary Left (those who espoused 'militant antifascism' and 'armed propaganda') and opt for targeted violence against symbols of the state, obliged the leadership to become clandestine and to avoid the environments in which the choice of terrorism had matured. Their inflexible application of Marxist-Leninist doctrine in a modern industrialized democracy proved anachronistic, and their increasing isolation made them incapable of interpreting the mood of those they claimed to represent. The indifference or even approval of factory workers to the kidnaps and kneecapping of managers, which they interpreted as consensus, 'meant nothing', according to brigadist Adriana Faranda, 'It didn't mean consensus with anything, all it signified was a non-committal expression of discontent'. In her view, their isolation from society and from former companions on the Left was a major factor in their defeat:

> It was absurd, suddenly there was a feeling almost of enmity [...] we became so far apart that they were seen as counter-revolutionaries. And you weren't just separated from a part of yourself, your own history, but from a whole area of people who like you were outside the system. You had the feeling of squeezing yourself into an ever tighter corner.
>
> (Faranda 1987)[4]

Their misinterpretation of political reality prevented the Red Brigades from exploiting their greatest coup, the 1978 kidnap of former prime minister Aldo Moro, whom they killed after 55 days of holding him hostage. Obsessed by the aim of political recognition through an exchange of prisoners, the brigadists did not understand how to manipulate to their own advantage the exhortations and accusations written by Moro in his 'people's prison', nor did they see that Moro's release would have caused more divisions within Italian political life than did his murder.

In the period 1992–3, *Cosa Nostra* lost consensus by exceeding the limits of violence tacitly accepted by its natural constituency, which as a consequence became afraid to deal with it. The organization became first isolated, then was weakened by effective law enforcement measures. It has re-acquired financial stability and a degree of social inclusion by abandoning the policies of confrontation and by reconstructing a new set of dynamic relationships with the society around it. Its capacity for preserving and adapting its core characteristics in the exploitation of new opportunities has been key to its survival. The state-within-a state coexistence paradigm has been re-established.

The Red Brigades' violence also went beyond the limits that were tolerated, firstly by their intended constituency, their idealized 'proletariat', and then by former companions on the Left, who during the Moro kidnap had called on them to release their prisoner. From 1980, failure and internal dissent fragmented the organization into vindictive factions defined more by their differences from each other than by a common enemy, paving the way for 'repentance' and dissociation from armed struggle. The Red Brigades' defeat was caused by an inability to reflect the concerns of an external constituency whilst at the same time preserving internal unity and ideological integrity. Militants calling themselves Red Brigades continue to carry out violent actions in Italy, including murder, but their 'constituency' barely extends beyond their own number.

Conclusion

The themes of this chapter are relevant to the wider issue of 'root causes of terrorism' in terms of perceptions and acceptability of violence. As this paper has tried to show, violent groups do not exist in a vacuum but require a degree of consensus to persist in time. Our knowledge of the causes of terrorism, and of what leads to its cessation, would be improved if we understood better how violence is perceived, firstly at a personal level by its perpetrators, and secondly, by the constituency on whose behalf violence is being exercised. There are, demonstrably, levels of violence that constituencies deem 'acceptable', when the motivation for violence or its consequences are shared by or benefit the society for whom it is perpetrated. Likewise there are levels deemed 'unacceptable'. Logically, therefore, it ought to be possible to bring some influence to bear on the continuum that runs from active support for violence through approval, tolerance and indifference to the point at which the group on behalf of which it is exercised actively rejects the use of violence in its name and alienates the perpetrators from its midst. Then it might be possible either to prevent terrorism or, if it were already underway, to introduce elements that would isolate violent actors from their intended constituents. An improved understanding of such mechanisms could contribute significantly to a reduction of terrorism in the future.

Notes

1   There are examples of 'reactive' right-wing terrorists who wish to preserve the status quo, such as the French OAS which tried to stop the French withdrawal from colonial rule of Algeria in the early 1960s, or the *Afrikaner Weerstandsbeweging* (AWB) which tried to preserve apartheid in the early 1990s. Some forms of vigilante terrorism may also be seen as attempts to preserve the old order, such as the lynchings and arsons committed by the Ku Klux Klan (see Bjørgo 1995).
2   Alberto Franceschini, founder member of the Red Brigades, in one of several informal conversations in Rome with the author during 1988–9.
3   Judge of juvenile criminal court in Palmi, Calabria. Extract quoted with permission in Jamieson (1999: 156–7).
4   Extract from an interview by the author with Adriana Faranda in Paliano high-security prison, 26 February 1987. Reproduced in full in Annex to Jamieson (1989).
5   Former militant Mario Massardi, in Annex to Jamieson (1989).

All translations from Italian into English are by the author.

Bibliography

Bjørgo, T. (1995) *Terror from the Extreme Right*. London: Frank Cass. Also published as a special issue in *Terrorism and Political Violence*, 7(1), Spring, 1995.
Catanzaro, R. (1988) *Il Delitto come Impresa: Storia sociale della Mafia*. Padua: Liviana Editrice, p.137.
Cipriani, A. (1999) *Il Riciclaggio del Denaro Sporco*. Rome: Casa Editrice Roberto Napoleone, p.97.
Fenzi, E. (1987) *Armi e Bagagli: un Diario delle Brigate Rosse*. Genoa: Costa & Nolan.
Gaeta, P. (1997) Paper given at the seminar *Criminal Organization and Exploitation of Minors* organized by the International Association of Juvenile and Family Court Magistrates, Naples, 4–6 April.

Jamieson, A. (1989) *The Heart Attacked: Terrorism and Conflict in the Italian State*. London/New York: Marion Boyars.

Jamieson, A. (1999) *The Anti-Mafia: Italy's Fight Against Organized Crime*. Basingstoke/New York: Palgrave, p.104.

Lupsha, P.A. (1996) 'Transnational organized crime versus the nation-state', *Transnational Organized Crime*, **2**(1), Spring, 1996, 31–2.

14 Patterns of state failure

The case of Lebanon

Farid el Khazen

States fail for several reasons ranging from the loss of monopolistic control over the means of legitimate coercion to the failure to deliver and regulate services. State failure falls in one or all three categories of state activities: extractive, protective/regulatory, and redistributive (Zartman 1995; Helman and Ratner 1993). There are also different degrees of state failure. First, one extreme degree of state failure is when centralized authority within internationally recognized borders of the state collapse (e.g. Somalia) or where a recognized authority exists but no borders are defined and the 'state' is ruled by another country (e.g. Palestine, Kuwait 1990–1). Second, deficit in the capacity of the state to exercise power (e.g. Cambodia, Sri Lanka, Haiti, Indonesia, Colombia). Third, states kept together by an authoritarian order (e.g. Tibet under Chinese rule, Iraq under the Saddam Hussein regime).

The literature on state failure is diverse, but according to Jean Germain Gros, five types of state failure can be identified: (1) anarchic states having no centralized government (Somalia, Liberia); (2) phantom states with semblance of authority (Zaire); (3) anaemic states where energy is sapped by counter-insurgency groups or deficient modernity (Indonesia); (4) captured states where centralized authority is captured by members of insecure and rival elites (Rwanda); and (5) failed states *in vitro* or aborted states, where failure occurs even prior to the process of state formation (Bosnia) (Gros 1996; see also Morton 2002).

Excluding the war years (1975–90), Lebanon has not witnessed state failure similar to that of African states; it had a weak state and its weakness was most visible when it had to interact with the largely authoritarian Arab state system, particularly in time of regional conflict such as the Arab–Israeli conflict and inter-Arab rivalries. Lebanon presents a case of state failure (or state weakness) with consequences that differ from those that occurred in countries such as Somalia, Haiti or Liberia on the scale of marginal states in their respective regional order, or in countries such as Kuwait in 1990–1 or Afghanistan after the al-Qaeda attacks in New York and Washington on 11 September 2001. In the former cases, state failure had no impact on the strategic interests of major powers, while in the latter cases, the interests and, above all, the security of major powers, notably the USA, were at stake.

We need to distinguish between three periods of state weakness (or failure) in Lebanon: the pre-war period (1943–75), the war years (1975–90) and the post-war period (1990 to present). Each period witnessed a different kind of state failure and had, therefore, different consequences on Lebanon and its regional order. When it occurred, state failure resulted in a security vacuum filled by several state and non-state actors with conflicting interests.

Pre-war period: 1943–75

Modern states in the Arab Middle East came into existence after the downfall of the Ottoman Empire in the First World War. Except for Egypt, states in the region were formed by colonial rule with or without support by the local elite, or by conquest, as was the case in Saudi Arabia (Fromkin 1984). Formed in 1920, the modern state of Lebanon emerged out of an existing nucleus, the *Mutasarrifiya* (Governorate) of Mount Lebanon, which was a legal and territorial entity recognized by the six major European powers. The two decades that followed the formation of the state were characterized by the struggle to achieve independence from French mandatory rule.

After independence, Lebanon, like other states in the region, embarked on an effort of state consolidation but, unlike its neighbouring Arab countries, it opted for competitive politics, open society and a functioning market economy, while in other countries the military took over and radical transformation dominated state and society. By the late 1950s the increasing gulf between Lebanon and the rest of the Arab state system was becoming a problem and Lebanon gradually parted ways with regional statist politics. The magnitude of change in Lebanon ceased to be commensurate with change in the region. Lebanon's approach to the expansion of state apparatus and, by extension, to state power, diverged from that of other Arab countries, particularly in the Arab East.

The notable development in Arab countries in the post-independence period was the rise of the authoritarian state (Ayubi 1995). It rested on five major pillars: military rule, single-party regimes, family rule, an official ideology of the state (which is generally a variant of Arab nationalism) and a state-dominated economic system. Arab states have had one form or another of authoritarian rule. State power increased and the scope of state activity continued to broaden and had a great impact on societies at all political, social and economic levels.

Lebanon, by contrast, was an exception in the region. As Arab regimes became more exclusive and Arab societies more closed, Lebanon became plural and increasingly open. As Arab regimes drifted toward radicalism, Lebanon drifted toward moderation. As Arab regimes opted for ideological politics, Lebanon opted for pragmatism. As Arab countries were the scene of rapid revolutionary change, Lebanon underwent gradual, non-violent change. And as other Arab states sought to lead the struggle for the liberation of Palestine, Lebanon confined its role to giving political support to the Palestinian cause and was content to stand on the sidelines. In short, as state–society relations in the Arab countries, notably in the Arab East, underwent political and social transformation in one direction, Lebanon's state–society relations moved both in form and substance in the opposite direction (el Khazen 2000: 89–121).

Lebanon's historic dilemma lies in the gap that separates its state and society from state and society in its regional order (the Arab state system) with which Lebanon has had to interact, politically and otherwise. Lebanon's consociational democracy and open society contrasted with authoritarian states and closed societies in its regional order. The gap between Lebanon and its regional order has continued to widen from independence in the mid-1940s until the outbreak of the war in the mid-1970s.

The turning point in the pre-war period was the 1967 Arab–Israeli war which had a devastating impact on Arab states and societies following the defeat of the Egyptian, Syrian and Jordanian armies and Israel's occupation of all Palestinian territory. One of the immediate consequences of the 1967 war was the emergence of a non-state actor, the Palestine Liberation Organization (PLO), under a new leadership and committed to the armed struggle through guerrilla warfare to liberate Palestine. Founded in 1964, the PLO was far more militant, nationalist and populist after the 1967 war than prior to this event (Sayigh 1997).

In a saturated political and territorial space in the age of the nation-state, the emergence of an armed non-state actor like PLO was bound to encounter opposition by the state, irrespective of the nature of the political system and relations between state and society. As the PLO sought to expand and to establish an autonomous military and political base, it was bound to clash with any power or authority (*Sulta*) where it was present, especially in the three 'confrontation states' neighbouring Israel: Jordan, Syria, and Lebanon.

Three options were available to the Lebanese state: the 'Jordan option', that is the use of force against the PLO irrespective of the outcome and the consequences on state and society, as was the case in 1970–1; the 'Syrian option', that is state control over the PLO in the name of Arab nationalist ideology and sponsorship of particular PLO factions loyal to the regime; and the 'Lebanese option', that is accommodation since the use of force was not always within reach in a divided, non-authoritarian Lebanese state. While the option of the use of force was possible in an authoritarian regime like that of Syria and Jordan, it was not possible in Lebanon's non-authoritarian political system and open society. Notwithstanding internal differences in Lebanon, communal and otherwise, the deepest divide in Lebanon on the eve of the war in the mid-1970s was over the PLO armed presence. Accommodation was possible on domestic issues but not on the PLO armed presence.

From 1969 until 1975, two major confrontations took place between the PLO and the Lebanese army. The first confrontation in 1969 led to a seven-month cabinet crisis which crippled the political process. The crisis ended following the signing of an agreement between the PLO and the Lebanese army (The Cairo Agreement) which gave the PLO control over the refugee camps and freedom of military action in the south (el Khazen 2000: 140–75). Another confrontation occurred in 1973, two years after the PLO's ouster from Jordan. The 1973 confrontation, in which Syria and other Arab countries intervened in support of the PLO, was ended with another agreement, negotiated by the Arab League. The 1973 agreement, like in 1969, aimed at regulating PLO armed presence and guerrilla operations across the Lebanese–Israeli borders. Both agreements were violated by the PLO, and conflict-resolution amounted to temporary ceasefires separating one confrontation from the other. This gave the PLO freedom of military action not only in south Lebanon but also in and around Palestinian camps throughout the country.

Short of a comprehensive settlement to the Arab–Israeli conflict, the clash between the Lebanese state and the PLO was inevitable under the circumstances that prevailed in the 1970s. War broke out in 1975, but it could have occurred before or after that date. The PLO's gradual political and military takeover in Lebanon in the first half of the 1970s was clearly a case of state failure since government authorities lost control over parts of Lebanese territory and lost monopoly over the means of legitimate coercion.

Wartime Lebanon: 1975–90

War in Lebanon evolved in several phases, each reflecting the changing power equation between the large number of internal and external actors involved in conflict (Hanf 1997). The war's objectives and targets were in constant mutation as political and military alliances underwent continuous change. Except for the 1982 Israeli invasion of Lebanon, which attracted international involvement, namely, the deployment of the Multinational Forces in 1982–4 and the active role of the USA in brokering the abortive 17 May 1983 Accord, Lebanon's multiple wars remained largely a local and regional affair.

During the first phase of the war (1975–6) state institutions were paralysed, and following the failure of the first attempt to end the war through the Syrian-sponsored February 1976 Constitutional Document, the Lebanese army was factionalized.

The entry of the Syrian army to Lebanon in Spring 1976 and the clash between Syrian forces and the PLO marked another escalation in conflict. In fact, PLO control over Lebanon constituted a direct political and security threat to the Asad regime in Syria. The 1975–6 war ended only when Syrian troops defeated PLO forces in Autumn 1976. By then, state institutions were dominated by Lebanese militia forces, PLO guerrilla organizations and Syrian forces. The Arab Deterrent Force (ADF), formed by the Arab League in Autumn 1976 with the objective of disarming the militias and enforcing the 1969 Cairo Agreement with the PLO, was inactive, and it gradually became a Syrian force as contingents from Arab states withdrew from the ADF in 1977–8.

The second phase of the war (1977–84) was far more complex. By then, the protagonists of all persuasions were fully mobilized and were in fact preparing for another round of fighting. To that we add a newcomer to the conflict: Israel, who, following the 1979 Camp David Accord (the peace treaty between Israel and Egypt) turned attention to Lebanon and, more specifically, to the PLO in Lebanon. It was during that period of the conflict that Lebanon became a base for various terrorist groups, including the Japanese Red Army, the Armenian Secret Army, Abu Nidal faction, Iranian militants affiliated with Khomeini prior to and after the 1979 Islamic revolution in Iran, and other groups. These groups operated closely with PLO organizations, particularly with Fateh, the Popular Front for the Liberation of Palestine (PFLP), and the Democratic Front for the Liberation of Palestine (DFLP).

Since the early 1980s, Iran's Islamic revolution became the breeding ground for a different kind of violence couched in religious slogans to liberate Lebanon from Israeli occupation and, ultimately, to end Israeli occupation of Palestine. The Israeli invasion in 1982 provided additional momentum for a new kind of terrorism motivated by religion. In the 1980s, Lebanon was turned into one of the major bases of operation for both 'secular' and 'religious' terrorist organizations.

Apart from Afghanistan, the major zone of operation for American-backed Islamist groups engaged in warfare to rid Afghanistan of Soviet occupation in the 1980s, Lebanon served as the major base of operation for Shia Islamist militants backed by Iran and Syria. Their task was facilitated by two factors, which could only be found in wartime Lebanon. First, with Lebanese government authorities controlling only a small part of the country, Lebanon's open borders with Syria and Israel facilitated the traffic of people and weapons in and out of the country. Lebanon, in other words, was entirely accessible to any state and non-state actor in the region seeking to engage in warfare in defence of any cause and in pursuit of any objective. Second, targets of great significance, such as the Multinational Forces made up of American, French, British and Italian troops, as well as the Israeli army occupying large parts of the country, were not only accessible, they were also irresistible for Syria, Iran and the Soviet Union, though for different reasons.

Whereas Israel was engaged in war with the PLO, Syria and Lebanese groups, the Multinational Forces were not involved in combat and were in a peace-keeping mission in support of the Lebanese government. But they were nonetheless accessible targets (McDermott and Skjelsbæk 1991). On 23 October 1983, suicide truck bombers attacked American and French forces in Beirut, killing 241 Marines in their sleep and over 50 French servicemen. Earlier, 18 April 1983, the US embassy was blown up by a suicide driver killing over 62 civilians, including senior American officials. In September 1984, the US embassy annex near Beirut was the target of another suicide attack.

Following the withdrawal of the Multinational Forces in February 1984 from Beirut, and the unilateral withdrawal of the Israeli army to its self-proclaimed security zone in the south in 1984–5, West Beirut was the scene of new kinds of terrorist act: political assassinations, the hijacking of a TWA plane in June 1985 and the killing and kidnapping of Westerners of different nationalities, beginning in July 1982 with the kidnapping of David Dodge, the acting president of the American University of Beirut. Hezbollah, with the backing of Syria and Iran, was involved in the abductions of several American, French and British citizens between July 1982 and May 1989 (Ranstorp 1997).

In the second half of the 1980s, Lebanon became the no man's land of the Middle East where no party could be held accountable for deeds by terrorist groups, although it was common knowledge that Syria and Iran were in control in areas of Lebanon where these deeds took place. Acts of violence that Iran and Syria would refrain from doing in Tehran and Damascus were carried out in Beirut. It was the kind of situation that disturbed Western powers but did not affect their strategic interests. Therefore, there was no incentive on the part of these powers to help the Lebanese state regain control in the country, nor would they intervene militarily against terrorist groups only three years after the Multinational Forces had been attacked.

In summary, the Lebanese state did not sponsor terrorism, nor were government officials directly involved in acts of terrorism. It was only after the state lost monopoly over the means of legitimate coercion that the PLO was able to entrench itself in Lebanon and to consolidate ties with various state and non-state actors in the region and elsewhere. The turning point for state failure prior to the outbreak of war was the inconclusive clash between the PLO and the Lebanese army in 1973. This clash marked the last abortive attempt by the Lebanese government to use force against the PLO. From then on, it became clear to all parties, particularly Lebanese government officials, that the state's capabilities to contain the PLO and PLO–Israeli warfare in south Lebanon were insufficient to deal with the loads on the political system, all the more so when Lebanon became the only de facto confrontation state with Israel after the Arab–Israeli war in October 1973. State failure was no longer reversible under the internal and regional circumstances that prevailed in the mid-1970s. At the same time it was also in the interest of several regional parties to invest in Lebanon's chaos.

The war years offer a typical case of a failed state captured by warring factions, Lebanese and non-Lebanese, pursuing objectives through the use of force. In particular phases of the war, total chaos prevailed, especially in the 1980s, when focus in regional conflict shifted to the Iran–Iraq war and away from the Arab–Israeli conflict. At that time Lebanon became the most accessible and cost-free dumping ground for all the unwanted causes in the region. It was also a marginalized conflict to which major powers gave little attention. Furthermore, this was a time when Hezbollah appeared on the war scene as the most effective military arm of Islamic Iran outside its borders. With access to Israel through the south, and with a large Shia community, Lebanon was the only Arab country where Iran could 'export' its Islamic revolution with no political impediment or military constraints.

Post-war period: 1990–present

War ended in 1990 not by peace conference but by an act of war, when the Syrian army and units of the Lebanese army overran units of the Lebanese army loyal to interim premier General Michel Aoun. The closest substitute to a peace conference was a political settlement embodied in the Document of National Understanding, commonly called the Ta'if Agreement, reached by Lebanese deputies who met in the Saudi city of Ta'if in November 1989.

The product of several years of deliberations involving Lebanese and non-Lebanese parties, the Ta'if Agreement has two components: political reforms and sovereignty (Maila 1992). Over a decade after the introduction of constitutional amendments based on the Ta'if Agreement, Ta'if has not been fully implemented and the component of sovereignty having to do with Syrian–Lebanese relations and Syrian military presence in Lebanon has been completely ignored (Mansour 1993). The outcome of this uneven relationship between Lebanon and Syria since the end of the war is that final decisions in domestic policy and, especially foreign policy, are made in Damascus and not in Beirut (Malik 2000).

Post-war Lebanon offers a unique situation of a satellite state in the post-cold war era. The state functions but it performs functions to the benefit of Lebanese and non-Lebanese parties, other than the state itself (el Khazen 2003). The Ta'if Agreement called for the dissolution of all armed groups in the country; all armed groups were dissolved in 1991 except two Lebanese parties (Hezbollah and, to a lesser extent, Amal, both Shia-based) and Palestinian camps. These exceptions were made not because the Lebanese army was not able to enter Palestinian camps or disarm militia forces but because there was no political decision to allow the army to do so. Indeed, the Lebanese army was rebuilt and it has tripled in size (about 50,000) compared with the pre-war Lebanese army, and the state has recovered control over all Lebanese territory, except Palestinian camps in the northern and southern parts of the country.

The Lebanese army was supposed to enter Palestinian camps in 1991 but was prevented from doing so by the Lebanese government, and it was ordered to deploy in southern Lebanon in 1993 with the consent of President Elias Hrawi, Prime Minister Rafiq Hariri, and Parliament Speaker Nabih Berri, but army deployment did not take place because it was opposed by Syria. The reasons for these exceptions are not difficult to discern: both Hezbollah and Palestinian groups help further Syria's objectives in regional and international politics. In the 1990s, south Lebanon was the only war zone in the Arab–Israeli conflict in the era of the Arab–Israeli peace talks in the 1990s, especially following the 1993 Oslo Agreement between Israel and the PLO.

The security vacuum in south Lebanon has been of strategic importance for Syria, for it served as a proxy battlefield at a time when Damascus has kept the Golan Heights calm since the signing of the 1974 Syrian–Israeli military disengagement agreement in the aftermath of the 1973 Arab–Israeli war. While warfare in south Lebanon dates back to late 1960s, the south Lebanon war zone gained additional importance in the 1990s following the launching of the peace talks between Israel and Arab countries. It was also the only war zone in the region accessible to Iran, Syria's strategic ally since the early 1980s and the major supporter of Hezbollah, financially and militarily. Hezbollah, in fact, was the only non-state actor engaged in warfare against the Israeli army and its client militia force, the South Lebanon Army. The intensity and frequency of military confrontations in the south were to the tune of the peace talks between Syria and Israel. All parties engaged in peace talks except Lebanon, even when Syria and Israel were about to reach agreement in 1996 and, subsequently, in March 2000 in the highly publicized meeting between presidents Assad and Clinton in Geneva.

An unusual development occurred in 1996 when Washington was instrumental in facilitating an agreement, known as the April Understanding, between Hezbollah and Israel. Brokered by the USA, France and Syria, the April Understanding was essentially an agreement to manage military confrontations between Hezbollah and Israel rather than a ceasefire between the two sides. Its main objectives were to avoid targeting civilian areas and to form a special committee co-chaired by the USA and France to monitor its implementation. In essence, the April Understanding legitimized warfare and gave it international recognition and, by implication, gave Hezbollah recognition as the de facto partner in the Understanding between Syria on the one hand and the USA and Israel on the other.

War continued until Israel was forced to withdraw from South Lebanon in May 2000 according to the 1978 United Nations Security Council (UNSC) resolutions

425 and 426. Israeli withdrawal, however, did not end conflict. The Lebanese government claimed that part of the Lebanese territory, the Shebaa farms, was still under Israeli occupation and, therefore, Hezbollah would have to resort to warfare to liberate it. For the United Nations, however, Shebaa farms are Syrian territory occupied by Israel in the 1967 war and not Lebanese (Kaufman 2002). Therefore, UNSC resolutions 242 and 338 apply to Shebaa farms and not UNSC 425. The Syrian and Lebanese governments were asked by the United Nations to officially demarcate the borderline between the two countries to prove whether or not Shebaa farms are Lebanese or Syrian, but the two governments have so far failed to do so. In short, for the Lebanese government, Syria and Hezbollah, Shebaa farms have constituted an instrument of pressure on Israel and the USA and were the only substitute to the south Lebanon war following the withdrawal of Israeli troops in 2000.

That instrument of pressure was used by Hezbollah in 2000 when three Israeli soldiers were killed in Shebaa farms (and a retired Israeli army officer was detained in an unknown location) and their bodies were kept in Hezbollah's custody. Freed from the burden of occupation and from being hostage to its occupation, Israel, now ruled by Prime Minister Ariel Sharon and a hardline cabinet, altered its policy of retaliation in Lebanon and targeted Syrian troops twice in Lebanon in 2001–2 and threatened to hit targets in Syria should Hezbollah's attacks continue. The message was not lost on the Syrian leadership and, as a result, Hezbollah's military operations became less frequent since they were no longer cost-free. This situation coincided with the death of Syrian President Hafez Assad in June 2000 and the coming to power of his son, Bashar, and with the collapse of the peace process and the beginning of the second uprising in the West Bank and Gaza, instigated by Sharon's defiant visit to the al-Aqsa Mosque.

September 11 and its aftermath

The event that radically transformed the status quo in south Lebanon and had a direct impact on Syrian and Iranian policies in Lebanon was al-Qaeda's terrorist attacks in New York and Washington on 11 September 2001 (Juergensmeyer 2000; Marty and Appleby 1995). The vacuum in south Lebanon, made possible by the policy of ambiguity designed by Syria, backed by Iran, and implemented by Hezbollah with the support of the Lebanese government, suddenly became a liability for all parties. It also became a security breach in the 'War on terrorism' declared by President George W. Bush. In other words, Syria's and Hezbollah's assumptions, based on the state of affairs that prevailed prior to the 9/11 attacks regarding their margin of manoeuvre in Shebaa farms, were not functional anymore.

The US-imposed rules of the game have changed and all parties had to adjust to that reality and operate accordingly. The state-designed failure by the Lebanese government in the south, which gave Hezbollah a free hand, was no longer a marginal issue that could be ignored. Just like state failure in Taliban-controlled Afghanistan, which provided the territorial base for bin Laden and al-Qaeda, was tolerated by the USA and seemed a manageable problem prior to September 11, what was business as usual in the Hezbollah–Syrian–Iran nexus in Lebanon prior to September 11 was no longer tolerated when the USA became the target of terrorism.

At the centre of the controversy in Lebanon is Hezbollah. Is Hezbollah a terrorist party, as claimed by Washington, or is it a party of the resistance to liberate south Lebanon from occupation, or is it simply a political party engaged in the political process like any other active party in Lebanon? (Sharara 1996; Saad-Gorayeb 2002).

Founded unofficially in the early 1980s and officially in 1985, Hezbollah has had three overlapping faces. First, Hezbollah is a Shia-based Islamist political party engaged in local and national politics. It mobilizes popular support and engages in clientelist politics and has taken part in the three parliamentary elections held since the end of the war. It is represented in the last elected parliament in 2000 by nine deputies (out of a total of 128) and is active in the educational and social domain within the Shia community.

Hezbollah has focused on ending Israeli occupation in south Lebanon and Palestine, but has advocated few domestic policies. Its participation in parliamentary and municipal elections was an act of moderation in form but not in substance since it continues to subscribe to its 1985 founding charter calling for the establishment of an Islamic state in Lebanon. Hezbollah is the only Islamist party in the Muslim world that fully espouses Iran's political and ideological agenda. Hezbollah's Iranian-funded satellite television station *al-Manar*, the only Arabic-language satellite station run by an Islamist party, has transformed Hezbollah into a global party with a worldwide audience.

The second face of Hezbollah is that of the party of the armed resistance, credited for ending Israeli occupation in south Lebanon. Since the Israeli withdrawal, Hezbollah has continued to acquire weapons and has maintained and even enlarged its military force, especially in areas that were under Israeli control. At present, the borderline line between Lebanon and Israel is manned by Hezbollah. The Lebanese army has not deployed in these areas.

Prior to the Israeli withdrawal in 2000, Hezbollah enjoyed popular support in the country beyond its Shia power base. But that support has greatly diminished since 2000. In fact, for many Lebanese, the Shebaa farms are not Lebanese territory and, if they are, they can be liberated by less costly means, that is, by non-military means, just like Syria's attempts to liberate the Golan Heights by negotiation rather than by warfare. In other words, many Lebanese, including the inhabitants of south Lebanon, have priorities other than warfare, at a time when Lebanon is in deep economic crisis (public debt is currently about US$35 billion, up from less than US$1 billion when war ended in 1990), and would like to see conflict end after thirty years of continuous turmoil in the south.

The third face of Hezbollah is the most problematic and the most difficult to define. Prior to the September 11 attacks, Hezbollah, like other Islamist organizations, was not officially on Washington's list of terrorist parties. Even Syria, which has been placed on the US Department of State's list of states sponsoring terrorism for many years, continued to have normal relations with the USA. All this suddenly changed after September 11 and Hezbollah was listed as a Foreign Terrorist Organization, and Syria has been accused of sponsoring terrorist groups such as Hamas, Islamic Jihad, and Ahmad Gibril's PFLP-GC. Hezbollah's involvement in clandestine operations goes back to the 1980s, and Imad Maghniya is frequently singled out in this regard as Hezbollah's major operator accused of being involved in the bombings of the US embassy and Marines compound in Beirut in 1983–4 and of other terrorist attacks. But Hezbollah's supporters reject the terrorist label as based mainly on Israeli concerns. They also point out that Israel recently took part in a German-mediated prisoner exchange with Hezbollah, and released 400 Lebanese and Palestinian prisoners to Hezbollah rather than to the Palestinian Authority: actions that are inconsistent with Israel's designation of Hezbollah as a terrorist organization.

State failure by design

The war in Iraq and subsequent developments have prevented any possibility of accommodation over the issue of terrorism as defined by the Bush administration. At present, the USA is a de facto regional power in addition to being a superpower capable of using force against the will of the international community, as it did in the Iraq war. Moreover, American–Syrian relations have sharply deteriorated since the toppling of Saddam Hussein's Ba'athist regime and Syria's backing of the insurgency in Iraq against Coalition Forces. In May 2004, President Bush approved the Syria Accountability Act and Sovereignty for Lebanon. That marked Washington's intention to exert further pressure on Syria.

Terrorism or not, the security vacuum made possible by the American-backed Syrian order in Lebanon since the early 1990s has served functions to the benefit of all parties, except the Lebanese state before September 11 and the USA after that date. Hezbollah is the only armed non-state actor in the international system that runs an autonomous military and security infrastructure with the full backing of its 'host' state.

Given this anomalous situation, the state in post-war Lebanon does not present a classic case of a failed state but a state that provides an arena for armed conflict involving several regional state and non-state actors. But unlike patterns of failures forced upon the state for political and/or military reasons, as was the case in wartime Lebanon or in countries such as Afghanistan, the Philippines, Indonesia, Pakistan and Liberia, to name only a few, state failure in post-war Lebanon is designed by the state to the benefit of Syrian and Iran. For Syria, state failure in Lebanon has multiple objectives including fighting proxy wars in Lebanon and/or pursuing political objectives ranging from maintaining close ties with the USA in an earlier period to a multifaceted regional agenda that relates to the Arab–Israeli conflict, Iran, and inter-Arab politics. Similarly, for Iran, Lebanon's state failure by design is no less rewarding, particularly for the hardliners in the Iranian regime in the aftermath of the Iraq war.

If not contained, this state-designed security vacuum provides the possibility of armed conflict and political violence: whether labelled terrorism or otherwise. Only when the vacuum is filled would the state in Lebanon be held accountable for its deeds and for whatever developments that occur over its territories. Similarly, Syria's field of action would then be confined to Syrian territory and would thus be held accountable for its deeds within its national borders.

Bibliography

Ayubi, N. (1995) *Overstating the Arab State: Politics and Society in the Middle East*. London: I.B. Tauris.

el Khazen, F. (2000) *The Breakdown of the State of Lebanon 1967–76*. Cambridge, MA: Harvard University Press.

el Khazen, F. (2003) 'The Post-war Political Process: Authoritarianism by Diffusion', in Hanf, T. and Salam, N. (eds) *Lebanon in Limbo: Post-war Society and State in an Uncertain Regional Environment*. Baden-Baden: Nomos, pp. 53–74.

Fromkin, D.A. (1984) *A Peace to End All Peace: The Fall of the Ottoman Empire and the Creation of the Modern Middle East*. New York: Avon Books.

Gros, J.G. (1996) 'Towards a taxonomy of failed states in the New Order world: decaying Somalia, Liberia, Rwanda and Haiti', *Third World Quarterly*, 455–71.

Juergensmeyer, M. (2000) *Terrorism in the Mind of God*. Berkeley, CA: University of California Press.

Kaufman, A. (2002) 'Who owns the Shebaa farms?', *The Middle East Journal*, **56**(4), Autumn, 579–96.

Hanf, T. (1993) *Coexistence in Wartime Lebanon: Decline of a State and Rise of a Nation*. London: The Center for Lebanese Studies and I.B. Tauris.

Harris, W. (1997) *Faces of Lebanon: Sects, Wars and Global Extensions*. Princeton, NJ: Marcus Wiener Publishers.

Helman, G.B. and Ratner, S.R. (1993) 'Saving failed states', *Foreign Policy*, Winter, 3–18.

McDermott, A. And Skjelsbæk, K. (eds) (1991) *The Multinational Forces in Beirut 1982–4*. Miami, FL: Florida International University Press.

Maila, J. (1992) *The Document of National Understanding: A Commentary*. Oxford: Centre for Lebanese Studies.

Malik, H.C. (2000) *Between Damascus and Jerusalem, Lebanon and Middle East peace*, policy paper 45, Washington, DC: The Washington Institute for Near East Policy, pp. 25–45.

Mansour, A. (1993) *Al Inqilab ala al-Taif*. Beirut: Dar al-Jadid.

Marty, M.E. and Appleby, R.S. (1995) *Fundamentalisms Comprehended*. Chicago: Chicago University Press.

Morton, A.D. (2002) 'Historicizing representations of failed states: beyond the cold war annexation of the social services', *Third World Quarterly*, 23 February, 55–81.

Ranstorp, M. (1997) *Hizb'Allah in Lebanon: The Politics of the Western Hostage Crisis*. London: Macmillan Press, pp. 60–109.

Saad-Gorayeb, A. (2002) *Hizbollah: Politics and Religion*. London: Pluto Press.

Sayigh, Y. (1997) *Armed Struggle and the Search for State: The Palestinian National Movement 1947–93*. Oxford: Oxford University Press.

Sharara, W. (1996) *Dawlat Hizbollah. Lubnan Mujtama'an Islamiyan*. Beirut: Dar al-Nahar.

Zartman, W. (1995) *Collapsed States: The Disintegration and Restoration of Legitimate Authority*. Boulder, CO: Lynne Reinner Publishers.

15 State sponsorship –
a root cause of terrorism?

Louise Richardson

In the 1980s it was an article of faith of US administrations and the US public, as reflected in repeated public opinion polls, that state-sponsored terrorism was the biggest security threat facing the USA. This polling data reflected the orientation of the Reagan administration, which brought the issue of state-sponsored terrorism to the top of the political agenda. In the 1980s, however, the image of state-sponsored terrorism was of the Communist terrorist trained and controlled by the Soviet Union who set out to undermine the West. Claire Sterling's book (1981), with its depiction of a global Communist conspiracy against the West, became the bible of the Reagan administration and especially Secretary of State Alexander Haig.[1]

With the implosion of the Soviet Union, yet the continuation of international terrorism, the view of Communism as the root cause of terrorism was undermined. Nevertheless, American policy makers have continued to focus on state sponsorship. In the much discussed, and eventually released, speech by the National Security Adviser scheduled for delivery on 11 September 2001,[2] Condoleezza Rice only mentioned terrorism as a danger posed by rogue states. Evidence that the Bush administration ignored mounting evidence of terrorist activity by Islamic fundamentalist movements while fixating, instead, on the states such as Iraq that they thought directed them, is provided in detail by Richard Clarke, one-time Coordinator for Counter-terrorism (Clarke 2004). Clarke also demonstrates, as do Wesley Clark and Bob Woodward, that the immediate reaction of the Bush administration to the September 11 attacks was to retaliate against states, not terrorist movements (Clarke 2004; Clark 2003; Woodward 2004). While the concept of the state sponsor as the root cause of terrorism has remained constant from the Reagan to the Bush administrations, the identity of those sponsors has largely changed. The modal type has changed from Communist to Islamist. Today the threat is perceived to come from radical Islamic fundamentalists directed by rogue states such as Iraq or Syria rather than Communists directed by Moscow. The attention on the state continues.[3]

Why the USA sees state sponsorship as a root cause of terrorism

There are at least three reasons, from the general to the specific, as to why the USA, far more than her allies, sees state sponsorship as a root cause of terrorism.

First, the most general explanation is that US administrations generally, and specifically this Bush administration, tend to have a simplified view of the world. They have not wanted to engage the internal complexities of other countries, preferring to deal with known states rather than either multilateral institutions on the one hand, or nebulous sub-state movements on the other.

The essence of this explanation is captured in the story of the drunk looking for his car keys under the streetlamp. A friend approaches and asks what he is doing? 'I'm looking for my car keys,' he replies. 'Did you lose them here?' asks the friend. 'No, I lost them over there,' he says. 'Then why are you looking here?' asks the surprised friend. 'Because the light is better here,' replies the drunk.

The light is better here. The USA has the most formidable fighting force in the world. This army can militarily defeat any army on the planet. It can bring down the Taliban regime in Afghanistan and the regime of Saddam Hussein in Iraq in a matter of weeks. But this army was built, trained and equipped to bring down other armies, other governments, not inchoate, clandestine terrorist movements.

It requires a real shift in thinking to contemplate using the enormous fighting force of the USA against these small but ferocious movements. This shift is gradually taking place in the minds of some military planners; but for political leaders, who are far more comfortable on the domestic political stage than on an international one, the appeal of seeing this in traditional state-against-state terms is enormous.

President Bush has said,

> Every nation now knows that we cannot accept – and we will not accept – states that harbor, finance, train, or equip the agents of terror. Those nations that violate this principle will be regarded as hostile regimes. They have been warned, they are being watched, and they will be held to account.
>
> (George W. Bush)[4]

This is very much a deliberate and self-conscious use of the Churchillian language of traditional warfare. The post-war difficulties in Iraq, however, are daily demonstrating the limitations of this perspective.

The second, and more narrowly focused, reason for the emphasis on state sponsorship of terrorism is the concern with weapons of mass destruction (WMD). President Bush has repeatedly said, as he did at The Citadel on 11 December 2001: 'Above all, we're acting to end the state sponsorship of terror. Rogue states are clearly the most likely sources of chemical and biological and nuclear weapons for terrorists'. The prevailing fear in the USA is that rogue states will hand over weapons of mass destruction to terrorists to use against them. Very little attention has been paid to explaining the nature of the relationships, the ideological affinity, between states and terrorist groups in an effort to establish how likely a scenario this is.

American policy makers have wondered whether Saddam Hussein did not simply hand over all his weapons of mass destruction to al-Qaeda in the dying days of the regime. No effort is made to understand the very real differences between the secular Hussein and the fundamentalist al-Qaeda, nor the history of enmity between them, not to mention the justified paranoia of Saddam Hussein, which would have militated against any such action, even if he had these weapons of mass destruction; and it is becoming increasingly apparent that he did not.

The third reason for the recent focus on state sponsorship has been the felt need to bring down the Saddam Hussein regime in Iraq. For all the arguments against Saddam Hussein, the only one which called for immediate action was the link with terrorism. This provided a source of legitimization for military action and it allowed the mobilization of the American public (though not the international community) behind the war.

In his speech to the UN Security Council on 5 February 2003, Secretary of State Colin Powell spelled out in detail the nature of Hussein's support for international terrorism, most critically the alleged links with al-Qaeda through Abu Musab Al Zarqawi. Very real effort (with surprisingly little effect) went into depicting the Iraqi link with terrorism. On many other occasions Iraq's failure to comply with UN resolutions on terrorism has been stressed, from the attempted assassination of President Bush Sr. in 1993, which was a key fact for this administration, to sheltering members of MKO, PLF and the Abu Nidal Organization. There were a number of reasons to wage war on Iraq. Iraq's support of al-Qaeda was far from being the most compelling, but it was the most immediate.

These three reasons (the need to mobilize support for the war in Iraq, the belief in rogue states as suppliers of weapons of mass destruction, and the preference for perceiving the world in traditional state-to-state terms with traditional forces such as military) explain the USA's preference for seeing state sponsorship as such a crucial aspect, if not necessarily the root cause, of terrorism.

The list of designated state sponsors

This focus on states as the source of the problem is reflected in US legislation. The US Department of State's Office of Counter-Terrorism is required by law to report to Congress every year, since 1979, on the state of terrorism and state-sponsored terrorism. The Secretary of State, in this report, designates a number of countries as state sponsors of terrorism. Currently seven states have this designation: Cuba, Libya, Iran, Iraq, North Korea, Sudan and Syria (US Department of State 2004). Governments that find themselves on this list are subject to four main sets of US sanctions:

- a ban on arms-related exports and sales;
- controls over exports of dual-use items;
- prohibitions on economic assistance;
- a range of financial restrictions including US opposition to loans from international institutions, denial of duty-free treatment, tax credits for companies and individuals, and so on.

The existence of this list and the organization of US policy around it, reflects the US tendency to see state sponsorship as a key element in the threat of international terrorism. This view was widely held in the USA in the mid-1980s, declined there-after, and is enjoying a resurgence today.

The list of state sponsors is a curious one, ranging as it does from Cuba, which provides little more than a few damp apartments in Havana to some superannuated members of the ETA, the ELN and the FARC; to Iran, which bankrolls powerful groups like Hezbollah, Hamas and Islamic Jihad, among many others. The inclusion of Cuba on the list undoubtedly has more to do with electoral policies in Florida than with Cuba's sponsorship of terrorists. The list has remained unchanged since 1993 and several of the countries have been on it since it was first created.

The 1979 law allows for the removal from the list of any country that has not spon-sored terrorism in the previous six months. Many of the countries currently on the list would appear to qualify. Even prior to its recent concessions on the Pam Am 103 case and its WMD facilities, Libya's expulsion of the Abu Nidal group and its public sever-ance of ties with terrorist groups in 1999 would appear to have warranted removal. Fear of opposition from the families of victims of the Lockerbie bombing (an atrocity committed in revenge for the US bombing of Tripoli) appears to keep Libya on the list.

An even stronger case could be made for the removal of North Korea, which has not supported external terrorists in almost twenty years. Like Cuba, North Korea is alleged to house former members of terrorist groups, in this instance, the Japanese Red Army, a social-revolutionary terrorist group that operated in the 1970s. North Korea remains on the list presumably because the government fears its nuclear policy and does not want to alienate South Korea.

The case for keeping Sudan on the list is also a weak one given Sudan's expulsion of the infamous European terrorist, Carlos the Jackal, and the even more infamous, Osama bin Laden, in 1994. Sudan also signed a number of anti-terrorist conventions, shut down two terrorist groups operating in the country, and since 2001 has been sharing intelligence files with the USA. Sudan apparently does, however, continue to provide refuge to some terrorist suspects. Its position on the list, however, has more to do with opposition to the war against Christians in the south of the country, than it does to sponsorship of terrorists outside the country.

In fact it is a great deal easier to get on the list than to get off it. The last time a country was removed was in 1990 when North Yemen was removed after it ceased to exist as a separate country. Despite playing host to significant numbers of terrorists, including those who carried out the attack on the USS Cole, the successor state, Yemen, has not made it onto the list.

One sure way to get off the list is to serve US geo-strategic interests. Iraq, for example, was removed from the list between 1982 and 1989, not because of any change in its relationship with terrorist groups, but because the USA was cultivating Iraq in a bid to balance against Iran during the Iran–Iraq war.

Almost as interesting as the list itself is the unwritten list of countries not included. Afghanistan, host to al-Qaeda from 1994 to the toppling of the Taliban, was not on the list, apparently because the US government did not want to recognize the Taliban as Afghanistan's government. A more objective list of state sponsors of terrorism would include Saudi Arabia and Pakistan, both allies of the USA and both sponsors of more terrorism than any governments on the list, except arguably Iran. Most of the 19 hijackers on 9/11 came from Saudi Arabia, indeed none of the hijackers came from any of the states on the list of state sponsors. Saudi Arabia has harboured militant Islamic fundamentalists for years and has funded terrorists groups overseas in an effort to ensure domestic stability. Pakistan has sponsored Kashmiri terrorist groups and several Jihadi groups have operated from Pakistani soil. The USA has not placed either country on the list for fear of jeopardizing relations with them.

Of the seven countries that have been on this list for years, only Iran, and to a lesser extent Syria, could objectively be conceived as state sponsors of terrorism. Moreover, many other countries, most notably Afghanistan under the Taliban, Saudi Arabia and Pakistan meet the criteria for inclusion far more closely than most members of the list. The obvious inequities and inconsistencies in the list call into question the credibility of the US commitment to the principles it espouses. Rather than being perceived as an objective list of state sponsors of terrorism warranting international ostracism the list is widely perceived as a list of countries the USA, for one reason or another, dislikes.

The one country widely and rightly perceived to be the most active state sponsor of terrorism is Iran. Yet the USA has not acted against Iran with any more force than against states who are only nominal sponsors. The lesson that is being derived from this fact is that the USA acts only against the weak. Iran's sponsorship of terrorism dates to the 1979 Iranian revolution and the efforts to export that revolution overseas. More recently, as pointed out repeatedly in the US Department of State's annual reports, Iran provides Lebanese Hezbollah and Palestinian rejectionist groups, particularly Hamas and Palestinian Islamic Jihad, with funding, weapons, training and refuge. For a brief moment after 9/11 the USA and Iran, united in their shared enmity with the Taliban and Iraq, cooperated in the war in Afghanistan. The collaboration ended with the discovery in January 2002 of a ship, the Karine-A, loaded with 50 tons of weapons being smuggled to the Palestinian Authority from Iran (US Department of State 2003; Bahgat 2003). While each of the groups supported by Iran is significantly strengthened by Iranian support, they are in no sense creatures of Iran. Iranian sponsorship enhances their lethality but is not a root cause of their terrorism. Iran rather capitalizes on their pre-existing conflicts in order to further its own interests.

Terrorism as an instrument of foreign policy

The relationships between states and terrorist movements might more objectively be considered in terms of the use of terrorism as an instrument of foreign policy rather than the more loaded term 'state sponsorship'. It is not hard to see the attraction for any government of sponsoring terrorism abroad. If one is fighting a much stronger enemy, then one must be creative and avoid a head-on clash, which one would lose. State sponsorship of terrorism has, first, relatively low cost; and second, may serve to achieve one's foreign policy objectives, and if it does not, is easily deniable. Moreover, the primacy placed on the value of human life by Western democracies leaves them very vulnerable to attack through their individual citizens, who are easy targets because there are so many of them, in so many places. State sponsorship, therefore, is often low cost, easy to deny, difficult to prove, and has a potential for a high pay-off. Thus, it should come as no surprise that relatively weak states resort to the tactic against their more powerful enemies.

It is really a political judgement as to who is, or is not, a sponsor of terrorism; and who does, or does not, use terrorism as an instrument of their foreign policy. If one were to ask most Americans to name the countries they associate with using terrorism to advance their foreign policy goals, topping the list today would be Iraq, Iran and Libya. Twenty years ago, topping the list would have been the USSR and Cuba. You would have to search long and hard to find the USA on the list. Yet, if you were to ask people in other countries, even in allied countries, you would have found the USA high on most people's list. If you were to ask people in countries hostile to us, you would find the USA at the top of their list.

The examples most people would cite to support the view that the USA has been a state sponsor of terrorism are the support for the *Contras* in Nicaragua and support for the mujahidin fighting the Soviets in Afghanistan. Historical cases would include the support to local groups trying to overthrow Castro in Cuba and Allende in Chile. Now, if you look at some of these cases, you see that the USA had very good reason to dislike the governments of Cuba, Chile and Nicaragua. Their ideological orientation was inimical to US interests, so the USA supported local groups who used whatever means were available to try to bring them down. To have engaged in open warfare against these governments, perceived as being unsavoury, would have provoked an international uproar.

These are very much the same type of justifications the contemporary sponsors of terrorism in the Middle East would use. They perceive the existence of the state of Israel to be inimical to their interests, they cannot directly and openly fight Israel, so they do so surreptitiously. The only real difference between their position and that of America is that if the latter had chosen to fight openly it could be confident of winning, but it was not prepared to pay the price. The Middle Eastern countries believe they cannot beat Israel openly, so they fight her in other ways. Moreover, given the nature of US economic and political power, the USA has many more options at their disposal in terms of isolating these governments than do the current sponsors of terrorism, who, in some ways, have a better case than the USA did for sponsoring terrorism. I make this point, not to indict American foreign policy, but only to emphasize that not only the 'bad guys' use terrorism as an instrument of their foreign policy. Sometimes the 'good guys' do too. Sometimes weak states use terrorism because they believe they have no other effective means available to them, and sometimes strong states do it because they do not want to display their strength openly. In every instance the state is capitalizing on the existence of pre-existing terrorist movements, not creating them.

Southern Africa is a part of the world not generally considered in discussions of state sponsorship of terrorism but it provides a number of illustrative examples. The ultimate success of the African National Congress, the ANC, can only be understood in terms of the external support it received. This support was not a root cause of ANC violence; the root cause of the formation of the ANC was the apartheid regime. The root cause of the ANC decision to adopt a military strategy was its exclusion from all political means of voicing opposition. The external support for the ANC can only be understood in the context of the success of decolonization that swept Africa during the 1960s. In the fourteen years between the Rivonia Trials and the emergence of the Black Consciousness movement in South Africa, the complexion of South Africa's neighbours changed dramatically. The British colonies achieved independence in the 1960s and the Portuguese colonies of Angola and Mozambique in 1974. The only exception was Rhodesia, which eventually came under majority rule as Zimbabwe in 1980.

In 1967 the ANC's military wing, MK, tried to infiltrate guerrillas through Rhodesia from bases in Zambia with the help of the ZAPU liberation movement. The Rhodesian forces tracked them down and handed them over to South Africa. Later, after the failure of the Soweto uprising and the increase in recruits to ANC camps, the South African government became more aggressive. The South African leader, P.W. Botha, launched a deliberate policy of destabilization against neighbouring states known to harbour ANC members. The South African army launched repeated attacks on ANC targets in the 'frontline' states of Angola, Mozambique, Tanzania, Zimbabwe and Zambia.

The South African government, therefore, used a two-pronged approach to counter the external support for the ANC. First was direct military action against ANC camps, much as Israel raided Hezbollah camps in Lebanon. Second was to sponsor terrorist groups in the frontline states who opposed the new post-independence governments. Unlike the Iranian policy of exporting revolution this was an effort to prevent the importation of revolution.

In Mozambique and Angola, the South African government sponsored terrorist movements RENAMO and UNITA against the governments of Samora Machal and Jonas Savimbi in order to undermine what it perceived to be a terrorist movement, the ANC, at home. This use of terrorism as an instrument of foreign policy only ended with the Nkomati Accord (1984) when Machal agreed to stop supporting the ANC in return for South Africa ceasing support for RENAMO. Similarly, as part of the Namibian peace settlement, South Africa ceased its support of UNITA in return for Angola expelling ANC members.

Strong states as well as weak states, and states of all political hues, in all regions of the world have used terrorism as an instrument of their foreign policy. They have done so to export revolution overseas, to prevent the importation of revolution, and to undermine revolutions abroad. In each instance they have capitalized on pre-existing conflicts rather than providing a root cause.

Relations between terrorists and their sponsors

Even when one accepts that there is a sponsoring relationship between a terrorist group and a state, it is very easy to exaggerate the influence the sponsor has on the movement. Terrorist movements usually guard their independence jealously and accept support from several sponsors in order to avoid dependence on one. Relations between state sponsors and terrorist movements can be imagined as falling along a spectrum of state control from very tight to very loose.

At one end of the spectrum is the covert action of intelligence agencies masquerading as terrorists, as in the murder of dissidents by Iran and Iraq. Here state control is complete and what we are really seeing is not terrorism but undercover action. Further along the continuum of control is the recruitment and training of operatives specifically for missions abroad. The murder of Kurdish dissidents in Berlin in 1992 by several Lebanese and an Iranian recruited by Iranian intelligence is an example. Murdering of dissidents, again, does not, in fact, constitute terrorism, though it is often perceived as such.

The third level is when a government closely controls a terrorist group and directs their actions. The Popular Front for the Liberation of Palestine-General Command, PFLP-GC, for example, is essentially directed by its main sponsor, Syria. Ahmad Jabril is a former captain in the Syrian Army and Syria provides headquarters, financial and logistical support. But these instances of close state control are quite rare.

The fourth level is by far the most common. It is when a government provides training, financing and safe haven for an autonomous terrorist group. This is the case, for example, for most Palestinian groups operating in the Middle East. Many of these groups jealously guard their independence. They accept assistance from several sponsors, in part to avoid being exclusively dependent on any one sponsor. Most groups, like Hamas, try to supplement their government funding, in this case from Iran, with support from private benefactors in places like Saudi Arabia and Egypt and from Palestinian expatriates. In some cases, groups accept help from sworn enemies. The PKK (Kurdistan Workers' Party), for example, accepted support from both Iran and Iraq as well as Syria. When one of these groups commits an atrocity there is a tendency to blame one of the sponsoring states. While the state may indeed be pleased by the action, they may not have known of it in advance. In this case, the sponsoring state may be responsible for the action in a normative or moral sense, in having supported the perpetrators, but it is not directly responsible for the action.

The fifth and final level on the continuum of state control is when the sponsoring state decides that the actions of a terrorist group will serve its ends. The state then supports the group financially because it identifies its interests with those of the group. The support of Libyan leader Muammar Qaddafi for the IRA can be seen in this light. He wanted to punish Britain for allowing American planes to take off from British airbases in their bombing of Tripoli in 1986 and financing the IRA was a means of doing so. He knew little of the IRA's campaign, caring only that they shared a common enemy, Britain.

In forging a successful policy to eliminate state sponsorship in specific instances it is essential to differentiate between the different types of relationship between terrorists and their state sponsors.

Conclusion

To summarize, state sponsorship is not a root cause of terrorism; state sponsorship itself is a more nuanced relationship than is generally appreciated, and the use of terrorism as an instrument of foreign policy has not historically been limited to rogue states, Islamist states or Communist states.

That said, it is impossible to deny that the financial, logistical and territorial support given terrorists by states enormously enhances the lethal potential of these groups and complicates the task of defeating them. Undermining that support is an entirely legitimate goal and should be a high priority for all governments engaged in a campaign against terrorism. No government should delude itself, however, that the elimination of state sponsorship will eliminate terrorism. To do that, the real root causes of terrorism must be addressed.

Notes

1 Apparently Secretary Haig kept dozens of copies of Sterling's book in his office and would hand out a copy to anyone who would accept it. Every academic's dream!
2 *The Washington Post*, 1 April 2004.
3 The Reagan administration did, of course, include non-Communist states such as Libya in the panoply of state sponsors. America bombed Tripoli in 1986 to punish Libya for sponsoring terrorism against the USA.
4 Remarks by President George W. Bush at The Citadel, Charleston, South Carolina, 11 December 2001.

Bibliography

Bahgat, G. (2003) 'Iran, the United States, and the war on terrorism', *Studies in Conflict & Terrorism*, **26**, 93–104.

Clark, W (2003) *Winning Modern Wars: Iraq, Terrorism and the American Empire*. New York: Perseus.

Clarke, R. (2004) *Against All Enemies: Inside America's War on Terror*. New York: Free Press.

Sterling, C. (1981) *The Terror Network: The Secret War of International Terrorism*. New York: Reader's Digest Press.

US Department of State (2003) *Patterns of global terrorism 2002*, 30 April.

US Department of State (2004) *Patterns of global terrorism 2003*, 30 April.

Woodward, R. (2004) *Plan of Attack*. New York: Simon and Schuster.

16 Expected utility and state terrorism

Michael Stohl[1]

I begin with two quotes, one from fiction and one which is used so often by defenders and opponents that it has almost achieved fictional status:

> The fault, dear Brutus, is not in our stars, but in ourselves.
>
> (Cassius to Brutus, Shakespeare's *Julius Caesar*
> (Act I, Scene ii, 139–40))

> Extremism in the defense of liberty is no vice ... Moderation in the pursuit of justice is no virtue.
>
> (Barry Goldwater
> Accepting the Republican presidential nomination, 16 July 1964)

Cassius's comment to Brutus should remind us to look carefully at ourselves, the choices we make and their consequences. Barry Goldwater's political rallying call reminds us of how easily political choices may be framed so as to marginalize the moderate voice and thus alter inhibitions to certain forms of action.

Twenty years ago, in an article published by the Peace Research Institute in Oslo, in the *Journal of Peace Research* (Stohl *et al.* 1984), my colleagues and I introduced a political terror scale with five data points by which, using the yearly reports prepared by Amnesty International and the US Department of State, we classified states on the basis of their respect for human rights.

Political terror scale

Level 1: Countries [...] under a secure rule of law, people are not imprisoned for their views, and torture is rare or exceptional ... Political murders are extraordinarily rare.

Level 2: There is a limited amount of imprisonment for non-violent political activity. However, few are affected, torture and beatings are exceptional ... Political murder is rare.

Level 3: There is extensive political imprisonment, or a recent history of such imprisonment. Execution or other political murders and brutality may be common. Unlimited detention, with or without trial, for political views is accepted ...

Level 4: The practices of Level 3 are expanded to larger numbers. Murders, disappearances and torture are a common part of life ... In spite of its generality, on this level violence affects primarily those who interest themselves in politics or ideas.

Level 5: The violence of Level 4 has been extended to the whole population ... The leaders of these societies place no limits on the means or thoroughness with which they pursue personal or ideological goals.

This scale focused on the impact on victims of violations. When we focus on state terror we focus on the perpetrators of the violations, many of which may be classified as terrorism. Almost all the other chapters in this book will focus on terrorism used by those who oppose the state. My purpose therefore will be to explore what we can learn from the use of terrorism by states as we consider the problem of the root causes of terrorism by those who oppose states.

In the list of questions suggested for our attention I hope to address two basic sets:

- Are there some root causes or fundamental processes that are common to all (or most) forms of terrorism?
- What role does the weakness or strength of the state play in state terrorism?

There is now a substantial body of case study literature which has documented the use of repression and terrorism by states against their own populations. Most of these studies concentrate on the most egregious violators of human rights and the most terroristic of states. There is thus a substantial body of literature on the use of state terror by the Communist Eastern European regimes of the twentieth century, the Nazis, the state terror of the Southern Cone and Central American right-wing regimes of the 1960s and 1970s and the 'fragile states' of Africa and Asia in the post independence era (see most recently Valentino 2004; and also Krain 1997; Rummel 1995; Hayner 2001; Ball *et al.* 1999). There is also a growing body of research involving cross-national quantitative measures of state violence, repression and terror, which rather than focusing on the particulars of any one case seeks patterns and theoretical causes across the cases. Both types of studies have contributed much to our knowledge of the very wide range of characteristics, dimensions and horrors of state behaviour. What is clear is that state terrorism has been practised by states which are rich and poor, revolutionary and reactionary, expansionist and reclusive, secular and religious, east and west, north and south. In short virtually all types of state have at some time engaged in or promoted behaviours which many would characterize as terrorism either within their own borders or in the wider international system. Given this diversity, it is not surprising that no clear single factor derived from a structural characteristic related to state terrorism has emerged. Or put another way, if we were to consider the various structural characteristics of states, there are very few analytic cells which would remain empty of the experience of state terrorism. Given the increasing ability of people to move across national boundaries and the increasing interconnectedness of states and peoples across those boundaries, there are few states that may be confident that they will experience first hand none of the conflicts that arise in their neighbours or even in distant states or be simply threatened from afar by them. Under such circumstances how will they react and how will they respond?

In this chapter, after an initial definitional and conceptual discussion, I introduce an expected utility approach to explore the conditions under which states have resorted to the use of violence, repression and terrorism against their own and others' populations, to detect the conditions that resulted in these behaviours and to explore different forms of state terrorist behaviour in both domestic and international affairs.

My intention is not to equate all state and non-state actors who employ terrorism in pursuit of political goals, nor is it to condemn such actors out of hand (though I would consistently deplore their choice of terrorism as a tactic or strategy) but rather to seek to understand the context in which state terrorism occurs and thus provide new insight into the conditions under which terrorism emerges as a political tactic or strategy. Hopefully, this will contribute to the discussion of the 'root causes' that are the focus of this book.

Before discussing the conditions under which governments choose to employ strategies and tactics which involve violence and terrorism it is useful to clarify how these concepts will be employed. The basic conceptual/theoretical principle with which I begin is that terrorism is intentional behaviour. As such, its explanation and prediction lie primarily with models of intentional or purposive behaviour.

With minor modification I follow the pre-1984 US Department of State's definition of terrorism:

> The threat or use of violence for political purposes by individuals or groups, whether acting for, or in opposition to, established governmental authority, when such actions are intended to influence a target group wider than the immediate victim or victims.
>
> (US Department of State 1983)

To make the intentionality more clear, I would simply add the term purposeful and thus consider terrorism as:

> The purposeful threat or use of violence for political purposes by individuals or groups, whether acting for, or in opposition to, established governmental authority, when such actions are intended to influence the victim and or a target group wider than the immediate victim or victims.[2]

Following Bissell *et al.* (1978), repression is considered as 'the use of coercion or the threat of coercion against opponents or potential opponents in order to prevent or weaken their capability to oppose the authorities and their policies'. This definition enables the recognition of the denial of rights (including the rights to food, shelter and security which are often characterized in terms of structural violence as different, but no less meaningful than physical acts). Violence is defined in accordance with the liberal tradition as an act of physical harm.

An important key to the understanding of how terrorism differs from 'ordinary' political violence is to recognize that in terrorism the act or the threat of the act of violence is but the first step. Terror is purposeful behaviour designed to influence targets beyond the moment of victimization and/or beyond the direct victims of the violent act. It is a conscious strategy or tactic of influence and not merely violent acts which cause death and destruction. The violence that is terrorism seeks to influence the behaviours of others, not merely to eliminate victims.

Thus, following the insights of Thomas Schelling (1966: 16–17), the position taken throughout this chapter is that we need to consider that the actions that are being described are concerned with the manipulation of violence and, in Schelling's words, 'the threat of pain and the promise of more' – making this consideration whether the terrorism undertaken by governments 'saves lives or wastes them …', whether punitive coercive violence is uglier than straightforward military force or more civilized, or 'whether terror is more or less humane than military destruction'. As such, I would contend that such acts are properly defined as terrorism and are there-fore quite simply unacceptable behaviour regardless of the actor.

An expected utility approach provides useful insights into the process of under-standing why a government might choose terrorism as a tactic or strategy. In a previous work (Duvall and Stohl 1983), Raymond Duvall and I argued that an expected utility model is useful for understanding a government's choice of terrorism as a tactic or strategy in domestic affairs. In a later work (Stohl 1986) I argued that it could be applied to state behaviours in the international realm as well. Underlying this approach is an argument that people who employ terrorism as a tactic or a strategy consider three things in making a decision. The first is the preferred outcome they seek. The second is their calculation that what they would choose to do will likely bring about the preferred outcome. The third is the cost of engaging in the action to bring about the preferred outcome. This approach does not require the analyst to believe that the actor who chooses to employ terrorism is a fanatic; merely that he is a 'rational actor' who has calculated that a terrorist action will bring about a desired outcome.

The argument is that if all other things (and most relevantly according to the argument, expected costs) are equal, a regime is more likely to employ terrorism as a means of governance when it believes that terrorism is more effective relative to other means of governance. This approach locates terrorism as a strategy of action in a conflict situation. State terrorism within the domestic context presupposes a regime in conflict with at least some of its citizenry. Almost certainly, this means eliminating, quieting, or mitigating an actual or perceived potential challenge or threat on the part of some identifiable segment of the citizenry to the structure, personnel, or policies of the regime. If terrorism is calculated as a relatively more effective means of gover-nance, then, the government must estimate that terrorism will perform better than alternative means in eliminating or quieting some actual or perceived potential chal-lenge or threat. Within the international realm, the same logic applies.

States (and other terrorist actors) might choose terrorism paradoxically both when they perceive themselves powerless (the sense that other policy instruments of rule are unavailable or less useful) and when they are in a situation that may be labelled confident strength (when the costs are perceived as low and the probability of success believed high in relation to other means) (Duvall and Stohl 1983). Following the same approach, Valentino (2004: 235) has examined eight cases of mass killing (The Soviet Union under Stalin, China under Mao, Cambodia, Turkish Armenia, Nazi Germany, Rwanda, Guatemala and Afghanistan) which he argues occurred because the decision makers concluded that 'other strategies for achieving their goals were impossible or impractical'.

The situation of powerlessness

Much discussion of terrorism begins with the assertion that terrorism is a weapon of the weak. The image is of a group so unable to engage successfully in political conflict through 'conventional' means that it adopts terrorism as a last resort out of frustration and a sense of powerlessness.

Whether or not this imagery is generally apt, it does contain an important lesson for the student of state terrorism. That is, a government may be 'driven' to the use of terror as a means of ruling out of a sense of relative hopelessness in attempting to meet the (actual or perceived potential) threat through alternative means of governance. The believed relative effectiveness of terrorism in this situation depends less on the perception of terror as highly efficacious than it does on the sense that other means of rule are quite inefficacious.

A sense of relative ineffectiveness of conventional means of rule depends on two factors: an inability of the regime to mobilize and employ the positive and negative inducements on which those means rely; and/or the non-receptivity of target groups to those inducements. A simple expectation is that the first of these factors is apt to be greatest where the regime is able to command relatively few resources and where it has relatively limited means (particularly organizational apparatus) to deliver those few resources it can command; that is to say, in the context of new, weak, fragile states. An equally simple expectation is that the second factor, the non-receptivity of target groups, depends overwhelmingly on the vulnerability of the group to the manipulation of positive and negative inducements by the government. Groups are less vulnerable, and hence less receptive, to conventional means of governance where they are a large proportion of the population or where they are strongly and zealously committed to the values about which they are in conflict with the regime, particularly if they are an elusive social group. This is because it is difficult for the government to buy off, coopt, make compromises with, directly repress, or engage in physical military combat with either a large proportion of its citizenry or a deeply committed, highly zealous, generally elusive adversary group. This interactive process is illustrated in Ron's (1997) analysis of the changing nature of Israeli repressive behaviours with respect to the Palestinian community during the period 1988–96.

Taken together, these considerations lead us to expect that a sense of relative governmental powerlessness potentially conducive to terrorism can occur in two closely related but distinct syndromes. One is the new fragile state in which the government perceives itself challenged or threatened by large portions of the society it is attempting to rule. The second is the new fragile state in (actual or perceived potential) conflict with a strongly committed, elusive adversary group. In both syndromes, moreover, one would expect whatever state terrorism occurs to be both intense and socially pervasive. This is due, in the one instance, to the large size of the target population, and, in the other instance, to the strength of commitment and elusiveness of the target. In either case, a great deal of terror would be required to be effective.

In summary, one path, in two distinct forms, that conduces to state terrorism of an especially intense and socially pervasive kind is the path of perceived powerlessness on the part of the regime: the sense that other means of governance are relatively less useful, indeed sometimes to the point of believed futility, in waging the conflict with societal challenges. The two distinct forms of this path correspond quite closely to the empirical patterns found in the immediately post-revolutionary Second World experience, on the one hand, and in the contemporary Third World experience of the government going after an amorphous, ill-defined political 'enemy' on the other hand. One, the post-revolutionary Second World, was the model of a new, fragile state in conflict with substantial portions of the population who were felt to be resisting the revolutionary transformation of society. The other, contemporary Third World regimes in conflict with an 'enemy' is the model of a fragile state facing multiple political challenges, often representing potentially significant ethnic and/or religious cleavages.

The situation of confident strength

A failing of much of the analysis of political terrorism is the implicit presumption that it is only the weapon of the weak. But it most certainly is not. Beliefs about the relative expected effectiveness of terrorism do not depend solely on a sense of inefficacy for alternative strategies of action. On the contrary, some political actors, including some governments, estimate that terrorism can and will itself be highly effective. In this situation, terrorism can be adopted out of a position of confidence and strength.

Again, the estimation of relative effectiveness depends on the two factors identified above: ability to command relevant resources; and receptivity, or vulnerability, of the target group. But here the factors are essentially reversed from their positions in defining a situation of powerlessness. Now we are talking about a government's belief that it can command, mobilize and employ the resources necessary to wage a campaign of terror (whether or not it can mobilize resources for conventional means of governance), and its belief that the target will be vulnerable and receptive to such a campaign (again, regardless of the group's vulnerability to other positive and negative inducements). This entails an estimation of both the extent to which the target is vulnerable to terror or to pressure or influence by some intermediary terrorized population, and the extent to which the actor is able to control or manage the processes of terrorizing and of translating the terror into desired action by the target and/or the intermediary population. The more vulnerable the target is believed to be and the more the government feels itself able to control the process, the greater the believed probability of effectiveness of terrorism.

Our simple expectation is that three considerations are most relevant to a determination of these two subjective factors. The first is a process of learning, by which we mean simply that believed probabilities are greater as terrorism has been judged to have been successful in past conflict situations. Learning can be based on either an actor's own past or reports of others' pasts. The former is apt to have strong impact, and leads to the obvious point that the more successfully a government has made use of terrorism as a means of rule in the past, the higher the expected utility it is apt to attach to terrorism for current conflicts. The other form of learning is an imitation principle. It is not apt to have as strong an impact, but nevertheless it acts to encourage the use of terrorism by a government to the extent that it is aware of successful terrorism in other regimes. As it becomes public knowledge that some governments have used or are using terrorism successfully to rule, the more common will state terrorism likely become. The converse also follows.

The second consideration is especially relevant to a government's beliefs about its ability to administer terror and to control the process of terrorism. Although this ability includes a technological component – 'does the government possess the means to target violence?' – we believe that its primary basis is of an organizational nature. That is, it rests on the extent to which the government has penetrated or has the means to penetrate the informational and politically relevant sectors of society. If a government maintains, or is capable of implementing, an extensive network of penetration of society, its decision makers are apt to believe themselves able to manage, with some fairly high probability of success, the process of terror. Governments that are most likely to satisfy this condition are those which are highly developed and maintain large bureaucratic establishments.

The third and perhaps most important consideration has to do with the features of the target population; features which increase its vulnerability to state terror. The most relevant of these would seem to be a lack of integration of the target group into the dominant social fabric. Socially marginal groups, without strong ties to and support from the mainstream of society, are especially vulnerable to victimization and, concomitantly, terror. Societies in which there is significant ethnic cleavage with political power concentrated within rather than across ethnic lines are equally likely to produce what are considered by those in power to be social marginal groups.

Taken together, these considerations lead us to expect that a situation of felt confidence and strength potentially conducive to terrorism on the part of the regime can occur in a particular syndrome. This is the syndrome of the polity with highly developed informational and organizational networks through which the regime penetrates society, and in which the government perceives itself in actual or potential conflict with some socially marginal group that is poorly integrated into (or 'disoriented' with respect to) the rest of society. In this syndrome, one would expect state terror to be limited in scope and generally of fairly low intensity, sufficient only to 'win' the conflict with the marginal social group. When the socially marginalized group is large and easily identifiable, terror is likely to be intense because of the scale of the potential opposition. At the same time, one would expect terror in this situation to be used more regularly and perhaps with greater intensity by governments who have learned its utility for rule through past experience.

The expected relative costs of terrorism

Certainly terrorism is not used to the same degree by all governments which find themselves either in a position of relative powerlessness to govern effectively through alternative means, or which believe themselves able effectively to employ terrorism as a means to govern socially marginal groups. There is considerable variance, even within these kinds of situations. That variance is due in part to the subjective probabilities of relative effectiveness of various means of governance. But beliefs about relative effectiveness are only part of the picture. They set situations conducive to the use of terrorism. But they are not sufficient to explain its actual occurrence.

Also necessary are the government's expectations about the costs it would have to bear in using terrorism relative to the costs of alternative means of governance. Two kinds of costs, response costs and productions costs, can be distinguished. Response costs are those costs which might be imposed by the target group and/or sympathetic or offended bystanders. The bystanders may include domestic and foreign audiences and the target audience may be wider than the attacking party may have intended when choosing the victims and the actions.

Production costs are the costs of taking the action regardless of the reactions of others. In addition to the economic costs (paying the participants, buying the weapons and the like) there is the psychological cost of behaving in a manner which most individuals would, under normal conditions, characterize as unacceptable behaviour.

Following Ted Gurr (1986: 62–7) we may identify three sets of conditions that affect the decision-making calculus of threatened elites:

- *Situational* conditions: include the political traits of challenges (the status and strategies of challengers) and the elite's own political resources for countering those challenges (regime strength and police apparatus).
- *Structural* conditions: those that define the elites' relations with their opponents and determine or constrain their response options. These include the state's position in the international system and the nature of social stratification and the elite's position within it.
- *Dispositional* variables: conditions that can be expected to influence how elites regard the acceptability of strategies of violence and terrorism. Norms supporting the use of violence are shaped by elites' direct or mediated experience with violent means of power and are inhibited by democratic values.

Response costs

When governments consider various means of governance, they are attentive to the expected responses of others. What others likely will do in reaction affects the utility of a particular strategy. Most relevant to a consideration of terrorism are what might be called punitive or retributive costs imposed by the target group and/or sympathetic or offended bystanders. State terrorists, as do insurgent terrorists, therefore consider how to make themselves relatively invulnerable to response. There are at least two means to this end. One is inaccessibility. Retaliators may know in general, or even in particular, who the terrorist is but be unable to locate him. The anonymity of refugee camps or urban areas, and physical mobility across national boundaries may provide this inaccessibility for insurgent terrorists. But governments and governmental decision makers are not, in general, inaccessible in these terms, except to the extent that they can completely insulate themselves from retaliation, and to the degree that they are immune to international pressure. States with fewer ties to potential interveners, those without significant international importance (lack of strategic geographic significance, important natural resources) or important international constituencies (émigrés, sponsors, etc.), and with a lack of openness and democratic structures are likely to be more invulnerable than other types of states.

States and some insurgents also rely on a second means of invulnerability, that is, secrecy of action. State terrorism can often be expected to be covert action, because in this way the government effectively reduces its vulnerability to retaliation even below its vulnerability to the (otherwise lesser) response costs expected for other means of governance. This means that, in general, state terrorism will not have 'publicity of its cause' as an objective. Also, it means that as public accessibility to governmental officials is greater, and/or as regime vulnerability to international pressure is greater, terrorism is more likely to be secretive, and, concomitantly, is less likely to be as extensive.

Thus, state terrorism appears to be greatest in reclusive states. Regime vulnerability, either to domestic retribution or to international pressure, is generally less important in such regimes and thus response costs are relatively low.

In addition, these considerations about response costs help to explain the ways in which state terrorism is carried out in relatively more vulnerable regimes. The terrorism itself is often targeted at socially marginal groups who are not expected to have many politically powerful sympathetic friends able to impose very high punitive costs on the government. The agents of the terror are likely to be clandestine, that is the secret police or its equivalent or parastatal vigilante squads, thereby reducing the extent to which the regime can be held directly accountable.

Production costs

This is the cost simply of taking the action regardless of the reactions of others. For terrorist action, which is not apt to be terribly expensive to undertake, this is most importantly a self-imposed cost. It takes the form of normative or moral constraint on action. Because this type of cost is less tangible, it is frequently overlooked. But it is quite important to an analysis of terrorism in that it may be quite high. That is because whatever moral/normative constraints have been internalized regarding the use of violence in general are supplemented by the fact that terrorism entails a special kind of violence. The victims of terrorist violence are incidental and instrumental. They are not, in general, the direct or particular objects of intense animosity. Thus something other than hatred must operate to break down whatever prohibitions have been internalized against the use of violence.

The psychological costs that an actor can expect from perpetrating violence on an incidental, instrumental, victim involve the extent to which the victim can be or has been dehumanized in the mind of the violent actor. Where victims can be viewed in other than human terms, the self-imposed costs of terrorist actions are apt to be low and hence the choice of terrorist actions more frequent.

The extent to which victims and potential victims can be dehumanized is affected by two important variables (for an extended discussion of this point see the seminal piece by Herbert Kelman, 1973). The first is the perceived social distance between the government and the victim population. The second is the extent to which action is routinely and bureaucratically authorized, so that personal responsibility is perceived, by all actors in the decisional chain, to be avoided. These production costs for terrorist action are apt to be lower for governments (a) in a conflict situation with those they define as 'inferior', or those that have initiated or protected those that have committed terrorist actions against them or on their soil, and/or (b) when policy-makers can justify their actions to themselves as acting 'in and for the best interests of the state and not as individuals'.[3]

For international relations scholars working within the realist tradition this is familiar ground. For realists states reside within an international system which is akin to the Hobbesian state of nature, with both lacking 'a political authority sufficiently powerful to assure people security and the means to have a felicitous life' (Beitz 1979: 21). Thus states have the right (and the responsibility in the realist tradition) to do what they must to preserve their existence and may expect other states to behave in the same manner. Charles Beitz argues that Hans Morgenthau, the leading realist scholar of the past half century, seems to claim that 'a state's pursuit of its own interests justifies disregard for moral standards that would otherwise constrain its action' (ibid.: 21) and indeed Morgenthau (1978: 10) asserts that the state 'has no right to let its moral disapprobation [...] get in the way of successful political action, itself inspired by the moral principle of national survival'. For realists, it would thus appear that there are no limits to actions which may be taken on behalf of the state when it is the national security of the state which is actually at risk.

In a previous work (Stohl 1986) I identified three broad forms of state terrorist behaviour in the international sphere. A terrorist form of coercive diplomacy constitutes the first. In terrorist coercive diplomacy the aim is to make non-compliance with a particular demand, in the words of Schelling (1966: 15), 'terrible beyond endurance'. While the threat is openly communicated by the actions of the state, the threat may be implicit and is quite often non-verbal. Terrorist coercive diplomacy is overt behaviour. The parties to the conflict are fully aware of the nature of the threat.

There are two types of covert state terrorism which constitute the second form of state terrorism: (1) clandestine state terrorism is a form of covert action which consists of direct participation by state agents in acts of terrorism; and (2) state-sponsored terrorism is a form of covert action which consists of state or private groups being employed to undertake terrorist actions on behalf of the sponsoring state.

The clandestine services of the national state are generally responsible for initiating, participating in, or coordinating these actions. Government agents operating across national boundaries may choose either national elites or the foreign society itself as the target. In this type of state terrorism, states may thus attempt to intimidate government officials directly through campaigns of bombing, attacks, assassinations and by sponsoring and participating in attempted *coups d'état*. Alternatively, national states participate in the destabilization of other societies with the purpose of creating chaos and the conditions for the collapse of governments, the weakening of the national state and changes in leadership. The threats to the regime and the society are obvious, but there is an attempt at deniability nonetheless. Both the pattern of such behaviour and the threat of such a pattern being initiated constitute the terroristic aspect of this type of action.

The third broad form of state terrorism involves assistance to another state or insurgent organization which makes it possible or 'improves' the capability of that actor to practise terrorism either at home or abroad. This form is labelled surrogate terrorism as the obvious effect and intent of the assistance provided is the improvement of the assisted actor's ability either to carry out terrorist actions to maintain a regime's rule or to create chaos and/or the eventual overthrow of an identified enemy-state regime.

There are two subcategories of this form of terrorism: (1) state supported terrorism exists when third parties undertake actions on their own which are subsequently supported by the interested state; and (2) state acquiescence to terrorism occurs when terrorism is undertaken by third parties and while not explicitly supported by the interested state, the actions are not condemned or openly opposed.

Terrorist coercive diplomacy

The defining characteristic of coercive diplomacy as distinct from both diplomacy and traditional military activity is that the force of coercive diplomacy is used ' … in an exemplary, demonstrative manner, in discrete and controlled increments, to induce the opponent to revise his calculations and agree to a mutually acceptable termination of the conflict' (George 1971: 18).

We may speak of terrorism as a subset of coercive diplomacy when violence or its threatened use is present. Not all coercive diplomacy employs violence and thus not all coercive diplomacy is terrorism. For example, one may employ economic sanctions in an allowed coercive manner, as did the members of the United Nations with respect to South Africa, without employing violent tactics. We will confine our analysis to the violence of coercive diplomacy whose central task has been described as 'how to create in the opponent the expectation of unacceptable costs of sufficient magnitude to erode his motivation to continue what he is doing' (ibid.: 26–7).

We must recognize that by convention (and it must be emphasized only by convention) great power use and the threat of the use of force is normally described as coercive diplomacy and not as a form of terrorism. But if we return to the US

Department of State's definition of terrorism introduced earlier, it is quite clear that certain forms of coercive diplomacy involve the threat and often the use of violence for what would be described as terroristic purposes were it not great powers who were pursuing the very same tactic.

We should also recognize that states, particularly great powers, find it a much easier task not only to bring force to bear for threats but also to communicate their ability to do so. It is thus less necessary for a state actually to carry out its threat than it is for an insurgent terrorist organization which has to work much harder to demonstrate the credibility (in both dimensions of capability, i.e. is the actor both willing and able to employ the threat?) of their threat to employ force.

Further we must also consider the question of innocents and non-combatants. When coercive diplomacy is in the nature of the traditional gunboat-diplomacy mode, when in principle gunboats face off against gunboats, we have what Schelling (1966: 3) described as brute force to overcome strength. However when the 'gunboat' is positioned so as to indicate the ability to strike at the civilian population and not a military target, we have what Schelling describes as the threat of pain to structure the opponent's motives. We should recognize that this inclusion of innocent non-combatants should not be considered to be any different in form from that of the insurgent terrorist who threatens to unleash a wave of bombings on city streets. When these innocents are citizens of non-democratic societies who are not considered responsible in any conceivable sense for their government's legitimacy or actions, then coercive power which threatens these citizens to coerce their governments surely involves threats to helpless innocents and must be considered as a form of terrorism.

One may argue that the virtues of such state terrorist coercive strategies illustrate, 'achieving one's objectives economically, with little bloodshed, for fewer psychological and political costs, and often with much less risk of escalation' (George 1971: 19). Saving lives is indeed a virtue. This virtue, however, does not alter the fact that the strategy is based on terror and the power to destroy if 'proper' responses are not engendered by the threats and/or the relatively low levels of violence employed. Coercive strategies which rely on the threat of violence should therefore be considered state terror policies, regardless of whether or not they save lives or we approve of them (see Schelling 1966: 16–17).

Covert state terrorism

Both the clandestine state terrorism and state-sponsored forms of covert state terrorism in international relations, unlike the coercive diplomacy discussed above, are usually aimed at producing, not compliance, but rather fear and chaos. In addition to the message that the act conveys about vulnerability and the assets (personal and material) that are destroyed, it is hoped that as a result of increased fear and chaos, governments at some later point will be in a weaker bargaining position or will be more willing to make concessions, given the costs that have become apparent. In relative terms, response and production costs are lower than for open coercive diplomacy. The attempt at deniability may create suspicions, but suspicions are generally less costly in the court of public opinion than are open admissions. It is also less expensive to mount most forms of covert operations than it is to 'send the fleet' or mobilize the resources necessary for a fully-open coercive operation. Further, if a covert operation fails the cost is likely to be less than that of the failure of an open coercive operation. Costs increase only as deniability and success become less possible and the various publics involved lessen their support and extract punishment for the failures and embarrassment. It is the threat of this type of behaviour in general that serves to keep governments fearful of outside interference. Operation Condor, a secret intelligence and operations system created in the 1970s by the military regimes of the Southern Cone may be the most notorious multinational example of such behaviours (see McSherry 2002).

States also employ private clandestine agents and there are differential response and production costs associated with these. It should be noted that both the line between these agents as state-sponsored versus state-supported terrorists as well as that between the two and clandestine state terrorism, may be easily blurred in the absence of reliable information. However, it should be clear that the distinguishing analytic criteria are temporal – was approval or instigation for an action granted prior to the decision to undertake the act? – and organizational – are the actors members of the state's covert organization or are they acting on their behalf or being supported after the fact? These analytically clear demarcations break down when agents purposefully outline acceptable goals and ambiguous limits to the means with a knowing wink and nod.

Surrogate terrorism

The third form of state terrorism in international affairs, surrogate terrorism, involves assistance to another state or insurgent organization which makes it possible for, or 'improves' the capability of, that actor to practise terrorism both at home and abroad. There are two forms of this type of terrorism. State-supported terrorism occurs when third parties undertake actions on their own which are subsequently supported by the interested state. State acquiescence to terrorism is identified when third parties, although not explicitly supported by the interested state, conduct operations which are either quietly approved (because they contribute to state objectives) and/or are not condemned or openly opposed by the interested state. Surrogate terrorism requires even lower response and production costs than the previous forms of state terrorism, but it also provides much less control and by its nature is least likely to lead to benefits that may be calculated in advance. States having few options, or finding themselves in situations where direct actions (even if they have a reasonable chance of deniability) would still be extremely dangerous were they either to fail or be discovered, often find the surrogate choice acceptable if they believe there is a chance, at the very least, to raise the costs of their adversaries. During the past twenty years, numerous states in the Middle East have provided safe havens for a variety of terrorist groups who have conducted operations against Israel and other Middle Eastern regimes with whom they have had foreign policy disagreements. Thus, for example, Syria has provided safe haven for Islamic Jihad, Hamas, Hezbollah and the PFLP General Command; Sudan provided a home for al-Qaeda, Islamic Jihad, Hamas and Hezbollah; and Libya for the PFLP General Command and Abu Nidal organization (see Pillar 2001: 157–96).

States as surrogate terrorists

Within the structures of dominance that exist in the international system, powerful states do not simply exert military force and threats to control all aspects of both the internal and external relations of subordinate states. I have already discussed the intervention of relatively powerful states in the affairs of the less powerful. Powerful states also aid the less powerful states in their domestic and international affairs. These less powerful states, in turn, assist the powerful to pursue their objectives. When states sell, grant and otherwise provide favourable terms by which their coalition partners, allies, client states (and at times neutrals and even adversaries) obtain equipment enabling their regimes to continue and/or expand practices of repression and terrorism, I would argue that in such cases states are practising a form of surrogate terrorism which at the very least may be considered as state acquiescence. When the terror serves purposes which have been discussed jointly, it spills over into state sponsorship. When the superpowers train the personnel that conducts the terror operations, consult with and advise (for 'reasons of state') the security services of 'friendly' states in their use of terrorism, this tool is a form of surrogate terrorism. As long ago as 1975, Brian Jenkins (1975) worried that nations might employ groups as surrogates for engaging in warfare with other nations. These surrogates (both state and non-state actors), he argued, might be employed:

- to provoke international incidents;
- to create alarm in an adversary;
- to destroy morale;
- to cause the diversion of an enemy's resources into security budgets;
- to effect specific forms of sabotage;
- to provoke repressive and reactive strategies and the revolutionary overthrow of targeted regimes (what we may designate as the Marighela strategy as applied by state rather than insurgent actors, see Marighela 1971).

We recognize that terrorism has become simpler for insurgents because of advances in transport, communications, weapons, technology and access to the media. We should also recognize that the vast resources of the state allow it to make far greater use of these developments than many individuals and insurgent groups. Thus we must create the conditions under which states will find it too costly to choose a policy of terrorism.

Conclusion

The preceding pages argue that strategies and tactics of terrorism are considered and employed by states in both the domestic and international policy realms. As with the case of insurgents, the practice of state terror, when identified as such, brings almost universal condemnation. But when it is the state that is the perpetrator of the terrorist act, few even pause to label the action as such. States and proponents of their actions shrink from labelling what they themselves or those they support do as 'terror', preferring more 'neutral' designations such as 'coercive diplomacy', 'assistance' to a friendly state in its pursuit of internal security or 'aid' to freedom fighters or wars of national liberation.

One final question brings us back to the beginning: if terrorism presupposes states within a conflict situation, what are the conditions then in which the expected utility model with its consideration of effectiveness and response and production costs produces empty cells, that is cells in which terrorism does not appear as a chosen policy?

As Gurr has argued:

> The disposition to use state terror is most effectively constrained if elites hold democratic values and are checked by democratic institutions. The relationship is not coincidental or spurious. Democratic political norms emphasize compromise in conflict and participation and responsiveness in relations between rulers and ruled, traits that are inconsistent with reliance on violence as an instrument of rule or opposition.
>
> (Gurr 1986: 58)

The cases in the domestic realm in which stable democracies resort to repression or even clandestine acts of terror within their borders have almost all occurred during times of extreme crises or in specific regional crises, which while 'explicable' go beyond what we expect the behaviour of democracies to be, particularly when looking from a distance of either years or miles. While repressive behaviour is the more likely extreme behaviour, even some of these states have also used terrorism against their own citizens.

If the theoretical framework employed to guide this analysis is useful, the management of the problem of states and terrorism will come in increasing the response and production costs of terrorism as a possible strategy within domestic and foreign-policy repertoires of states. The first step in such a process is the delegitimization of the option. It is necessary to tear away at the protective clothing that allows agents of the state and the public to ignore the human consequences that state terrorist behaviour generates. If we may delegitimize such behaviour, we increase the psychic production costs for state decision-makers. By challenging the behaviour and raising public awareness both at home and abroad we increase the possibilities of bystanders of the terrorism challenging the behaviour. This will contribute to an increase in the response costs that policy-makers will have to add to their decision calculus.

The raising of the issue will obviously be more effective in pluralistic Western societies than elsewhere in the international system. While these states are less likely to employ terrorist strategies within their own states, their acceptance of the international rules of the game has enabled engagement in terrorist strategies abroad and also to ignore, except in politically selected cases, terrorism by states and insurgents of which they approve.

Not all state-terrorist behaviours can be managed or countered in the same way. While all states can operate at levels equivalent to insurgents, it is quite often the case that the costs of doing so are larger than the expected benefits and thus they choose not to do so. It is our task to find useful procedures to increase the costs of terrorist operations across the board. Twenty years ago when my colleagues and I began scoring Amnesty International's and the US Department of State's reports on the five point scale concerned with states' human rights behaviours the number of states that would receive scores of 1 or 2 was significantly lower than it is today. As the number of democracies has increased, the opportunities for increased response and production costs for those that would choose terrorism also increases.

When looking across time and space at the varieties of states, the variance in circumstance and contending political and social groupings, the expected utility approach forces us to contend with the willingness of decision makers to use not simply violence instrumentally but victims instrumentally. By thinking about the processes and structures that constrain such behaviours, it is clear that calculations about not only the response of enemies but also of supporters are a key component in restraining the instrumental use of victims.

Notes

1   This chapter is based on an argument first presented in Duvall and Stohl (1983).

2   This definition of terrorism is, on the one hand, slightly expansive in relation to that of the US Department of State's in that it allows for the possibility that the victim as well as the wider target may be terrorized. It is important to note that both the 1983 Department of State definition and the modi-fied form adopted here allow for both the state and individuals or groups to be a terrorist actor and for both states and individuals or groups to be potential victims. The US Department of State adopted a new definition after 1984 and now defines terrorism as 'premeditated, politically motivated violence perpetrated against noncombatant targets by subnational groups or clandestine state agents, usually intended to influence an audience'. This new definition, whether intentional or not, dramatically restricts the definition of state terrorism by eliminating all reference to open activities of states in the violent repression of their populations. By this definition actions by state agents which are 'advertised' would not be terrorism.

3   Walzer refers to this problem as the Problem of *Dirty Hands*, the concept deriving its label from Sartre's play of that name. 'It means that a particular act of government (in a political party or in the state) may be exactly the right thing to do in utilitarian terms and yet leave the man who does it guilty of a moral wrong' (Walzer 1974: 63).

Bibliography

Ball, P., Kobrak, P. and Spirer, H.F. (1999) *State Violence in Guatemala 1960–1996: A Quantitative Reflection*. Washington, DC: American Association for the Advancement of Science.

Betts, R.K. (2002) 'The soft underbelly of American primacy: tactical advantages of terror', *Political Science Quarterly*, **117**(1), 10–36.

Beitz, C. (1979) *Political Theory and International Relations*. Princeton, NJ: Princeton University Press.

Bissell, R., Haignere, C., McCamant, J. and Piklo, M. (1978) *Varieties of political repression*, unpublished manuscript prepared for the US Department of State, p.6.

Brownlee, J. (2002) '… and yet they persist: explaining survival and transition in neo-patrimonial regimes', *Studies in Comparative International Development*, **37**(3), 35–63.

Campbell, B.B. and Brenner, A.D. (eds) (2000) *Death Squads in Global Perspective*. New York: St Martin's Press.

Davenport, C. and Ball, P. (2002) 'Views to a kill: exploring the implications of source selection in the case of Guatemalan state terror, 1977–1995', *Journal of Conflict Resolution*: **46**(3), 427–50.

Duvall, R.D. and Stohl, M. (1983) 'Governance by Terror', in Stohl, M. (ed.) *The Politics of Terrorism* (2nd edn.). New York: Marcel Dekker, pp. 179–219.

George, A. (1971) 'The Development of Doctrine and Strategy', in George, A., Hall, D. and Simons, W.R (eds) *The Limits of Coercive Diplomacy*. Boston, MA: Little Brown.

Gurr, T. R. (1986) 'The Political Origins of State Violence and Terror: A Theoretical Analysis', in Stohl, M. and Lopez, G.A (eds) *Government Violence and Repression: An Agenda for Research*. Westport, CT: Greenwood Press, pp. 45–71.

Hayner, P. (2001) *Unspeakable Truths: Confronting State Terror and Atrocity*. New York: Routledge.

Jenkins, B. (1975) 'International terrorism: a new mode of conflict', *California Seminar on Arms Control and Foreign Policy*, research paper no. 48, Santa Monica: Rand Corporation.

Kelman, H. (1973) 'Violence without moral restraint: reflection on the dehumanization of the victims and victimizers', *Journal of Social Issues*, **29**(4), 25–61.

Krain, M. (1997) 'State sponsored mass murder: the onset and severity of genocides and politicides', *Journal of Conflict Resolution*, **41**(3), 331–60.

McSherry, P. (2002) 'Tracking the origins of a state terror network: Operation Condor', *Latin American Perspectives*, **29**(1), 38–60.

Marighela, C. (1971) *The Mini-manual of the Urban Guerrilla*. London: Penguin.

Morgenthau, H. (1978) *Politics Among Nations* (5th edn.). New York: Alfred A. Knopf.

Pillar, P. (2001) *Terrorism and US Foreign Policy*. Washington, DC: Brookings Institution Press.

Ron, J. (1997) 'Varying methods of state violence,' *International Organization*, **51**(2), 275–300.

Rummel, R. (1995) 'Democracy, power, genocide and mass murder', *Journal of Conflict Resolution*, **39**(1), 3–26.

Schelling, T. (1966) *Arms and Influence*. New Haven, CT: Yale University Press

Stohl, M. (1986) 'The Superpowers and International Terrorism', in Stohl, M. and Lopez, G.A. (eds) *Government Violence and Repression: An Agenda for Research*. Westport, CT: Greenwood Press, pp. 207–28.

Stohl, M., Carleton, D. and Johnson, S.E. (1984) 'Human rights and US foreign assistance from Nixon to Carter', *Journal of Peace Research*, **3**, 1–11.

US Department of State (1983) *Terrorist bombings: a statistical overview of international terrorist bombing incidents from January 1977 through May 1983*, Office for Combating Terrorism.

Valentino, B.A. (2004) *Final Solutions: Mass Killing and Genocide in the 20th Century*. Ithaca, NY: Cornell University Press.

Walter, E.V. (1969) *Terror and Resistance*. Oxford: Oxford University Press.

Walzer, M. (1974) 'Political Action: The Problem of Dirty Hands', in Cohen, M., Nagel, T. and Scanlon, T. (eds) *War and Moral Responsibility*. Princeton, NJ: Princeton University Press, pp. 62–82.

Wardlaw, G. (1986) 'Terrorism, Counter-terrorism and the Democratic Society', in Stohl, M. and Lopez, G. (eds) *Government Violence and Repression: An Agenda for Research*. Westport, CT: Greenwood Press, pp. 189–206.

17 A conceptual framework for resolving terrorism's root causes

Joshua Sinai

To effectively resolve the violent challenges presented by terrorist[1] groups to the security and well-being of their state adversaries, it is crucial to develop an appropriate understanding of all the root causes underlying such conflicts because terrorist insurgencies do not emerge in a political, socio-economic, religious or even psychological vacuum.[2] It could be argued, in fact, that the root causes underlying an insurgency are the initial components driving the terrorist life cycle (TLC) and the terrorist attack cycle (TAC). The TLC refers to why and how terrorist groups are formed, led and organized, the nature of their grievances, motivations, strategies and demands vis-à-vis their adversaries, and the linkages that terrorist groups form with their supporting constituency. These components of the TLC, in turn, affect the TAC (a group's modus operandi, how they conduct the spectrum of operations, ranging from non-violent to violent activities, and their choice of weaponry and targeting).

To understand the context in which root causes relate to the TLC and TAC, it is necessary to conduct a comprehensive study of the magnitude of the warfare threat posed by a terrorist group against its adversary. The manifestations of the threat would then be 'drilled down' into their component warfare elements, such as conventional low impact (e.g. warfare in which a few persons will be killed in a single attack involving conventional weapons warfare, such as explosives or shootings), conventional high impact (e.g. warfare in which conventional means are used to cause hundreds or thousands of fatalities), or warfare employing chemical, biological, radiological or nuclear (CBRN, e.g. utilizing 'unconventional' means to inflict catastrophic damages). It is here, for example, where the latest advances in social science conceptual approaches, such as social network theory, would be applied to model how terrorist groups organize themselves, plan attacks, conduct recruitment, develop operational capabilities, link up with counterparts, etc.[3] Other components of the TLC and TAC also would need to be addressed, such as why certain groups choose to embark on 'martyr'-driven suicide terrorism, as opposed to other forms of warfare where operatives seek to stay alive and escape from the scene of the incident.

Once the magnitude of the terrorist threat is identified and outlined (i.e. whether conventional low impact, conventional high impact, CBRN or a combination of the three), then one could begin the process of trying to understand the underlying conditions, or root causes, for why such warfare is being waged against a specific adversary (or adversaries). Thus, to understand how to anticipate and, in the most ideal cases preemptively contain or defeat on-going or emerging terrorist insurgencies, understanding the root causes underlying such conflicts must constitute the first line of analysis in a government's combating terrorism campaign's strategies and programmes.

Therefore, to resolve terrorist insurgencies it is essential to research and systematically map the spectrum of root causes underlying a rebellion's origins, grievances and demands. In ideal cases, it is hoped that such mapping of root causes will then produce the knowledge and insight on the part of governments to formulate appropriate responses that would be most effective in terminating a terrorist insurgency,[4] whether peacefully, militarily, by law enforcement, or through a combination of these measures. By incorporating such an understanding of a conflict's underlying root causes into a government's combating terrorism campaign,[5] such response strategies and tactics could be effectively calibrated to address their specific challenges and threats. It is this chapter's objective to provide an analytic framework to enable the combating terrorism community, whether in government or the academic sectors, to develop the conceptual capability and tools to resolve terrorist insurgencies using the most appropriate mix of coercive and conciliatory measures that address the general and specific root causes and other underlying factors that give rise to such insurgencies. Without understanding how to utilize such a root causes-based conceptual capability and tools, combating terrorism campaigns are likely to be ineffectual and terrorist insurgencies will become, due to lack of effective resolution, increasingly protracted and lethal in their warfare.

Why root causes are significant?

Terrorists, whether operating as small or large groups, are generally driven to commit acts of terrorism due to a variety of factors, whether rational or irrational, in which extreme forms of violence are utilized to express and redress specific grievances and demands. Root causes are the factors and circumstances underlying insurgencies that radicalize and drive terrorists, whether they are consciously or unconsciously aware of these root causes, into carrying out their violent actions (Bjørgo, Chapter 1). Root causes consist of multiple combinations of factors and circumstances, ranging from general to specific, global, regional or local, governmental-regime, societal or individual levels, structural or psychological, dynamic or static, facilitating or triggering, or other possible variations, some of which may be more important and fundamental than others (ibid.).

Addressing a conflict's underlying root causes may not necessarily automatically lead to conflict termination. For example, there may not be a direct correlation in every case between a specific root cause and a terrorist rebellion because of the myriad of alternative forms of action, ranging from non-violent to violent, that may be available to a group to express the underlying grievances and demands driving their group. In fact, a terrorist rebellion is likely to occur only when certain significant propitious circumstances in the form of political, economic, social, military, and other underlying trends coincide and coalesce, but even these trends may not be sufficient to launch such rebellions unless they are buttressed by the availability of effective leaders, organizational formations, including a willing cadre, access to particular types of weaponry and the logistical and other covert capabilities to carry out an operation against its adversary.

Nevertheless, it is still important to understand and map the spectrum of root causes underlying a terrorist rebellion because they influence a group's choice of targeting and degree of lethality in its warfare. Thus, the intensity of how a group perceives its adversary and the strategies that it believes are required to redress the grievances against it, will affect the types of tactics and weaponry it will employ in the warfare against its stronger adversary. This is particularly the case in determining whether a group's warfare proclivity will be characterized by conventional low impact, conventional high impact, or CBRN warfare, with the latter form of warfare exponentially escalating the lethality threshold of casualties.

Another important consideration in understanding a rebellion's underlying root causes is to identify them from the varying perspectives of the insurgents, the threatened governments, and independent academic experts (who are likely to disagree among themselves) because these three general perspectives are likely to differ and, in some cases, even clash. Thus, for example, what the insurgents consider to be the underlying causes to their rebellion may be perceived entirely differently by the challenged government, which may deny the existence of such underlying factors. For example, while both Palestinians and Israelis agree that the central root cause underlying their conflict is the contention by two peoples over the same territory, there is disagreement over other possible root causes. To the Palestinian insurgents, the continued presence and expansion of Israeli settlements in the heart of the West Bank is claimed to constitute one of the primary root causes of their rebellion, whereas certain factions in the Israeli government may claim that such settlements should remain and are not an obstacle to reaching a peace accord. Independent academic experts may agree that such settlements may in fact represent an important root cause driving the conflict, because of the refusal by a minority of Israelis, in the form of the Jewish settlers, to give up their idea of a 'Greater Israel' and live within the pre-June 1967 War confines of the Jewish state. At the same time, academic experts may find that the Palestinian insurgents engage in subterfuge on this issue because even if the settlements were evacuated many Palestinians would still refuse to ever recognize the legitimacy of Israeli rights to a homeland in a re-partitioned historical Palestine. Moreover, the Israeli government and academic experts, but not the Palestinian insurgents, may argue that an important root cause is the unresolved generational conflict among the Palestinians, with the younger generation, which is highly frustrated, much more militant and extremist than their elders, desiring to impose an Islamic theocracy over Palestinian society and reject a negotiated compromise with Israel.

To bridge the different interpretations between a government and its insurgent adversary, it is necessary for academic experts, who, as pointed out earlier, may even disagree among themselves, to provide as independent, impartial and objective as possible assessments of a conflict's root causes in order to assist the two adversaries to better understand the underlying problems that require resolution of their conflict.

In another important step, identifying and categorizing a conflict's underlying root causes will make it possible to hypothesize whether or not it may be possible to influence or resolve them so that long-term insurgency termination may take hold.

How to resolve root causes

Once the spectrum of a conflict's underlying root causes is mapped and identified (initially, as in most cases, at the academic level, and then at the governmental level) then it is up to governments and their security and military organizations to formulate the appropriate combating terrorism response measures to resolve these underlying problems. For the underlying factors to be resolved, however, it is also up to the insurgents to incorporate into their demands grievances and other objectives that are amenable to the 'give and take' of compromise and negotiations because otherwise even addressing a conflict's root causes may not succeed in terminating the insurgency.

In this analytic approach, a government's combating terrorism campaign against an insurgent movement that utilizes terrorist tactics in order to overthrow that government, punish it for alleged transgressions, or seek independence against foreign rule, must be comprehensive and holistic in scope. This is because resolving terrorist insurgencies requires a much more thoroughgoing response than the narrower military or law enforcement orientations of most counter-guerrilla or counter-terrorist operations, which generally do not include crucial political, diplomatic, and socio-economic dimensions that are required to resolve a conflict's underlying root causes.

The objective of the government's combating terrorism campaign therefore is to employ a mix of coercive (e.g. military or law enforcement) and conciliatory (e.g. political, diplomatic or socio-economic) measures that either will militarily defeat the insurgents on the battlefield or peacefully terminate the insurgency by resolving the root causes and conditions that may prolong the conflict.

A successful combating terrorism campaign that seeks to address a conflict's underlying root causes must be based on the following three measures:

1   Governments need to map, identify and prioritize what they consider to be the most significant underlying root causes driving the terrorist insurgency threatening them. To conduct such an assessment, combating terrorism planners need to take into account their own perspectives, those of the insurgents, and academic experts. Once such a prioritized assessment is finalized, then the most appropriate measures need to be formulated on how these discrete root causes can be influenced and resolved. In fact, in determining the root causes associated with a terrorist insurgency, it is crucial to map all possible root causes, not just a select few that may be perceived as most likely. Such a comprehensive mapping effort will then generate the basis from which one could select those root causes whose resolution might yield the greatest benefit to eventual conflict termination. In this process, all perceived underlying root causes in a conflict would be itemized and categorized (e.g. poverty, lack of education, political inequality, foreign subjugation, religious

extremism, psychological distress, nihilism, etc.) and codified (e.g. first-order root cause, second-order root cause, third-order root cause, etc.).

2   Governments then need to formulate a clear definition in their directives and policies about the combating terrorism campaign's short-, medium- and long-term strategic objectives, including, as the final component, formulating a methodology to measure the effectiveness of their responses to the underlying root causes driving the terrorist insurgency. This involves formulating a mission area assessment that provides a roadmap for how strategic objectives can be implemented tactically on the ground for insurgency resolution to take place.

3   The combating terrorism campaign must be coordinated and integrated at all levels of government, especially among the political, diplomatic, law enforcement, intelligence, and military establishments, resulting in a 'unity of effort'.

In ideal cases, when such a three-pronged combating terrorism campaign is implemented, in situations where an insurgent conflict is caused by political or socio-economic deprivations or disparities that are exploited by the insurgents, a government's conciliatory policies that address and resolve that conflict's root causes may succeed in peacefully winning the affected populations 'hearts and minds'. Also in ideal cases where a foreign power controls a territory that is inhabited by a hostile population, then a combating campaign's conciliatory components may succeed in terminating the insurgency by providing autonomy or independence to that territory, following a consensual peace accord between the government and the insurgents.

Thus, in ideal cases, a conflict resolution-based combating terrorism strategy may be the most effective way to resolve a protracted terrorist-based insurgency where the insurgents represent 'genuine' grievances that succeed in mobilizing the local population to support their cause. This does not imply that coercive measures are not necessary as an initial governmental response to nip the insurgency in the bud. In fact, during the initial phase, coercive measures are required to counteract the insurgency's violent threats to the maintenance of law and order. These coercive measures will likely take the form of military, police and intelligence operations against the insurgent forces; governments will insist that no concessions be made to insurgent demands, which they perceive as illegitimate because violent means are used to express them; insurgent movements will be declared illegal; a state of emergency accompanied by prevention of terrorism laws will be imposed, particularly in insurgent areas; and diplomatic pressure will be exerted on the external patrons or supporters of the insurgency to cease such support.

While these coercive measures may be necessary in the initial stages of an insurgency, there are limits to the degree of coercion that democratic governments will employ in their combating terrorism campaign. Thus, for example, democratic governments, such as Israel, will refrain from employing crushing military force to wipe out civilian populations that provide the insurgents with support because of the damage that such devastation would inflict on their own democratic constitutional nature. This is the situation currently confronting Israel in its response to the al-Aqsa Intifada, where even the deployment of massive Israeli military force in Spring 2002 against Palestinian cities and towns in response to devastating Palestinian suicide terrorism against Israelis was not intended to massacre Palestinian civilians, but to ensure that terrorists, their operational handlers, and infrastructures were uprooted and destroyed so that a political settlement might be possible when conditions were considered ripe.

Moreover, even during the initial coercive phase of their response, democratic governments are likely to include certain limited conciliatory measures. These conciliatory measures will be restricted in scope, and will likely consist of limited degrees of political, legal, and socio-economic reforms, including permitting human rights groups to monitor the impact of the combating terrorism campaign on the affected population.

Authoritarian governments, on the other hand, are less inclined to act with such restraint against civilian supporters of an insurgency, as demonstrated by the crushing by Syrian forces of the Muslim Brotherhood insurgents in Hama in 1982, the Iraqi use of chemical weapons against the Kurdish villagers in early 1988, the 1998 bombardment by Serbian forces against the rebellious ethnic Albanian villagers in Kosovo, and Russia's military campaign against the Chechen terrorist separatists.

However, when an insurgency, even when it employs terrorism to achieve its objectives, succeeds in gaining the support of a significant segment of the population to its cause and in protracting the insurgency, and the government's coercive measures, accompanied by limited conciliation, are unable either to decisively defeat the insurgents on the battlefield or to resolve the insurgency peacefully, then a new combating terrorism strategy is required to resolve the conflict. Based on my research, I believe that in a situation of a protracted 'hurting stalemate' that is damaging to both sides, in which there is no military solution to end the insurgency, long-term resolution can only come about when governments begin to address the conflict's underlying root causes; but only when the insurgents' grievances are considered legitimate and grounded in some aspects of international law.

This recommendation does not imply that resolving a conflict's root causes will automatically terminate the insurgency peacefully. Some insurgent movements are inherently extremist and not interested in compromising their demands, such as militant religious fundamentalists who are intent on establishing highly authoritarian theocratic states (e.g. in Algeria, Egypt, Jordan and Lebanon[6]), or are filled with unrelenting rage against a superpower (e.g. Osama bin Laden's al-Qaeda group and its network of affiliates), while other insurgents may be using narcotrafficking means to fund their political activities (e.g. the FARC in Colombia). Thus, in such cases no peaceful accommodation may be possible between governments and insurgents even when governments are willing to resolve a conflict's 'root causes', such as socio-economic and political inequalities.

One way to determine whether it is possible for governments and insurgents to arrive at a negotiated compromise is by distinguishing between insurgents' legitimate and illegitimate grievances.[7] Legitimate grievances may be defined as those that are anchored in international law, particularly in the areas of constitutionalism and human rights, and are politically, legally, economically and geographically equitable to all relevant parties affected by the conflict. Illegitimate grievances, on the other hand, generally are based on anti-democratic, theocratic, religiously exclusionary, or criminal principles and objectives, as well as desiring the destruction or annihilation of the adversary.

Because of the different responses that are necessary to address legitimate and illegitimate demands being espoused by terrorist groups, employing conciliation to resolve a terrorist rebellion can be applied to certain types of insurgencies, but not others. In the case of the insurgency mounted by al-Qaeda, for example, there may be no alternative but to pursue a full-scale military campaign, backed by intelligence and law enforcement measures, to round up as many of their insurgents as possible, because of their operatives' single-minded pursuit of causing as much catastrophic damage to their adversaries as possible, regardless of the consequences to their own societies. In fact, even under these circumstances, it is still possible to address the underlying conditions that facilitate recruitment and support for al-Qaeda (such as the prevalence of Arab regimes that stifle opportunities for educated youths to attain socio-economic and political advancement) without giving in to al-Qaeda's demands or long-term goals.[8]

Similarly, for Israel, while it may be difficult to negotiate with insurgents such as Hamas, the Palestinian Islamic Jihad and the al-Aqsa Martyrs Brigade, because of their determination to sabotage all efforts at a peace process by launching wave upon wave of suicide bombers to achieve their goal of a theocratic Palestinian state in all of historical Palestine, the underlying conditions that perpetuate that conflict still need to be addressed. Thus, in spite of extremist demands by its terrorist adversaries, Israeli counter-terrorism planners must map that conflict's root causes in order to generate responses that will effectively terminate or mitigate that insurgency. For example, if the presence of Jewish settlers in the heart of Palestinian territories in the West Bank and Gaza Strip is considered to constitute one of the underlying root causes for continued Palestinian hostility, then evacuating and resettling those settlers in Israel 'proper' may prove to be a solution to addressing those Palestinian demands that may be judged to be 'legitimate'. In fact, there is a substantial segment of the Israeli leadership that supports the notion of 'unilateral disengagement' from such territories, even without a negotiating process with a counterpart Palestinian peace partner. However imperfect such an approach to conflict resolution, at least it recognizes that certain underlying problem areas can be resolved without appeasing the insurgents' extremist demands. Here, as in other cases, intransigence by insurgents should not preclude the need for the threatened governments facing protracted insurgencies to strive to resolve their conflicts' underlying problems by using as many creative and 'out of the box' measures as possible, because the alternative is continued suffering for all contending sides.

Notes

1   In this framework, terrorism is defined as 'a form or tactic of warfare characterized by the deliberate acts of violence, such as killing persons and causing physical damage, perpetrated by sub-state or non-state groups against all citizens of a state, whether civilian or military, to achieve a myriad of

objectives'. This definition is not intended to demonize a group that uses violence to achieve its goals or to delegitimize its grievances and demands, but merely to highlight its chosen form of tactical warfare, which is distinguished from guerrilla warfare, which deploys different sets of tactics and objectives, such as using paramilitary forces against government forces to increase territory under insurgent control.

2   In the academic literature on terrorism, several important studies have been published on the need to understand the root causes of terrorism, including Gurr (1970), Reich (1998), Smelser and Mitchel (2002).

3   For an example of how social network theory can be applied to excavating how terrorist groups such as al-Qaeda and its affiliates are organized and led see Sageman (2004).

4   The term 'terrorist insurgency' is used because generally incidents of terrorism are not single or isolated acts but are part of a protracted rebellion that employs terrorist tactics against its stronger adversary.

5   Combating terrorism (CbT) is an umbrella concept incorporating anti-terrorism, which is defensively oriented, and counter-terrorism, which is offensively oriented.

6   In the case of Lebanon, Hezbollah's political party is part of the country's confessional democratic political system, but a major intangible element is whether at some point it will seek to overthrow the political system and impose Iranian-based theocracy over the country.

7   Such operationalizing of the distinction between legitimate and illegitimate grievances was suggested by Dr Alex Schmid in a personal discussion with the author in 1995.

8   This insight was suggested by Tore Bjørgo, this book's editor, in correspondence with the author.

Bibliography

Gurr, T.R. (1970) *Why Men Rebel*. Princeton, NJ: Princeton University Press.

Reich, W. (ed.) (1990) *Origins of Terrorism: Psychologies, Ideologies, Theologies, States of Mind*. Baltimore, MD: The John Hopkins University Press.

Sageman, M. (2004) *Understanding Terror Networks*. Philadelphia: University of Pennsylvania Press.

Smelser, J. and Mitchel, F. (eds) (2002) *Terrorism: Perspectives from the Behavioral and Social Sciences*. Washington, DC: The National Academies Press.

18 Prevention of terrorism

Towards a multi-pronged approach

Alex P. Schmid[1]

The root causes of terrorism are a subject that offers some intellectual challenges.[2] When the United Nations first took up the issue of terrorism in 1972, there were two schools of thought. On the one hand there were those who were primarily interested in addressing the causes of terrorism. On the other hand, there were those who were more concerned with fighting the manifestations of terrorism itself. The second school of thought has become much more prominent over the last three decades. Today we even hear voices that plead for a disregard of causes of terrorism, perhaps for fear that addressing them could somehow justify terrorism and encourage those who engage in acts of violence to continue their atrocities.

Yet when one wants to prevent terrorism, there is really no way that one can disregard the conditions that enable terrorism, whether these are called breeding grounds of terrorism or root causes. Yet concern for the origins of terrorism and motivations of terrorists should be balanced with concern for victims and other affected groups. The study of root causes has to be placed within a broad spectrum of inquiries and activities that range from prevention and early warning to dissuasion and deterrence and, if these fail, to prosecution and retribution. An effective counter-terrorism strategy ought to be comprehensive, with full coordination between the parts and the parties concerned.

Combating terrorism is not easy since we might have to deal with a constantly changing phenomenon. A senior French intelligence officer responsible for counter-terrorism observed some three months before 11 September 2001: 'Terrorism is always changing. The way I am looking at terrorism today, is not the way I looked at it yesterday'.[3]

Is terrorism or our perception of it changing? Or are both subject to change? Some argue that 'The 11 September 2001 changed everything'.[4] It would be foolish to say that 9/11 'changed nothing'. In little more than one hour, almost 3,000 people from more than 80 states were killed in the al-Qaeda attack on the Twin Towers of the World Trade Center of New York. Yet we have to look at terrorism in a broader way than just focusing on al-Qaeda and 9/11. A number of trends can be discerned. Terrorism/terrorists:[5]

- are becoming more lethal;
- have become less dependent on state sponsorship;
- have become increasingly non-secular;

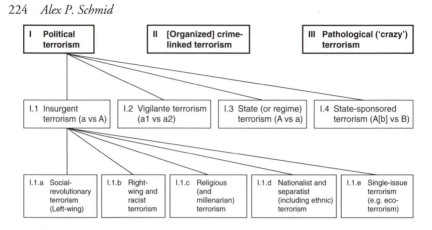

Figure 18.1 Schmid's typology of terrorism.

Source: Schmid and Jongman (1998).

- have become more suicidal;
- link increasingly up with transnational organized crime groups;
- are organized in more loosely affiliated groups; and
- allegedly strive to obtain Weapons of Mass Destruction.

When it comes to perception of terrorism, it is a fact that within the more than 190 Member States of the United Nations there is still no consensus as to what exactly should be labelled 'terrorism'. The formula 'terrorism in all its forms and manifestations' is sometimes used to offer Member States with different perceptions a 'container term' which allows for a spectrum of interpretations. Indeed, there are different types of terrorism, as this typology reminds us.

Some UN Member States perceive 'state' and 'state-sponsored terrorism' to be covered by the formula 'terrorism in all its forms and manifestations'. Some also differentiate between 'terrorism' and 'legitimate struggle for self-determination and against foreign occupation'. Other member states do not wish that the term terrorism be applied to activities of official armed forces. Yet, despite these differences, there is already considerable consensus on some key ingredients of terrorism. The negotiations in the United Nations Ad Hoc Committee on Terrorism have produced this interim draft definition:[6]

1 Any person commits an offence within the meaning of this Convention if that person, by any means, unlawfully and intentionally, causes:

(a) Death or serious bodily injury to any person; or

(b) Serious damage to public or private property, including a place of public use, a State or government facility, a public transportation system, an infrastructure facility or the environment; or

(c) Damage to property, places, facilities, or systems referred to in paragraph 1 (b) of this article, resulting or likely to result in major economic loss, when the purpose of the conduct, by its nature or context, is to intimidate a population, or to compel a Government or an international organization to do or abstain from doing any act.

This UN draft definition is approaching terrorism as a very serious crime and would, if accepted, outlaw two things: (1) the intimidation of a population, and (2) compelling a government or international organization by means of unlawful and intentional violence. These are broad and somewhat abstract categories. The existing twelve universal conventions and protocols related to the prevention and suppression of international terrorism, on the other hand, are much more concrete. These international legal instruments outlaw specific offences such as hijacking, hostage-taking and bombing (UN Office of Legal Affairs 2001):

- Unlawful acts aboard aircraft;
- Unlawful seizure of aircraft;
- Unlawful acts against the safety of civil aviation;
- Crime against internationally protected persons, including diplomatic agents;
- The taking of hostages;
- Attacks against the safety of nuclear material;
- Attacks against airports;
- Attacks against the safety of maritime navigation;
- Attacks against fixed platforms;
- Making of plastic explosives;
- Terrorist bombings;
- The financing of terrorism.

However, outlawing specific terrorist crimes is not enough. Acts of terrorism usually also have political, communicational and other features. Next to criminal justice measures, there is, therefore, a range of other measures that can be taken to combat this phenomenon of provocative, punctuated, blind, and sometimes revenge-driven violence against non-combatants. When we think of prevention and control of terrorism, we therefore have to look not just at criminal justice responses but at the whole spectrum of possible responses.

The following lists eight categories from a *Toolbox of Measures to Prevent and Suppress Terrorism*,[7] which was developed by the Terrorism Prevention Branch of the United Nations Office on Drugs and Crime in Vienna (see the appendix to this chapter) (Schmid 2001):

- Politics and Governance (e.g. negotiations, amnesty);
- Economic and Social (e.g. asset freezing, grievance removal);
- Psychological-Communicational-Educational (e.g. use of 'wanted' posters);
- Military (e.g. rescue operations);

- Judicial and Legal (e.g. use of crown witnesses, witness protection);
- Police and Prison System (e.g. stationing liaison officers abroad);
- Intelligence and Secret Service (e.g. *'Rasterfahndung'*, infiltration);
- Other (e.g. immigration measures, victim support).

Let me make some comments on one or two tools in each of these eight categories.

Politics and governance

While terrorism is a crime, it is more often than not also meant to affect politics; the process of give and take in pursuit of power within and between communities. As such, it becomes subject to measures that go beyond law enforcement. While the declaratory policy of governments often excludes negotiations with politically-motivated murderers, in reality there have been numerous instances of negotiations; if not always with the terrorists themselves then with front organizations or representatives of political parties with similar political goals as those of the terrorists who, in a sense, can themselves be seen as violent political parties. Negotiations might not be possible with organizations such as al-Qaeda which are only interested in polarization not in rapprochement, accommodation and compromise. Yet with groups that use terrorism as a tactic in an effort to share power rather than to take over political power in a totalitarian way, there is usually some room for negotiation. In such situations amnesties have been proclaimed once an interim or final political solution has been found, as in the case of Northern Ireland. Such settlements are often hard to accept for victims of terrorism as they see some of their tormentors rewarded. From a moral justice point of view it would be much better to apply preventive political measures to curb political hotheads rather than accommodate them after they have moved from radicalism to extremism and have made themselves guilty of serious politically-motivated crimes.

Prevention of violent crime strategies and prevention of terrorist crime strategies cannot be the same in all respects. While the opportunity factor plays a role in both, and the skills and tools needed to commit a violent crime are often not too different, the motivation is generally different: profit in one case and ideology in the other.[8] In my view, there are four pillars on which successful preventive national anti-terrorist measures should be built:

- good governance;
- democracy;
- rule of law;
- social justice.

Why these four? The reasons are simple:

- When governance is bad, resistance against corrupt rule gains followers and support.

- When unpopular rulers cannot be voted away in democratic procedures, advocates of political violence find a wide audience.
- When rulers stand above the law and use the law as a political instrument against their opponents, the law loses its credibility.
- When long-standing injustices in society are not resolved but allowed to continue for years, without any light in sight at the end of the tunnel, we should not be amazed that desperate people, and some others championing their cause, are willing to die and to kill for what they perceive to be a just cause.

These four principles are the foundations on which one should build policies aimed at the prevention and suppression of domestic terrorism.[9] However, they are no panacea against international terrorism.

Economic and social measures

Let us look at the second category where prevention and countermeasures might be of use: economic and social measures. Again, these are broad and somewhat diverse categories. Much attention is currently being paid to the suppression of the financing of terrorism. This is an important way of starving terrorists and their supporters of their funding. Since it is widely discussed elsewhere, I will not discuss this here.[10] Instead, I would like to turn, for a moment, to one alleged cause of terrorism frequently cited, namely the existence of poverty as a motive for terrorism. Looking at the alleged nexus between poverty and terrorism in statistical terms, I tried to combine indicators of poverty with indicators of terrorism for some 70 countries.

There are several ways of measuring poverty. One indicator of poverty is provided by the Human Development Index which UN Development Programme (UNDP) developed. It consists of three indicators, measuring respectively per capita income, life expectancy and level of education. In parallel, I created a Terrorism Index[11] which is also based on three indicators:

- severity: number of casualties (killed and injured people) per year;
- frequency: number of terrorist incidents per year; and
- scope: number of active terrorist groups in a country.

Looking at the data and comparing data from the Human Development Index of UNDP and the Terrorism Index, the correlation shown in Figure 18.2 emerges. The result, 0.25, represents a rather low correlation between the occurrence of terrorism and the occurrence of poverty.

Let us now look at the correlation between a Gross Human Rights Violations Index and the Terrorism Index (Figure 18.3).

What emerges is that while the direct correlation between the presence of poverty and the incidence of terrorism at the country level is quite low, the correlation between observance of human rights and absence of terrorism is significantly higher. While democracy itself is not a sufficient guarantee against terrorism, the presence of a

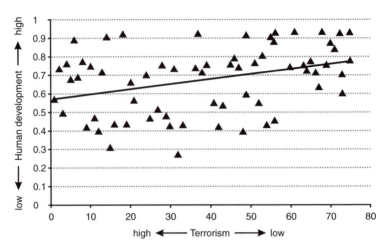

Figure 18.2 Poverty and terrorism compared.

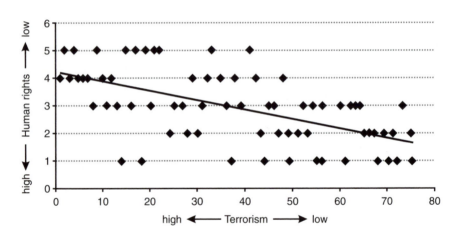

Figure 18.3 Human rights and terrorism compared.

solid rule of law regime seems to reduce the incidence of terrorism. This is not to say that poverty itself is not a very serious problem. Yet poverty should be fought in its own right, not for the purpose of preventing terrorism.

One area where poverty plays a contributory role is probably the area of unemployment, especially among relatively highly educated young men. When they see no solution to their situation in the prevailing political and economic circumstances, they become more susceptible to the false promises of those who favour terrorist methods to bring about social and political change. Table 18.1 is suggestive of such a link: almost a quarter of the recruits of insurgent groups in Kashmir cited 'joblessness' as a recruiting motive.

Table 18.1 Recruitment motives of guerrillas/terrorists from Jammu and Kashmir

Motive	
Force or threat	15.00%
Peer/family pressure	10.00%
Gentle persuasion	12.00%
Attraction	10.00%
Religious/political conviction	20.00%
Enemy/agent	0.25%
Opportunist	8.75%
Jobless	24.00%
Other	3.00%

Source: Medhurst 2000.

Countries with a 'youth bulge', a relatively open system of higher education and high unemployment rates among university graduates, would seem to be at a higher risk of seeing young men attracted to political violence, including terrorism.

Poverty might also indirectly contribute to terrorism, in that some relatively well-to-do young men and women strongly identifying with the fate of the poor begin to act as self-appointed champions of their cause, without being part of their class or ethnic group and often without asking them whether it is in their best interest. They then recruit young people on the margins of society from impoverished shanty towns, some of them petty criminals, and indoctrinate them and use them for their purposes (Cembrero 2003: 4–5).

There might be yet another way in which poverty and terrorism are indirectly linked: the massive investments into counter-terrorist measures since 9/11 draw scarce resources from social welfare and development programmes, which, in turn, might lead to greater social pressures that translate into a willingness to protest and revolt in various ways, including by acts of terrorism.

A word about 'grievances'. Genuine grievances can lead to political revolt, including acts of terrorism. Addressing the social grievances on which terrorism feeds, is necessary. However, it is sometimes difficult in practice because the demands of terrorists are often extreme. Not infrequently, the terrorists have eliminated moderates in their own political movement in their trajectory from radicalism to extremism. Their claims for a theocratic religious state or for ethnic homogeneity clash with the claims of others whose claims might be equally or even more valid. Compromise is not what many terrorists usually have in mind except as part of a 'salami' tactic to inch closer towards achieving all their professed goals. These 'dangerous dreamers of the absolute' (as Karl Marx once called them) are often totalitarian in their mindset. Their ideology must therefore be targeted.

Psychological-Communicational-Educational measures

Terrorism is more than violence. The direct targets of violence are not the primary targets, they serve mainly as message generators to impress, coerce or terrorize one or several audiences, sometimes simultaneously. A recent unpublished study of five terrorist groups found that 'terrorist propaganda is the key to escalation' as it 'leads to recruitment both of members and supporters and [helps in] raising funds' (Gunaratna).[13] The following lists terrorist target audiences:

- Those who already identify positively with the terrorist group (goal: to maintain or increase their support).
- Those who are their declared opponents (goal: to demoralize, intimidate or coerce them).
- Uncommitted members of the local community or external audiences (goal: to impress them).
- The terrorists' own organization (goal: to keep it united through planning 'the bigger one').
- Rival groups (goal: to show them who is 'number one').

The fact that an act of terrorism is more than an act of violence, that it is first and foremost an act of violence-induced communication, makes the public affairs and propaganda dimension of both terrorism and counter-terrorism crucial. Nevertheless, psychological operations in the fight against terrorism are receiving often only minor consideration. In my view, this is the single biggest shortcoming in strategies against terrorist violence.

Communication strategies can be divided into offensive and defensive operations, directed at one's own community or at the constituency of the terrorists. Israel's counter-terrorism strategy, for instance, includes efforts to strengthen the psychological resilience of its own civilian population through a campaign of education in schools (Tucker 2003);[14] efforts which would fall under the following internal psychological operations (Crelinsten and Schmid 1992):

- *Offensive internal psyops:* aimed to *promote* desired perceptions, images, opinions or attitudes among members of the society under attack.
- *Defensive internal psyops:* aiming to *prevent* undesired perceptions, images, opinions or attitudes among the members of the targeted society.
- *Offensive external psyops:* aiming to *promote* desired perceptions, images, opinions or attitudes among members of the terrorist constituency.
- *Defensive external psyops:* aiming to *prevent* undesired perceptions, images, opinions or attitudes among terrorists and their constituency.

Elements of a psychological strategy along the lines just sketched can be found in the report of a High-level Policy Working Group on the United Nations and Terrorism, which was made public on 10 September 2002. It proposes a three-pronged strategy involving dissuasion:

The Organization's activities should be part of a tripartite strategy supporting global efforts to:

(a) dissuade disaffected groups from embracing terrorism;

(b) deny groups or individuals the means to carry out acts of terrorism;

(c) sustain broad-based international cooperation in the struggle against terrorism.

(UN Security Council 2002: 1)

In the context of the first point, the Secretary-General requested the UN Department of Public Information to 'initiate a review of how the United Nations can reach local populations that support terrorist aims, in a form that is designed to be "heard" by those communities' (UN Security Council 2002: 1 & 11). In the same vein, the United Nations Education, Scientific and Cultural Organization (UNESCO) also began to promote activities and materials which can contribute as preventive measures to counteract terrorism: activities on education for human rights, tolerance, dialogue among civilizations and the *Decade for a Culture of Peace and Non-Violence* (Doyle 2002: 50).

Military measures

Let me make a few remarks on the military response to terrorism. For many people a war on terrorism model appears to be the preferred model. The war model is, in some quarters, more popular than a lower-key law enforcement model. However, when the terrorists are elusive, avoid confrontation and prefer the asymmetrical strategy of attacking civilians, the role the military can play against a clandestine organization controlling no specific territory might be limited. At times the use of the armed forces might even be counter-productive, especially when terrorists try to militarize a conflict situation in the hope that overreaction of the security forces would drive the population in their arms as the government is perceived as making little or no distinction between supporters of the terrorists and the population at large. The terrorists risk, however, that the military response might crush the terrorist organization without mobilizing popular support. Such has been the case in Argentina between 1976 and 1983. The choice between military maximum use of force (which tends to become indiscriminate) and minimum use of force (as is the police force doctrine) has important implications for the relationship between government and society. These implications needs to be considered carefully. Putting the military in control of countering terrorists tends to lead to a neglect of addressing the social and political causes of conflict and can lead to a protracted war on terror lasting a decade or longer.

Judicial and legal measures

If one views acts of terrorism not primarily as acts of warfare but as violations of the public order and acts of serious crime, a judicial response in the framework of a criminal justice model is called for. Terrorists challenge the monopoly of violence which the state claims. By levying 'revolutionary taxes' they also challenge the state's prerogative of taxation. Faced with a domestic terrorist challenge, the state, certainly the liberal-democratic state, ought to react within the limits of the rule of law while adhering to basic human rights and humanitarian law standards. However, when states are weak or failing, an exclusive law enforcement response becomes difficult to maintain. In such cases the authority of the state does not extend to all corners of the country; guerrilla groups create 'liberated zones' and even terrorists manage to create de facto no-go areas for those not belonging to their constituency and representatives of the authorities, at least during night-time.

The strong decline in interstate war in the last decades and the rise of civil disturbances and internal conflict has not led to a large-scale resource transfer from the military armed forces to police and law enforcement. The judicial apparatus of many states requires strengthening. This is often only possible with the help of bilateral or multilateral international legislative assistance and capacity-building. It is here that the Counter Terrorism Committee (CTC) of the Security Council is playing an important role. The CTC has inventorized national anti-terrorist shortcomings and is facilitating the provision of technical assistance to those states lacking sufficient resources of their own to prevent and counter terrorism. The actual legislative assistance and capacity-building work, however, is delegated by the CTC to other parts of the UN system such as the International Monetary Fund and the UN Office on Drugs and Crime in Vienna with its Terrorism Prevention Branch (TPB).

The TPB's Global Programme against Terrorism provides legislative assistance to Member States. No less than 140 out of 192 UN Member States have asked the CTC for help and support of one sort or another. The assistance which the TPB provides consists of legislative drafting, training of judges and prosecutors in using the new laws and in the introduction of measures enhancing international legal cooperation, for example in the area of extradition. The basic principle to create a strong regime against international terrorism is the *aut dedere aut judicare* principle: either you extradite a known terrorist to another country willing to bring him or her to trial or you prosecute him or her in your own country. The TPB has been working on a Global Programme against Terrorism (GPT), which engages *inter alia* in:

- analysis of effectiveness of anti-terrorist legislation;
- assistance in drafting enabling laws, and preparation of model legislation;
- strengthening the legal regime against terrorism with new tools contained in the conventions against illicit drugs and transnational organized crime;
- preparation of legislative guidelines on the basis of relevant instruments;
- preparation of implementation kits;
- technical assistance for capacity-building for international cooperation;
- promoting enabling operational structures for international cooperation;
- strengthening international cooperation for common border control;
- establishment of coordination agencies.

Police and prison system

An encompassing, multi-pronged strategy against terrorism will also have to include special training of the police to deal with terrorists. Perhaps the most important issue here is to ensure correct and lawful police behaviour and the strict application of the principle of minimum force, that is restrict the use of deadly force to what is reasonable, justified and proportionate to prevent further harm in a given situation (Bailey 1995: 754). A police that is respected and trusted by the public because it reacts adequately without overreacting tends to obtain voluntarily information on criminals in general and terrorists in particular from society. If this source of information dries up, the police acts as if it were in the dark and it will always be too short of manpower to cope with terrorist challenges.

Equally important is that good prison policies are in place. In a number of countries whole prison wings have de facto been run by the terrorists themselves who keep up indoctrination and even recruit new members to the movement behind prison walls. Measures to inhibit the formation and perpetuation of terrorist networks in prison are therefore called for. Prisons ought to be places were criminals, including terrorists, are not only punished by depriving them of their freedom. Prisons ought to be also places of rehabilitation.

Some terrorists have, paradoxically, found their prison period 'liberating': the group pressure on them is gone, the constant fear of being caught in a gunfight is gone. Imprisoned terrorists can learn a trade or study and have a chance to think about their lives and reorient themselves. Repentant terrorists (*pentiti* in Italian) are a priceless asset in the destruction of terrorist movements and ought therefore be cultivated. If a terrorist suspect has been tortured into confessions by either police or prison wardens, he or she is not likely to become 'repentant'. Torture to extract confessions is not only a gross human rights violation and, as such, a crime, it is also counterproductive. The building up of a trustful relationship with the imprisoned terrorist is time-consuming but is ultimately more rewarding, both in terms of information-gathering and in terms of preventing that he or she becomes a recidivist.

Intelligence and Secret Service

Good intelligence is the most important resource against clandestine underground organizations which are compartmentalized into cells and utilize foreign or coded language to communicate with each other. Even carefully built terrorist networks have points were they surface: cell members need safe houses, transportation, money, identification and travel documents, weapons, explosives and, above all, they need to communicate with each other and supporters from whom they can recruit new members to refill their ranks. Their modus operandi leaves certain 'footprints' which identify them even when their real names are not yet known. Before becoming terrorists, they have followed certain life-paths which also reveal characteristic patterns. Through certain investigative techniques such as *Rasterfahndung* (matrix investigations) suspects can be filtered out from larger, innocent populations. The system of

Rasterfahndung which scrutinizes data from hundreds of thousands of completely innocent people to find a few suspects poses, of course, certain privacy problems. These can, however, be resolved if due diligence is observed and regular monitoring by an independent review commission is assured.

The main problem with intelligence is that it is not widely enough and timely enough shared with others services at home and abroad for reasons of bureaucratic turf wars and for fear of revealing sources. Often the flow of intelligence between intelligence services is unidirectional rather than going in both directions in a balanced way. As a consequence, such flow tends to dry up. Another problem, especially with signal intelligence, is the huge quantity of electronically collected material and the imbalance between information and intelligence gathering on the one hand and analysis and contextual interpretation on the other hand. Timely analysis of foreign intelligence is immensely complicated by the absence of sufficient language skills within intelligence agencies (US Government 2003).

Other

Among the remaining measures listed in the *Toolbox of Measures to Prevent and Suppress Terrorism* are figures relating to victim support. Victim support is, in my view, of crucial importance. The victim of terrorism is often only, to use a crude, but telling, metaphor, the skin on a drum beaten to reach a wider audience. He or she is generally innocent, non-combatant and trusting in the protection of the state. If the state not only fails to protect him or her from an attack, but after the attack fails to care for the surviving victim and its relatives, this is bound to decrease confidence in the political system and in the solidarity of society. We are all potential victims and if we do not show care for each other, the cement that holds the community together will become brittle as we feel powerless in the face of the sudden, unprovoked attacks of terrorists. The quality of our care for the victims of terrorism will also determine our perseverance in the fight against terrorism. It is a fight we cannot afford to lose because we would lose those standards and norms that separate civilization from barbarism. As a British report on victim support put it in 1993:[15]

> A civilized society denounces violence and seeks to protect the innocent against the guilty and, to the extent that it can do so, it will be more stable and confident than one which does not.

Generous support for victims also makes sense for another reason: if the state will not defend victim group rights, they might take the law in their own hand and engage in vigilante activities which might make them resemble more and more the terrorists. As a consequence, the government might have to deal with two terrorist challenges where there was only one.

Table 18.2 Number of armed conflicts worldwide, mid-1998–mid-2001

Type	mid-1998	mid-1999	mid-2000	mid-2001
High-intensity conflict	16	22	26	23
Low-intensity conflict	70	77	78	79
Violent political conflicts	114	151	178	176
Total armed conflicts	200	250	282	278
Political tension situations	—	—	—	331

Source: PIOOM 2002.

Outlook

There are no simple solutions to the problem of terrorism.[16] As armed terrorists attack unarmed civilians in peacetime without warning, we must opt for a multi-pronged approach to terrorism and utilize a broad repertoire of responses. We must keep in mind that terrorism thrives on conflict and that we have to address the underlying conflict issues. In many cases we will not be able to solve these conflicts. The number of ongoing armed conflict is much higher than commonly assumed if one looks not only at inter-state conflicts but also at domestic conflicts in many of which the state is often not even a party (Table 18.2).

Conflict is part of human existence as groups of people have different creeds, needs and goals. What we can try to do is to provide enough conflict resolution mechanisms and tools to the conflict parties for addressing contentious issues in and between societies that the resort to violence can be minimized (Lund 1996). Democracy is a tool to conflict resolution, especially when it results in proportional rather than winner-takes-all rule. The rule of law and human rights observance (good governance) is a powerful tool against terrorism of a domestic nature, which is almost 90 per cent of all terrorism by non-state actors, depending on the region of the world (Table 18.3).

Not all domestic political conflicts are accompanied by manifestations of terrorism. Not all wars are marred by widespread war crimes. Why this is so, is an intriguing question, the answer to which might hold a key to improving our ability to prevent and control terrorism. Yet we should be under no illusion that there is a quick solution to terrorism. There are too many enabling factors and conditions at work to hope for that (Alexander and Alexander 2003):

- the absence of a universal definition of terrorism;
- disagreement as to the root causes of terrorism;
- religionization of politics;
- exploitation of the media;
- double standards of morality;
- loss of resolve by governments to take effective action against terrorism;
- weak punishment of terrorists;

Table 18.3 Terrorist incidents by region from 26 December 1997 to 8 March 2003

Region	International	Domestic ('national')	Total (= global)
North America	4	33	37
Western Europe	182	1,853	2,035
Eastern Europe	43	555	598
Latin America	77	1,103	1,180
East and Central Asia	13	43	56
South Asia	61	1,122	1,183
South-east Asia and Oceania	35	241	276
Middle East/Persian Gulf	333	1,209	1,542
Africa	29	117	146

Notes: Total incidents: 7,053
        Total fatalities: 9,856
        Total injuries: 19,129
Source: MIPT 2003;

- violation of international law by, and promotion of, terrorism by some nations;
- complexities of modern societies; and
- high cost of security in democracies.

Long as this list is, there is no ground for despair: many of the factors listed are wide open to social engineering and can be dealt with by the international community if there is enough political will and international cooperation.

Appendix

A toolbox of measures to prevent and suppress terrorism

This abbreviated list (an unabridged version can be found in Schmid (2001)), developed within the Terrorism Prevention Branch of the UN Office on Drugs and Crime, is simply meant to identify and classify possible preventive and counter-terrorist measures, regardless of their use, efficacy or rate of success. The United Nations does not necessarily endorse specific measures from this list. Some measures listed are objectionable on moral and legal grounds but have been included because examples of such practices could be found in the literature on counter-terrorism.

1. Politics and Governance

1.1 Address specific political grievance of terrorists
1.2 Engage in conflict resolution
1.3 Offer political concessions
1.4 Participation in broader political process

1.5 Amnesty
1.6 Diplomatic pressure on state sponsors to decrease their support

2. Economic and Social

2.1 Address specific socio-economic grievances
2.2 Engage in socio-economic policies that reduce inclination to engage in political violence
2.3 Address financial/monetary aspects of terrorism
2.4 Other

3. Psychological-Communicational-Educational

3.1 Attempts to establish a common value base with political opponents
3.2 Providing a forum for freedom of expression
3.3 Use of media
3.4 Counter-terrorism public relations campaign
3.5 Other

4. Military

4.1 Use of strikes/operations
4.2 Use of armed forces for protecting potential victims and objects
4.3 Recruitment/training/maintenance of personnel
4.4 Operating procedures and policies

5. Judicial and Legal

5.1 International efforts
5.2 Domestic legislation
5.3 Witnesses
5.4 Courts

6. Police and Prison System

6.1 Target hardening
6.2 Enhance international police cooperation
6.3 Enhance capacity of law enforcement officials
6.4 Informants/infiltrators
6.5 Police behaviour
6.6 Police powers
6.7 Measures to inhibit the formation and perpetuation of terrorist networks in prison

7. Intelligence and Secret Services

7.1 Use of technology (traditional and newly developed) and human intelligence (HUMINT)
7.2 Engage in exchange of intelligence
7.3 Intelligence/infiltration
7.4 Use of secret negotiations
7.5 Develop an early warning system based on indicators of public violence

8. Other

8.1   Concessions/deals
8.2   Immigration measures
8.3   Victim support
8.4   Governmental strategy

Notes

1   The views and opinions expressed in this chapter are solely those of the author and do not necessarily represent official positions of the United Nations and its Terrorism Prevention Branch.

2   William O'Neill (2002) noted in this regard: 'Proponents of looking for root causes of terrorism have three difficult tasks. First, they must make clear that understanding or explaining is not the same as justifying or excusing terrorism. Second, they must explain why some terrorist groups operate in wealthy, economically vibrant and well-governed democracies (France, Italy, Germany, USA, Japan, Spain) and why so many poor countries do not experience terrorism. And third, even when terrorism plagues poor countries, why are so many of its leaders are relatively wealthy and well educated (Hamas, Hezbollah, al-Qaeda, Sendero Luminoso)?'

3   In interview with Bruce Hoffman (RAND Corporation), Paris, May 2001 (Hoffman 2001).

4   Remark made by Maurice Bigar, an Independent expert and Advisor of the Counter-Terrorism committee at a presentation held at OLA/UNITAR seminar, 27–8 May 2003.

5   Sources: US General Accounting Office (2003) and Schmid (2002).

6   UN Ad Hoc Committee on Terrorism: Informal Texts of Art. 2 and 2 bis of the draft Comprehensive Convention, prepared by the Coordinator. Reproduced from document A/C.6/56/L.9 Annex I.B. These texts represent the stage of consideration reached at the 2001 session of the Working Group of the Sixth Committee. It is understood that further consideration will be given to these texts in future discussions, including on outstanding issues. –A/57/37 Annex II.

7   See the appendix to this chapter for an unabridged version of the *Toolbox of Measures to Prevent and Suppress Terrorism*.

8   For a discussion of prevention see, for example, US National Crime Prevention Institute (2001), Gilligan (2001), and Schmid and Melup (1998).

9   This view closely parallels that of the late UN High Commissioner for Human Rights, Mr Sergio Vieira de Mello, who said (2002), 'I am convinced that the best, the only, strategy to isolate and defeat terrorism is by respecting human rights, fostering social justice, enhancing democracy and upholding the primacy of the rule of law. We need to invest more vigorously in promoting the sanctity and worth of every human life; we need to show that we care about the security of all and not just a few; we need to ensure that those who govern and those who are governed understand and appreciate that they must act within the law'.

10   See, for example, European Center for Security Studies (2003).

11   I used a two-based logarithmic transformation, $f(X) = \log 2(2 + X)$, (adding 2 is necessary because some cases have a zero value and so do not allow a logarithm to be taken). The two-based index levels extreme values in any one variable, as shown below:

12   The Human Rights Index was originally developed by Michael S. Stohl of the University of California. It is based on the Human Rights Country Reports of the US Department of State. The data here are taken from the World Conflicts and Human Rights Map of PIOOM, Leiden University (2002).

	Incidents	Groups	Victims	Index
Country 1	10	10	1,000	17.14
Country 2	100	100	100	20.02

13 Conversely, the study found that 'the government reaching out to terrorists in different states of mind was paramount to weaken terrorist cohesion, confuse terrorist thinking and facilitate terrorist desertions. Thus sustained information operations aimed at weakening the motivation of individual terrorists can contribute towards permanently de-escalating the fight. [...] As long as the ideology of a group remains undefeated, the opportunity for survival and making a return in some other form, often with renewed vigour, is high'.

14 The other four elements of Israeli counter-terrorism strategy comprise: (1) intelligence collection and analysis; (2) military and paramilitary operations to disrupt terrorist infrastructure; (3) commercial aviation security: and (4) defence against chemical and biological attacks (Tucker 2003).

15 Victim Support (1993) cited in Goodey (2003).

16 Based on a comparative study, Y. Alexander (2002) concluded, 'First, there are no simplistic or complete solutions to the problem of terrorism. As the tactics utilized to challenge authority of the state are, and continue to be, novel, so too must be the response by the instruments of the state. We must also be cautious to avoid the kinds of overreaction that could lead to repression and the ultimate weakening of the democratic institutions we seek to protect'.

Bibliography

Alexander, D.C. and Alexander , Y. (2003) *Terrorism and Business: The Impact of 11 September 2001*. Ardsley, NY: Transnational Publishers, p.195.

Alexander, Y. (2002) *Combating Terrorism: Strategies of Ten Countries*. Ann Arbor: University of Michigan Press.

Bailey, W.G. (1995) *The Encyclopedia of Police Science* (2nd. ed.). York: Garland Publishing.

Cembrero, I. (2003) *The Roots of Violence Within Moroccan Youth*. El Pais.

Crelinsten, R.D. and Schmid, A.P. (1992) 'Western responses to terrorism: a twenty-five year balance sheet', in Schmid, A.P. (ed.) *Western Responses to Terrorism*, special issue of *Terrorism and Political Violence*, 4(4), Winter, pp. 322–3.

de Mello, S.V. (2002) *Statement before the Counter-terrorism Committee of the UN Security Council*, 21 October.

Doyle, M.W. (2003) 'Toward a long-term United Nations strategy to combat terrorism. Part 1: The United Nations system and terrorism: current activities', in *Combating international terrorism: the contribution of the United Nations*, New York: United Nations Office on Drugs and Crime.

European Center for Security Studies (2003) *The economic war on terrorism: money laundering and terrorist financing*, international conference sponsored by the Conference Center of the George C. Marshall European Center for Security Studies, co-sponsored by the US Department of the Treasury, the US Federal Bureau of Investigation and the US Department of Justice, Garmisch-Partenkirchen, Germany, 21–4 July. http://www.marshallcenter.org

Gilligan, J. (2001) *Preventing Violence*. New York: Thames & Hudson.

Goodey, J. (2003) *Compensating Victims of Violent Crime in the European Union*'. Washington, DC: National Roundtable on Victim Compensation.

Gunaratna, R. Unpublished draft.

Hoffman, B. (2001) *Combating terrorism: in search of a national strategy*, Washington, DC, RAND, 27 March. Testimony before the Sub-committee on National Security, Veterans Affairs and International Relations, House Committee on Government Reform, Washington, DC: US Congress.

Lund, M.S. (1996) *Preventing Violent Conflicts: A Strategy for Preventive Diplomacy*. Washington, DC: US Institute of Peace Press.

Medhurst, P. (2000) *Global terrorism*, a course produced by UNITAR, New York: UNITAR, p.68.

MIPT (2003) Oklahoma City National Memorial Institute for the Prevention of Terrorism, Spring 2003.

O'Neill, W.G. (2002) 'Beyond slogans: how can the UN respond to terrorism?', in *International Peace Academy Responding to Terrorism: What Role for the United Nations?*, Proceedings of a conference, New York, 25–6 October, p.7.

PIOOM (2002) *World conflict and human rights map 2001/2002*, Leiden University.

Schmid, A.P. (2001) 'Towards Joint Political Strategies for Delegitimizing the Use of Terrorism', in Schmid, A.P. *et al.* (eds) *Countering Terrorism Through International Cooperation*. Milan: ISPAC. The toolbox is also available at http://www.nupi.no/IPS/filestore/UN-Toolboxantiterrorism.pdf

Schmid, A.P. (2002) *Links between terrorist and organized crime networks: emerging patterns and trends*, ISPAC conference paper, Courmayeur, 6–8 December.

Schmid, A.P. and Jongman, A.J. (1988) *Political Terrorism: A New Guide to Actors, Authors, Concepts, Databases, Theories and Literature*. Amsterdam: SWIDOC, North Holland Publishing Company.

Schmid, A.P. and Melup, I. (eds) (1998) *Violent Crime and Conflict*. Milan: ISPAC.

Tucker, J.B. (2003) *Strategies for countering terrorism: lessons from the Israeli experience*, http://www.homelandsecurity.org/journal/articles/tucker-israel.html

UN Office of Legal Affairs (2001) *International Instruments Related to the Prevention and Suppression of International Terrorism*. New York: United Nations.

UN Security Council (2002) *Measures to eliminate international terrorism*, item 162 of the provisional agenda, report of the High-level Policy Working Group on the United Nations and Terrorism, Annex to A/57/273–S/2002/875: General Assembly/Security Council, New York: United Nations.

US General Accounting Office (2003) *Combating terrorism: interagency framework and agency programs to address the overseas threat*, Report (GAO-03-165) to Congressional Requesters, Washington, DC, May, pp. 28–30.

US Government (2003) *Report of the Joint Inquiry into the Terrorist Attacks of 11 September 2001 to Congress*, by the House Permanent Select Committee on Intelligence and the Senate Select Committee on Intelligence, Washington, DC: Government Printing Office, July.

US National Crime Prevention Institute (2001) *Understanding Crime Prevention*. Boston, MA: Butterworth & Heinemann.

Victim Support (1993) *Compensating the victim of crime*, report of an Independent Working Party, London: Victim Support, p.4.

19 Fire of Iolaus

The role of state countermeasures in causing terrorism and what needs to be done

Andrew Silke

Introduction

In the nineteenth century, puerperal fever was one of the most feared diseases for women who were planning to deliver a child in a public hospital. Even in the most modern hospitals of the age, as many as one quarter of the patients would die as a result of this disease. Yet what were the root causes of the illness? On one level, childbirth itself was a cause. This, after all, was the reason the mothers were hospitalized and why they were receiving treatment. Yet, in 1847, an Austrian doctor, Ignaz Semmelweis, made a profound breakthrough. He discovered that while the hospital may be treating these women because of childbirth, vast numbers were dying not because labour itself was inherently so dangerous, but because the manner in which the hospitals treated these women was so misguided. Poor sanitary conditions and misguided medical practices rapidly spread infection and disease among patients. One could not solve the problem of patients dying from puerperal fever without first tackling the major cause of these deaths: the way in which hospitals managed people who came for treatment. When Semmelweis introduced the use of proper disinfectants, the death rate plummeted from nearly a quarter of all women to just one patient in a hundred.

The flawed manner in which the medical profession had responded to puerperal fever was a major cause of the disease's spread and lethality. Similarly, the issue of how states respond to terrorism raises questions about the nature of the drivers for terrorist violence. It has been argued by some that state countermeasures should not be seen as a root cause of terrorism. After all, they are primarily a reaction to something which is already occurring. Yet, as with the early medical countermeasures to puerperal fever, while a problem exists in some form before the countermeasures are introduced, these measures themselves can profoundly affect the nature and lethality of that problem. As a driver and facilitator of terrorist campaigns, state countermeasures can have a negative impact far greater than many of the issues which are traditionally seen as root causes of terror. Any comprehensive analysis of the causes of terrorism which does not consider state responses, runs the risk of being as limited and flawed as an analysis of puerperal fever which did not consider the practices of doctors and hospitals in the treatment of that disease.

Fortunately, there already exists in the literature on terrorism some appreciation that countermeasures can inadvertently play a major role in causing and sustaining terrorism. Mythology often provides insight into modern life, and the fight against terrorism has on more than one occasion been likened to the mythological struggle against the monstrous Hydra (e.g. Wilkinson 1986). The Hydra was a beast with formidable resilience. In battle it could recover from even the fiercest strikes. When one of its heads was knocked off, two more would grow swiftly in place. Thus the creature could survive a barrage of savage blows, growing stronger in the aftermath of each one, until eventually its foe was exhausted and overwhelmed. Here is a form of violence which rather than being crushed by strong aggressive countermeasures can actually be stimulated and become an even greater threat. Yet, why exactly is this the case? And what lessons are there to be taken away at a time when a so-called 'War on Terror' is being prosecuted across the globe?

Ultimately, there is no simple and single solution to terrorism, just as there is no simple and single cause. Responding effectively to terrorism is a very complex matter: a considerable array of responses are available to any regime facing a terrorist threat. As with many things in life, the easy and popular options are often also the most useless and unhelpful. Terrorism, itself the extreme use of violence and force, encourages a view that forceful and violent responses are not simply justified in combating it but are also obligatory. Such reactions are understandable but they can show a poor awareness of human psychology.

One conflict which has shown the painful consequences of forceful (yet popular) responses is that surrounding Northern Ireland. The 'troubles' here offer many lessons for anyone interested in solving stubborn and costly terrorist campaigns, but a critical feature is that to get a useful answer one needs first to ask a useful question.

In 1968, the Irish Republican Army (IRA) was a moribund, shrivelled and irrelevant organization. Its membership was tiny and in long decline, its bantam resources diminished further with each year, and its political front, Sinn Fein, was an irrelevance boasting little electoral mandate. How, in the space of a handful of years, could this senile group turn into the largest, best equipped, best funded terrorist organisation in the Western world? From being a parochial joke, how did the IRA become a fiercely supported organization which enjoyed massive local endorsement and tolerance and become the benefactor of millions of pounds of donations from sympathizers spread around the world? A major factor in the growth of the IRA was not the skill and acumen of its leaders and members, but more the ineptitude of the manner in which the state chose to subdue it. As Seán MacStiofáin, the Provisional IRA's first Chief of Staff put it:

> It has been said that most revolutions are not caused by revolutionaries in the first place, but by the stupidity and brutality of governments. Well, you had that to start with in the North all right.
>
> (MacStiofáin 1975: 115)

In 1969, the Catholic minority in Northern Ireland were suffering considerable discrimination at the hands of the Protestant majority. Catholics were kept out of the civil service, the judiciary and managerial positions in Ulster's industries. Catholic families had more trouble acquiring state housing than their Protestant counterparts, and even in higher education Catholics were seriously underrepresented. Added to this, Protestant politicians manipulated voting boundaries to minimize Catholic influence in elections.

In August 1969, events came to a head as serious riots erupted first in Derry, then in Belfast. The riots followed in the wake of the annual Apprentice Boys March in Derry. Catholic crowds stoned the marchers and then were attacked themselves in a violent counter-reaction from the Royal Ulster Constabulary (RUC, the largely Protestant police force). The RUC actions were caught on television and led to a strong condemnation from the Irish government, which hinted they would invade the North to protect the Catholic population. Such hints provoked Protestant rioting in Belfast, and Protestant mobs invaded Catholic areas causing widespread violence. Three and a half thousand families (3,000 of them Catholic) were driven from their homes in Belfast during August and September. At least as many Catholics again would be driven from their homes over the next four years, in the largest case of ethnic cleansing in Europe since the Second World War. Protestants in their turn would be driven out of their enclaves in Catholic areas. The principle was the same. It just so happened that more Catholics were at risk (Lee 1989: 429).

As already stated, the IRA had been in serious decline since a failed campaign of violence in the North's border areas which lasted from 1956–62. By the time of the 1969 riots, the organization was lethargic and lacked a clear structure and focus. The fervent republican ethos had become diluted with socialism, and even the traditional ban prohibiting active involvement in parliamentary politics was being reconsidered. When Protestant mobs swept into Catholic areas, the IRA lacked the manpower or the weapons to offer any kind of resistance. In the aftermath, the letters 'IRA' became in Catholic minds, 'I Ran Away'.

Help for the beleaguered Catholics instead came from the British Army: in hindsight, a surprising source. In mid-August, to the frustration of the Protestants and the relief of the Catholics 10,000 British troops were sent to the North and the rioting was quelled. In the wake of the Army, the British Government imposed substantive reforms meeting virtually all of the demands of the civil rights movement (which shortly disbanded, its aims essentially achieved).

However, the Catholic experience at the hands of the Protestant mobs and the security forces in August meant the matter would not simply dissipate there. In Belfast, disgust at the IRA's failure during the riots led to a split in the organization, with a more focused and militant Provisional IRA (PIRA) abandoning the socialism and emerging-politicization that characterized the 1969 IRA. The Provisionals provided a far more attractive and comprehensible façade to their Catholic neighbours, than the older IRA had. Initially they were almost a single-issue group, there largely just to protect the Catholic population. However, a united Ireland offered a long-term solution to this problem as well, and the Republican dimension was quickly to the fore again. Apart from being ideologically more accessible and acceptable, the PIRA benefited from a superior ability to acquire weapons and funds.

The emergence of such a vigorous militant force led to crackdown from the security forces, but this would have unforeseen repercussions. The PIRA benefited enormously from a massive influx of young recruits, who collectively became known as the 'Sixty-niners' within Republican vocabulary (Bishop and Mallie 1987). However, it was only in 1970, when crude and oppressive security policies gave many previously uninvolved Catholics ample reason to hate the RUC and British Army, that the recruits began joining up en masse.

For example, in one two month period, over 1,183 Catholic homes were extensively vandalized by the security forces searching for weapons. The searches may not have been as extreme as Israeli demolitions of militants' homes in Gaza and the West Bank, but they were still highly ruinous. Carpets and floorboards were pulled up, doors kicked in, walls and ceilings knocked open with drills and sledgehammers. Yet in just 47 cases were weapons actually found. In 1971 alone, 17,262 Catholic houses were searched in this manner (Lee 1989: 433). The IRA themselves worked to provoke harsh measures from the unfortunate security forces, knowing full well the benefits it would reap in terms of support and recruits. For example, the IRA provoked a riot in Ballymurphy in April 1970. The security forces responded with the widespread use of CS gas alienating Catholics living in the area as well as the rioters.

As Bishop and Mallie astutely observe, it was not deeply felt republicanism which led to the IRA recruitment boom of the early 1970s,

> ... usually it was an experience or series of experiences at the hands of the Army, the police or the Protestants that left them with a desire to protect themselves in the future and also to get back at the state.
>
> (Bishop and Mallie 1987: 151–2)

The trend continued throughout the early 1970s, the IRA provoking the security services who generally lacked the restraint necessary to win the propaganda war. By the end of 1970, PIRA membership had grown from 100 to over 800 in the Belfast area alone. In an attempt to control the burgeoning growth of the PIRA, internment without trial was introduced by the Stormont government in August 1971. Theoretically internment was meant to allow the imprisonment of PIRA activists quickly and efficiently. The reality was that internment was the biggest miscalculation made in an attempt to end the violence. The intelligence on which people were detained was often appallingly poor. Of the first 2,357 people arrested, 1,600 were released without charge after humiliating interrogation (in some cases involving torture), leaving the innocent with a deeply unpleasant, offensive and bitter encounter with the security forces. In its wake and for as long as it continued, PIRA recruitment soared. The killing of 13 people on Bloody Sunday, 30 January 1972, by British Paratroopers in Derry added further to the vilification of the security forces, and did much to cement international support for the PIRA, particularly in the USA. Strong local support, ample manpower, and newly acquired funds and weapons allowed the PIRA to conduct an unprecedented campaign of violence against the RUC, judiciary and Army. The destruction and death toll escalated dramatically. Finally, the British

Government stepped in and dissolved Stormont, implementing direct rule. Ultimately, the opportunity to bring about an end to the bloodshed had been lost for decades.

Feeding the Hydra

It has long been recognized that for most members a key motivation for joining a terrorist organization ultimately revolves around a desire for revenge (Schmid and Longman 1988). Humans certainly have an incredibly strong sense of justice and a desire for vengeance represents a persistent darker side to this. It is not just humans either who can feel this way. Research on our nearest primate relatives reveals similar patterns. For example, Jennifer Scott at the Wesleyan University in Connecticut has found comparable behaviour in gorillas. Physically massive alpha males, can still be given a hard time by their subordinates if they appear to behave unjustly (Tudge 2002).

Cota-McKinley *et al.* (2001: 343) define vengeance as 'the infliction of harm in return for perceived injury or insult or as simply getting back at another person'. These researchers carried out one of the few psychological studies on the subject in recent years and their thoughts on the subject are worth considering in more detail.

One important element of the desire for vengeance is the surprising willingness of individuals to sacrifice and suffer in order to carry out an act of revenge. As Cota-McKinley *et al.* (ibid.: 343) comment:

> Vengeance can have many irrational and destructive consequences for the person seeking vengeance as well as for the target. The person seeking vengeance will often compromise his or her own integrity, social standing, and personal safety for the sake of revenge.

This observation is supported by a number of research studies. For example, in one Swiss study, researchers gave students a cooperative task of the 'prisoner's dilemma' kind: all students in the study benefit provided each behaves honourably, but those who cheat will benefit more provided they are not caught. The students were rewarded with real money if they did well and fined if they did not. They were also able to punish fellow players by imposing fines but could only do this by forfeiting money themselves. This meant that those who punished others frequently would end up with considerably less than those who punished others only a little. Despite this, the research found that the participants tended to punish cheats severely, even though they lost out by doing so. People seem to hate cheats so much that they are prepared to incur significant losses themselves in order to inflict some punishment on the transgressors (Tudge 2002).

The principle goes well beyond gorillas and university students. James Gilligan, a prison psychiatrist who encountered some incredibly violent and dangerous individuals during his career, judged that:

> I have yet to see a serious act of violence that was not provoked by the experience of feeling shamed and humiliated, disrespected and ridiculed, and that did not

represent the attempt to prevent or undo this 'loss of face': no matter how severe the punishment, even if it includes death. For we misunderstand these men, at our peril, if we do not realize they mean it literally when they say they would rather kill or mutilate others, be killed or mutilated themselves, than live without pride, dignity and self-respect.

(Gilligan 2000: 110)

Yet why are people willing to pay such costs? What ends are served by a process which brings such cost to oneself? Cota-McKinley *et al.* (2001) highlight that revenge can fulfil a range of goals, including righting perceived injustice, restoring the self-worth of the vengeful individual, and deterring future injustice. Lying at the heart of the whole process are perceptions of personal harm, unfairness, and injustice and the 'anger, indignation and hatred' associated with the perceived injustice (Kim and Smith 1993: 38).

Ultimately, the desire for revenge and the willingness to violently carry it out are tied both to the self-worth of the originally offended individual and also to a deterrent role against future unjust treatment. The vengeful individual 'sends the message that harmful acts will not go unanswered' (Kim and Smith 1993: 40). Not only is the goal to stop this particular form of maltreatment in the future, it is to deter the transgressor from wanting to commit similar crimes; additionally, vengeance may stop other potential offenders from committing similar crimes or from even considering similar crimes.

Not everyone though is equally content with the idea of vengeance or equally prepared to act in a vengeful manner. What little research that does exist indicates that some groups are more vengeance prone than others. Men hold more positive attitudes towards vengeance than women, and young people are much more prepared to act in a vengeful manner than older individuals (Cota-McKinley *et al.* 2001). It is not surprising to find that most recruits to terrorist groups then are both young and male. Some evidence exists too to suggest that religious belief also affects one's attitude to vengeance, with more secular individuals showing less approval to vengeful attitudes.

In-group and out-group stereotyping however can leave both sides depressingly blind to this reality. As Cota-McKinley *et al.* (2001) emphasized in their writing, revenge revolves around the idea of injustice and more particularly redressing injustice. However, appreciating this reality, involves accepting that your in-group has behaved in an unjust manner. In a conflict situation, however, stereotyping does not easily allow for accepting ignoble behaviour of the in-group. We are good, they are bad. God is on our side. Everything we do is justified, everything they do is provocative, inhumane and cruel. We are innocent, they are guilty. Or at least, we are more innocent than they are.

Living in denial

In Northern Ireland, even after policies such as internment without trial were abandoned, there were many who continued to argue their benefits. It was argued that the aggressive tactics had after all resulted in weapons seizures and the incarceration of actual terrorists. These were significant achievements against a very serious problem. The counter-productive elements of such policies were ignored or dismissed. As a result throughout the conflict there remained voices who constantly advocated for these policies to be used. After the Shankill bombing in 1993, when a botched IRA bombing killed nine Protestant civilians (including two young girls), mainstream Unionist politicians argued strenuously in public that internment should be reintroduced. This was an understandable reaction given the human needs for justice and revenge. But it also displayed a blindness to the formidable costs hard-line policies bring in their wake. Northern Ireland is not the only arena to show such blindness, however.

On 5 April 1986, a bomb was detonated at La Belle discothèque club in West Berlin, a popular venue with off-duty American soldiers. The explosion killed three people and wounded more than 200 others. Two of the dead and some 80 of the injured were American servicemen. Intercepted embassy messages indicated that the Libyan government had been involved in the attack. In retaliation, the Reagan administration authorized a direct military strike on Libya, codenamed *Operation El Dorado Canyon*.

Ten days later, in the early morning of 15 April, over 40 US warplanes entered Libyan airspace. Flying just over 200 feet above the ground and at speeds of around 540 miles per hour, the planes closed in on targets in Tripoli and the important port city of Benghazi. The Americans devoted special attention to attacking Libyan leader Qaddafi's personal compound at the Sidi Balal naval base, dropping 2,000 pound, laser-guided bombs on buildings Qaddafi was believed to use. After the raid, the Libyans claimed that 37 people had been killed and nearly 100 wounded. Among the dead was Qaddafi's adopted daughter, and two of his sons were among those seriously injured. Qaddafi himself escaped the attack unharmed.

The military strike was extremely popular in the USA. Most Americans believed that the strike sent a powerful warning to states and groups who were contemplating terrorist attacks against American targets. The international community though reacted badly to the bombings and it was condemned outright by Arab nations. In Europe, only the UK provided support for the US action. The British Government allowed the Americans to use airfields in England to launch the attack. In contrast, other European countries, such as France and Spain, refused to even allow the US planes to fly through their airspace.

In the eyes of many experts and professionals, the raid came to be seen as having had a valuable deterrent effect on terrorist activity. For example, a research study conducted at Harvard University by Mark Kosnik (2000), a US Navy commander, concluded that the attack

> left Qaddafi weak, vulnerable, isolated and less able to engage in terrorism ... it put Qaddafi's terrorist apparatus on the defensive, rendering it less able to focus on new terrorist activities ... following the raid Qaddafi reduced his terrorist activity ... [and the attack] did not trigger a new cycle of violence against America.

Similar views are very common in the literature on terrorism and seen in such terms, the retaliation seems an unequivocal success. But is this an accurate assessment?

Many experts expressed serious doubts about the frequent claims of success surrounding *El Dorado Canyon*. Writing shortly after the attack, Michael Stohl (1987) warned against the back-slapping and congratulatory tone which dominated US political discourse on the bombing. The raid was being widely cited as being immediately effective in fighting terrorism, though Stohl pointed out that there was no reasonable evidence to support such claims. By 1998, Bruce Hoffman was able to comment that contrary to many claims, Libyan involvement in terrorism detectably increased in the immediate years after the raid (Hoffman 1998). He could not understand on what basis the original claims of a decrease were being made. Other studies agreed with Hoffman and judged that the accepted view of *El Dorado Canyon* being a success was badly misplaced (Enders *et al.* 1990; Enders and Sandler 1993). These studies were based on trends in international terrorism, and had uncovered that the retaliatory strike led to a significant short-term increase in terrorism directed against the USA and its close ally the UK. In the three months after the raid, terrorist bombings and assassinations against US and UK targets nearly doubled. Significant disruption was also caused when hoax attacks increased by 600 per cent. Libya, far from being cowed into submission, actually increased its commitment to terrorism and started to sponsor even more acts of terrorism than before. These new efforts included an attempt to launch a bomb attack in New York in 1988 (an attempt which was only foiled when the terrorist delivering the bombs was pulled over for a traffic offence in New Jersey). More tragically, the new terror campaign also included the bombing of Pan Am flight 103 in December 1988 over Lockerbie, Scotland, which left 270 people dead. In terms of saving lives, the *El Dorado Canyon* was a dismal failure. In the four years prior to the strikes, Libyan-supported terrorism killed 136 people. In the four years after the strikes, Libyan terrorism left 599 people dead (Collins 2004).

The UK also paid in other ways for its support of the US action. In the months after the raid, Libya secretly shipped an estimated 130 tonnes of weapons and munitions to the Provisional IRA. This haul included at least 5 tonnes of Semtex-H explosive (the bomb which brought down Pan Am 103 is believed to have contained just eight ounces of Semtex-H). Such a massive injection of weaponry virtually guaranteed that the IRA would have the means to continue their terrorist campaign for decades to come if they wished.

Stohl (1987) pointed out that the doctrine the USA adopted for responding to Libyan-sponsored terrorism in 1986 had been consciously modelled on the Israeli approach to tackling terrorism. The Israelis certainly had a deserved reputation for responding to terrorism in a highly aggressive and punitive manner. But how wise was the USA to follow in their wake?

On 11 March 1978, a team of Palestinian terrorists landed on the Israeli coast twenty miles south of Haifa. They promptly killed a US tourist, shot dead the occupants of a taxi, took hostage the passengers of a bus and then drove the bus to Tel Aviv, firing randomly at passing traffic as they went. The event ended in a violent shoot-out with the authorities. By the time it was all finished, 25 civilians were dead, as were nine of the 11 terrorists, and over 70 people had been injured. In response Israel launched a massive invasion of Southern Lebanon. Over 20,000 troops poured over the border backed up by tanks and jets. In the resulting fighting the Israelis killed 2,000 people and left a further 250,000 homeless.

Yet, Brophy-Baermann and Conybeare (1994) in an analysis of terrorist trends, found that the invasion, despite all the ferocity, failed to produce the expected decrease in terrorist attacks against Israeli targets. On the contrary, the level of attacks against the Israelis remained stubbornly stable. In the face of massive international condemnation the Israelis slowly pulled their troops back across the border. However, irked by continuing terrorist attacks, Israel invaded again a few years later in June 1982. This time they were determined to teach an even harsher lesson. In Operation *Peace in Galilee*, the Israelis forced their way deep into Lebanon and after four days of fighting they reached Beirut which was put under siege. The bombardment of the city lasted for over four weeks and casualties were horrendous. Over 18,000 people, most of them civilians, were killed and at least 30,000 were injured. Yasser Arafat and the PLO, the main targets of the Israelis, fled Beirut into exile. In the aftermath, over 1,000 Palestinian refugees were massacred in the city at the hands of paramilitaries allied to the Israeli army. Yet what did all this bloodshed achieve? Did terrorist attacks against Israel decline afterwards? Despite the violence, Brophy-Baermann and Conybeare (1994) again found that *Peace in Galilee* failed entirely to stop or reduce terrorism: attacks continued unabated and undiminished.

Though many continued to portray the various retaliations as successes, there was now mounting evidence that they were distinctly failing to deter terrorism. Worse, they could provoke a backlash of violence, a backlash which often included acts of terror more destructive and more costly than those which had originally goaded the Americans and Israelis to action. The retaliations, rather than cowing the Libyans and the Palestinians away from terrorism, had served only to increase support for extremists.

Why do military retaliations, pre-emptive strikes and other aggressive policies so often struggle to have more of an obvious detrimental impact on terrorism? Though many writers, analysts and security practitioners argue that they do work, the reality as testified by the actual records of terrorist attacks and activity is that retaliations do not have this effect. Why is this the case? The answer lies in understanding why people become terrorists and support terrorist groups to begin with. Labels like extremism, fundamentalism and fanaticism all work to help dismiss terrorism as the aberrant behaviour of an isolated few.

The true irony of retaliation and military force as a tool of counter-terrorism is that in the one moment it is a child of, and a father to, the cycle of vengeance and the common human desire for revenge and retribution. Social psychology has long appreciated that groups in conflicts become extremely polarized in their views of each other. There is a pervasive tendency to show increased appreciation of the traits and characteristics of the in-group (the group to which you as an individual identify with) and to denigrate the members of the out-group. Such denigration includes a tendency to dehumanize members of the out-group. Their members are described as 'animals' or 'monsters' rather than as people, and their psychology is regarded in suitably similar terms.

One unfortunate result of this common phenomenon is that as well as making it easier to tolerate and support the killing, suffering and harsh treatment of the out-group, it also lulls members of the in-group into thinking that the psychological response of out-group members to events will be qualitatively different to their own. For example, if the out-group kills our members we will not surrender but will continue to struggle on and will persevere to the end. However, if we kill members of the out-group, that will teach them that they cannot win against us and that they must surrender and give in to our will.

Colin Powell, as US Secretary of State, highlighted in his autobiography the dangers of such thinking. He made the point while discussing his reaction to the suicide attack against the Marine Barracks in Beirut in 1983 that killed 241 Marines. In the weeks prior to the attack, US ships of the coast of Lebanon had fired hundreds of shells into the hills around Beirut. This massive bombardment was supposed to support US allies in the area and deter attacks against US positions. Yet as Powell commented:

> What we tend to overlook in such situations is that other people will react much as we would. When the shells started falling on the Shi'ites, they assumed the American 'referee' had taken sides against them. And since they could not reach the battleship, they found a more vulnerable target, the exposed Marines at the airport.

> (Powell 1996: 281)

Powell's point is an important one. Inevitably, both the out-group and the in-group are composed of people, and how they react to events will not escape this simple fact. The human desire for justice and for vengeance is an extremely common one. Indeed, it is arguably a universal trait of the human condition regardless of language, culture or racial background. Thus when Jews kill Arabs, and Arabs kill Jews, both sides can be expected to be equally vulnerable to issues pertaining to the psychology of vengeance and retribution.

A question of popularity

Because harsh countermeasures attend so closely with the human desire for revenge, they also possess an additional characteristic: they are very popular with domestic audiences. Though not commonly used by most Western democracies, military retaliations have generally been widely approved of in home opinion when they have been employed. In polls and surveys carried out in the aftermath of terrorist attacks, a clear majority consistently voice approval of their own government's use of military force against terrorism. In the USA, for example, although the government has only rarely resorted to such methods in recent decades, each occasion has been regarded with warm and overwhelming domestic approval. Though condemned internationally, the American strike against Libya in 1986 was approved by 77 per cent of US citizens polled. The two strikes authorized by the Clinton administration, first against Iraq in

1993 and then against alleged al-Qaeda interests in 1998, had approval ratings of 66 and 77 per cent, respectively, even though the latter occurred at a time when the president himself was embroiled in humiliating personal scandal (Kosnick 2000). After the terrorist attacks of September 11, the use of American military force in Afghanistan received massive domestic support with 87 per cent of the US population expressing approval. This high level of support remained solid over the following months of fighting as the Taliban collapsed and US troops scoured the countryside for al-Qaeda remnants. The levels of public support for these actions, from Libya to Afghanistan, have always been considerably higher than that seen for other harsh measures democracies utilize in the interests of security and law enforcement. For example, support for the use of capital punishment in the USA has normally fluctuated between 59 and 75 per cent. These are comfortable majorities, but the figures are less than those seen for the various retaliations. It is interesting that there is less public support for the killing of offenders whose culpability has been established by a rigorous, overt and lengthy judicial process, than for the swift elimination of alleged terrorist adversaries in a process which enjoys no such safeguards.

In Israel, too, support for retaliatory measures in response to terrorism has traditionally been high. Friedland and Merari (1985) found that 92 per cent of Israelis surveyed supported the assassination of terrorist leaders, 75 per cent supported the bombing of terrorist bases (even if it jeopardized civilian life), and 79 per cent supported the demolition of houses which harboured terrorists. Friedland and Merari found that males tended to support these measures more strongly than females. Also, religious respondents expressed more support for them compared to secular respondents.

The surveys and polls indicate, again, just how common vengeful attitudes are, and one does not have to be a terrorist (or support a terrorist group) to believe that the use of violence is appropriate and justified even when it incurs the loss of innocent life and bypasses non-violent means of responding to the problem. Ultimately, for any government which wishes to make a widely popular response to terrorist violence (at least among its own domestic population), aggressive military force is by far the most obvious choice.

Yet, despite this, the reality is that liberal democracies in general have tended to avoid overt military retaliations. Countries which have embraced the approach more fully have tended to be states whose status sits uncomfortably with the concept of a liberal democracy. Arguably, the two most ardent users in recent decades were the already much discussed Israelis followed then by apartheid South Africa. The USA, though siding with these two on many international counter-terrorism issues in the 1970s and 1980s, has been far more restrained. Between 1983 and 1998, there were some 2,400 terrorism incidents directed against US citizens and interests throughout the world. More than 600 US citizens were killed in these attacks and another 1,900 were injured (a casualty list which does not include the many non-US citizens killed and injured). Yet, in response to these 2,400 acts of terrorism the US government decided to take overt military reaction in just three cases.

The first of these three terrorist incidents was the already discussed bombing of a West Berlin discothèque in April 1986 which led to a retaliatory strike against Libya a few weeks later. The second was the attempt by Iraqi agents to assassinate former President George Bush using a car bomb when he visited Kuwait in April 1993. The third incident was the near-simultaneous destruction of the US embassies in Kenya and Tanzania by al-Qaeda terrorists in August 1998. These attacks killed 224 people, including 12 Americans, and more than 4,000 were injured.

It is revealing to ask why the USA responded violently to just these three incidents? After all, during that period the country and its citizens had endured thousands of terrorist attacks, but did not use overt military force in response. What was different about these three? Malvesti (2001) argued that while governments spoke about deterring and preventing terrorism in justifying the use of retaliatory military force, the reality was that there were other factors which actually predicted when the USA at least would resort to such measures. Malvesti identified six factors which were common to the three terrorist attacks but which were not seen in the others. She argued that it was this combination of factors which was important in leading to the use of military force. The factors she identified were:

- Relatively immediate positive perpetrator identification: the US authorities were quickly able to identify who they thought was responsible for the attack.
- Perpetrator repetition: this incident was not the first time the perpetrators had attacked US interests.
- Direct targeting of a US citizen working in an official US government-related capacity: Malvesti found that attacks against government officials, military servicemen, etc. seemed to ellicit a retaliatory response whereas attacks against civilians only did not.
- The fait accompli nature of the incident: it was completed by the time the response was being contemplated. So for example, retaliation was not used in response to sieges or kidnappings.
- Flagrant anti-US perpetrator behaviour: the perpetrator had a history of defying and denigrating US interests in a high-profile and open manner.
- The political and military vulnerability of the perpetrator.

The last factor is a particularly important one. When terrorist groups are not vulnerable in these terms, the USA did not move against them. Most of these factors probably also play a major role in explaining the decisions of other states to strike back. For example, these factors appear to be present for most Israeli strikes. The anti-Israeli terrorist groups, whether in the Palestinian territories, Lebanon or further afield are certainly militarily vulnerable to Israel's overwhelming conventional forces. This was proved in the invasions in the 1970s and 1980s and again more recently with the relative ease with which Israeli troops have been able to take control of towns and camps in the Palestinian Authority even when faced with determined opponents such as at Jenin in April 2002.

The political vulnerability of the groups is also well established. While most of the Islamic and Arab world is sympathetic to the Palestinian plight, and hostile towards Israeli military retaliations, the reality is that such states exert little political influence over Israel. The only foreign state with real political clout in Israel is the USA, and US governments have traditionally been tolerant or else largely ambivalent about hard-line Israeli measures in combating terrorism. While this is the case, the terrorist groups themselves will remain politically vulnerable and thus one can expect Israel to feel relatively unrestrained in considering military responses to terrorism.

While government spokespersons will make various defences of retaliatory responses to terrorism, Malvesti's research highlights that other undisclosed factors play an important role in the decision to use these measures. We have already seen though that retaliation does not seem to prevent or deter future acts of terrorism.

Conclusions

In considering the risks associated with the use of harsh measures to combat terrorism, it is worth returning to story of the Hydra. As we have seen in this review, harsh blows administered in response to Irish, Palestinian and Libyan terrorism, did not quell the conflict or subdue the protagonists. The violence continued, often more destructive and intense than before, consuming more lives and resources. How then does one overcome a Hydra?

According to myth, the Hydra was defeated by the most powerful of all the Greek heroes: Hercules. Yet crucially, it was not Hercules' great strength and power which proved the key to victory. In an insane rage, Hercules had killed his family. In order to atone for this act, the oracle of Delphi assigned him a series of labours and the second of these involved going to Lerna to kill the Hydra. The Hydra was the result of a mating between the monster Typhon and the Echidna, and was an enormous serpent with nine heads. Its den was a marsh near Lerna in Peloponnese. It would issue forth to ravage the herds and crops, and its breath was so poisonous that whoever smelt it fell dead. With the help of Athena (goddess of wisdom and prudent warfare), Hercules located the monster's lair. Accompanied by his nephew Iolaus, Hercules forced the monster to emerge from the marshes by means of flaming arrows. Hercules rushed forward to attack the beast, but every time he struck off one of the Hydra's heads two more grew in its place. Iolaus looked on in anxiety as his uncle became ever more entangled in the Hydra's growing heads. The tremendous power and force of Hercules' blows were proving useless in the struggle. Finally, with the great hero engulfed and on the verge of defeat, Iolaus grabbed a burning torch and dashed into the fray. Now, when Hercules cut off one of the Hydra's heads, Iolaus seared the wounded neck with flame, and prevented further heads from sprouting. Hercules cut off the heads one by one, with Iolaus cauterizing the wounds. Hercules succeeded in lopping off the last head, supposedly immortal, and buried it deep beneath a rock from where it could never do harm again.

Ultimately harsh, aggressive policies in response to terrorism fail so often in their stated aims, because they so badly misunderstand and ignore the basic psychology of the enemy and of observers. Strength and power alone are not enough to defeat terrorism. The Greeks had many gods of war, but the one who guided Hercules in his struggle with the Hydra was Athena, the goddess of prudent war. Athena, unlike the god Ares, did not glory in destruction and chaos. For her, violence had to have a clear and calm purpose and had to be guided in an effective and principled manner. Without the intervention of Iolaus, Hercules, for all his mighty strength, would have been undone. Aggression and force are too crude to resolve terrorist conflicts. They deceive by meeting the psychological needs of the state and its constituents and by offering up apparent indications of success. Their popularity gives the politicians and leaders who authorize them wider support, and the short-term results provide the security forces with evidence of apparent success: terrorists disabled, weapons and resources confiscated; operations and networks disrupted.

Yet, appearances and accolades can be deceiving. It is as if Hercules, when fighting with the Hydra, had paused to show each decapitated head to a cheering crowd. 'Look another head ... and another ... and another ... surely we are winning'. But relying on such an approach brought Hercules to the edge of ruination. Without the fire of Iolaus, the great hero would have been vanquished.

Terrorist groups can endure military strikes, 'targeted assassinations' and other harsh measures not because the people and resources lost are not important, but because the violence works to increase the motivation of more members than it decreases, and works to attract more support and sympathy to the group than it frightens away.

During the 1980s, the apartheid regime in South Africa sanctioned an organized campaign of assassination of Black activists and their prominent supporters, which resulted in scores of people being killed. The assassination campaign was intended to give the government better control over the process of change. However, as O'Brien (2001) argues the policy in all likelihood hastened the collapse of the system as wider support for the ANC and other opposition groups burgeoned in the face of the perceived injustice of the policy. When the British introduced harsh measures to tackle the IRA, recruits and support flooded to the organization. When the USA bombed Libya, the Libyans increased their involvement and buttressing of terrorism rather than pulling away from it. When Israel kills Hamas members and imposes other sanctions on Palestinian communities, they increase the sense of perceived injustice, particularly considering the high loss of innocent life, driving more recruits into extremist groups and facilitating increased sympathy and support for these groups not only within the West Bank and Gaza, but further afield among the international community. As a result, Israel may win skirmish after skirmish in these terms but still find itself unable to establish lasting peace and stability until other counter-terrorism policies are given greater priority and prominence. For similar reasons, the USA, aggressively chasing down al-Qaeda and its affiliates throughout the world, may find that a lasting resolution to the pursuit eludes it, regardless of how much energy and military force it invests in the campaign.

Ultimately, the use of aggressive measures to combat terrorism can be both justifiable and legal. Frequently, they also successfully fulfil a number of important (though usually short-term) objectives. However, if past experience is anything to go by, defeating or diminishing the threat of terrorism in the long-term is not something that such measures are proficient at doing.

Though Hercules won the battle at Lerna, leaving the Hydra crushed and ruined in his wake, the monster nonetheless played a crucial part in the hero's eventual demise. After he had killed the beast, Hercules cut the snake's body open and dipped his arrows in the poisonous venom. Many years later, while living happily with his new wife, Hercules killed a centaur with one of the poisoned arrows. Before it died, the centaur tricked Hercules' wife into thinking that his now-poisoned blood was a love potion that would keep her husband faithful. She dipped one of Hercules' shirts in the centaur's poisoned blood and gave it to him later. When Hercules put it on, it burned his body to the bone and he died in agony. The ancients understood well that the apparent victory of today may simply be unlocking the door to future defeat.

Bibliography

Bishop, P. and Mallie, E. (1987) *The Provisional IRA*. London: Corgi.

Brophy-Baermann, B. and Conybeare, J.A.C. (1994) 'Retaliating against terrorism: rational expectations and the optimality of rules versus discretion', *American Journal of Political Science*, **38**, 196–210.

Collins, S. (2004) 'Dissuading state support of terrorism: strikes or sanctions? (An analysis of dissuasion measures employed against Libya)', *Studies in Conflict and Terrorism*, **27**, 1–18.

Cota-McKinley, A., Woody, W. and Bell, P. (2001) 'Vengeance: effects of gender, age and religious background', *Aggressive Behavior*, **27**, 343–50.

Enders, W., Sandler, T. and Cauley, J. (1990) 'UN conventions, technology and retaliation in the fight against terrorism: an econometric evaluation', *Terrorism and Political Violence*, **2**, 83–105.

Enders, W. and Sandler, T. (1993) 'The effectiveness of antiterrorism policies: a vector-autoregression-intervention analysis', *American Political Science Review*, **87**, 829–44.

Friedland, N. and Merari, A. (1985) 'The psychological impact of terrorism: a double-edged sword', *Political Psychology*, **6**, 591–604.

Gilligan, J. (2000) *Violence: Reflections on Our Deadliest Epidemic*. London: Jessica Kingsley.

Hoffman, B. (1998) *Inside Terrorism*. London: Victor Gollancz.

Kim, S. and Smith, R. (1993) 'Revenge and conflict escalation', *Negotiation Journal*, **9**, 37–43.

Kosnick, M. (2000) 'The military response to terrorism', *Naval War College Review*, **53**, 13–39.

Lee, J.J. (1989) *Ireland 1912–1985: Politics and Society*. Cambridge: Cambridge University Press.

MacStiofain, S. (1975) *Memoirs of a Revolutionary*. Edinburgh: Gordon Cremonesi.

Malvesti, M. (2001) 'Explaining the United States' decision to strike back at terrorists', *Terrorism and Political Violence*, **13**, 85–106.

O'Brien, K. (2001) 'The use of assassination as a tool of state policy: South Africa's counter-revolutionary strategy 1979–92 (Part 2)', *Terrorism and Political Violence*, **13**, 107–42.

Powell, C. (with Persico, J.) (1996) *My American Journey*. New York: Ballantine.

Schmid, A. and Jongman, A. (1988) *Political Terrorism* (2nd edn.). Oxford: North-Holland Publishing Company.

Stohl, M. (1987) 'Terrorism, states and state terrorism: The Reagan administration in the Middle East', *Arab Studies Quarterly*, **9**, 162–72.

Taylor, P. (1993) *States of Terror*. London: BBC Books.

Tudge, C. (2002) 'Natural born killers', *New Scientist*, **174**, 36–9.

Wilkinson, P. (1986) 'Fighting the Hydra: International Terrorism and The Rule of Law', in O'Sullivan, N. (ed.) *Terrorism, Ideology and Revolution: The Origins of Modern Political Violence*. Boulder, CO: Westview Press.

20 Conclusions

Tore Bjørgo[1]

Addressing factors that cause a recurring problem is usually preferable to dealing with symptoms and consequences. If an area suffers from mosquitoes, draining the swamps where they breed is usually a more effective strategy than trying to kill all the individual insects.[2] This principle applies to terrorism as well as to many other problem areas. The approach requires, however, that we can identify causes and mechanisms that are of such a nature that they are available for intervention and possible to change. For this approach to be effective, it requires that the causes identified for intervention should be specific and have a direct causal relationship to the problem. This is by no means easy to achieve with such a complex and multifarious phenomenon as terrorism. Nevertheless, it has been a main objective of this book to explore these possibilities.

Given the diverse views and backgrounds of the contributors to this book, it would not be realistic to achieve a consensus on what constitutes the root causes of terrorism. Still, to a surprising degree, the preceding chapters point in the same direction on many critical issues.

Debunking myths about root causes of terrorism

A main accomplishment of this book was to invalidate several widely held ideas about what causes terrorism. There is broad agreement that:

- *There is only a weak and indirect relationship between poverty and terrorism.*[3] At the individual level, terrorists are generally not drawn from the poorest segments of their societies. Typically, they are at average or above-average levels in terms of education and socio-economic background. Poor people are more likely to take part in other or simpler forms of political violence than terrorist campaigns, such as riots and civil wars (which may certainly involve acts of terrorist violence). The level of terrorism is not particularly high in the poorest countries of the world. Terrorism is more commonly associated with countries with a medium level of economic development, often emerging in societies characterized by rapid modernization and transition. On the other hand, poverty has frequently been used as justification for violence by social-revolutionary terrorists, who may claim to represent the poor and marginalized without being poor themselves. Some data also suggest that poverty may be a factor of some significance for the recruitment of certain types of terrorist actors (or possibly, into particular roles within a terrorist group).[4] Although not a general root cause of terrorism, poverty is a social evil that should be fought for its own reasons.

- *State sponsorship is not a root cause of terrorism.*[5] Used as an instrument in their foreign policies, some states have capitalized on pre-existing terrorist groups rather than creating them. Terrorist groups have often been the initiators of these relationships, at times courting several potential state sponsors in order to enhance their own independence. State sponsorship is clearly an enabling factor of terrorism, giving terrorist groups a far greater capacity and lethality than they would have had on their own. States have exercised varying degrees of control over the groups they have sponsored, ranging from using terrorists as 'guns for hire' to having virtually no influence at all over their operations. Tight state control is rare. Also Western democratic governments have occasionally supported terrorist organizations as a foreign policy means.

- *Suicide terrorism is not caused by religion (or more specifically Islam) as such.*[6] Many suicide terrorists around the world are secular, or belong to other religions than Islam. Suicide terrorists are motivated mainly by political goals, usually to end foreign occupation or domestic domination by a different ethnic group. Their 'martyrdom' is, however, frequently legitimized and glorified with reference to religious ideas and values.

- *Terrorists are not insane or irrational actors.*[7] Symptoms of psychopathology are not common among terrorists. Neither do suicide terrorists, as individuals, possess the typical risk factors of suicide. There is no common personality profile that characterizes most terrorists, who appear to be relatively normal individuals. Terrorists may follow their own rationalities based on extremist ideologies or particular terrorist logics, but they are not irrational.

What causes terrorism?

The notion of terrorism is applied to a great diversity of groups with different origins and goals. Terrorism occurs in wealthy countries as well as in poor countries, in democracies as well as in authoritarian states. Thus, there exists no single root cause of terrorism, or even a common set of causes. There are, however, a number of preconditions and precipitants for the emergence of various forms of terrorism.

One limitation of the 'root cause' approach is the underlying idea that terrorists are just passive pawns of the social, economic and psychological forces around them; doing what these 'causes' compel them to do. It is more useful to see terrorists as rational and intentional actors who develop deliberate strategies to achieve political objectives. They make their choices between different options and tactics, on the basis of the limitations and possibilities of the situation. Terrorism is better understood as emerging from a process of interaction between different parties, than as a mechanical cause-and-effect relationship.

With these reservations in mind, it is nevertheless useful to try to identify some conditions and circumstances that give rise to terrorism, or that at least provide a fertile ground for radical groups wanting to use terrorist methods to achieve their objectives. One can distinguish between preconditions and precipitants as two ends of a continuum.

Preconditions set the stage for terrorism in the long run. They are of a relatively general and structural nature, producing a wide range of social outcomes of which terrorism is only one. Preconditions alone are not sufficient to cause the outbreak of terrorism. *Precipitants* much more directly affect the emergence of terrorism. These are the specific events or situations that immediately precede, motivate or trigger the outbreak of terrorism.[8] The first set of causes listed below have more the character of being preconditions, whereas the latter causes are closer to precipitants. (The following list is not all-inclusive.)

- *Lack of democracy, civil liberties and the rule of law* is a precondition for many forms of domestic terrorism.[9] The relationship between government coercion and political violence is essentially shaped like an inverted-U; the most democratic and the most totalitarian societies have the lowest levels of oppositional violence. Moderate levels of coercive violence from the government tend to fuel the fire of dissent, while dissident activities can be brought down by governments willing to resort to extreme forces of coercive brutality. Such draconian force is beyond the limits of what democratic nations are willing to use: and rightfully so.[10]

- *Failed or weak states* lack the capacity or will to exercise territorial control and maintain a monopoly of violence.[11] This leaves a power vacuum that terrorist organizations may exploit to maintain safe havens, training facilities and bases for launching terrorist operations. On the other hand, terrorists may also find safe havens and carry out support functions in strong and stable democracies, due to the greater liberties that residents enjoy there.

- *Rapid modernization* in the form of high economic growth has also been found to correlate strongly with the emergence of ideological terrorism, but not with ethno-nationalist terrorism.[12] This may be particularly important in countries where sudden wealth (e.g. from oil) has precipitated a change from tribal to high-tech societies in one generation or less. When traditional norms and social patterns crumble or are made to seem irrelevant, new radical ideologies (sometimes based on religion and/or nostalgia for a glorious past) may become attractive to certain segments of society. Modern society also facilitates terrorism by providing access to rapid transportation and communication, news media, weapons, etc.

- *Extremist ideologies* of a secular or religious nature are at least an intermediate cause of terrorism, although people usually adopt such extremist ideologies as a consequence of more fundamental political or personal reasons.[13] When these worldviews are adopted and applied in order to interpret situations and guide action, they tend to take on a dynamic of their own, and may serve to dehumanize the enemy and justify atrocities.

- *Historical antecedents of political violence, civil wars, revolutions, dictatorships or occupation* may lower the threshold for acceptance of political violence and terrorism, and impede the development of non-violent norms among all segments of society. The victim role as well as longstanding historical injustices and grievances may be constructed to serve as justifications for terrorism. When young children are socialized into cultural value systems that celebrate martyrdom, revenge and hatred of other ethnic or national groups, this is likely to increase their readiness to support or commit violent atrocities when they grow up.[14]

- *Hegemony and inequality of power.* When local or international powers possess an overwhelming power compared to oppositional groups, and the latter see no other realistic ways to forward their cause by normal political or military means, 'asymmetrical warfare' can represent a tempting option.[15] By attacking the 'soft underbelly' of the enemy, such as unprotected and vulnerable civilian targets, terrorism offers the possibility of achieving high political impact with limited means.

- *Illegitimate or corrupt governments* frequently give rise to opposition that may turn to terrorist means if other avenues are not seen as realistic options for replacing these regimes with a more credible and legitimate government,[16] or at least a regime which represents the values and interests of the opposition movement.

- *Powerful external actors upholding illegitimate governments* may be seen as an insurmountable obstacle to needed regime change.[17] Such external support to illegitimate governments is frequently seen as foreign domination through puppet regimes serving the political and economic interests of foreign sponsors.

- *Repression by foreign occupation or by colonial powers* has given rise to a great many national liberation movements that have sought recourse in terrorist tactics, guerrilla warfare, and other political means.[18] Despite their use of terrorist methods, some liberation movements enjoy considerable support and legitimacy among their own constituencies, and sometimes also from segments of international public opinion.

- *The experience of discrimination on the basis of ethnic or religious origin* is the chief root cause of ethno-nationalist terrorism.[19] When sizeable minorities are systematically deprived of their rights to equal social and economic opportunities, obstructed from expressing their cultural identities (e.g. forbidden to use their language or practise their religion), or excluded from political influence, this can give rise to secessionist movements that may turn to terrorism or other forms of violent struggle. This is particularly the case when the conflict becomes longstanding and bitter, with few prospects for a resolution acceptable for both sides. Ethnic nationalisms are more likely to give rise to (and justify) terrorism than are moderate and inclusive civic nationalisms.

- *Failure or unwillingness by the state to integrate dissident groups or emerging social classes* may lead to their alienation from the political system.[20] Some groups are excluded because they hold views or represent political traditions considered irreconcilable with the basic values of the state. Large groups of highly educated young people with few prospects of meaningful careers within a blocked system will tend to feel alienated and frustrated. Excluded groups are likely to search for alternative channels through which to express and promote political influence and change. To some, terrorism can seem the most effective and tempting option.

- *The experience of social injustice* is a main motivating cause behind social-revolutionary terrorism. Relative deprivation or great differences in income distribution (rather than absolute deprivation or poverty) in a society have in some studies been found to correlate rather strongly with the emergence of social-revolutionary political violence and terrorism, but less with ethno-nationalist terrorism.[21]
- *The presence of charismatic ideological leaders* able to transform widespread grievances and frustrations into a political agenda for violent struggle is a decisive factor behind the emergence of a terrorist movement or group. The existence of grievances alone is only a precondition: someone is needed who can translate that into a programme for violent action.[22]
- *Triggering events* are the direct precipitators of terrorist acts. Such a trigger can be an outrageous act committed by the enemy, lost wars, massacres, contested elections, police brutality, or other provocative events that call for revenge or action.[23] Even peace talks may trigger terrorist action by spoilers on both sides.

Individuals join extremist groups for different reasons. Some are true believers who are motivated by ideology and political goals, whereas others get involved for selfish interests, or because belonging to a strong group is important to their identity.

Factors sustaining terrorism

Terrorism is often sustained for reasons other than those which gave birth to it in the first place. It is therefore not certain that terrorism will end even if the grievances that gave rise to it, or the root causes, are somehow dealt with.[24] Terrorist groups may change purpose, goals and motivation over time.[25]

- *Cycles of revenge.* As a response to terrorist atrocities, reprisals are generally popular with broad segments of the public. However, this tends to be the case on both sides, which often try to outdo each other in taking revenge to satisfy their respective constituencies. Deterrence often does not work against non-state terrorist actors. Violent reprisals may even have the opposite effect of deterrence because many terrorist groups want to provoke overreactions. Policies of military reprisal to terrorist actions may become an incentive to more terrorism, as uncompromising militants seek to undermine moderation and political compromise.[26]
- *The need of the group to provide for its members or for the survival of the group itself* may also cause a terrorist group to change its main objectives or to continue its struggle longer than it otherwise would have, for example to effect the release of imprisoned members or to sustain its members economically.[27]

- *Profitable criminal activities* to finance their political and terrorist campaigns may eventually give terrorist groups vested interests in continuing their actions long after they realize that their political cause is lost.[28] Alternatively, some continue even if many of their political demands have been met.
- *No exit*. With 'blood on their hands' and having burnt all bridges back to mainstream society, some terrorist groups and individuals continue their underground struggle because the only alternative is long-term imprisonment or death.[29] Serious consideration should be given to ways of bringing the insurgent movement back into the political process, or at least offering individual terrorists a way out (such as reduced sentences or amnesty) if they break with their terrorist past and cooperate with the authorities. Such policies have in fact helped to bring terrorism to an end in several countries.

Final remarks

Several of the causes of terrorism described above are of such a nature that they might be addressed and influenced in a direction that would make them less likely to produce terrorism; or more precisely, to induce persons and groups to choose other modes of action than terrorist violence. However, there are also a number of root causes (or preconditions) of terrorism that cannot be 'removed' because they are beyond our capacity to change.

Many terrorist insurgencies will not come to an end before their root causes are addressed and fundamental grievances and rights are provided for. However, terrorism will not necessarily disappear even if the root causes are dealt with, because terrorism is often sustained for reasons other than those which produced it. That is why we should pay particular attention to the factors that *sustain* terrorist campaigns. Moreover, we are often not in a position to address terrorist grievances as such until the terrorist campaign has developed.[30]

In counter-terrorism efforts, it is crucial to uphold democratic principles and maintain moral and ethical standards while fighting terrorism. Increased repression and coercion are likely to feed terrorism, rather than reduce it.[31] Extremist ideologies that promote hatred and terrorism should be confronted on ideological grounds by investing more effort into challenging them politically, and not only by the use of coercive force.

Many of the causes of terrorism are also the causes of rebellious guerrilla warfare, riots and other forms of political violence. What distinguishes terrorist violence from other forms of violence used in waging political and armed conflict is its criminal and normless character, with deliberate attacks on civilians, indiscriminate bombings, the taking of hostages: tactics that would qualify as war crimes in conventional armed conflicts. Thus, acts of terrorism can be seen as the peace-time equivalents of war crimes.[32]

We need insights into the conditions and processes leading up to terrorist atrocities if we are to identify possible avenues of prevention, early intervention, or ways of breaking the vicious circle of terrorist revenge and counter-revenge. Such understanding does not mean accepting or justifying the use of terrorist methods. The political goals for which terrorists wage conflict may be legitimate in some cases and unjust in others; but deliberate and indiscriminate targeting of civilians as a tactic to achieve these goals is never acceptable.

Target hardening and suppressing terrorism by law enforcement or military means are short-term but often indispensable measures to respond to specific terrorist threats. At its best, competent police work and intelligence have prevented many planned terrorist actions from being carried through.[33] Still, redressing the grievances that give rise to terrorism offers the best prospects for reducing terrorist violence in the long run. However, given the complexity of the phenomenon and the difficulties involved in changing deep-seated structures and patterns of domination, the run may sometimes become very long. Committed terrorists are not likely to change their views or mode of action due to political reforms, but their social and political support base is far more likely to dry up.[34] To reduce the conditions that provide recruitment and popular support for international Jihadist terrorism, we will probably have to think in terms of decades rather than months or years, involving a wide range of social and political changes. There are no quick fixes to this problem. Other terrorist campaigns, concerning conflicts over a share of power or independence rather than totalitarian demands, are often more amenable for political initiatives and compromise.[35] To avoid rewarding terrorism, it is preferable to direct offers and negotiations towards non-terrorist parts of the insurgency. This is not always possible, though. Sometimes groups involved in terrorism will have to be parties to a political settlement if such a solution shall be achieved.[36] When terrorist demands are extreme and totalitarian, a wiser political response would often be to isolate the extremists and talk with more moderate factions, and avoid branding as terrorist everyone promoting the political case.

Trying to deal with the causes of terrorism in its general form is less rewarding than addressing the causes of specific forms of terrorism or specific terrorist campaigns. If such insights shall be of practical use, the challenge is twofold. At the preventive level, the challenge is to identify at an early stage grievances, factors and developments that make a certain conflict escalate in such a direction that some elements are likely to turn to terrorist methods, and then try to influence these causes. If a terrorist campaign has already developed, the challenge is to identify factors which sustain the ongoing campaign, and remove them or alleviate their negative consequences.

The notion of 'addressing the root causes of terrorism' may become a dead end if by 'root' we mean the distant and general issues such as poverty, globalization and modernization that are far removed from the actual acts of terrorism and extremely difficult to change. The approach is far more promising if we focus on the more immediate causes and circumstances that motivate and facilitate specific campaigns and acts of terrorism.[37] Future research and efforts should move in this direction.

Notes

1   The findings described in this chapter are conclusions drawn by the editor/chairman of the *Oslo Expert Conference on Root Causes of Terrorism* on the basis of presentations and discussions. Thus each individual expert on the panel may not necessarily agree with every single conclusion or statement.

2   Addressing causes of problems rather than symptoms and consequences, being proactive rather than

reactive, is also at the core of new approaches to policing, health care and a number of other fields (see Goldstein 1990).

3   See Gupta (Chapter 2), Malečková (Chapter 3), Merari (Chapter 6), Mohammad (Chapter 8) and Schmid (Chapter 18).
4   See Post (Chapter 5) and Schmid (Chapter 18) in relation to Horgan's discussion (Chapter 4) about different types and roles of terrorists.
5   See Richardson (Chapter 15) and Schmid (Chapter 18).
6   See Merari (Chapter 6), Ahmad (Chapter 7) and Mohammad (Chapter 8).
7   See Gupta (Chapter 2), Post (Chapter 5), Merari (Chapter 6) and Ahmad (Chapter 7).
8   The distinction between preconditions and precipitants is taken from Crenshaw (1990).
9   See, for example, Schmid (Chapter 18), Gupta (Chapter 2), Stohl (Chapter 16) and Mohammad (Chapter 8).
10 This point is made by Gupta (Chapter 2), but also by Sinai (Chapter 17).
11 See l Khazen (Chapter 14), Jamieson (Chapter 13), and Zartman (1995).
12 See Engene (1998).
13 See Post (Chapter 5), Waldmann (Chapter 12) and Bjørgo (1997).
14 See Post (Chapter 5), Ahmad (Chapter 7) and Lia (2005).
15 See Waldmann (Chapter 12), Ahmad (Chapter 7), Lia (2005) and Volgy *et al.* (1997).
16 See Schmid (Chapter 18) and Engene (1998).
17 See Mohammad (Chapter 8) and el Khazen (Chapter 14).
18 See Ahmad (Chapter 7) and Gurr (1970).
19 See Reinares (Chapter 9), Ahmad (Chapter 7) and Kaarthikeyan (Chapter 10).
20 See Mohammad (Chapter 8) and Rubenstein (1987).
21 See Waldman (Chapter 12), Engene (1998) and Malečková (Chapter 3).
22 See Gupta (Chapter 2), Kaarthikeyan (Chapter 10) and Bjørgo (1997: 143).
23 See Bjørgo (Chapter 1), Kaarthikeyan (Chapter 10), Sinai (Chapter 17) and Silke (Chapter 19).
24 See Horgan (Chapter 4)
25 See Bjørgo and Heradstveit (1993).
26 This dynamic of retaliation is discussed, in particular, by Silke (Chapter 19), Horgan (Chapter 4), Ahmad (Chapter 7) and Kaarthikeyan (Chapter 10).
27 See Horgan (Chapter 4), Waldman (Chapter 12) and Bjørgo and Heradstveit (1993: 92–104).
28 See Horgan (Chapter 4) and Waldmann (Chapter 12).
29 See Post (Chapter 6), Bjørgo and Heradstveit (1993), Bjørgo (1997: Chapter 6) and Horgan (2003).
30 This argument is made by Horgan (Chapter 4).
31 See Silke (Chapter 19).
32 See Schmid (Chapter 18).
33 In the period 11 September 2001 until the end of 2004, around 30 major terrorist plots by Jihadist activists have been prevented by police and intelligence action in Europe, whereas only two major attacks were carried through: the Madrid bombings (11 March 2004) and the murder of the Dutch filmmaker Theo van Gogh (2 November 2004). For an analysis see Nesser (2004).
34 This was argued by Gurr (2003).
35 See Sinai (Chapter 17).
36 See Schmid (Chapter 18).
37 See, for example, Mærli (2004).

Bibliography

Bjørgo, T. (1997) *Racist and Right-wing Violence in Scandinavia: Patterns, Perpetrators and Responses*. Oslo: Tano Aschehoug.
Bjørgo, T. and Heradstveit, D. (1993) *Politisk Terrorisme*, Oslo: Tano.
Crenshaw, M. (1990) 'The Logic of Terrorism: Terrorist Behaviour as a Product of Strategic

Choice', in Reich, W. (ed.) (1990) *Origins of Terrorism: Psychologies, Ideologies, Theologies, States of Mind*. Cambridge: Cambridge University Press.

Crenshaw, M. (2003) 'Why is America the Primary Target?: Terrorism as Globalized Civil War', in Kegley, C.W. (ed.) *The New Global Terrorism: Characteristics, Causes, Controls*. Upper Saddle River, NJ: Prentice Hall.

Engene, J.O. (1998) *Patterns of terrorism in Western Europe, 1950–95*, doctoral dissertation. Bergen: Department of Comparative Politics, University of Bergen.

Goldstein, H. (1990) *Problem-oriented Policing*. New York: McGraw-Hill.

Gurr, T.R. (1970) *Why Men Rebel*. Princeton, NJ: Princeton University Press.

Gurr, T.R. (2003) 'Terrorism in Democracies: When It Occurs, Why It Fails', in Kegley, C.W. (ed.) *The New Global Terrorism: Characteristics, Causes, Controls*. Upper Saddle River, NJ: Prentice-Hall.

Horgan, J. (2003) 'Leaving Terrorism Behind', in Silke, A. (ed.) *Terrorism, Victims, Society: Psychological Perspectives on Terrorism and its Consequences*. London: Wiley.

Laqueur, W. (1987) *The Age of Terrorism*. London: Weidenfeld & Nicolson.

Lia, B. (2005) *Globalization and the Future of Terrorism: Patterns and Prediction*. London: Routledge.

Mærli, M.B. (2004) *Crude nukes on the loose? Preventing nuclear terrorism by means of optimum nuclear husbandry, transparency and non-intrusive fissile material verification*, doctor7al dissertation, Faculty of Mathematics and Natural Sciences, University of Oslo, Norway, March. Http://www.nupi.no/IPS/filestore/664.pdf

Nesser, P. (2004) *Jihad in Europe: A survey of the motivations for Sunni Islamist terrorism in post-millennium Europe*, FFI/Rapport – 2004/01146, also available at http://www.nupi.no/IPS/filestore/01146.pdf

Rubenstein, R.E. (1987) *Alchemists of Revolution*. New York: Basic Books.

Volgy, T.J., Imwalle, L.E. And Corntallel, J.J. (1997) 'Structural determinants of international terrorism: the effects of hegemony and polarity on terrorist activity', *International Interactions*, **23**(2), 207–31.

Zartman, W. (ed.) (1995) *Collapsed States: The Disintegration and Restoration of Legitimate Authority*. Boulder, CO: Lynne Rienner Publishers.

Index